Managing Information and Statistics

Second edition

Frances Bee read mathematics at Somerville College, Oxford before going on to take a postgraduate diploma in statistics at London University and an MBA at the Management College, Henley-on-Thames. She has worked as a statistician, a corporate planner and also in the personnel, training and finance functions. Her experience has included local government and a major building society, a stint as the general manager of a large department store and a period as a university lecturer.

Roland Bee has worked as an industrial chemist, served as a navigator in the RAF and then spent several years in human resource and management services roles. He has worked as a chief personnel officer ....overnment and h.... senior posts in housing and the electricity supply industry. .... in Man..... mei..... m the Management College, Henley-on-Thames and has taught hr and management subjects at a number of universities.

Frances and Roland are Managing Consultants at Time for People, a learning consultancy specialising in information management, learning needs analysis and evaluation. They have written *Learning needs analysis and evaluation, The complete learning evaluation toolkit, Facilitation skills, Project management: the people challenge, Customer care* and *Constructive feedback*, all for the CIPD. They work from a converted barn in the grounds of their late medieval/early Tudor farmhouse in Suffolk, surrounded by 10 acres of land which they are managing for conservation and wildlife.

The CIPD would like to thank the following members of the CIPD Publishing Editorial Board for their help and advice:

- Pauline Dibben, Middlesex University Business School
- Edwina Hollings, Staffordshire University Business School
- Caroline Hook, Huddersfield University Business School
- Vincenza Priola, Wolverhampton Business School
- John Sinclair, Napier University Business School

Managing Information and Statistics

Second edition

Frances and Roland Bee

Chartered Institute of Personnel and Development

Published by the Chartered Institute of Personnel and Development,
151 The Broadway, London, SW19 1JQ

This edition published 2005
First published 1999
Reprinted 1999, 2001, 2002, 2003 (twice), 2006

Typeset by Curran Publishing Services, Norwich, Norfolk
Printed in Great Britain by Cromwell Press, Trowbridge, Wiltshire

British Library Cataloguing in Publication Data
A catalogue of this publication is available from the British Library

ISBN 0-85292-995-1

Chartered Institute of Personnel and Development
151 The Broadway, London, SW19 1JQ
Tel 020 8612 6200
E-mail cipd@cipd.co.uk Website: www.cipd.co.uk
Incorporated by Royal Charter. Registered Charity No. 1079797

In memory of our beautiful and beloved daughter

Elizabeth Alice Bee

5 April 1988

Contents

Foreword   xiii
Preface   xv

Part 1   Introduction to information systems   1

Chapter 1   The philosophy of managing information   3
              Chapter objectives   3
              Introduction   3
              Key issues for information systems   4
              Classes of management information report   8
              Impact of organisational factors on information systems 10
              Managing information for competitive advantage   13
              Decision-making and information systems   15
              Conclusion   18
              Review questions   19

Chapter 2   Information systems concepts   20
              Chapter objectives   20
              Introduction   20
              Definition of a systems approach   20
              System boundaries   21
              Open and closed systems   22
              Holism and emergent properties   22
              Systems entropy   23
              Hard and soft properties   23
              Hard and soft systems   24
              Systems thinking and complexity   29
              Conclusion   30
              Review questions   30

Chapter 3   Information systems for planning and organising   31
              Chapter objectives   31
              Introduction   31
              Information strategy   31
              Levels of planning   32
              Problems with planning   32
              Types and sources of information for planning   36
              Mathematical modelling   37
              Sensitivity analysis   40
              Conclusion   41
              Review questions   41

Chapter 4   Information systems for review and control   42
              Chapter objectives   42

	Introduction	42
	Elements of control systems	42
	Monitoring, controlling and revising the plan	45
	Conclusion	47
	Review questions	47
Chapter 5	**Storing data**	**48**
	Chapter objectives	48
	Introduction	48
	Collection and storage of data	48
	Databases	50
	Database management systems	51
	Database structures	51
	Conclusion	55
	Review questions	55
Chapter 6	**Designing, developing and implementing your information system**	**56**
	Chapter objectives	56
	Introduction	56
	Basic project model	57
	Techniques for requirements analysis	64
	Issues affecting the design and development of information systems	67
	Project management	69
	Conclusion	70
	Review questions	72
Chapter 7	**Data security**	**73**
	Chapter objectives	73
	Introduction	73
	Protection	74
	Disaster recovery	75
	The UK law relating to data security	75
	Conclusion	78
	Review questions	79
Chapter 8	**Human resource information systems**	**80**
	Chapter objectives	80
	Introduction	80
	Core features of HR information systems	81
	Learning from experience	82
	Recruitment modules	90
	Learning and development modules	90
	Other modules	92
	Conclusion	93
	Review questions	93
Chapter 9	**Knowledge management systems**	**94**
	Chapter objectives	94
	Introduction	94
	Defining knowledge and knowledge management	95

Systems and infrastructure for knowledge management   98
Some approaches to knowledge management   99
Conclusion   103
Review questions   103

Chapter 10   The e-organisation   104
Chapter objectives   104
Introduction   104
Electronic mail (e-mail) and the World Wide Web (WWW)   105
E-business and e-commerce   106
B2C e-commerce   107
B2B e-commerce   108
E-HR   110
E-government   111
Other applications   113
Conclusion   115
Review questions   115

Chapter 11   Looking ahead   116
Introduction   116
How will it all work?   116
Our organisations   119
Some future directions for HR   120
Conclusion   120

Part 2   Introduction to statistics   123
Numbers into information   123

Chapter 12   Tabulations   125
Chapter objectives   125
Introduction   125
Arrays   125
Frequency distributions   126
Conclusion   130
Review questions   130

Chapter 13   Diagrammatic methods   131
Chapter objectives   131
Introduction   131
Bar diagrams   131
Pie charts   133
Pictograms   133
Histograms   136
Frequency polygons   138
Ogives   139
Graphs   140
Radar diagrams   141
Conclusion   143
Review questions   144

Chapter 14	**Numerical methods**	**145**
	Chapter objectives	145
	Introduction	145
	Measures of location	145
	Measures of dispersion	151
	Conclusion	155
	Review questions	155

Chapter 15	**Introduction to probability and probability distributions**	**156**
	Chapter objectives	156
	Introduction	156
	Experiments and outcomes	156
	Experimental outcomes and their probabilities	158
	Events and their probabilities	158
	Random variables	159
	Probability distributions	159
	The Normal distribution	164
	Conclusion	165
	Review questions	166

Chapter 16	**Sampling, estimation and inference**	**167**
	Chapter objectives	167
	Introduction	167
	How to choose a sample	168
	Point estimates	171
	Sampling distributions and confidence limits	173
	Calculating sample size	178
	Conclusion	179
	Review questions	179

Chapter 17	**Hypothesis testing**	**180**
	Chapter objectives	180
	Introduction	180
	Null and alternative hypotheses	180
	Types of error	182
	Two-tailed hypothesis testing	182
	Statistical process control	184
	Two-population inference (independent samples)	185
	Chi-squared tests	186
	Conclusion	192
	Review questions	192

Chapter 18	**Regression and correlation**	**193**
	Chapter objectives	193
	Introduction	193
	Regression analysis	193
	Simple linear regression	194
	Correlation	199
	Multiple regression	201
	Conclusion	202
	Review questions	203

Chapter 19	**Forecasting and time series**	**204**
	Chapter objectives	204
	Introduction	204
	Quantitative methods	205
	Qualitative methods	205
	Structure of a time series	206
	Smoothing methods	209
	Trend projections	211
	Forecasting with seasonal elements	214
	Conclusion	218
	Review questions	218
Chapter 20	**Index numbers, published indices and sources of data**	**219**
	Chapter objectives	219
	Introduction	219
	The Retail Price Index (RPI) and Consumer Price Index (CPI)	222
	Stock market indices	228
	Sources of data	229
	Government statistical publications	230
	Private market research	231
	Organisation information	231
	Conclusion	232
	Review questions	232
Chapter 21	**Decision theory**	**234**
	Chapter objectives	234
	Introduction	234
	Pay-off tables	234
	Expected monetary value	236
	Decision trees	237
	Risk and utility	239
	Conclusion	240
	Review questions	240
Chapter 22	**Using a computer package for statistical analysis**	**241**
	Chapter objectives	241
	Introduction	241
	Frequency distributions	242
	Diagrammatic methods	243
	Numerical methods	244
	Sampling	246
	Regression and correlation	248
	Forecasting	250
	Conclusion	252
Answers to review questions		**253**
References		290
Index		293

Foreword

This latest edition of *Managing information and statistics* has been prepared specifically to meet the new leadership and management standards of the core management module Managing Information for Competitive Advantage.

The significant updating takes in the wider view of information management explicit in the new standards, incorporating as it does new chapters dealing with knowledge management systems and the e-organisation, with the latter covering the more mainstream technological developments of e-commerce. The very important chapter on developing new information systems now includes a section on key project management principles as well as setting out the basic project model and techniques.

This edition contains a thorough treatment of the important theoretical models and thinking associated with information management, and also shows how the theory relates to human resource management systems and practice. This balanced approach allows the student to meet the CIPD requirements of the thinking performer: that is, to be able to make convincing and sophisticated decisions in complex and unpredictable situations, and to be aware of the limitations of concept and theory in relation to problem complexity.

The first part of this book deals with information systems generally, the second with the transformation of numerical data into information for decision-making. One of the great strengths of the second part, from a student's perspective, is the way that the reader is taken gently and almost, I suspect, painlessly through a selection of the most useful statistical techniques for management decision-making.

This book must be viewed as essential reading not only for all those who aspire to pass the CIPD module Managing Information for Competitive Advantage, but for anyone who wants to become an effective manager and problem solver.

The reader should note that this is a companion volume to the other main text for this module, *Managing financial information* by David Davies.

David Allen
CIPD Chief Examiner, Managing Information for Competitive Advantage

Publisher's acknowledgements

We are grateful for the permission to reproduce the following copyright material:

Figures 1.1 and 9.1: WARD, J. and PEPPARD, J. (2002) *Strategic planning for information systems*. 3rd ed. Chichester: Wiley.

Figure 2.2: CHECKLAND, P. and SCHOLES, J. (1999) *Soft systems methodology in action*. Chichester: Wiley.

Figure 9.2: ALAVI, M. (1997) *KPMG Peat Marwick U.S.: One Giant Brain*. Harvard Business School, Case 9–39–08, Boston, Mass: Harvard Business School Press.

Figure 9.3: NONAKA, I and TAKEUCHI, H. (2001) "Organisational knowledge creation." In J. HENRY (ed.), *Creative management*. London: Sage.

Figure 9.4: ALAVI, M. and LEIDNER, D. (2001) "Knowledge management and knowledge management systems: conceptual foundations and research issues." *MIS Quarterly*. Vol. 25, No. 1.

Preface

When we wrote our original book on this subject, *Management information and statistics* (Bee and Bee, 1990), we said we were living in a time of great change. Then in the first edition of this book, we commented that, if anything in the intervening years, the pace of change had accelerated. There can be little doubt that the pace of change has accelerated yet further and also that we are all living and working in an increasingly complex world. Managers and specialists have to assimilate masses of data, convert that data into information and knowledge and make decisions leading to the achievement of business objectives – all in double-quick time. They may often be working in an environment where the issues are not clear cut, where there may be many and conflicting objectives, and where there is great uncertainty about the future. All of this continues to take place against the background of a fiercely competitive environment and increasingly global markets!

There is no doubt that we are operating in an information dominated world and where competitive advantage will depend on the ability of today's managers and specialists to harness the power of that information.

We would emphasise that the aim of this book is not to turn you into an information management specialist or a statistician (you will probably be pleased to hear!). It is aimed at giving you:

- a sound understanding of the concepts that underpin this key area which now permeates every part of our organisational life
- the confidence to contribute to the development of information and knowledge systems
- the ability to make the best possible use of the information in and around your organisation.

We continue to use the terms managers and specialists to recognise the fact that it is not only managers who use information systems, but there is also a wide range of specialist professionals who are not managers but who routinely use business information in the course of their work. We also continue to draw on examples from across the general business world, with some concentration on human resource management. Sometimes in the book we have used the word business to describe the organisation in which the information system works and in which the quantitative methods are used. We mean the word to include both the profit-making part of the economy and the not-for-profit sector – local government, charities, schools, hospitals, etc. In this edition we have introduced chapter objectives to help the reader understand the key learning issues covered by each chapter and included review questions for Part 1 (in the previous edition these were only provided in Part 2).

Part 1 of this book is about the concepts and applications of information systems. We would make the point that information systems now are so sophisticated and complex, that writing about them can, and does, fill the pages of many, very thick textbooks. We have the space only to provide an introduction to this fascinating and vital subject but hope that it will provide a foundation on which you will be able to build and develop your knowledge and skills. In this edition we have introduced new chapters on the exciting areas of knowledge management systems and the e-organisation. Also, in recognition of the issues posed by data security we have now devoted a whole chapter to this subject.

In Part 2, the section on statistics, we look at a range of quantitative approaches to managing our information. Our approach is to assume that you know little about the subjects, other than being able to cope with the basic mathematical functions, and to take you gently through to a reasonable level of understanding. We aim to give you sufficient understanding of some of the most useful statistical techniques to enable you to recognise when they might be helpful in your business or professional activities and to be sufficiently knowledgeable to use the output from statistical packages. Some of the techniques are straightforward enough for anyone to apply themselves, others may require the help of a friendly neighbourhood (or in your case, organisation) statistician.

We are not going to blind you with jargon. We shall try to explain the terms as we go along, using italics for emphasis when we introduce a term in its relevant section for the first time. There may be occasions when, for the sake of simplicity in our explanations, we will offend the pure statistician and mathematician or ICT specialist. We make no apology for this! When you get to the final line, when the ICT specialist and professional statistician have delivered 'x' equal to something and achieved their purpose, you the business manager and specialist will go on to use this computed or calculated value of 'x' to make your inferences about what is happening in your business.

The techniques are only a means to an end – they are not an end in themselves. They are a means of taking you from the chaos of the Dark Ages of data through to the Renaissance of information and knowledge. Data on its own is meaningless, it must be converted into information and then knowledge before it can be used in the decision-making process. We suggest that you think of the techniques as an engine converting raw fuel into usable energy and then into power. As you will appreciate, information is power and that is what information systems and statistics, properly applied, can give you. The core philosophy of our approach is that information systems, statistics and ICT technology are not theoretical subjects, ends in themselves, but the means to a greater understanding of the business process.

We would like to thank John Bevan of the Kent Business School at the University of Kent for all his help on this edition. We would also like to thank Michaela Maycock, Alastair Ramsay and the many other busy people who took the time and trouble to share with us their views on the opportunities and challenges posed by our information world and who provided the material for our case studies. We could not have written this edition without you all.

Frances and Roland Bee
Newsons Farm
June 2005

Introduction to Information Systems

Information systems is a very grand title for a very basic but vital concept. Information is the lifeblood of any business or organisation. It can range from simple reports on sales and profits for a small business through to complex systems covering all aspects of a vast conglomerate or large public sector organisation. Information is in essence what you, whether a manager or specialist in your profession, need to know to run your 'business' (or part of it) successfully. The system is merely the mechanism to ensure that information is available to you in the form you want it and when you need it.

In this new edition, we have attempted to reflect the new ideas and innovations of the past few years. Most of the basic concepts remain unchanged, however the technology for their implementation has inevitably moved forward. Interestingly, although generally life appears to be getting more complicated, most of the changes in our information systems are helping to reduce their complexity and to make them more understandable and simple to use by the non-specialist. Good news! Many of the changes happening now, and on the horizon, reflect the ever-increasing pace of life, with the need to have good quality information available within seconds (or even nanoseconds) and the ability to access this information from almost anywhere – across the globe, in one's home, when on the move, etc.

A new feature of this part of the book is the inclusion of review questions at the end of each chapter. The aim of these, as the name suggests, is to encourage you to reflect on what you have read and develop your understanding of the issues. They are intended to take no more than 30 minutes to complete in total per chapter and full specimen answers are provided at the end of the book. We strongly recommend that you take the time to tackle these questions and also to read the answers provided. We hope this process will enhance your learning about this fascinating subject.

Chapter 1 is an overview of information systems. It examines the content, form and timing of the information we need in order to make decisions and the management of information in the context of the organisation – its structures and cultures, the different levels of need, the decision-making processes. In Chapter 2 we explore some of the major systems concepts – the features of a systems approach, system boundaries, open and closed systems, holism, emergent properties, hard and soft properties, hard and soft systems and systems entropy. In Chapter 3 we move on to look at how information systems can help us in our planning processes – discussing levels of planning, types and sources of information for planning, modelling and simulation, and sensitivity analysis. Chapter 4 then examines the information requirements for monitoring and control – the use of information in controlling, monitoring/reviewing and revising the plan. Chapter 5 is about the processing and storage of data, the structure of databases and database management systems. In Chapter 6 we look at some of the issues that are considered important in the design, development and maintenance of information systems. We go through a basic project model for designing information systems and focus on the key area of requirements analysis. Chapter 7 offers some words of wisdom about data security, data protection and, when the seemingly inevitable worst thing happens, some thoughts on disaster recovery to help get your organisation back on its feet. Chapter 8 looks specifically at information systems for the Human Resource (HR) professional. In Chapter 9 we cover the exciting and developing area of knowledge management systems, where we search for that holy grail of harnessing the knowledge assets in our organisations. Then, in Chapter 10 we discuss the impact of the e-revolution on all aspects of our life. Finally, we conclude Part 1 in Chapter 11 with a glance into the future.

The philosophy of managing information

CHAPTER 1

CHAPTER OBJECTIVES

When you have studied this chapter, you will be able to:

- distinguish between data, information and knowledge
- analyse the issues that affect the content, presentation and timing of information
- describe different types of report
- define the impact of organisational factors on information systems
- explain how information can be used for competitive advantage
- describe the relationship between different types of decision-making and information systems.

INTRODUCTION

Developments in computer technology, and the way this technology is used by organisations, have taken us from the twentieth century – where personal computers (PCs) performing simple tasks on individuals' desks have been used to improve local efficiency – into the twenty-first century, where managing information effectively will be a key contribution to the achievement of organisational objectives.

The late twentieth century also saw the development of the concept of 'knowledge'. Most of us will be familiar with the concept of data – the raw facts obtained by various types of measurement; and the concept of information – data which has been transformed by various processes, such as statistical analysis, which we describe in the Part 2 of this book, so as to provide meaningful information that can be used for decision-making. Knowledge can be defined in various ways but one of the best definitions we have found is in Ward and Peppard (2002), who describe it as 'information combined with experience, context, interpretation and reflection'. Simplistically, you can imagine data, information and knowledge on a continuum with the degree of human involvement increasing as you move from data through information to knowledge. Ward and Peppard go a further step with their description of the DIKAR model – see Figure 1.1.

As you go from left to right you can see the model from an information systems perspective – you move from data to information to knowledge, and hence to action and results for the organisation.

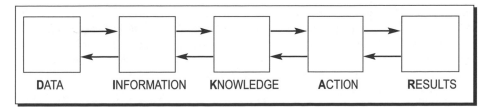

Figure 1.1 The DIKAR model
Source: Ward and Peppard (2002), reproduced with permission.

If you go from right to left you can see it from the business perspective, as the model explains how the organisation's objectives (*results*) can be achieved by asking the basic questions: What *action* is required to achieve the results? What do we need to *know* to perform those actions? Then finally, what *information* and hence *data* do we need to provide us with that knowledge?

It is now widely accepted that knowledge is a key resource of any organisation. The issue of how to retain and share knowledge within organisations has been the subject of much interest and debate. We discuss the area of knowledge management in Chapter 9. However, in this book we are essentially concerned with the issues of transforming data into information and the systems you need to manage that information. Clearly when we discuss the use of information for decision-making we are encroaching into the arena of the use of knowledge, but we shall continue to use the language of information. Good information management is a key component in knowledge management.

KEY ISSUES FOR INFORMATION SYSTEMS

The principal objective of any information system is to satisfy the demand for information needed by the organisation to achieve its objectives. Thus, the key issue for any information system is what information is actually required, and the starting point for understanding what information is required is the realisation that this is critically dependent on:

- who requires the information, and
- for what purpose.

In reality, of course, there will be many users of an information system, and the vital stage in the development of any information system is identifying all the potential users and analysing their needs for information. We discuss approaches to exploring and codifying information requirements in Chapter 7.

The needs of the users will in turn determine:

- the *content* of that information
- the *form* in which it is presented
- the *timing* of its presentation.

For our purposes we choose to define a successful information system as one that provides the right information in the right form and at the right time, to enable the users effectively and efficiently to do their jobs. We fully support the emphasis by Lucey (1997) that information systems are all about the use to which the information is put, rather than the way it is produced, ie the software and hardware that support the system.

We are living in a time of great change, and this will be reflected in the continually evolving needs for information. Any system for delivering information must be flexible and allow for easy updating and amendment. In an ideal world an information system would be tailored to the needs of the individual user. In the past this has not always been possible. Managers and other users often had to make do with data that was produced for other purposes and convert it as best they could to meet their own requirements. However, developments in computer technology have increasingly made it possible for users to select the information they require, in the form best suited to their needs, and when they want it.

While we shall be concerned in this book with formal information systems, we need to be careful not to ignore the capture and integration of informal information derived from, for example, networking within and outside the organisation. When we are operating at a more strategic level, or in situations of uncertainty, information from informal systems will assume a far greater profile.

Content of information systems

Clearly the content of an information system provides the basic building materials for it. There are a number of key issues that impact on the content:

- The *scope* of the information system – what areas of information it is covering, for example HR information, production information, internal or external information.
- The *accuracy* of the underlying data. The old adage 'garbage in, garbage out' is so very true. If you have no confidence in the underlying data, you should have no confidence in the resulting information. A really good example was when were told by a large financial organisation operating on the European stage that it did not have an absence problem. We were rather surprised by the information being generated from its HR information system, which did indeed suggest low levels of absence. However, further research identified that managers in the organisation did not consider supplying absence data on their staff to be a high priority, and therefore the underlying data was unsound. There can be a surprisingly high level of error in even simple, straightforward data. One organisation did a sample survey of the data on employees and found a significant level of error in the data on gender!
- The *coverage* of the data – is the data available across all departments, all regions, for all employees, etc?
- The *consistency* of the data as it relates to the coverage. Does the data mean the same in different parts of the organisation? For example, when costing learning events, are all the learning administrators including the same costs, such as the travel costs of the learners, the costs of producing the handouts, and the cost of learners' time?
- The *clarity* of the data. Are there clear and unambiguous definitions for all the data? For example, when headcount information is produced, who should be included? In many organisations, there is a wide variety of ways in which people work for the organisation – as traditional employees, as contractors, on short-term employment contracts, as secondees, as trainees, and so on.

As the foundations of the information system, it is vital that the content is right – that you have the relevant data for your users, and that you have confidence that the data is sound. Often this relies on setting up good supporting systems for capturing the basic data, characterised by clear documentation, regular monitoring and checks. However, most of all it depends on everyone involved understanding the purpose and value of the information system, and being committed to ensuring that the data is of the highest quality.

Presentation of information

If the content of information systems provides the basic building blocks, we believe that getting the presentation of information right lies at the heart of designing a really successful information system. Let us take a simple example of a company that manufactures glass bottles in 20 factories across the country. Consider the information needs, say, of the supervisor of a particular production line, and compare these with the information needs of the managing director (MD). The supervisor will need detailed information on the production line for which he or she is responsible. The MD will be more concerned with total production for the whole company and will probably not routinely need to have information broken down to less than factory level. So both managers will need information on production, but at quite different levels of detail. The MD's powers of under-standing, analysis and decision-making will be completely swamped by the sheer volume of infor-mation provided if it comes to him or her in the same degree of detail needed by the supervisor. On the other hand, the supervisor would find that the lack of detail provided for the MD would be totally inappropriate for his or her needs.

Lucey (1997) describes the different levels of management decision-making as operational, tactical and strategic. The characteristics of the decisions taken at the different levels will be discussed later in this chapter, but clearly as the spectrum shifts from operational to strategic, as characterised by the example above, the attributes of the information needed change.

So we can see that there are important issues affecting the way in which information is assem-bled and presented. Also, we can see that there can be as much danger in having too much infor-mation as in having too little. Indeed, with the use of Information and Communications Technology (ICT) in the routine operation of business processes, we have the ability to produce masses of information, often as a by-product, and the problem often becomes one of too much information rather than not enough. It is easier to churn it out than to think about how it should be modified to meet the needs of individual managers. Ackoff (1967), in a classic article 'Management misinfor-mation systems', argued that most such systems were designed on the assumption that man-agers lacked the relevant information, whereas he believed that most managers suffered from an over-abundance of irrelevant information! There is evidence that suggests that Ackoff's message has still not been heard. We still see weighty management reports full of tables of detailed figures. Managers of today are now confronted with massive databases of information and the tools to extract almost anything they want. Therefore, the emphasis shifts from supplying relevant infor-mation to eliminating irrelevant information, and the two most important activities become filtration and condensation – we *filter* out the irrelevant and *condense* the relevant into manageable form.

The use of statistical techniques, described in Part 2 of this book, is also key to the successful conversion of data into information and to its presentation in a usable format. These techniques can be used to analyse data – by summarising it, comparing data, looking for relationships and so on – in order to provide useful information in a form that highlights the significant points of interest, thereby aiding their use in decision-making. Let us look at some simple examples in Case Studies 1.1 and 1.2, where we have been asked to advise on the preparation of meaningful information for the management team .

CASE STUDY 1.1

One of the areas of interest is the number of working days lost through employee absen-teeism. The basic data would be the number of days lost, perhaps broken down by depart-ment. This can be pretty meaningless on its own. However, we can use simple statistical techniques to present information in a way which means something immediately to the user: for example, by presenting the absentee figures as a proportion of days lost com-pared with working days available. If these proportions are broken down by department, we can compare the figures and take appropriate action. For example:

There are two departments, A and B. A has 200 days lost through absence during the year while department B has only 75 days lost. Which department has the better absence figures?

At first sight we might be tempted to say that department B has the better figure because 75 is less than 200.

However, as suggested, compare the absences with the possible working days available. Let us assume that department A had 5,000 working days while department B had 1,250 working days available. The comparison looks like this:

Department A   Department B

$$\frac{200}{5,000} = 0.04\ (4\%) \qquad \frac{75}{1,250} = 0.06\ (6\%)$$

Department B, far from being better, is now shown to be half as bad again in percentage terms as department A (6%:4%), so management would probably decide to concentrate attention on Department B.

By presenting the absence figures in this way we actually produce information on which management can take action. In the above example, the absence rates expressed as a proportion (or percentage) of days lost against employee availability give a much more useful picture of the absence levels in the two departments than the raw absence figures.

CASE STUDY 1.2

Often an item of information is meaningless on its own. For example, suppose we are interested in the productivity of a sales representative measured in terms of sales per year. Let us imagine Ms X achieves sales of £100,000 per year. Is this a good, bad or indifferent performance? We just do not know. How can we possibly tell? Well, we could compare her results with the other sales representatives. However, if there are 100 sales reps, it could be a bit difficult to compare 100 sales per year figures and make much sense out of it all. So what do we do? These are some possibilities.

■ Rank the results of all the sales people – in order from the highest results at the top, down to the lowest sales per year at the bottom – and see where Ms X's result falls.
■ Compare her performance with the average performance of all sales representatives.
■ As a complete alternative, compare her performance over time. What sales results did she achieve last year, or over the last five years? Are her sales increasing or decreasing? How does this compare with the other reps?

As should be evident, managing information is a vast and complex subject. However, as we have seen, the basic principles are fairly simple, and as long as these are kept in mind we shall be neither overwhelmed nor disappointed in our quest to manage information effectively.

So far we have looked at some of the issues surrounding the content and presentation of information systems. We look next at the third key issue, *when* it is required.

Timeliness of information

Timeliness is often something that is overlooked in the search for the right information in the right form. No matter how good the information is or how well it is presented, if it is provided too soon it may be ignored; too late and it is useless. A good example of the timeliness of information is the difference between financial accounting and management accounting. While both are useful, the distinction between them is that financial accounting gives a very accurate historical record of the results of the previous year's trading activities, and management accounting gives an up-to-date comparison of how the business is performing against budgeted targets. Management accounting aims to give information to managers in time for them to take corrective action, where necessary, to secure the results they are aiming for.

The frequency with which the information is presented to users is also very important. If it arrives too often, it can overload the user. If the intervals between its arrival are too long then it is possible that it will arrive too late for its purpose. For example, if we are a manager who is concerned about meeting a weekly target, we will probably want information on a daily basis, and want the latest information on our desk when we get into work in the morning. If it is yearly sales that are particularly important then monthly reports will probably suffice, and the timing of their arrival will not be critical, at least at the beginning of the yearly cycle. Perhaps later in the year, we may need reports more frequently, because there is so little time left for the manager to take corrective action to ensure that targets are met.

A really good example which sums up the importance of getting the content, presentation and timing of information right is highlighted in the Higgs report (Higgs 2003) on the role of non-executive directors (NEDs). Higgs rightly identifies the importance of the quality of information available to NEDs and the board generally. He suggests that directors must ask themselves, 'Is appropriate, timely information of the right length and quality provided to the board ...?'

So, having looked at what information is needed, in what form and when it is required, we now look at how the users of information receive their information – the different types, or classes, of report that are generally used.

CLASSES OF MANAGEMENT INFORMATION REPORT

There are usually considered to be four main classes of report through which information can be made available to managers and specialists. We shall consider them in turn. These are:

- routine reports
- exception reports
- request reports
- special reports.

Routine reports

As the name suggests, *routine reports* are the regular reports that are the bedrock of any information system. They are characterised by the fact that they are usually provided at regular, predetermined time intervals, and contain the same type of information, presented in exactly the same format, on each occasion. Examples are weekly sales reports, monthly reports on absenteeism, half-yearly reports on staff turnover, annual reports to staff and shareholders, etc.

Exception reports

The second class of report, the *exception report*, is generated as the result of some exceptional situation. For example, it could be that as production manager we are interested in the performance of each production line. But are we? In fact, we may only be interested in receiving reports from those production lines that, by exception, are not achieving their targets. By asking only for these exception reports we would cut down the amount of information we have to study and concentrate our attention on those parts of the operation that are not going according to plan.

Another example could be where we are managing a shop or a store with a vast number of product lines. We are clearly interested to know from time to time exactly how many items we have available in each stock line but we would want to know *immediately* the details of any item that is about to go out of stock. Hence we would probably want, by exception, daily reports only on low or out-of-stock items. If we are conscious of the costs of overstocking we would probably also want exceptional, weekly reports on those item lines that exceed particular limits.

Alternatively, we might be an HR manager responsible for a number of factories or premises. Suppose absenteeism is a concern. We would probably be inundated with information if we received detailed reports from all factories. So we would seek exception reports only from those factories where the absentee rate (expressed as the number of days lost through absenteeism as a proportion of possible working days available – see earlier) is greater than a particular level, say, 5 per cent. What we have decided is that we are not worried about those premises with absentee rates below 5 per cent – they require no action to be taken by us at the present time. However, we are worried about all those premises with absentee rates over 5 per cent and will wish to take action on them, or at least monitor closely what is going on.

Finance professionals are always interested in variances from budget, on either the income or the cost side. With detailed budgets, there can be a vast range of variances to look at, so it makes sense to report on exceptional variances – perhaps those that are, say, more than 5 per cent above or below the budgeted figure.

With the growth in the use of performance indicators, particularly in the public sector (for example in the health service and the police service), when managers are faced with a large number of indicators to monitor it makes a lot of sense to focus attention on those that are 'significantly' different from their target.

Exception reports are really a more sophisticated version of routine reports. They have the advantage that they focus on the problem areas – the areas where action or decisions may be required. They take a lot more effort to set up but can be worth their weight in gold to the user!

Request reports

Request reports are produced as a result of a specific request for information that is thought to be available, but which is not usually included in a routine report. They may provide information in more detail: for example, staff turnover shown by production line rather than as an overall figure. They may provide information required for a specific timescale: for example, we might be interested in one particular month's figures on profitability rather than waiting for the half-yearly report. A request report could be a report that other people receive as a routine report but we do not. An example of this could be where, as the finance manager, we might not routinely receive information on market trends, whereas the marketing manager would. However, we could find such information invaluable at certain times, such as when putting together the budget for next year.

Modern information systems provide the flexibility to produce request reports much more easily than was the case even a few years ago. In parallel with the developments in ICT, there is a growing school of thought that most reports should be request reports and that routine reports should be kept to a minimum. Most managers and many staff have ready access to a PC or computer terminal and the facility to call up the specific information they need, in the form they want it, when they want it. Moves in this direction are being accompanied by a shift away from what might be thought of as the more traditional management information systems, towards the concept of the corporate database. More of this later.

Special reports

Finally, we come to the *special report*. As the name implies, the need for this type of report usually arises out of some special or unusual situation. It may also require information that is not readily available from the organisation's database, and so call for a special exercise in data capture. By their very nature, the need for special reports should arise infrequently, at least in those organisations that have sorted out their information requirements! Special reports will usually be designed from scratch specifically for the particular requirement and can be expensive to produce.

A typical example is when a factory puts out a particularly poor production result one month. There could be a call by managers for a lot of detailed information on that factory: for example, details of employees, the condition of plant and equipment, specific production line figures, etc. Another example could be where an opportunity has arisen to sell our product for the first time in a foreign country. We will want information on that country, eg, its economy, its markets, its import regulations. That information will almost certainly not be available within our organisation and considerable external research will be required.

In this section we have looked at the types or classes of reports through which information can be made available to managers and specialists. You will be starting to get a feel for both the potential for managing information effectively and the sort of choices that have to be made in designing your information system. We next look at the sorts of organisational factors that influence information systems.

IMPACT OF ORGANISATIONAL FACTORS ON INFORMATION SYSTEMS

When an organisation is a small, simple set-up, the need for sophisticated information can be virtually non-existent. In a small firm with an owner/manager, a small number of staff and customers, that manager will probably know every aspect of the business in detail and will probably keep his or her own records of useful information in his or her informal information system. The situation becomes trickier if within this one business there are two different types of activity. For example, suppose the manager runs a decorating business and also has a shop selling paint, wallpaper and the like. Add to this a further dimension – say a redevelopment is planned of the premises where the business is located – and now the manager could really start to think that things are getting a little out of hand. The manager might begin to feel the need for some formal systems for managing information in order to allow him or her to prioritise the use of time and concentrate on the important indicators of business success.

This is a very simple and obvious example, but we have used it to introduce the very important concept that *the need for information increases with the complexity of the organisation, the complexity of the tasks carried out and the rate of change in the environment of the organisation*. From this statement it can be readily understood why there is an increasing emphasis on managing information today. We have seen the growth of large complex organisations – vast conglomerates of many different, disparate businesses. We have also seen that companies that we normally associate with one particular activity are actually also engaging in a variety of other activities. Take, for example, gas and electricity suppliers. They are now selling each other's products, as total energy suppliers. Similarly, supermarkets have diversified from food into other products such as clothes and petrol, and then into different business areas altogether, such as financial services.

Another important factor is that we continue to live and work in an climate of great change. Let's look at some of these changes:

- Technological change: for example, increasing use of computers in all aspects of our lives. This ranges from the ability to buy and sell almost anything through the Internet, to the exponential growth in mobile phones with ever-increasing facilities, to robot production lines and information systems that can out-think experts.
- Demographic change: for example, there is an ageing population in the UK, and a trend to smaller households; there is also rapid population growth in the developing world.
- International change: for example, the breakdown of national barriers, the growth of international companies or companies with worldwide interests, and the emergence of global markets.
- Changes in social values: for example, a greater concern for protecting the environment.

Organisation structure and culture

So not only are organisations becoming more complex and their activities more varied, but this is against a background of enormous changes in their environment. Hence there has come to be a burgeoning need for information and more emphasis on effectively managing that information.

So, what factors influence the type of information system required? One factor is the type of activity the organisation is involved in – for example manufacturing or services – but equally important will be the management structure and the culture within the organisation itself. By 'structure' we mean the way in which an organisation is physically organised in terms of units such as departments and/or locations. By culture we subscribe to the definition set out by Stonich (1982), which takes culture to be 'the set of traditional and habitual ways of thinking, feeling, reacting to opportunities and problems that confront an organisation.' Or perhaps put more succinctly 'the way things are done around here'. Both structure and culture will influence the way information flows through the organisation.

There are one or two clear principles that apply in the development of all information systems. Generally, the simpler the structure and the culture, the more straightforward it is to work out the information needs and develop an overall information system. Organisations where responsibilities are clearly defined and understood will also find it much easier to set up effective information systems, as will those where the structure and culture are not in conflict. In practice, it is a rare organisation that achieves these conditions. There will always be some blurring of the edges as far as managers' or departmental responsibilities are concerned. Indeed, some organisations that operate in very dynamic environments adopt looser styles of organisation structure to cope with their ever-changing environments: for example, moving towards multidisciplinary project teams. So there will need to be a very different approach to developing an information system depending on how an organisation is structured – whether it has a traditional structure, a matrix management structure or whatever.

In the past, the traditional and probably most common organisational structure was based on functional lines. Consequently, information systems have tended to develop within each function. For example, the director of HR might have under his or her control payroll and information relating to all aspects of the staffing of the organisation. The director of finance might have systems for budgetary control, the treasury function, etc. These systems were usually developed with only one purpose in mind – to suit their particular departmental or functional needs. They are known as *dedicated systems*, in that they are dedicated to one specific purpose, and may have been developed independently of each other.

As the organisation has grown both in size and complexity, so will the individual systems have grown and developed, often putting an almost impossible burden on an outdated computer system. This is assuming that there is one computer system in the organisation – but it is just as likely that, as the separate information needs have been identified, they will have been met by the development of information systems on different types of computer hardware and computer software. Many organisations have rued the detrimental effects on their efficiency of this type of sporadic development of their overall information system strategy. As well as being inefficient in meeting the traditional departmental needs, this functional approach to information is ineffective in meeting the needs of today's structures with their emphasis on multidisciplinary approaches.

Corporate databases and information independence

What is the alternative to this ad hoc approach to the development of different types of information systems? One answer is the development of more sophisticated *corporate* database systems, with the aim of providing a common pool of data to meet the information needs of all users in the organisation. The advantages of this approach are enormous and are discussed in detail in Chapter 5. However, another important concept is that of *information independence*. This means that the storage of information/data is independent of how it is processed and used in different parts of the organisation. The implications of this independence are that it should be possible to vary the requirement for information without this affecting the way it is stored; and vice versa, restructuring the underlying database should not affect access by the users.

Information culture

Key to the success of any information strategy is what might be described as the information culture of the organisation. Ward and Peppard (2002) define information culture 'as the values, attitudes and behaviours that influence the way employees at all levels in the organisation sense, collect, organise, process, communicate and use information'. They go on to outline four common types of culture found in organisations:

- functional culture – where information is used as a means of exerting power over others
- sharing culture – where information is willingly shared and used to improve performance
- enquiring culture – where people actively search for better information about the future and ways of doing things differently
- discovery culture – where people are open to information on new ideas and radical changes.

We suspect that all too many readers will have experienced the functional culture and appreciate the advantages of a more positive and constructive approach to the use of information. It is all too easy to concentrate on the technical aspects of information systems and forget that an information system is only as good as the people that use it. Changing the information culture, as with any aspect of organisational culture, is hard work. As HR professionals we need to be particularly aware of these issues, as we can make a key contribution in helping to develop the appropriate culture. Marchand *et al* (2000) (in Ward and Peppard 2002) introduce the concept of *information orientation* as a measure of how effectively an organisation manages its information, and they have developed a set of competencies associated with the effective management of information.

Impact of information on structures

A further interesting issue is the effect of better and more accessible information on structures. Johnson and Scholes (2002) talk about the impact of better information through ICT on the roles of some of the traditional information 'gatekeepers' in organisations. Staff can now obtain the information to do their jobs directly without it passing through the conduit and filter of middle managers; customers no longer need rely on sales staff as they access information through the Internet; the role of unions will change as they cease to be the main source of information to their members; the role of HR staff will change as they no longer are the gatekeepers of all that information on policies and procedures and all that vital information on employees. Johnson and Scholes suggest that this will lead to flatter structures, and much greater interaction at lower levels across the organisation and with outside stakeholders. In Chapters 10 and 11 we develop some of these ideas of how structures may change in the future.

MANAGING INFORMATION FOR COMPETITIVE ADVANTAGE

So far we have discussed information systems and the management of information as a fairly abstract concept. Now we need to come down to earth and ask why managing information is so important as to justify the cost and attention we suggest is needed!

In this respect, all organisations exist for a purpose:

- in the commercial sector, to survive and grow, thus providing good returns to investors over time
- in the not-for-profit sector, to provide the highest quality services in the most cost-effective way.

In both sectors there is fierce competition for resources (human, financial, plant and equipment), suppliers and most of all customers, in every meaning of that word. Most books on business strategy (eg Porter 2004, Johnson and Scholes 2002) talk about the need for organisations to gain and maintain strategic or competitive advantage and the key role that information plays in achieving this. There are a number of basic strategies that organisations can adopt:

- *Overall cost leadership*: providing goods or services at the lowest cost through reduced production costs and/or increased productivity. An example is the first marketing firm to sort the information in its customer database into specific interest segments for targeted mail shots, thus securing the same response but at lower mailing costs. Organisations using the Internet and e-business provide numerous examples. Among the most striking are the low-cost airlines, which have driven down costs by doing all their ticket sales online and providing a no-frills service.
- *Differentiation*: the ability to add value or some unique feature(s) to a product or service to improve its image and/or quality. An example is the market research information that led the first bank to decide to offer 24-hour banking over the telephone. This gave customers instant access to information about their accounts, allowing them to pay bills, transfer money and so on at any time of the day or night. A further differentiation was to

allow access to customers to make the changes themselves, online from the computer in their own home or office.

- *Focus* (sometimes regarded as a combination of cost leadership and differentiation): that is, specialisation and concentration on a particular market or product niche. Organisations analyse market information in order to focus on being the lowest-cost supplier to that segment, or to meet a particular requirement of the segment that allows a premium to be added to the 'normal' price. Examples are businesses that specialise in certain vehicle repairs such as exhaust systems or tyres, or farmers that have opted for organic markets, perhaps in specialist areas as well, such as supply of organic asparagus. These organisations develop their operational information as they move along their specialist learning curves through the repetitive nature of their activities. They become big fish in their small pools.

Porter's generic strategies are applied so as to overcome the strategic competitive threats faced by organisations. These threats are two-sided depending on whether we see them as applied to us or to our competitors. The main competitive forces at work have been described as:

- Threat to entry: barriers created by, for example, strict government legislation or the high cost of setting up.
- The power of suppliers and buyers. A monopoly supplier can, in theory, charge a high premium, thereby driving our costs up. If there is only one customer for our goods and services, that customer can drive a hard price and quality bargain.
- Threat of substitutes: if customers can obtain supplies, whether goods or services, from sources other than ourselves.
- Rivalry between competitors, possibly setting off a price war.

It is interesting that this approach to competitive advantage has stood the test of time. Porter (2004) argued cogently that despite the massive changes in technology, development of new growth industries, changes in government policies and so on, the 'underlying framework for understanding competition' set out in his classic text of 1980 still remains as valid today, over two decades later. Each of these strategies will generate its own information requirements, and if an organisation is going to be successful in achieving competitive advantage then it will need to be effective in managing the information required to support them.

In the public sector an interesting development has been the introduction of the concept and activities of *Best Value*. All local authorities in England, and police and fire authorities in England and Wales, are required to undertake Best Value reviews of their services using the structure of the 4Cs to:

- *challenge* why, how and by whom the service should be provided
- *compare* the processes and performance of others, taking account of views of service users and potential suppliers and against 'best performers'
- *consult* local people; service users; staff, staff associations and trade unions; partners; and the wider business community (that is, their stakeholders) about the service and how it can be improved
- use fair and open *competition*, where appropriate, to secure efficient and effective services.

A fifth C – *collaborating* with public and private sector organisations and the voluntary sector as a means of securing efficient and effective services – is also usually applied.

The undertaking of these reviews has generated the need for large quantities of information and has often highlighted quite serious gaps in knowledge about how efficient and effective services currently are, and about the lack of reliable information to enable comparisons with other organisations. It can be hoped that one of the positive by-products of these reviews will be to build a comprehensive picture of the information needs of these organisations and the information systems required to support these needs. (We are not sure that this opportunity is actually currently being grasped!)

It is perhaps self-evident that the purpose of your information system is to support the organisation's objectives, at the strategic, tactical and operational levels. Your information system has to help answer the questions:

- Which 'business' or 'businesses' should we be in?
- How should these businesses be financed?
- How should the organisation be structured?
- How should resources be allocated?
- How should we organise these resources?
- How should people be rewarded for their performance?
- How should we integrate with others in the supply chain, our suppliers and customers?

DECISION-MAKING AND INFORMATION SYSTEMS

There is no point in having information for its own sake. The main purpose for having an information system is to support the decision-making processes of the organisation. This process can be set out in a simple way (see also the hard and soft systems approach in Chapter 2):

Identifying the problem	– scanning the external environment and monitoring the internal environment
Defining the problem	– analysing the problem, developing models to represent the problem, developing success criteria
Generating solutions	– using the model to identify solutions, explore the outcomes and implications
Choosing a solution	– selecting the best or optimum solution using the model
Implementing the solution	– putting the solution into practice
Evaluating the solution	– assessing the effectiveness of the solution in meeting the success criteria, learning from the process

In a business environment there is a range of very different problems depending where on the spectrum of operational decisions to strategic decisions we are working. The decision attributes, therefore, will follow the same spectrum, and in turn so will the information attributes – see Figure 1.2.

Level	Decision-making attributes	Information attributes
Operational	Operation specific, frequent, repetitive, short time scale, short-term implications, small scale resources, low impact, highly structured, clear decision rules, little or no discretion.	Detailed, precise, comprehensive, mostly quantitative, available frequently and quickly, usually on a routine basis, mainly internal, mainly historic, high levels of certainty.
Tactical	↓ ↑	↓ ↑
Strategic	Organisation wide, infrequent, one-off, long-time horizons, long-term implications, large-scale resources, high impact, difficult problem definition, complex, unstructured/ambiguous, high uncertainty, requiring judgement and creativity.	Broad brush, summarised, often incomplete, often qualitative, forward looking, heavy external emphasis, high levels of uncertainty, wide range of sources including informal.

Figure 1.2

There is an issue about the cost of information. Clearly, this has to be related to the value added by the information to the decision-making process. There has to be a balance between the cost of the information and the value of the decision. Often the cost of information increases as you move up the spectrum from operational to strategic – however, so too does the cost of making a wrong decision!

Decisions are also characterised by the amount of information or degree of certainty we have about the outcomes of our choices, ranging from:

- *Certainty:* where there is only one outcome from each choice of action and we have complete and unequivocal information about the outcomes. For example, someone deciding to purchase an item at a specific price using cash from her wallet can be certain that the amount of cash she has left in her wallet will be reduced by that amount.
- *Risk:* where each choice of action may result in one of several identified possible outcomes and a probability of occurrence can be attached to each outcome. In the simple example of deciding to throw a dice, we know there are six possible outcomes and the probability of each outcome is 1/6. In the treatment of an illness, previous studies will have shown the likelihood of success of the treatment.
- *Uncertainty:* where the number of outcomes, their values and the probabilities of them occurring are not known. For example, the decision to join the euro or not is plagued by uncertainty. It may be possible to estimate the likely impact on certain financial indicators, but the wider ramifications in terms of relationships with the rest of Europe, world trade, and the political implications at home cannot easily be listed as series of outcomes whose probabilities can be estimated.

The degree of uncertainty surrounding decisions is often closely associated with the levels of decision-making. At the operational levels there are high degrees of certainty – we are often repeating decisions that we have made before, on the basis of detailed and accurate information. At the tactical level, more uncertainty creeps in, over the impact of a pricing decision, or a particular allocation of resources. At the strategic level, almost all the decisions have quite a high level of uncertainty associated with them. Do we really know what the impact will be of selecting a particular chief executive, or going into a new market, or developing a new product, or trying a new system of government such as regionalisation?

Despite the obvious issues surrounding risk and uncertainty, there is still some inclination on the part of designers of information systems to assume that all decision-making takes place in a rational way. By this we mean that:

- there is a single clear objective that can be described in positivist numerical or financial terms
- there is complete and perfect information available
- all the possible outcomes are known, and can be quantified and described in relation to the objectives
- the outcomes are ranked against the specific criteria describing the objectives
- the best outcome is chosen.

While this rational approach in its pure form may suit lower levels of decision-making, that is, decisions on operational and some tactical occasions, where there is more certainty and structure, it is not always appropriate at the strategic level. Here, as we have shown, there is less certainty, there may be conflicting objectives and all the outcomes are not known. It is likely that other qualitative factors such as political, social and psychological issues will be included in the decision-making process. Indeed, when we were involved in the relocation of an organisation some years ago, the deciding factor was the extent to which the managing director felt the proposed locations would meet his family's requirements!

These fuzzy, uncertain situations we face, so lacking in clarity of objective and with incomplete and imperfect information, probably respond best to the *limited rationality* approach. In these cases a comprehensive analysis is either not worth doing or is impossible. Possibly the best use of the busy manager/specialist's time here is to make a start searching for a possible solution and stop searching when he or she finds something that appears to work. They will make decisions that are sensible or rational given the incomplete information they have and taking into account the high costs of getting better information. They then refine this decision as they go along through a series of incremental steps known as *logical incrementalism.*

This conflict between objectives and between the socio-political issues surrounding them often continues after the decision has been made, into and through the implementation stages, so that our decisions need to be thought of as processes rather than as single events. In fact, particularly in strategic decision-making, we often make our decisions in a piecemeal and unstructured manner. In other words, rather than being deliberate and rational, the decisions are emergent.

In practice, this is probably the situation that faces most of us operating day-to-day in the real world. We rarely analyse the problems we encounter, generate all the possible options for their solution and then scientifically identify the best solution. There is so much disorder in our decision-making, problems are not clear-cut and discrete, they interact with each other and we vacillate between the problems and their possible solution(s). The level of disorder can be such that, instead of simply having a problem in need of a solution, the solution of one problem causes other problems (or opportunities) for us to address. For example, the introduction of our HR information system (see Chapter 8) may lead to a speedier, more efficient administration of personnel records, but where can we redeploy the staff who previously worked on the paper files?

Sometimes the situation in which we are trying to make our decisions is such that, unlike the rational decision-making model where the decision itself is seen as all-important, there can be cases where the way in which we are seen to make the decisions is more important. For example, when we are trying to win the hearts and minds of our stakeholders, we might consult them and involve them in the decision-making process. A wise organisation planning a restructuring may well decide that consulting the staff – seeking their views on the way forward, the issues that need to be addressed – will pay dividends when implementing the changes. Many public bodies will undertake public consultation exercises on sensitive decisions such as level of charges, closure of facilities. They may well involve high profile, senior staff to indicate the importance they attach to the consultation exercise. In other words, the way in which we are seen to be arriving at our decision is symbolic of the degree of importance we attach to the decision itself.

All of these factors, and others, demonstrate the complexity of decision-making and the distance, in reality, between the way we actually make decisions and the structured, rational model. This is not to say that we ignore the rational model but that we need to identify which, if any, of the aspects surrounding our decision-making respond to the rational model and how best we can cope with those that do not. In Chapter 2 we discuss a rather different approach, the Soft Systems Methodology, which helps us make sense of, and make decisions in, the highly complex world in which we live. In Chapter 21, we discuss decision theory – another approach to structuring our decision-making processes.

CONCLUSION

In this chapter we have covered some of the important issues that affect the development of information systems. We have distinguished between the concepts of data, information and knowledge. We have analysed the issues affecting the content, presentation and timing of information. We have considered the different types of report through which information can be made available. We have focused on the information needs of the individual users, however as most people work as part of an organisation, we have also considered how the structure and culture in an organisation can influence the development of its information system.

This chapter also covered the key issue of how information can give competitive advantage, and finally we have introduced some of the concepts of decision-making, touching on risk and uncertainty. One final point is that some people might argue that the cost of getting the right information in the right form at the right time is very high. We believe the cost of not doing so could be much higher.

Having looked at the some of the general principles and philosophy underpinning our use of information, in the next chapter we consider some of the key systems concepts involved in designing an information system.

REVIEW QUESTIONS

1. Information is required on the number of leavers in your organisation. Discuss the key issues concerning the content, presentation and timeliness of providing this information.

2. In the context of a decision to move the HQ of an organisation, discuss the decision in terms of certainty, risk and uncertainty.

Information systems concepts

INTRODUCTION

Before we go much further in describing the processing and uses of information, or the design and development of systems for managing that information, it will be useful to set out some of the key concepts, and the terms used to describe them, which are common to all systems. As key players in the specification of requirements for the system and end users, it is essential that we understand and speak the language of the ICT specialist.

Some of the concepts we describe may appear relevant only to the simple and straightforward world of physical systems. However systems thinking provides a very powerful approach and a rich source of insight into the complex world within which we live and work. In the last section of this chapter we set out some thoughts about systems and complexity.

DEFINITION OF A SYSTEMS APPROACH

There are many types of system but essentially all systems are made up of various parts that are connected together in a particular way in order for the parts to interact so as to achieve a specific purpose. Examples of systems range from a simple system such as a central heating system, which through the combination of parts – pipes, radiators, boiler, working together – provides heating for a building, through to complex systems such as an organisation – which through its component parts of people, buildings, equipment, financial resources, etc work together to meet the objectives of that organisation.

The function of a system is to receive inputs and transform them into outputs:

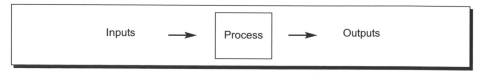

Inputs → Process → Outputs

Figure 2.1

In the case of *information systems* the inputs are the data – for example on sales, production and people – and the outputs are the information that can be used for decision-making in the organisation. The process involves storing and manipulating the data in order to transform the raw data into usable information. The process uses a combination of computer and communications technology.

The key features of a system are:

- All systems are made up of component parts and/or subsystems, and can only be described in terms of the whole.
- The components/subsystems of a system work towards a collective goal.
- The subsystems are arranged in a hierarchy, where moving up the structure provides a wider view and descending the structure provides greater detail.
- No part of the system can be changed without some effect being felt throughout the whole system.

A systems approach or systems thinking provides a method or framework for analysing the various systems that surround us. It is an approach that emphasises the connections between the various parts of the system and is essentially about relationships and processes.

SYSTEM BOUNDARIES

Systems do not operate in isolation. They are contained with an *environment* consisting of other systems and external agencies. *System boundaries* define the scope of the system itself. Everything within the system boundary is part of the system and everything outside the boundary forms part of the system's environment. This provides a very wide definition of environment, and in practice we are normally concerned only with those parts of the environment that impact on the system, that is, where changes in the environment will affect the state of the system, and those parts of the environment that are affected by the system, that is, where changes in the behaviour of the system cause changes in the environment.

In a business context a production manager will be responsible within the boundary of motivating, controlling and rewarding production staff in the effective performance of their duties to achieve production objectives. A sales manager will have similar responsibilities for the sales force. These boundaries seem clear and well defined. However problems can arise where there is ambiguity and responsibilities overlap. Also, boundaries may change, for example, when there is organisational restructuring, takeovers, etc.

As everyone who has worked in the real world of organisations, of whatever size and in whatever type of 'business' appreciates, boundaries are rarely clear cut. Where processes and problems are complex, the boundaries between systems and their environments are often ill-defined and continuously shifting. A good example of this is the work/life balance, where the systems defined by work and home are becoming increasing flexible as people choose to work from home, adopt variable working patterns, etc. Also, as many organisations move to a more project-based way of working, the traditional departmental boundaries no longer apply and the 'subsystem' becomes the project rather than the organisational unit. As we discuss in Chapter 10, the concept of partnership sourcing is changing the boundaries between organisations in the supply chain. All these flexible and changing boundaries will impact on the way we design and operate our information systems.

OPEN AND CLOSED SYSTEMS

First, we need to clarify what we mean by open systems in the context of this book. We are *not* describing the open architecture systems of computer hardware that can run any form of software. When the business applications of computers first started to develop, different hardware required its own dedicated operating systems and software. The open systems movement grew during the late 1980s and great strides have now been made towards standardisation of computer operating systems.

For our purposes:

- *Open systems* are those that interact with the external environment, outside the system boundary.
- *Closed systems* are self-contained and neither influence, nor are influenced by, the external environment.

For example, a marketing system, which is an open system, operates in an environment affected by competitors. If a competitor introduces new features for a product or changes the way it advertises a product, then our marketing function must adapt to the change in the external environment or we will remain at a competitive disadvantage.

Schultheis and Sumner (1998) wonder why closed systems, which by definition do not interact with their environment, exist at all and surmise that they exist largely by accident in that the 'participants become closed to external feedback without fully being aware of it'. They use the example of a university offering courses that might attract mature students but only offering these during the daytime like its normal undergraduate courses. If the university was more aware of potential student needs (that is, was open to external feedback), it might offer the courses in the evenings and/or at weekends!

In the organisational context, most systems are open systems. In the strictest sense, while it is possible to visualise mechanical systems as being isolated from their environment, it is difficult to imagine social systems, with all their complex interactions, as ever being 'closed'. However, in organisations there may be some attempts to keep some systems closed from each other, for example those concerned with the audit function from those concerned with authorising expenditure.

HOLISM AND EMERGENT PROPERTIES

We have already explained that under systems theory, all systems are made up of component parts or subsystems but because of their connectedness the system can only be described in terms of the whole. The whole system operates in a way that is greater than the sum of its parts. This is *holism*. The interaction of the separate parts can produce *emergent* properties or behaviours that could not obviously been predicted by looking at each part on its own. A commonly used example is that the wetness of water cannot be readily understood in terms of its component parts of the gases oxygen and hydrogen. Another, perhaps more frivolous, example is the exquisite taste of the drink, a gin and tonic – the sharpness of the gin and the bitterness of the tonic promote the emergence of that gastronomic experience, the G&T. An interesting emergent property of the eBay system (see Chapter 10), with the growth of individuals selling items in this way, has been an increase in parcel post with benefits to our rural Post Office (much to the delight of our local postmistress!).

The emergent properties of a system can be also be both unexpected and unwanted. As we deal with more complex systems, it is usually more difficult to predict all the emergent properties. Social and planning policies are littered with examples of unexpected and sometimes detrimental outcomes. A classic and powerful example is the prison system, which depending on your perspective could be seen as a system for either punishing people or rehabilitating them. However, prisons were never envisaged as operating as schools for crime! The building of high-rise flats, which allowed large numbers of homes to be provided very efficiently on small areas of land, overlooked the effects of the design on community structures, with resulting increases in anti-social behaviour.

Holism and the associated concept of emergent properties means that it is difficult to fully understand and explain how the system will operate as a whole. To be able to do so would imply having complete knowledge and therefore being omniscient. It could be argued that the issues surrounding holism and emergent properties lie at the heart of complexity.

SYSTEMS ENTROPY

All systems, whether they are mechanical, social, biological or information systems, can deteriorate if they are not maintained. Business environments are subject to great change and our information systems need to be sufficiently robust to cope with this change. Like the planned maintenance of our cars we need to include maintenance of information systems in their design, or they will cease to do the things we designed them for, possibly even break down on the information highway! This running down of information systems leads to what is known as *systems entropy*. Information systems are particularly prone to systems entropy. We have all experienced systems where the processing and generation of information slows down, where security precautions fail to meet new threats and where the system ceases to meet all the information needs of its users.

It is possible to draw parallels between having diagnostic tools for plant and equipment – with the consequent reduction in downtime and avoidance of delays in production, with their associated costs – and having similar tools for reviewing information systems. While there is a cost to having such a process for information systems maintenance, there is potentially a much bigger cost in terms of business performance if the system is allowed to deteriorate. In Chapter 6 we discuss the importance of maintaining information systems and planning to do so as part of the overall initial design of the system.

HARD AND SOFT PROPERTIES

Most business or organisational problems can be defined in terms of information with both hard and soft properties. Whatever sector we work in, some of the issues we face can be precisely measured, for example the cost of an item, the strength of a particular piece of material, or the number of employees in our organisation – and the answer is not conditioned by the measurer's sense of value. This data is said to have *hard properties*.

On the other hand, some issues are not capable of such precise measurement, and the assessment contains at least an element of judgement or is subjective in some way. Information such as whether a material looks attractive, whether we should recruit a particular person or what the average rate of price inflation will be over the next 10 years is subjective and we say that it has *soft properties*.

Needless to say these definitions can get blurred. For example, when we are measuring absences from the workplace, whether someone is absent or not would appear to be clear cut and not a matter of judgement, so we might be inclined to consider this information as having hard properties.

However as we discussed earlier, we cannot always be sure we are picking up all absences or correctly allocating them to the appropriate category of absence. The first problem can simply be the result of human error; the second may be caused by unclear definitions. A more fundamental blurring can take place when we try to attribute *meanings* to hard property data, for example, if we try to assess the level of morale in an organisation by the level of sickness absence or perhaps by the level of labour turnover.

HARD AND SOFT SYSTEMS

These terms are generally used in the context of approaches to solving problems or dealing with issues, ie you will read about the hard/soft systems approach or hard/soft systems methodology. The *hard systems methodology* has its roots in the physical sciences and engineering and takes a systematic approach to problem solving. The *soft systems methodology* has its roots in the work of Checkland (1981) and takes a *systemic* approach to dealing with *issues* rather than clear-cut problems.

Hard systems methodology

We will probably all recognise the traditional hard systems approach to problem solving, which is set out below as a series of stages:

- What is the problem or opportunity? (Set out the problem/opportunity.)
- Where are we now? (Describe the existing system.)
- Where would we like to be and what is stopping us? (Define objectives and constraints.)
- How will we know when we get there? (Formulate measures of performance/success criteria.)
- How can we get there? (Generate alternative routes/solutions.)
- How can we assess the outcomes? (Build a model.)
- What are the outcomes? (Evaluate the alternative routes/solutions.)
- Choose the best route/solution.
- Implement.
- Review and learn lessons.

This methodology takes what can be considered to be a rational and logical approach to solving the problem. It usually assumes that there is one overall 'owner' of the problem, and that it is possible to 'agree' a set of objectives which can be defined in terms of 'hard' measures of performance. This quickly leads on to seeking out alternative solutions that can then be evaluated against the performance measures. The aim is to try to find the 'best' solution, which is usually defined in terms of optimising against the performance measures.

Done properly, this is a rigorous approach designed to produce solutions to well-defined problems, and many managers will feel very comfortable with it. However, it works best in situations where all these assumptions apply. Many writers and practitioners would argue that in our complex organisations of today, operating in ever more complex environments which are changing continually, this model of problem-solving is not always the most appropriate. It was concerns of this nature that led to the development of soft systems methodology.

Soft systems methodology (SSM)

Before we start our description of SSM, we must emphasise that we cannot really do justice to the subject in this brief account. In practice it is a radically different way of organising our thinking around a 'problem situation' and reference to some of the other texts mentioned below will be essential before you move on to using SSM on a specific project.

We explained earlier that the hard systems approach works best on problems where the outcome objectives can be clearly defined and it would be splendid if all situations had such structure and clarity. However, clearly this is not the case and SSM was developed by Checkland (1981) to cope with the analysis of unstructured and poorly defined problems. As Checkland and Scholes (1999) put it rather well, 'it is an organised way of tackling a messy situation', that is, a system in which problems are interrelated. Checkland and Holwell (1998), who go on to reflect on the application of SSM in a number of arenas, assert that in fact the real world of most organisations is messy and that SSM offers the appropriate 'methodological approach to tackling real-world problems'.

SSM is in fact a structured way of dealing with complexity. SSM starts from the premise that there is no such thing as reality, individuals' real worlds being a composite of their previous experience. Their realities change as people gain further experiences. This, combined with Checkland and Holwell's (1998) definition of information, that 'data is transformed into information when meaning is attributed to it', suggests that information and information needs will be perceived differently by different people, and differently by the same person at different times. The holy grail of the 'right information' can rarely exist in organisations staffed by human beings (who are all unique). An example is the school system viewed through the eyes of students, parents, teachers, school governors, the education authority and community representatives. Each group sees a different world from the others, since each has different priorities and objectives. There is no single static organisational world in which you can define actions or decisions that in turn can be supported by a set of 'information requirements'.

A number of variants from Checkland's original methodology have developed over the years since 1981 but for convenience we shall stick largely to his original for ease of explaining the concepts. Checkland set out a seven-stage process. He never expected that the SSM analyst would go steadily through all seven stages but thought that there would be refinement of earlier ideas and iteration backwards and forwards (and possibly even across the stages) as clarification developed. We set out the stages below (and put Checkland's SSM terms in italics when they are first used). They are shown in diagrammatic format in Figure 2.2.

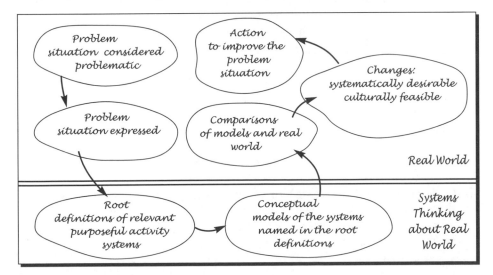

Figure 2.2 The conventional seven-stage model of SSM
Source: Checkland and Scholes (1999), reproduced with permission.

Stage 1

The enquiry starts, not so much with a problem but with a *messy* organisational situation in which someone in authority believes a *problem situation*, or situations, exists. The analyst gathers all the information, both quantitative and qualitative, through interviews, desk research, original research study, whatever.

Stage 2

The analyst combines all this information into a representation, or *rich picture* of the problem situation, without deciding on any analytical methodology or objectives at this point. This stage really does involve drawing a picture using images and symbols to represent the different stakeholders, entities, relationships, tensions and so on. At this stage, the analyst resists all temptation to start seeing solutions to the problem situation. Having drawn the rich picture, the analyst looks for generalised patterns that allow the characteristics of the situation to be described – the *primary tasks* that are the *raisons d'être* of the organisation, and the issues that can be matters of dispute/concern. Case Study 2.1 sets out an example of how one organisation tackled its messy situation.

CASE STUDY 2.1

A parish council was concerned about reports of the development of a 'yob culture' in its village, which was starting to affect relations between different groups. This was particularly evident between the youths in the village and the older residents but also affected relations between parents and other villagers. Vandalism had increased dramatically, as had other types of anti-social behaviour, and the local police had been called to address several incidents. The parish council decided that the answer was more police patrols in the village. However the police force, which had limited resources, was unable to provide much additional cover and the problems persisted, including damage to parish council property. The parish council considered employing private security guards for the village, but this was an expensive option.

One of the parishioners, a lecturer at the local university, had experience of soft systems analysis and identified that the issues involved were likely to be rather more complex than could be addressed by the single solution of security guards. She offered to carry out a review with colleagues and report back to the interested parties. The parish councillors, who were at a loss as to what to do, readily accepted the offer.

The team started without any assumptions about the problem(s) but instead recognised it was a messy situation involving the community as a whole. They set out to gather together all the information that was available, including carrying out additional research. The data/information gathered was very wide-ranging and comprehensive. It included:

- existing sources such as crime records, census data on demographics, and parish council minutes
- new sources: for example the team carried out a village appraisal seeking views on a range of issues such as the provision of leisure facilities, transport, people's expectations of community life, and perceptions of the village
- information from a series of village meetings that were held to explore the issues in more depth.

The team then drew a *rich picture* to capture the different perspectives of the various stakeholders involved – the young people in the village, older residents, the police, the parish council and so on. They resisted the temptation to see answers but wanted the general characteristics of the situation to emerge. The sample representation of the rich picture is set out in Figure 2.3.

Stage 3

Having studied the rich picture at length, the analyst needs to develop a systematic style of describing it from the various viewpoints or *Weltanschauungen* (world-views). These descriptions are known as *relevant systems* in the terminology of SSM and give an insight into the problem situation. The analyst then goes on to describe the chosen relevant systems in words that are as precise as possible, to produce the *root definitions*. Lucey (1997) describes a root definition as a 'concise, verbal description of a system that captures its essential nature and core purpose'. Establishing the root definitions, which are helpful in exposing the differing views of the people who are affected by the system, is a key stage in the process.

Stage 4

The analyst continues by constructing activity models from all the tasks that the hypothetical relevant system would logically contain in order to achieve its outcome(s). These models are called *conceptual models.*

Stage 5

The conceptual models are then compared with the rich picture, the visual model of the real world problem situation derived from the information that the analyst gathered in Stage 2. Checkland suggests that this is a stage where most iteration takes place, depending on the inconsistencies between the conceptual model and the real world. The iteration might lead to changes in the analyst's view of the problem situation, possibly some altered ideas for relevant systems, and 'an agenda for possible changes' for discussion with the stakeholders of the problem situation, the *participants*.

Stage 6

The debate with the participants sets out to identify those possible changes that all concerned agree are both desirable and feasible. Such agreed changes are taken forward to the final stage.

Stage 7

In the final state, the agreed changes are implemented.

To those of us who have been weaned on the need for instant results, SSM may appear at first sight to be incredibly complex, drawn out and, rather than bringing light into 'messiness', totally obliterates any early understanding of what might have been the problem! However, a moment's thought on some of those instant solutions – what about all those projects that have gone over time, over budget, or have been implemented without solving the core problems they were set up to solve – will show that somewhere along the line something has gone very wrong. It is not so much paralysis by analysis but maybe slow, expensive death by inadequate analysis in the desire to get quick results in problem situations that lack clarity, or where the view of too few stakeholders is given sufficient attention.

SSM is no panacea. However, carried out by well-trained and experienced analysts, who combine it with appropriate hard systems methodologies where appropriate, SSM has much to offer to our multi-faceted business systems.

Some of the key differences between hard and soft systems methodologies are set out in Table 2.1.

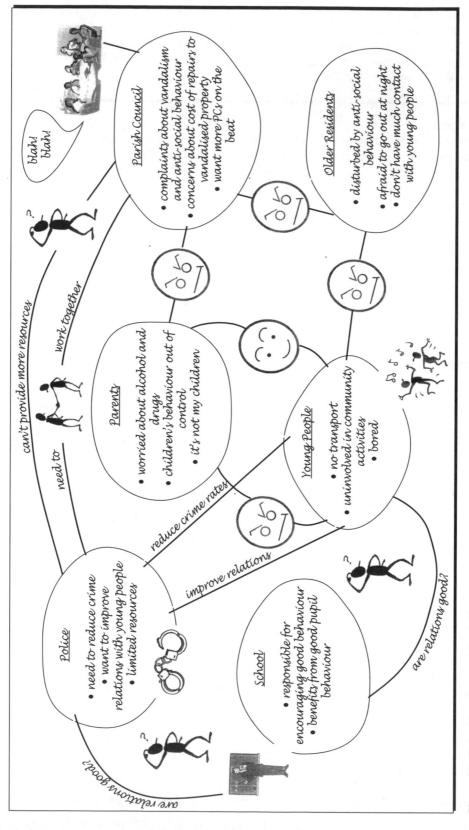

Figure 2.3 Rich picture – a vandalised village

Table 2.1

Hard systems	Soft systems
Have clear and agreed objectives.	Have unclear objectives, different perspectives.
Use the language of 'problems' and 'solutions'	Use the language of 'issues' and 'accommodations'
Deal with problems that can be clearly defined and structured	Deal with messy and complex situations.
Concentrate on the quantifiable, hard properties	Are good at dealing with unquantifiable, soft properties
Are geared to seeking the optimum solution	Are geared to exploring, understanding and explaining the situation
Assume there is one view of the world	Assume there are multiple views of the world
Assume systems are 'concrete models' of the real world	Assume systems are 'intellectual constructs'
Use an analytical approach	Use a contextual approach

SYSTEMS THINKING AND COMPLEXITY

Systems thinking, and particularly soft systems approaches, provide a very helpful way of dealing with complexity. Complexity occurs when there are many and various non-linear interactions between the different component parts of the system, and between the system and its environment. Systems thinking is all about how the different parts relate to and impact on each other. It is fundamentally about the connections between things, ideas and events. So systems thinking is very good at helping us understand the relationships, patterns and processes involved in any problem situation.

The soft systems approach both encourages and requires the user to focus on the big picture. Traditionally, we are often taught to break down problems into their component parts and set about finding the solutions to these individual parts. However, while this approach is useful in some situations it is less helpful in others. On the grand scale of problems, such as climate change or terrorism, there are so many interdependent factors that it can be very difficult to break down the problem into discrete parts. The old adage of 'How do you eat an elephant? In bite-sized chunks!' can actually be counterproductive when dealing with a complex problem. We need first to focus on the big picture and understand it, in order to appreciate its complexity. If we get bogged down too quickly in the detail of individual parts, we are likely to miss the overall patterns and inter-relationships, and the emergent properties of the whole system. The tendency to try and decompose problems into their component parts before having understood the overall picture and inter-relationships may well explain the number of embarrassing failures of large complex information systems.

Dealing with complex issues can be extremely daunting because in many ways we are programmed to be quickly into seeking solutions. Soft systems thinking requires us to step back from solutions and concentrate on exploring the issues, using a variety of models/systems to explain and reflect the multiplicity of stakeholders and their perspectives or views on the issue. It acknowledges that one's own understanding of the issues is both likely to be incomplete and to be different from other people's. Indeed one person's problem can be another person's opportunity!

CONCLUSION

In this chapter we have set out some of the important principles underpinning a systems approach to managing information. We have defined some of the less well-known terms and explained some of the key concepts. These are all concepts that the experts, the information systems professionals, take into account when designing, developing and maintaining information systems. In order to make the most constructive contribution to an information system's design and development, it is essential for users, too, to understand these basic concepts. We have also introduced you to the fascinating world of hard and soft systems methodologies, and the contribution these approaches can play in dealing with the complex world we live in.

REVIEW QUESTIONS

1. For each of the items below identify two inputs, processes and outputs:
   a. A human being.
   b. A photocopier.

2. Give two examples of hard properties and two of soft properties for the following systems:
   a. An HR performance management information system.
   b. A stock control system.
   Comment on your examples.

Information systems for planning and organising

CHAPTER 3

CHAPTER OBJECTIVES

When you have studied this chapter, you will be able to:

- define the elements of an information strategy
- describe the different levels of planning
- set out the issues associated with information and decision-making for planning
- identify types and sources of information for planning decisions
- explain the concept and purpose of a range of mathematical models used to support planning activities.

INTRODUCTION

Traditionally, the core activities of management are set out as:

- planning and organising
- reviewing and controlling.

In this chapter we concentrate primarily on the planning function, which Lucey (1997) defines as 'all activities leading to the formulation of objectives or goals and deciding on the means of meeting them'.

This is a very broad description, and it is helpful to consider the different levels of planning – strategic, tactical and operational (see Chapter 1) – and their requirements for information. Planning is a vital activity at every level: to fail to plan is to plan to fail. However, there is considerable evidence, which is supported by our own experience of working in a wide range of organisations, that suggests we do not devote enough time to planning nor are we very skilled at it. Good information and information systems can play a very important part in improving our planning capabilities. An essential ingredient to ensuring that our information systems make the most efficient and effective contribution to achieving the organisation's objectives is to have an information strategy.

INFORMATION STRATEGY

Given the key role played by information in today's organisations, one of the important outputs from an organisation's business strategy should be an *information strategy*. Bocij *et al* (2003) define an information strategy as setting out 'how information, knowledge, and the applications portfolio will be used to support business objectives'. The strategy examines the state of the organisation's information systems and ICT, and asks to what extent they provide the business information support needed for the achievement of the organisation's objectives.

The information strategy in turn sets out two substrategies:

- An *information systems (IS) strategy*, which basically defines how IT is used within the organisation, and is produced to ensure that the appropriate processes and all the necessary resources are in place to support the business strategy. Ward and Peppard (2002) refer to it in terms of setting out the *demand* side for information and systems to support the overall business strategy.
- An *information and communications technology (ICT) strategy*, which determines the most appropriate technological infrastructure: that is, the hardware, networks and software applications required to support the overall information strategy. Ward and Peppard (2002) refer to it as being concerned with the *supply* side – providing the ICT capability.

In essence the information strategy should specify the information needs of the organisation. The two substrategies are about how to deliver these. In practice, there can be an overlap between the ICT and IS strategies and some organisations choose to consider these together.

You might like to find out whether your organisation has an information strategy, and if it does, how well it meets Bocij *et al*'s definition.

LEVELS OF PLANNING

In Chapter 1 we identified three levels of management decision-making: operational, tactical and strategic. Clearly there are direct parallels in the planning processes. As we move up the spectrum from operational to strategic planning, the planning horizon shifts from being very focused, very narrowly centred on the immediate, the day-to-day activities of the organisation, to being very broadly spread across the whole organisation, as well as looking far into the future. The distinguishing features at the ends of the spectrum of the information requirements for planning are that:

- for operational planning we will usually focus internally and on accurate, historical data, with a high degree of detail.
- strategic planning we will be less concerned with absolute accuracy but will focus on external sources and build up our total information from all our environment.

Table 3.1 sets out in a clear diagrammatic way the implications of the three planning levels in terms of:

- the type of questions that need to be addressed/decisions that need to be made
- the time horizon
- the characteristics of the information in terms of scope and detail.

PROBLEMS WITH PLANNING

Our experience of consulting with, and running learning programmes for, a wide range of managers and specialists in a variety of organisations for many years has led us to conclude that few of us are natural planners. As Individual managers, we seem ready to let all sorts of excuses deflect us from taking the time to formulate our plans. It is almost as though we do not see planning as the real job. Examples of the reasons we give for not planning are:

- I don't know enough about where the organisation should be going.
- I don't have the information to plan properly.
- Even when I do plan, the future is so dynamic and uncertain that I have to keep changing the plan, so basically it's not worth planning.

Table 3.1 Levels of planning and information

Strategic	Tactical	Operational
Time horizon, say, as far into the future as we can see.	Time horizon, say one to three years.	Time horizon, say now to 12 months.
Greater breadth and scope of information ←		
What 'business(es)' should we be in? How should we organise/structure/finance the strategic plans and allocate resources? What information strategy do we need to support the strategic objectives?	What are the implications for the way we currently run our 'business(es)'? What new plant, equipment, information systems and working methods are needed to implement the new plans? What new staff, skills are required to implement the plans? What interventions are required to enhance motivation and morale?	How should we plan and organise the day-to-day activities of the organisation? What finance, materials, plant and equipment are needed for the immediate future? What are the required staffing levels? What specific issues in terms of motivation and morale need to be addressed?
Greater depth and detail of information →		

- Nobody takes notice of plans once they are written.
- Having a plan could tie me to targets which might prove difficult to meet.
- Having a plan reduces my freedom of action and restrains my creativity.
- Planning is a time-consuming task and I do not have the time at present.
- There are more urgent tasks to be done.
- Taking action on tasks feels better than thinking about them – at least I am achieving something.
- Planning requires a clear head, and I need to get all these small jobs done to clear the decks.
- Planning looks like and feels like hard mental exercise.
- My boss wants action now!

Whether we recognise these as excuses or call them reasons, we need to address them. Planning at every level is the key to the efficient and effective running of an organisation.

To use the analogy of a holiday, first we need to decide where we want to go (our objective). This is planning at a strategic level, and for that we will need information on issues such as:

- what we want from the holiday (market research on customer needs)
- availability of different types of holiday and what they can offer (information on suppliers)

- other environmental factors that might affect the decision, such as political turmoil in a country we would like to visit, and the currency exchange rate (environmental information).

The next stage in the planning process is at the tactical level. We need information to help us address issues such as:

- Do we go for a package holiday, a tailored holiday or a do-it-yourself holiday?
- How might we finance the holiday? For example we could use existing savings, set up a specific savings account and save towards the holiday, or take out a loan.
- What is the most appropriate timing, taking into account school holidays, work commitments and the like?
- Do we have the right equipment, such as suitcases, skis or snorkels?

The final planning stage, the operational level, deals with issues such as:

- What clothes do we need to take?
- How much foreign currency do we need?
- How will we get to the airport? If for example we plan to go by train we shall need to check train times; if by car, to investigate parking sites and costs; if by taxi, to check on availability.
- Do we have the right documentation: passports, tickets and so on?

None of us (we think) would choose to skimp on this planning if we wanted to have the holiday of our dreams, although some people might say, 'Oh no, I never plan my holiday. I just set off or take a cheap, last-minute package.' However, we all realise that this approach involves a certain risk. Now a poor holiday, or one that is not quite up to standard, is not too serious. However, in the organisational context much more may be at stake, and it is important to try to minimise risk. Not quite achieving our objectives, meeting customers' expectations or realising our quality standards might make all the difference between success and failure for the organisation. It could jeopardise the very survival of the organisation and, of course, our own jobs.

Many of the issues that arise in holiday planning can be mirrored at the different levels of organisational planning:

- At the strategic level, forecasting many years ahead in an environment that is subject to rapid change is very difficult. The lead times for introducing strategic change in large organisations can be very long. To use the analogy of a large oil tanker, changing direction is not a quick process, and the tanker will have travelled many miles before the change in direction is achieved. There may be very real concerns that by the time the change has taken place it will be too late to make the most of the market conditions or technological developments. Interestingly this can be a real issue in the development of information systems. There has been a number of classic examples in the public sector where by the time the system has been developed the processes and problems it is addressing have changed. (See Case Study 3.1.)

CASE STUDY 3.1

The police forces in England and Wales have been engaged for many years in trying to develop a co-ordinated package of information systems that will support the work of all police forces and the associated civil justice system. It is a highly laudable aim as it would appear to make no economic sense for each police force to develop its own system to do basically the same job. Also, by 'joining forces' they would have considerable power in purchasing both hardware and software to support the systems, and therefore achieve significant savings. Additionally, and very importantly, having one system used by all would ensure the easy transfer of data and information between forces.

However the co-ordinated approach has faced enormous difficulties. It has proved hard to agree a specification that is acceptable to all 43 police forces, and this process of negotiation has taken a long time. The systems keep being overtaken by events in the environment, such as policy changes. As individual forces' systems have become obsolete or they simply have got fed up with waiting, some forces have gone ahead independently with their own systems.

- At the tactical level, it requires a real team approach and hard work to translate strategic plans into coordinated tactical plans for different parts of the organisation. It only takes one part of this jigsaw of plans to be flawed for it to jeopardise the whole strategy. Again, it can often be the planning for new technology that proves the weak link – see Case Study 3.2.

CASE STUDY 3.2

Many banks and building societies identified the strategic advantage offered by providing Internet banking facilities so that customers could manage their accounts online using their own computers. Not only did such a service provide considerably greater convenience to the customer, it potentially represented big savings in terms of the reduced need for branches, call answering facilities and so on. However, many early online service offerings were fraught with problems. Some people could not access them using their existing software, the processes were very slow, and they terminated for no apparent reason. They were good examples of poor tactical planning.

- At the operational level, planning is usually much less of a problem. There are usually good quality information, well-established planning processes and relative stability over the planning period. However, it is at this level that the individual's reluctance to plan, or to keep putting it off, can cause problems – see Case Study 3.3.

CASE STUDY 3.3

A learning manager was asked to produce an evaluation report on a major learning programme that was taking place within the organisation. The report was required for a review meeting which was arranged many months ahead of time. The manager was very busy, and left the writing of the report until a few days before the deadline. It was only when he started to put the report together that he realised that an important section of the evaluation data was missing. He did not have the results of a survey of the views of learners' managers. The review meeting, involving a large number of stakeholders, had to be cancelled. Had the learning manager sat down at an early stage, planned the report and identified what information was required, the outcome would have been very different.

TYPES AND SOURCES OF INFORMATION FOR PLANNING

It goes without saying that without the right information our planning will be fatally flawed. Short-term operational plans need accurate, historical, mostly internal information. Longer-term strategic plans need more comprehensive external, environmental information. The tactical planning stage often combines aspects of both, but usually needs broad-brush internal information.

The types of *external* information we need are to provide answers to questions such as:

- What is happening in the sectors and markets that interest us? What is happening in the global environment which might affect these sectors and markets? What are the forecasts for growth/decline within the sector and our markets? Is the market new or is it close to maturity? Can the market be segmented? What should be our size/place in the market? What are the barriers to entry into the sector and the markets? What competition already exists or might we face in the foreseeable future? What are their plans and their likely counters to our initiatives? Are our competitors growing, shrinking or stable? Does a single organisation or small group of organisations dominate the sector? Are smaller organisations joining with others or are larger organisations demerging?
- What are the demographic changes we might encounter during the timescale of our plan? Are there any geographical movements of population that are of interest to us? How might the age profile change in our population(s) of interest? What are the implications of changing employment structures? How might these demographic changes impact on our organisation?
- What is happening to society as a whole? Will there be changes in the role of the family? Will there be significant changes in consumption, eg in the consumption of organic food, convenience foods, etc? Will there be a growth in ethical investment?
- What will be the political changes in our market countries? Will we be operating in a stable political climate? Will there be trends towards political combination or political separation?
- What are the implications of future legislation, for example on safety, working practice, trade regulations, etc?
- What impact will ICT have on our plans? Do we have the skills available to take advantage of ICT? Can ICT be harnessed as a positive competitive force? What will be the impact of technological change on our HR plans?

Typical sources of external information are government and trade association statistics; company reports; commercial organisations set up for the purpose of collecting and selling business information; scientific and technical papers; specific research investigations; conferences and working parties; meetings and discussions, as well as informal business and social contacts. Increasingly the World Wide Web provides ready access to a wide range of such information.

The types of *internal* information we need are to provide answers to questions such as:

- How do sales compare with targets? What is the production performance when compared with capacity? What are the delivery times and finished stock levels? How well are we meeting our quality standards? How up-to-date are our plant, machinery and equipment? How effective are our marketing campaigns? How do our distribution and logistics systems compare with those of our competitors?
- What is the size, range of skills, age profile and so on of our workforce? How stable is our workforce? How many people, and with what skills, do we need to recruit? How well do our people perform? What learning and development needs are there? How well do our

HR plans and succession plans support business development needs? How do our salary structures compare with the market?

- What is the financial state of our organisation? How profitable is it? What are the projected levels of cash flows? What is the level of debt? Should we invest in a new factory or warehouse, for example?
- What is the state of our research and development activities? How do they compare with the industry/sector norms? To what extent is the organisation a leader in products and technology?

Typical sources of internal information are everything that comes out of the organisation's formal information system. This can include:

- the results of the statistical analysis of raw business data
- comparison of budgets/targets with actual performance
- modelling and simulation exercises
- special investigation reports
- intra-company comparisons
- intercompany comparisons
- plus informal sources such as walking the floor to get a feel for the state of organisational morale, networking to pick up new ideas, etc.

Even a cursory comparison of the above types and sources of information with what information is actually available in your organisation for planning could reveal some interesting results!

MATHEMATICAL MODELLING

Most of us are familiar with the use of physical models in business processes. Architects and production engineers use models of factories and offices to enable them to plan efficient workplace layouts. Aeronautical engineers use models of aeroplanes in wind tunnels to give data on how the real aeroplane will fly, and chemical engineers use models of chemical plants to try out their process before going to the expense of building the real thing. These scale models are often called *iconic* models: that is, they are created in the image of something. However, in addition to these physical models there are mathematical models, which are being used increasingly by managers and other professionals to help in their business planning. They use mathematical equations and algebra to model situations. These models are often known as *symbolic* models. The idea is to develop a set of equations describing how the variables interact with each other, and answer 'what if' questions by examining different scenarios represented by different values of the variables involved.

The ability of computers to cope with thousands of mathematical calculations per second has made it possible to model very complex situations, and the developments in end-user applications have extended the use of these modelling techniques beyond the realm of the specialist mathematician or operational researcher to ordinary mortals. As a result managers now have a wide range of mathematical modelling approaches available to enable them to improve their planning decision-making.

Financial models

Perhaps the most familiar models in organisations are the financial models which represent the financial intricacies of an organisation, showing what might happen to its finances against a range of different assumptions such as trading levels, interest rates, input costs and prices. A computerised spreadsheet is an application that represents a simple financial model of a part of an organisation's finances, for example the cash flow. The spreadsheet can help us with our financial planning, for example, showing what cash flows to expect at different levels of sales, or showing what will happen to profit with changes in the price of raw materials. On the wider level, econometric models are a set of mathematical equations that attempt to describe, or model, the economy. They try to set out the many complex relationships that exist within the economy. Economists use econometric models to test out different policy alternatives and to forecast the future economic situation based on different views or scenarios of the future. The techniques have been extended to other economic planning activities and even to areas outside economics.

Optimisation models

Two models, most commonly used at the operational and tactical levels of planning and decision-making, are:

- linear programming models
- network/PERT/CPA models.

Linear programming is used in situations where the aim is to optimise the value of a single objective function: for example to maximise operational profit or minimise cost, and where there are a number of factors involved which are subject to a limit or constraint. The technique can be used in a wide range of situations where allocation of resources is required, such as production planning. See Case Study 3.4 for an example. This is a typical example of using a linear programming mathematical model to solve a business problem.

CASE STUDY 3.4

A small craft company makes fabric bags with arboreal themes out of remnants of heavyweight fabrics. It makes two types, a small handbag size with more ornate finishes, called the Leaf bag, and a larger size of a simpler design, called the Tree bag. It has plenty of orders, but has suddenly experienced staffing problems, and wants to make the best use of its specialist staff resources. The production manager estimates that she has the following resources available over the next month:

Cutting staff: 300 hours

Sewing staff: 700 hours

Finishing staff: 300 hours

Each bag requires the following input of labour:

Bag	Cutting (hours/bag)	Sewing (hours/bag)	Finishing (hours/bag)
Leaf	0.3	0.9	0.5
Tree	0.5	1.0	0.2

The finance manager advises that each bag generates the following profit:

Bag	Profit/bag (£)
Leaf	3.30
Tree	3.00

The managing director wants to know how production should be spread across the two types of bag in order to maximise profit.

This problem was set out in the form of mathematical equations as follows, where x is the number of Leaf bags to be produced and y is the number of Tree bags to be produced:

maximise $3.3x + 3.0y$

subject to the following constraints

$0.3x + 0.5y \leq 300$ (cutting time constraint)

$0.9x + 1.0y \leq 700$ (sewing time constraint)

$0.5x + 0.2y \leq 300$ (finishing time constraint)

The decision resulting from solving these equations was to make 500 leaf bags and 250 tree bags.

Network/PERT/CPA models are used for the planning and controlling of projects. The project is defined by a number of activities that are related to each other, for example they precede, follow after, or run in parallel with other activities. This then enables the project to be modelled using a network diagram of activities. Using PERT (Project Evaluation and Review Technique) and CPA (Critical Path Analysis) approaches, it is possible to determine the shortest time that the project will take, identify those activities which will be critical in terms of meeting the shortest project time, plan the requirement for resources over the project life, etc. These types of model are invaluable for project managers. The use of computers and specialist packages has enabled both the modelling of very large complex models (for example the development of a new town) and enabled managers at all levels to model relatively simple projects (for example an office move, or the launch of a new product). The models are used extensively to plan and manage information systems projects (see Chapter 6).

Simulation models

Simulation is an experimental process that helps us understand how a system will behave in reality by imitating its behaviour in an artificial environment. The basic idea is to build a model that approximates to the real world system, then carry out sampling experiments to see how it performs in various situations. Running the simulation generates representative samples of the system outcomes/performance measures, and therefore is said to *describe* what happens, rather than provide a 'best' or optimal option. Simulation techniques are particularly useful in situations that are too complex to be solved using some form of analytical process.

One of the most common simulation techniques, the Monte Carlo method, relied in the past on the use of thrown dice (hence its name) to generate random quantities representing the incidence of certain events. (Random number tables and computer random number generators are the modern equivalent!) Let us look at the example of managing the refuelling of airliners at a major airport – see Case Study 3.5.

> **CASE STUDY 3.5**
>
> The arrival intervals of the airplanes for refuelling and the volumes of fuel they require are known as the random variables. (Read more about these in Chapter 15.) Let us assume that our capacity to meet the refuelling needs of the aircraft depends on the availability of refuelling tankers, their capacity to carry fuel and the speed with which we can refill the tankers when they are emptied and get them back to their refuelling duties. In order to find the best combination of refuelling tankers and load carried to meet their task, we can construct a model of the relationship between the constraints: for example, the rate of arrivals of the aircraft and the refuelling demands made upon the tankers. We can build into the model aspects such as the capacities of the fuel tankers, and by throwing the dice time and time again and, by varying the constraints, find by trial and error which combination of tanker sizes and other factors produces the least delay in refuelling the aircraft.
>
> This would be at best a very lengthy and frustrating process and it could take days or weeks of calculations to get the optimum result. Our salvation lies in the ability of the computer, which makes it possible for us to design a model of the whole process, programme in a random number generator, ask it to simulate all the schedules and produce a schedule to give the best fit within all the constraints.

So, by processing the available data through our simulation we produce information on which to base our planning.

The use of models of all types can provide managers with powerful information to aid their decision-making. It is clearly an essential prerequisite that the model is realistic and effectively represents the real world situation it is modelling. There can be many reasons for using models. It can be cheaper than using the real thing. A good example is the use of simulators for training pilots to fly complex airliners or warplanes. It can also be safer: for example, using virtual models of underground railway stations to train emergency staff in handling disaster scenarios. Perhaps the most powerful use is the ability of models to provide an understanding of the real world they represent, by making it possible to try out, see the effects of almost unlimited different scenarios and therefore their use in forecasting. An important and interesting use of simulation models has been the work carried out on predicting the impact of carbon dioxide emissions on climate change.

SENSITIVITY ANALYSIS

Before we leave the subjects of modelling and simulation, we would like to say just a few words about the technique called *sensitivity analysis* and its use for decision-making in the planning process. In sensitivity analysis all the variables in a model are held constant except one. Each one can be varied in turn, and altering that variable by steady incremental steps enables the modeller to observe the effect on the outcome of interest. The object of this analysis is to determine to which of the variables the outcome is sensitive: in other words, relatively small changes in that factor have a disproportionate effect on the end result.

A good example of the use of sensitivity analysis is in our HR planning model. It can be used to test the sensitivity of the forecasts for different types of personnel required to the different variables in the model: for example to changes in wastage rates, or productivity assumptions. Another example is exploring the sensitivity of a capital investment decision – for example, to build a new department store – to different assumptions about interest rates, demand forecasts and the like.

CONCLUSION

In this chapter we have looked at the importance of planning, the need for an information strategy, the different levels of planning, types and sources of information required to inform our panning decisions and some of the issues that can impact on our planning abilities. We have also considered how ICT and mathematical models can help our planning by modelling and simulating the real environment. We end with the thought that, while planning can often be a challenging activity, the benefits are very great:

- consistently higher chances of meeting organisational objectives
- better use of resources of all types
- greater flexibility to respond when the real world situation turns out to be different from the one forecast
- greater personal effectiveness.

So, what happens next? Having produced our well-thought-out plans, the next key issue is whether we are achieving them. We look at this in the next chapter, which covers information systems for review and control.

REVIEW QUESTIONS

1. Take a simple example of a planning activity, for example:
   - an office or house move
   - an office party or outing
   - the purchase of a piece of equipment/household appliance.
   Identify the decisions required and the types of information needed to support them at the three levels of strategic, tactical and operational.

2. Give three examples of:
   a. external information
   b. internal information
   used for planning purposes in your organisation, or an organisation with which you are familiar. Set out their sources and explain how the information is used.

Information systems for review and control

INTRODUCTION

We have completed our plans and set in progress the activities needed to achieve the objectives that have been agreed. Now, if we had used perfect data in terms of accuracy and relevance in our planning, used appropriate statistical techniques to process this data into information, and operated in a certain (totally known) environment, we could sit back and await the achievement of our objectives. However, we rarely have these perfect conditions even at the operational level, because, for example, our plant and equipment break down, require maintenance and resetting, and our employees are subject to a whole raft of variability that affects their performance. Add to this the tactical and strategic actions of our competitors and customers in response to our plans, the unpredictability of local and global economies, and we have what Harry (1997) calls *environmental disturbances*. It is pretty obvious that we can never fully take these disturbances into account in our planning process. To emphasise the point, Harry suggests that the only reason we need control systems at all is because of the existence of these environmental disturbances.

So to ensure the achievement of our objectives and plans, we need to have information systems to *review* and *monitor* how well we are meeting our targets, etc and then take action in the event that there is a variance, to *control* the process involved. That action might be in the form of minor adjustments at the operational level – perhaps the resetting of our machines, changing the hours worked, the quality of supervision, the layout of the workplace. Or, if there is a more serious variance it may require a revision of the plan at the tactical level – perhaps our pricing policies need to be changed as we are not achieving the target market share. Or the review may show such fundamental differences that we need to revisit our strategic plans and overall objectives for the organisation – perhaps to consider further diversification or a major retrenchment. In this chapter we discuss the information systems that support the review and control function.

ELEMENTS OF CONTROL SYSTEMS

All control systems are made up of a basic set of elements. These are:

- some form of performance standard or target that has resulted from a planning process
- a measure of the level of performance achieved

- the calculation of the effect of environmental disturbances, variance or performance gap between expected and actual results
- the feedback of these variances to the control system
- action by the control system to return to the plan
- the opportunity to send feedback to a higher control unit if the environmental disturbances are so great that the original plan and/or objectives are no longer appropriate.

Feedback loops

In the above list of elements a *sensor* of some sort reports the actual level of performance. The sensor, which can be human or inanimate, generates the feedback that is measured against the *comparator* – a target or a standard. This forms the *feedback loop* (see Figure 4.1).

When the feedback acts on the control system to return the performance to plan, it is known as *single-loop feedback.* When the variance is so great that the feedback goes to some higher level for revision of the plan or the objectives themselves, it is known as *double-loop* or *higher-order feedback*. An example of single-loop feedback is a stock control system that automatically reorders stock against predefined reorder levels and quantities. If external conditions change so that the demand for stock items changes dramatically, this could result in overstocking or stock shortages. In such cases there needs to be a higher order of control which can review the low-level control system and adjust the reorder levels, quantities, and so on.

Another example is a recruitment system. A junior manager puts in a request for a member of staff to be recruited. The single-level feedback control in the system checks whether there is a vacancy in the manager's establishment. The double-loop feedback comes into play if there is not a vacancy and the request goes to a higher level of manager who has the authority to vary the establishment level.

Closed-loop and open-loop systems

Two other terms used to describe control systems are whether they are open or closed. Closed feedback loops exist as integral parts of the control system. Feedback, based on measurement of performance and comparison with the target or standard, is used to make appropriate changes to

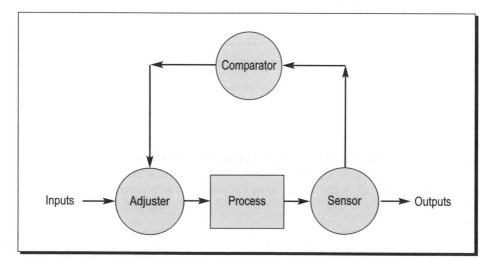

Figure 4.1 A simple feedback loop

the system inputs – a *closed-loop system*. The alternative, the *open-loop system,* exists where no feedback loop exists and control is exercised from outside the system.

A simple example of a closed-loop system is the thermostat on our central heating system – it measures the temperature against a pre-set standard and turns the heating system on or off accordingly. A similar example, but with an open-loop system, is a greenhouse with a thermometer to show the temperature. At a certain temperature level the gardener intervenes and takes action, perhaps opening a window or putting in a heater. An example of how these loops can work to advantage or disadvantage is the computer systems used for trading stocks and shares. Some years ago the traders' systems in the stock exchange were closed systems, programmed to sell a particular share when its value had dropped by a particular percentage or to a particular level. On 'Black Monday' in the late 1980s, when shares crashed worldwide, the systems were blamed for exacerbating an already difficult situation. They were reprogrammed to allow external control to be exercised by the traders when share values generally were in decline. In other words, they were turned into open-loop systems.

Case Studies 4.1 and 4.2 later in this chapter set out examples of both types of system operating in an organisational environment.

Negative and positive feedback

In most situations, fluctuations in our systems around a norm are regarded as normal. Let us take again the example of our heating system, where a temperature-sensing device monitors the environment. Once the thermostat is set to a given level, fluctuations in temperature are controlled by applying heat when the temperature falls below this norm, and applying cooling when it rises above the norm. The tendency is to dampen down wide fluctuations in temperature, and in this situation, the feedback is known as *negative feedback* – corrections are applied in the opposite direction to the original deviation. Another example is the levels of stock in your warehouse. If stocks are high you reduce your orders for new stocks. If they are low, you increase your order levels.

Positive feedback, on the other hand, acts in the same direction as the deviation and reinforces the direction of movement caused by the environmental disturbance. People rarely plan to have positive feedback in an automatic closed-loop system, as this would cause instability in the system, possibly leading to loss of control.

Positive feedback needs human intervention via an open-loop system. An example is a publisher is launching a range of books, who knows from the market research information that there is only room for one of them to be a worldwide success. Initial sales information show which book is likely to be the number one best-seller and the publisher reacts by increasing the promotion efforts on this book.

Feedforward loops

Based on the preceding sections, you might think that information flow for control involves only reacting to what has already happened. However, this is well wide of the mark. There are in fact two types of control loop, feedback loops as we have described earlier and *feedforward loops*. As the name suggests, feedforward loops are all about reacting to events that may occur in the future and making changes to the system in advance.

Feedforward loops scan the horizon for environmental disturbances (such as new legislation or potential shortages of key resources) to determine how these will affect the organisation in the future, and gather information as feedforward rather than feedback – allowing action to be taken in anticipation of environmental disturbances rather than after the effects are experienced. Feedforward control requires judgement and a sound insight into the business – and inevitably operates as an open-loop system.

Feedforward control can often involve a degree of risk – for example, anticipating a shortage of a key material and stockpiling in advance. This would increase stock holding costs, but these are likely to be considerably less than the costs of lost production should there be a shortage of materials. Most successful organisations use both feedback and feedforward control. Case Study 4.3, later in this chapter, sets out how one organisation used feedforward information that ensured its very survival.

MONITORING, CONTROLLING AND REVISING THE PLAN

We saw in Chapter 3 that planning was defined as all the activities leading to the formulation of objectives and deciding on the means of meeting those objectives. So for monitoring and controlling the plan, the first prerequisite is to have clear, unambiguous and measurable objectives. Next, we need to implement the plan, linking the strategic, through tactical to operational levels. Each level will have its targets or milestones at an appropriate degree of detail so that we can measure progress against the plan. Our feedback loops convey the variance information to the *actuator*, who (or which: the actuator is not necessarily human) will make adjustments to maintain or regain the progress of the plan towards the target.

If it is acceptable and achievable, the plan may be revised to achieve results above target. If the environmental disturbance is so great that it appears impossible for us to achieve the original objective(s) we may even abandon the plan and set new objectives, going round the system until we achieve a degree of stability which we can sustain with the resources that are available.

Monitoring, control and revision at the operational level may well be built into the plan as an automatic activity: for example, the sensing of temperature variance from the norm and getting feedback via a closed loop. This would lead to the automatic application of heat or cooling to maintain the norm. However, in most cases at the tactical level and almost certainly at the strategic level, where the situation is complex and the environmental disturbance and the degree of judgement needed is less predictable, the feedback will usually be via an open loop. This requires (or allows) control to be exercised externally to the system itself, by human intervention.

Case Studies 4.1, 4.2 and 4.3 set out some examples of control systems in action.

CASE STUDY 4.1

A good example of how single-loop closed systems of control can cause problems in situations where human beings are the recipient of the control action is the invoicing systems operated by organisations such as mobile phone companies. Here the system is programmed to react to non-payment of a bill after a set period of time by sending out various levels of reminders. Many of these systems appear not to be able to deal with situations where the customer has queried a bill or made a complaint of some sort. So customers who are being dealt with by the 'complaints department' have the added frustration of receiving these automatic reminders, with their escalating threats of action such as legal proceedings and disconnection. This does not lead to good customer relations!

> **CASE STUDY 4.2**
>
> A good example of where open loop systems are normally used at the operational level is the HR area of absence control. Many organisations monitor levels of absence and have procedures where a certain level of absence will trigger management action – perhaps counselling at the earlier stages, then followed by various levels of disciplinary action. HR systems normally work by generating reports on high absence levels. However, action is not usually taken automatically, but a manager will make a judgement on how to proceed.

> **CASE STUDY 4.3**
>
> A small charity set up to provide support and work opportunities for young adults had survived and developed on the basis of grant funding from a wide range of organisations. The chief executive was highly skilled at networking both with the staff from the donor organisations and senior staff in other charities. As a result she identified that a major source of grant funding was likely to disappear in 18 months' time, and that grant funding generally was becoming tougher to find. Identifying this key feedforward information well in advance allowed her to develop a strategy of self-sufficiency by steering the organisation towards profit-making activities. The advance notice gave the organisation time to create and develop these activities. Simply reacting to the feedback information of the withdrawal of the grants would not have given the organisation sufficient time to generate this new funding stream.

One of the factors we discussed in Chapter 1 was the timeliness of information. We saw that too frequent or infrequent, and too early or late, information was not conducive to effective decision-making. Similarly, once we have feedback on how our processes are performing against target, the timing of our control action can seriously affect the scale and effectiveness of the action taken. For example, when the space shuttles have climbed just a few miles they can often be seen to make some minor corrections to their direction before they leave the atmosphere. This small correction at the beginning of the flight is instrumental in their reaching the exact spot in space where they are planning to do their work. Leaving the direction correction until later could create a need for a much bigger correction or even make it impossible to reach the target position at all. The same principle applies to our earthbound activities – the sooner we take action on a variance, the smaller corrective action we need to take and the more effective the correction will be. For those of us involved in the management of people and their performance, this principle is all too easily recognisable. The sooner we take action to deal with a poor performance problem, the more likely it will be effective. Wherever there are delays in the receipt of information, there will also be delays:

- in formulating decisions about taking control actions
- about implementing those control actions
- in getting the benefit of moving towards our objective(s).

The human aspects of control

We have already mentioned the importance of human intervention in taking control action where there are open-loop systems. Human intervention can also be used to override automatic control mechanisms where it is clear that all is not well with the control system. For example, a pilot will take over manual control of the aircraft if a 'bug' gets into the autopilot. The so-called 'millennium bug' is another example where human control was needed to sort out computerised systems before the new millennium, or to manage the effects of any remaining bugs at the moment of changeover. Another example is where utility companies have automatic systems that generate letters and action in respect of non-payment of bills. However, at the final stage when the customer is facing disconnection, there is usually human intervention to review the case.

Yet another example will be of particular interest to those interested in the motivation of people in organisations. The objectives and performance measures we developed in our planning phase are used to monitor and control our processes and provide guidance on the activities needed to achieve the objectives. Clearly motivation will be present when control induces behaviour in the employee to work positively towards the objective(s). There is also plenty of evidence to show that people tend to be more motivated when they are involved in the setting of their own objectives. This comes, in part, from the quality of the communication between the manager and the managed, leading to an understanding by all the parties of the relevance of the objectives to individuals and to the organisation. This means that ideally, if an incentive scheme is to work in the way intended, the design of the scheme needs to be considered at the same time that the control system is designed, if the control systems are not to be ignored or at least used ineffectively.

Conflicting objectives can also have an impact here. We know of a number of customer call centres where a target is expressed as a number of calls taken per hour. This can cause conflict with standards for customer care if the operator concentrates on meeting the target rather than customer needs.

CONCLUSION

In this chapter we have looked at the basic elements of control systems and explained several terms used widely in describing the monitoring and control process of our information systems. We have discussed how control systems can be used in organisations and seen how automatic systems can review and control our environmental disturbances. However, we have also seen that there are many areas in our organisations where the disturbance is so great or our automatic treatment (electromechanical or otherwise) of the variance can be inadequate, or even exacerbate the situation. In these areas we need to build in the manual override that allows human intervention in the control process. We ended by discussing the importance of taking human factors, such as motivation, into account in the design of information systems for review and control.

REVIEW QUESTIONS

1. Considering the performance management system in your organisation (or an organisation with which you are familiar), describe how effective it is at reviewing and controlling the performance of the staff.

2. Give two examples of how control systems work in your organisation (or an organisation with which you are familiar).

Storing data

INTRODUCTION

So far we have looked at some of the underlying concepts of information systems and the crucial role they play in helping managers and specialists make decisions in the areas of planning and control. In this chapter we look at some of the operational and structural aspects of information systems, before going on in the next chapter to address the very important subject of designing your information system. So in this chapter we discuss issues such as the collection and storage of data, and the use of databases.

COLLECTION AND STORAGE OF DATA

Throughout our organisations we are constantly measuring, counting, observing activities, reading dials and scales and so on, then recording this data as 'facts'. These compilations of facts give us the basic or *raw data*, as it is most often known, about our organisations. Data from internal sources can be generated by capturing it automatically as a part of the process or activity to which it relates, or as the result of a special data capturing activity. Similarly, data is produced from external sources such as specialist researchers and banks, and provided in a form in which it is readily usable without any further processing. All this data provides the building blocks for our information systems. Consequently the quality of the data is crucial, and this can be far more important than the technical mechanics of processing. If the raw data is flawed, then however sophisticated our processing, the eventual information produced will be worthless.

In a sense, the data within and around our organisations is almost limitless, and as we discussed in Chapter 1, it is more a case of filtering and condensing it so that the user is presented with information that is relevant to his or her needs. We discuss this key issue of clearly specifying our information requirements in Chapter 6.

Storage devices have come on a long way since we wrote the first book in this series (*Management information systems and statistics*, Bee and Bee 1990). Developments in technology since then have led to the miniaturisation of components, allowing massive amounts of data to be stored in the smallest pieces of hardware. Computers for processing business information have come down in size from the mainframe to the personal computer, to the laptop and now to the palmtop. We can store masses of data in the smallest of 'boxes', and when this is combined with developments in communications technology, it puts information processing and storage, and communication worldwide, into the hands (literally) of the average person in the street.

However, the principles of data storage remain largely unchanged. Storage devices are essentially used to store programs, data awaiting processing and the results of that processing. Storage devices can be categorised as providing primary and secondary storage, the difference being similar to that between short-term and long-term memories in humans. *Primary* storage holds the data as it is being processed. *Secondary* storage devices hold data, programs, etc, that are not required to be worked on within the computer itself at that time. Rather than losing this data when the computer is switched off at the end of a shift, or losing it by overwriting it with the next set of data, it can be stored for safekeeping or archiving.

Secondary storage can be on a variety of media, but the most commonly used are:

- *Hard disks*, which are capable of storing ever-greater amounts of data and software. They have grown in size from many megabytes (1 Mb = 1 million characters or bytes) to many gigabytes (1 Gb = 1 billion characters or bytes), and commonly range up to over 50 Gb. They are used to store the computer's operating system, software applications and data. Hard disk drives are an integral part of a personal computer system. They provide a relatively fast means of storing and retrieving data.
- *Floppy disks* that were available in the past to most computers for backup and the use of external software. Floppy disks are portable; so provide a means of transferring data between machines and also a way of storing data separate from the main computer system so that in the event of a disaster, such as a fire, a copy of the data is still available. However, their storage capacity is relatively small (currently around 1.5 Mb), and saving and retrieving can be relatively slow. CDs and USB personal storage devices are now replacing them – see below.
- *Zip disks* that are capable of handling 100 Mb of data or more. Not only are they portable, but they work with portable disk drives, and are faster than floppy disks. However, CDs and USB personal storage devices also replacing zip disks – see below.
- *CD-ROM*, which stands for 'compact disc – read only memory'. Compact discs have a very high storage capacity – a standard disk can start at about 650 Mb of data. Like floppy disks they are relatively slow and of course provide a read-only medium. However, it is now possible to get a variation on the traditional CD-ROM drive, the CD recordable drive, which enables data to be written to special compact disks. These discs are known as write-once, read many (WORM) discs, as data cannot be erased or changed after it has been stored. Yet a further development has been the CD rewritable drive, which as the name suggests allows the use of special CDs on which data can be written, erased and altered many times.
- *DVDs*, which stands for 'digital versatile discs', gained popularity in the late 1990s, and the drives are now a standard feature of most new personal computers. DVDs have the advantage over CD-ROMs that they offer very high storage capacities – typically at present between 4 and 7 Gb – and data can be accessed very quickly. They are commonly used for storing full-length feature films.
- *Flash 'disks'*, which are really memory chips and do not require power to retain the data stored on them. Because of their physical size (smaller than a credit card) and high data capacity, flash disks are used with the newer palmtop computers and applications such as digital cameras.

- *USB* personal storage devices are a development of flash disks that are plugged into a USB port on a computer to provide extra storage space of up to 2 Gb at present. In the future it will be possible to store applications on them, and it should be possible to have a stripped-down version of your own computer's operating system held on one that can then be plugged into any other suitable computer so that you can operate from it as if from your own computer.
- *RFID* (radio frequency identification) tags consist of a tiny chip, the size of a pinhead, containing an RFID code and a tiny antenna that can receive and transmit data by means of radio waves. Currently, each chip can hold up to 2 Kb of data. The data transmitted can include the location of the tag as well as the data held on the chip. Possible uses include tracking items through the supply chain.
- *Magnetic tape* is mainly used these days for archiving purposes, that is, the storage of huge amounts of data and software that is not required on a regular basis. Tapes can take the entire contents from hard disks as a security process, in case the hard disk is damaged in some way or the data or software held on it are corrupted and become unusable.

The inventiveness of ICT scientists and the pace of development mean that we shall constantly have the benefits of improved storage devices and the future holds no bounds. The mobile phone can already double as a small computer, and the wristwatch-sized powerful computer and communication device may be just beyond the horizon as we write this book!

DATABASES

Before the advent of computers, those organisations that required information on customers, suppliers, etc tended to use card index systems to hold the data. These systems were very good but required considerable clerical work to keep them up to date. It was also a slow process to get at the data and convert it into the information needed for decision-making – and therefore an obvious case for computerisation. So in the early days of computing, databases were largely electronic card index systems. They made life considerably easier for the holder of large volumes of data on clients, customers, spare parts and so on, that were subject to regular amendment and updating. For example, staff records or customer information might be filed by surname in alphabetic order, or by salary record number, or customer number, or by some sort of code to indicate department, location, etc.

However, all was not perfect, even with this ability to update the records, sort and resort them, and to print out the records or parts of the records selectively. The main problem was that the records could only be sorted or accessed according to the actual file (the unique storage area for that data) or database in which they were held, and usually without reference to information held in other files. For example, details about an employee might be spread across several files – salary on the payroll file, age and length of service in the pension file, personal and job details on the personnel file, etc, effectively all in different databases. Particular applications or management reports made it necessary to interrogate every database separately to bring together all the data about one person, held in different files. Also it was usually necessary to amend the details of that person on every file in the system whenever a single piece of data changed. Without doubt this was a tedious and often long-winded process, and it was frequently the cause of the information system falling into disrepute because no one could guarantee that all the files had been updated and were accurate. Apart from any other reason for requiring accurate data, the Data Protection Act 1998 (see Chapter 7) places a legal obligation upon users to ensure that the data they hold on living individuals is accurate.

With the early systems it was also necessary to be very specific about the reports that were to be output from the database and to obtain the help of a systems designer and/or programmer to design these reports. Because of this, any changes in requirements for information from a database necessitated reprograming to obtain the new report or the new report format. This was often a long and costly business and not one beloved by computer programmers and systems analysts, who would much rather be developing exciting new applications than maintaining boring old ones!

Fortunately, developments in computer technology have come to our rescue, with the development of database management systems (DBMSs) and associated database structures. We shall discuss each of these concepts in turn.

DATABASE MANAGEMENT SYSTEMS

There is sometimes confusion between the terms *database* and *database management system* (DBMS). However, the distinction is quite straightforward: data is *held* on an electronic database and is *accessed* using a DMBS. Bocij *et al* (2003) define a DBMS as 'one or more computer programs that allows users to enter, store, organise, manipulate and retrieve data in a database'.

To explain what this actually means, we need to consider how data was traditionally accessed from dedicated databases in the past. Users typically had their reports programed for them by a computer specialist and were stuck with the report in that format until the system was reprogramed for a new report. With a DBMS the well-trained user became independent of the computer specialist, and could call for his or her own reports with a structured query language (SQL).

Harry (1997) draws an analogy with two types of coffee vending machine. The first machine, rather like the dedicated database, produces a beverage according to an expert's opinion of what premixed combinations of ingredients we find desirable. Choose 'white coffee with sugar', and the coffee cup, preloaded with set amounts of coffee, milk powder and sugar, falls down the chute to have water added to the mix. The second machine, where there is a 'DBMS' in control, enables users to choose separately what amounts of coffee, milk and sugar they prefer. The empty coffee cup is set in place, then the chosen amount of each ingredient falls down the chute and into it, so users can choose extra-milky or extra-sugary (or simply extra strong) coffee if that is what they prefer.

With a DBMS, our application software does not obtain the data needed direct from the storage medium. Instead it requests the data from the DBMS. The DBMS retrieves the data from the specific database or databases and provides them to the application we are using. In other words the DBMS operates between our software and the data in the database. Many modern database systems include a number of tools that automate the processes of answering queries and commonly used data analysis tasks such as producing tables and charts.

DATABASE STRUCTURES

Database structures assist users in the tasks of organising large databases logically into records and establishing the relationships between these records. This can be a complex and time-consuming process, as even the smallest businesses will have large numbers of records, each of which is related to other records in the database. For example, a mail-order firm will have records relating to the customer who bought a particular item, the distribution company that transported the item, the picker who drew down the item from the store and the company that manufactured the item. However, this example – showing only single relationships, eg the distribution company who transported the item to the customer – is not realistic. The reality is that there is a range of customers who bought a range of items, transported by one or more distribution companies. The items had been picked by several pickers from a range of items manufactured by several companies. In other words there could be a very complex set of relationships between the data, and this complexity must be taken into account when the information is processed.

We can represent the different types of relationships in our database using family relationship terminology as shown in Figure 5.1:

- one-to-one
- one-to-many
- many-to-one
- many-to-many.

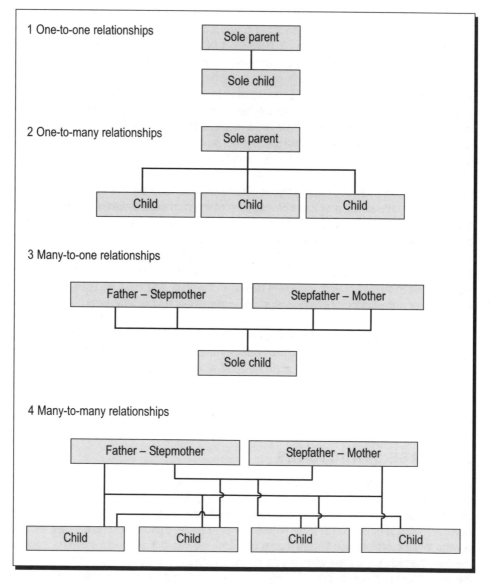

Figure 5.1 Relationships

There have been many approaches to organising the records and their relationships logically, for example:

- hierarchical database structure
- network database structure
- relational database structure
- object-orientated structure.

We shall briefly describe each in turn.

All records in a *hierarchical* database are called nodes. The structure starts from the top with what is known as the root record. The root record is the most generalised record, and each layer in the hierarchy becomes progressively more specific (see Figure 5.2). Records that are at a higher level in the hierarchy are known as the parents of those in the next layer down and those in this layer are known as the children of those in the layer above them. The parents are said to *own* the children. The relationships are fixed by the structure, and this tends to make hierarchical databases relatively less flexible than the other structures. However, they are relatively quick to process day-to-day, large-batch operational data, such as payroll or invoicing.

The next form of structure is the *network* database, which views all its records in sets. Each set has an owner record and one or more member records, analogous to the relationship of a sole parent to several children (see Figure 5.1). A record in this structure may be a member of more than one set. In other words a record may have more than one owner, so allowing us to implement one-to-one, one-to-many, many-to-one and many-to-many relationships. However, these relationships need to be decided in advance because they are physically established by the DBMS when storage space is allocated on the hard disk. Because of the way the relationships are installed in advance, large batch processing and the production of routine reports is fairly quick. However, the production of ad hoc reports requiring relationships that are not established in the structure may take a long time, and may not even be possible at all in some situations.

Both the hierarchical and networks models have largely been superseded by what is now perhaps the most commonly used database structure, the *relational* database. This differs from the previous two in that it does not require the specification of explicit relationships between the records, nor is it necessary to process the records one at a time. Data is stored as individual records in files of like records. The user can select a single record, specific records or all records from each file, to analyse with a single record, specific records or all records from any other file, and save the results in a third, combined file. This process may be repeated as often as required until the user has examined all the data necessary to provide the answer(s) to the information queries posed. Thus the relational database structure is much more flexible than the hierarchical or network database structures but, because the relationships between data are not determined in advance, large batch processing tends to be relatively slow. To a certain extent 'you pays your money and takes your choice', but the flexibility given to the non-IT specialist and the freedom from the need to constantly re-engage the IT expert has made this option attractive to most managers/specialists.

The last database structure we shall discuss is the *object-oriented* database (OODB). None of the structures we have mentioned so far are particularly well suited to many business applications, particularly those in engineering, where data in the form of images, drawings, videos, etc cannot be stored in the same way as data in the text form. OODB technology was developed to meet this need. This approach has been extended to the more traditional business applications, so that a customer or an employee is described as an object in much the same way as an image.

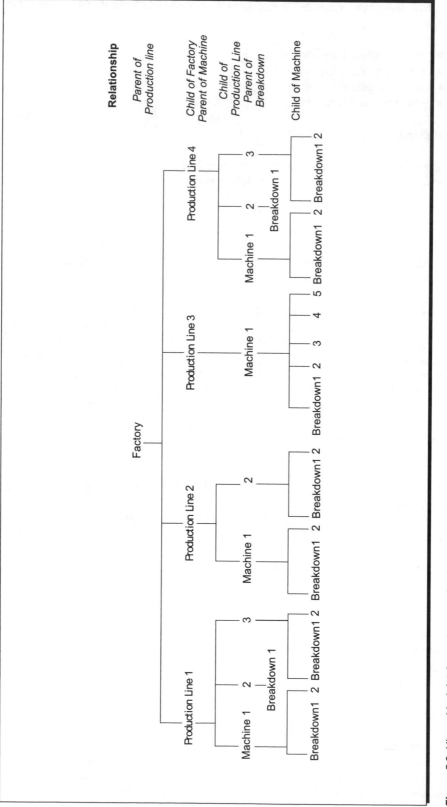

Figure 5.2 Hierarchical database structure showing relationships

This technology is substantially different from that in the other types of database structure. As Schultheis and Sumner (1998) describe it, 'each object in the database is bound together with its own data and a set of instructions that describes the behaviour and attributes of the object'. It results in large libraries of objects that can be used time and again. New business applications can use these off-the-shelf objects in the same way that different machines can be assembled using off-the-shelf parts.

Our modern databases are capable of easy amendment, capable of being used by lay professionals and managers with minimum intervention from the IT expert and, through the use of communications technology, can be accessed from almost anywhere and at any time. The result is modern information systems that are very flexible, very robust to change and very accessible. They are admirably suited to an environment where change is the order of the day and, as such, our information systems have really come of age.

The capability to store, access and manipulate large quantities of data efficiently provides the opportunity to refine and improve activities at all levels – strategic, tactical and operational. A good example is database marketing, where the detailed buying patterns of individuals can be identified, making it possible for marketers to target individuals very precisely. An interesting personal example is the mail-order wine companies, which have identified the sort of wine we like to buy and direct specific types of wine offers to us.

A further development has been the concept of data mining. Tools and techniques have been developed to identify hidden patterns or relationships in data, and this has uses in many areas, for example in credit analysis and crime pattern analysis.

CONCLUSION

In this chapter we have tried to do justice to what is becoming a massive field of activity. Developments in the storage, processing and accessing of data has opened up a wide range of opportunities. Commercial pressures and customer convenience are causing most organisations to examine carefully how best they can maximise the information that is available to them through the effective use of databases. In the next chapter we look at the key issue of how information systems are designed and developed.

REVIEW QUESTIONS

1. The trend towards the miniaturisation of storage devices is revolutionising the way organisations operate. Give three examples of how this development has affected your organisation, or an organisation with which you are familiar.

2. Taking a database with which you are familiar, briefly discuss:
   a. the type of information for which you use it
   b. how that information is used
   c. its structure
   d. its ease of use.

Designing, developing and implementing your information system

6

When you have studied this chapter, you will be able to:

- describe the stages in the basic project model for developing an information system, including the contribution of SSADM
- explain the different approaches to requirements analysis, including data flow diagrams and logical data modelling
- outline the key issues in project managing the design and development of an information system
- contribute to the design, development and implementation of an information system.

INTRODUCTION

Designing and implementing information systems in large organisations is a major and complex activity, and in the past it was often the sole province of the ICT specialist. However, when we carried out our research for *Project management: the people challenge* (Bee and Bee 1997), we found that there is a healthier variant of this, the multidisciplinary team approach. The simple point is that information systems are too important to us to leave them to the IT specialists. As a manager, specialist or a professional in our own right, we will be the users of the information system, and will want to make sure that it is designed to meet our needs and those of our customers (both internal and external). As top management, we will wish to ensure that our strategic needs are catered for in the system. At senior to middle grades we will typically more interested in tactical issues and, unless the information system actually makes our job easier we will be unlikely to 'buy in' to it. And at the operational level people have become adept at getting round or ignoring systems that they think get in the way of actually doing the job!

Consultation with all the stakeholders is essential, and this requires hard work and co-operation throughout all the stages of the basic project model, from the requirements analysis – the analysis of the business processes and the associated information needs – to handover and review. There is a variety of proven methods that can help us with these activities – however, always remember that they need the active involvement of the final users of the system. The users' needs are paramount in designing, developing and maintaining our information systems. The emphasis must be on designing the system *with* the users, not *for* the users. In this chapter we discuss each of the stages of the basic project model in turn.

The approach outlined is particularly useful and important for the design of large and complex information systems. However, the basic principles are also helpful in the design of smaller and simpler information systems.

BASIC PROJECT MODEL

We advocate a systematic approach to the design of an information system. This is so that there is a decent chance of ending up with a system that actually makes life easier rather than more difficult! Local circumstances might well dictate some variation on this process but being systematic actually improves the odds of our success. With this in mind we set out below the typical project stages (including the deliverables) that need to be followed in the development of any information system:

- project initiation
- requirements analysis
- system design
- system build
- system integration and testing
- user acceptance testing
- system handover and implementation
- system review, amend and maintain the system
- evaluation.

Most models of systems development follow similar stages, sometimes using slightly different terminology, and sometimes combining or subdividing some of the stages. For example, 'requirements analysis' is often referred to as 'systems analysis'. Figure 6.1 sets out these project stages and the level of involvement of both users and ICT specialists at each stage of a typical project.

Project initiation

The deliverable from the project initiation stage is the feasibility report. There needs to be extensive discussion between prospective users and technical staff on the need for the particular information system. In order to decide its objectives we need answers to the following questions:

- What 'business(es)' are we in and will be in, in the future?
- What are the information requirements of the 'business' now and in the future?
- What are the required outcomes from the system?
- What will the system do for the business?

As part of the wider management system, it is important to recognise that the information system will help managers and specialists plan, control and review, and replan their operational functions against corporate business standards.

The feasibility study will also consider:

- the scope of the new information system, its boundaries, etc
- the timing of the project
- the anticipated risks
- data and system security issues, including disaster recovery/business continuity measures (see Chapter 7)
- costs and benefits in designing the new system when compared with the existing system and other options for managing the business information.

It is at this stage that the balance of involvement between potential users and ICT specialists will be thrashed out. It is important to identify who is the client. In one organisation developing an HR

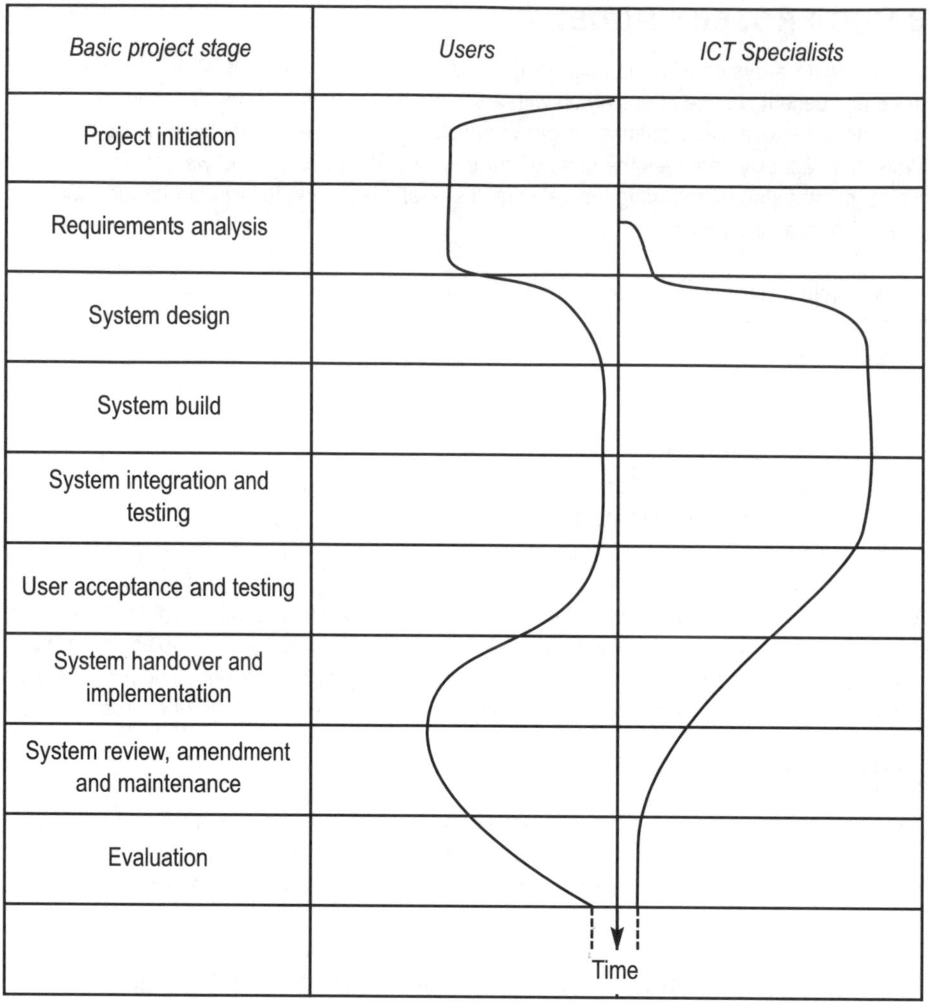

Basic project stage	Users	ICT Specialists
Project initiation		
Requirements analysis		
System design		
System build		
System integration and testing		
User acceptance and testing		
System handover and implementation		
System review, amendment and maintenance		
Evaluation		
	Time	

Figure 6.1 The basic project model showing an example of the relative involvement of users and ICT specialists

information system (HRIS) this issue was particularly highlighted. The lead in the development of their new HRIS was clearly identified as the HR department, with an HR manager taking on the role of project manager. In previous developments the project had been led and managed by the IT department, which had caused a number of problems (see Case Study 8.2, page 85, on Merseytravel's HRIS).

It is vital that the focus is on the client's needs right from the outset. It is from the client's needs that the hierarchy of objectives for the project overall will be established, and this provides the basis for identifying the critical success factors that will help keep the project on course and help with its evaluation.

Requirements analysis

The next stage is to carry out the detailed analysis of requirements. The main deliverables from this stage are a clear and very specific statement of the requirements to be met by the information system, and the standards for acceptance and evaluation. It is very tempting for the experts on the project team to decide that they know best, and that the simplest approach is to produce an outline system and then ask the managers or the other professionals, the users, to comment. This approach is fraught with dangers! Apart from the likelihood that it will not win the commitment of the other managers/users to using and supporting the system, it is approaching the problem from the wrong direction. Checkland and Holwell (1998) helpfully describe an information system as in fact made up of two systems:

- 'the system which is served' – which represents the domain of the user, the people taking the decisions and action and who have the information needs
- 'the system which serves' – which is all about the data processing activities which supply those needs.

They argue that all too often the emphasis is on the 'system which serves' rather than 'the system which is served'. This is often because it is this latter system that the ICT professional understands really well and feels very comfortable with. However, the key to a successful information system is building up a rich picture of the 'the system which is served', or in other words, developing a real understanding of the usually complex world of the users. It requires a partnership between the ICT specialist and the potential users to explore their user world and arrive at the users' information needs. The soft systems methodology described in Chapter 2 can provide a very effective approach to this key area.

The interviewing/facilitation skills of the system analysts need to be of the highest order and they may use a variety of tools, such as tailored questionnaires, to assist them in this process. At its most basic level, they will cover the key areas of:

- what the manager/specialist does, what his or her responsibilities are
- what decisions the manager/specialist takes, and therefore for what purposes the manager requires the information
- what the most useful form is for the presentation of the information to the manager/ specialist
- how often, and when, the manager/specialist needs the information.

The close involvement and commitment of the users is crucial to the success of this stage. It can be hard work and is sometimes very frustrating. Many managers and specialists may initially be unclear on what information they need, even supposing they are perfectly clear about their exact responsibilities! There may be sensitive issues around confidentiality and what information should be included – see Case Study 6.1.

CASE STUDY 6.1

The current major NHS IT project to create electronic patient records raises important and difficult issues about what data on patients should be shared and with whom. The extent of the issue has been recognised by the setting up of the Care Records Development Board specifically to formulate policy in this area. It began by holding stakeholder conferences involving people with a wide range of interests in the design of healthcare information, including doctors and patients.

Some potential users may have difficulty in seeing the usefulness and/or the relevance of the information system, and will probably change their minds on their requirements as the systems review proceeds and they develop their knowledge about what the system can do for them. Our experience is that this is par for the course, and again, it is vital that sufficient time and other resources are devoted to getting this stage right. Because of the importance and complexity of this stage, we discuss some of the methods and techniques available in detail later in this chapter.

The focus of this stage often tends to be on the *information* requirements or the 'content' of the system. However, it is equally important to specify what we refer to as the *user-friendly* requirements of the system. By this we mean the ease with which users, and particularly occasional users, can find their way around and make use the system. (This is particularly well illustrated in Case Study 8.2 on page 85.)

System design

At the system design stage the deliverable is a detailed specification of the output, input and processes needed to satisfy the user requirements clarified in the requirements analysis. This stage has been described as creating 'the bridge between the user's need and the hardware and software capability' (Edwards *et al* 1995). The task of the project team here is to take the results of the earlier research and consultations and turn them into the information system. Often the process will require frequent returns to the users, to clarify points and to test out ideas and output reports. It is at this stage that collaboration between users and ICT specialists can be strained, as the users struggle to understand the technicalities involved. While the computing side is clearly the province of the ICT specialist, the users have an obligation to achieve at least a working level of technical knowledge. Achievement of the project objectives will depend on both sets of colleagues ensuring that effective communication and understanding is maintained throughout the project.

As well as providing the detailed technical specification for the programing stage, the system design stage may finalise the format in which the documentation will be set out, both for users and for technical staff, and define the system testing stage, described later.

System build

This stage involves the creation or procurement of the software and consideration of the hardware required for the information system. It is the province of the technical experts. It is the stage where the users are least involved. There will be a number of software options to be considered, these are to:

- use a standard, predesigned package if one is available
- use a standard, predesigned package adapted to deal with the particular needs of our information system
- design the software from scratch, specifically tailored to our needs.

It is rare that a standard package will completely meet an individual organisation's needs, and considerable problems can occur if you try to shoehorn your information requirements to fit the package. This route is often chosen because it is perceived as a low-cost option. However, it can be a false economy if the system does not meet user needs! The third option is usually very expensive although, done properly, it can ensure that the system design actually does match the information needs. In practice the second option is the one most often adopted and, although a compromise, it can work well. However, the choice of the package is still very important, as too many alterations and adaptations to the original can be expensive and may well prejudice the overall robustness of the system.

There is also the issue of whether the organisation should opt for a single integrated system – often referred to as an enterprise planning resource (ERP) system – to meet all its information system needs. We discuss this issue in more detail in the context of the development of HRISs in Chapter 8.

It is at this stage that the hardware requirements are considered. The overall size of the proposed system and the choice of software will usually dictate the type of hardware required. The other key issue will be the degree of accessibility desired: for example, whether all users will have their own terminal, or whether there will be shared use within work groups.

The main deliverable at this stage is the creation/procurement of the individual program modules and their documentation. This is also the time for some initial thoughts to be given to the learning needs for both ICT staff and end-users.

System integration and testing

While the individual modules might work by themselves, there is a need to test them when the system is running as a whole. Tests will be used to ensure that the system meets its technical specification correctly and operates at the right speed. A range of data will be fed in to reflect the range of expected conditions, to test that the system can cope with any demands put upon it in operation. It needs to be understood by all concerned that these tests are designed to assess how the system works, and not whether it meets the business needs; that comes later in user-acceptance testing.

It is important that the system can deliver information on an appropriate timescale. There is nothing more frustrating than a system that appears slow to the user. Customer expectations here are increasing all the time. In the early days of mainframe computing it was acceptable for users to wait overnight for their reports. Nowadays, users often expect information to be delivered within seconds. We are aware of one e-HR project which faced major problems due to line managers' dissatisfaction with the slow speed of processing. This was associated with the use of firewalls (see Chapter 7) that were designed to protect the data on the system!

There are some non-technical activities that can be planned and scheduled at this stage, for example:

- learning activities
- communication with all concerned
- any parallel running of old and new systems
- important housekeeping issues of existing data file conversion and data cleansing
- production of documentation
- reviewing the implications for existing processes, for example the way data is collected and input.

The main deliverable of this stage is a system that works under the range of typical user conditions.

User-acceptance testing

This stage in the design process brings together all the disparate requirements of the users into a total system and ensures that it has the following principal attributes:

- It provides all managers and specialists with the information they require, in the right form and at the right time.
- The system is sufficiently robust to allow modification to meet changing needs relatively quickly and at a reasonable cost.
- The system is sufficiently user-friendly and intuitive to allow managers and/or specialists to make efficient and effective use of it (including occasional users where relevant).

It is a key stage in the development of the information system, and users will be closely involved with the ICT specialists in ensuring that the system does what is intended. All the stakeholders will need to give an appropriate amount of time, and such time is usually well spent. It is the time when all users learn how to use the system, when the documentation is issued and when arrangements are made for the 'help desk' queries that will inevitably arise. It is also a key stage in ensuring a smooth handover to the users.

We cannot overemphasise the need for the following:

- Really good communications between the parties to keep all the stakeholders – the main users, any support staff, technical staff – informed about progress and the resolution of any problems.
- Ensuring that the learning programes meet the needs of the users and are delivered at an appropriate time. There is a multitude of sad stories of learning interventions being delivered too soon, before there is any opportunity to practise on the system, or too late, when users have struggled to operate the system and have become frustrated and disillusioned.
- The documentation needs to be really good, comprehensive, easy to understand and with good indexing to help the users find their way around the manuals. Also, as users become more sophisticated, many of them may prefer to have good on-screen help at their fingertips.
- Good support through having good technical staff on hand, good help-desk facilities.

The main deliverables of this stage are:

- a system that the users are confident will meet their needs
- users having the required knowledge and skills to use the system
- all the support mechanisms in place.

System implementation and handover

The big day has arrived; the system is live, or at least parts are live! With major systems, it is often considered sensible to implement them in phased stages. Implementation might be phased by type of users, for example department by department, or by type of use, starting with the core system and then adding in additional modules one at a time. This is where the results of all the hard work and skilled project management show themselves. The information system is up and running and paying its way – or so you hope! The main deliverable is a system that works in practice! However, it is not yet time for the project team to pack it bags, since there are two more important stages to complete.

System review, amendment and maintenance

This is the stage when the system is reviewed to check whether there are any small amendments that need to be made now it has become operational. Also, amendments may be needed where the business needs have changed during the time taken to develop the information system, or perhaps where estimates of volumes of transactions or timings have proved to be inadequate. Great care needs to be taken with making any amendments and those that are made should be subject to the same rigour as the original project. Where errors, breakdowns and/or other glitches occur they should be carefully logged, analysed and brought to the attention of management at an appropriate level. This is also the stage to initiate the maintenance programme that all systems need to ensure that the system continues to meet the identified (and modified) business requirements. In a sense, this stage is never finished but is ongoing throughout the life of the system. The main deliverable is a system that continues to meet the information needs of its users efficiently and effectively, and avoids systems entropy (see Chapter 2).

Evaluation

In the initiation stage of the development project, we stressed the need for clear business objectives that the information system should help achieve, and for critical success factors to be defined by the managers and specialists who will use the system. We can now close the circle on these objectives and assess the extent to which they are being met. This is a very important stage. When we carried out our research for *Project management: the people challenge* (Bee and Bee 1997), one of our findings was that there was a tendency for project teams, at the conclusion of a project, to move quickly on to their next project. We could understand why this was so – the previous project was history, while the next project was the brave new exciting world of tomorrow! However, we found that a lot of potential organisational and individual learning was lost as a result of this failure systematically to review:

- whether the system had met the objectives and success criteria set out in the original feasibility study/business case
- whether the project had come in within budget and on time
- what had hindered the project along the way
- what had contributed to project success.

The results of this type of evaluation are set out in a survey published in 2004. It revealed that 'IT projects within large companies generally deliver only 59 per cent of their promised benefits' and one of the most frequently identified reasons for this was that staff were inappropriately qualified for the projects undertaken (*Manager* 2004).

A situation can arise at any of the stages in the process described above when it may be necessary to return to an earlier stage, or very occasionally to abandon the current project and go back to the drawing board. This does happen, and it is important to grasp the nettle as soon as possible, or the result will be an information system that never works satisfactorily and probably falls quickly into disuse. Also, and even worse, the failure can bring the whole concept of the information system into disrepute. During our research for this book we came across a number of such examples. One of the most unfortunate was an HRIS that was abandoned during the implementation phase. A number of problems arose because the system, which was a standard predesigned package, did not in the end prove flexible enough to meet the needs of the organisation.

Structured Systems Analysis and Design Methodology (SSADM)

Structured Systems Analysis and Design Methodology (SSADM) is one of a number of brand-name methodologies available in this field. However SSADM is probably the methodology used most frequently for IT developments in the United Kingdom, particularly in the public sector. SSADM focuses on the first three stages of the model described above, concentrating on the feasibility, analysis and design aspects. As the name suggests, it provides a highly structured approach. There are five modules encompassing six stages, and each stage has a set of activities and clearly stated deliverables.

Many of the techniques used by SSADM are used in other structured approaches. The main feature of SSADM's core techniques is their diagrammatic nature. Three of these techniques – data flow modelling, logical data modelling and entity behaviour modelling – are discussed in the next section on requirements analysis. SSADM works best on projects where it is possible to set out clearly defined objectives. The proponents of the soft systems approach set out in Chapter 2 would argue that SSADM focuses too much on the 'serving system' described earlier in this chapter and does not 'embody the kind of in-depth exploration of organisational thinking which is necessary if information requirements are to be richly captured' (Checkland and Holwell 1998).

Anyone who might be involved in using the SSADM approach may find it helpful to read Weaver *et al* (2004), which sets out the whole methodology in detail.

TECHNIQUES FOR REQUIREMENTS ANALYSIS

We now come to analysis techniques, as we promised on the section on requirements analysis. Many of the techniques are highly sophisticated and can be the subjects of books in themselves. Formal training is needed in order to become proficient in the use of most of them. Here we cover them only in summary form, and point readers to sources of further reading where more detail is available.

In very general terms the techniques for analysing system requirements fall into two categories, process analysis techniques and information analysis techniques.

Most proprietary analysis systems available are based on these two approaches. Process analysis techniques show in diagrammatic form what people are doing, what is actually happening with items or documents. Information analysis techniques, on the other hand, concentrate on the information flows that support those activities. The techniques we look at are:

- procedure narratives
- data flow diagrams (DFDs)
- logical data modelling (LDM).

Essentially, these are all techniques for recording the information gathered from the stakeholders in the proposed system. There are a number of ways of collecting the basic data, such as interviews, observation, and reviewing existing documentation. Clearly it is vital that this first stage in the process is conducted professionally to ensure that the data collected is valid. The output from the techniques we describe is only as good as the data that feeds into them.

Procedure narratives

The *procedure narrative* is a very basic analysis technique, much used in the past. It sets out in text form exactly what happens in the process. For example:

A customer orders an item from a supplier.

The supplier checks the stocks and, if sufficient, picks the order and delivers it to the customer.

The supplier adjusts the stock record.

The supplier raises an invoice and sends it to the customer.

The customer pays the invoice.

If the item is not in stock, the supplier notifies the customer and places the order in 'pending'.

The supplier obtains more stock.

The supplier updates the stock record.

The supplier picks the order and delivers it to the customer.

The supplier adjusts the stock record.

The supplier raises an invoice and sends to the customer.

The customer pays the invoice.

In a complex system the procedure narrative can go on for pages, and while it provides a comprehensive record of what happens, it does not show the dynamic nature and interdependence of the activities. In the sense that 'every picture paints a thousand words', data flow diagrams (DFDs) have been developed to translate the narrative into a diagrammatic format.

Data flow diagrams (DFDs)

Data flow diagrams (DFDs) represent the information flows in a system and between the system and its environment, together with the functions that are performed. They are very effective in defining data needs and clarifying any inconsistencies in the process and in the flow of data. They are one of the main charting methods used in SSADM for showing information flows. DFDs start with a high-level diagram followed by progressively more detailed diagrams showing linkages to the higher diagram. An example of how DFDs work is given in Figure 6.2, using the details from the procedure narrative above.

Logical data modelling (LDM)

A DFD is most useful for documenting the way the existing information flows operate. It provides a model of how things actually work at present. This often draws attention to inadequacies, confusions, duplications and inconsistencies. However, it does not show the underlying meaning and structure of the data. *Logical data modelling* (LDM) aims to set out the underlying picture: what the system actually holds data about and how the data really interrelates. This technique involves creating a diagram called the logical data structure (LDS) and a set of associated text descriptions. The LDS can be used to provide an understanding of both the existing system and the required system.

LDM's main building blocks are *entities*. Bocij *et al* (2003) define an entity as 'an object such as a person, place, thing or event about which we need to capture and store data'. Examples of entities are customers, employees, suppliers, factories, departments, products and orders. Each item of data that is held about an entity is referred to as an *attribute*. Examples of attributes of a customer are customer number, name and address. There are a number of possible relationships between entities – one-to-one, one-to-many and many-to-many – and which are represented by symbols – see Figure 6.3.

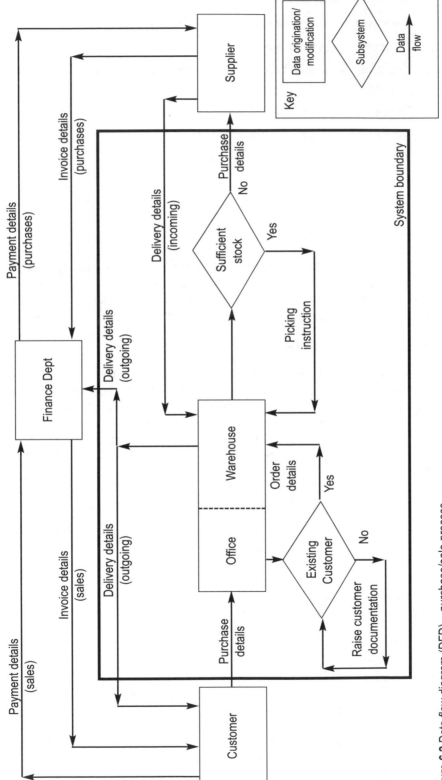

Figure 6.2 Data-flow diagram (DFD) – purchase/sale process

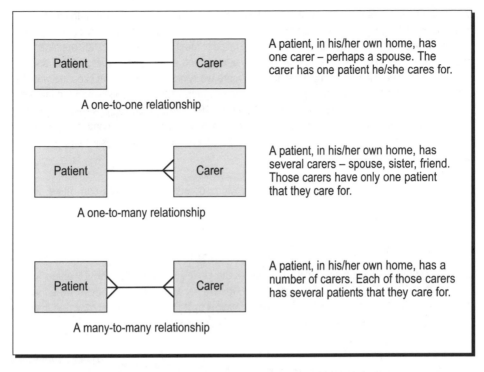

Figure 6.3 Entity relationships

SSADM also uses the concept of *entity life histories* (ELHs), which document how information relating to an entity changes by tracking the events that effect an entity during its life history in the system. For example, an ELH for a supplier might consist of a sequence of three events: supplier registration (as a new supplier is identified), supplier approval (as the checks on a new supplier are completed and the supplier becomes live), and supplier ceases trading or is dropped (as a supplier either goes out of business or the decision is taken to stop using that supplier).

ISSUES AFFECTING THE DESIGN AND DEVELOPMENT OF INFORMATION SYSTEMS

If you talk to anyone who has been involved in any way or at any level in the development of an information system, it is likely that the key issues that will be highlighted are:

- Project slippage – the project taking far longer than planned. Often the bigger and more ambitious the system, the greater the slippage. There are innumerable large government projects that have overrun, sometimes by years.
- The project coming in over budget – and again there can be massive overspends.
- The information system not performing to expectation, which may be in terms of the quality of information produced, the speed with which the system can be accessed, its user-friendliness or its reliability.

There has been a number of high-profile information systems failures. In 2004 there was publicity about a system that had been developed for the Child Support Agency at a cost of £465 million. In the first 18 months of its introduction, an enormous backlog of claims built up and waiting times escalated. The system was described by its own suppliers as 'badly designed, badly delivered, badly tested and badly implemented' (Hall 2004)! Only months later another system was in the news (part of a massive NHS project – see Chapter 10), which is being developed to allow patient choice and e-enabled booking of hospital appointments. It had failed to meet its target (of 205,000 appointments booked using the system by the end of 2004) by a large and embarrassing margin, with only 63 bookings achieved. However, what was perhaps more worrying than the project slippage was the survey carried out by the National Audit Office which suggested that some GPs had fundamental reservations about the whole system. Some felt that the GPs doing the bookings were taking up too much of the patient consultation time, and that other approaches should be adopted. This may be a 'teething' reaction to a new system or it may mean that the requirements analysis stage was fatally flawed. We shall report back in our next edition!

There is no doubt that good planning and following some basic principles can make all the difference – see Case Study 6.1.

CASE STUDY 6.1

A major leisure group with many sites across the United Kingdom decided it wanted to introduce a new HR information system that was web-enabled. The main driver was the need to update a complex and old-fashioned payroll system, but it was also decided that this was the right time to introduce an integrated overall HR system.

The company approached a number of major suppliers of integrated HR systems. In the final selection the ability of both partners to work together was seen as the crucial criterion. The new system was introduced on time, within budget and with no significant user issues. The keys to the success of the project were identified as the following:

- The selection of a supplier who saw customer care and sound project management as its unique selling points.
- A partnership approach was adopted throughout the project, with consistency of personnel on both sides throughout the project lifetime.
- A project board was established at the outset, which consisted of the key operational decision-makers and the key supplier representatives. This ensured that decisions could be taken quickly and by the right people.
- A dedicated (ie full-time) project team was established with its own project office.
- A detailed and realistic project plan and budget was developed, which took into account the business cycles, availability of key staff, and so on.
- The need to get buy-in across the organisation and manage any culture change was identified as a high priority. Demonstrations of the system were organised early on, and feedback was encouraged and incorporated.
- Proactive risk assessment and risk management was undertaken. One of the highest risks was identified as the people resource. It was agreed that the best and most appropriate people should be available to work on the project when required, and that their regular jobs should be back-filled with additional staff.
- There were regular review meetings with a good interchange of information between the project team and the departments involved, so that everyone knew the state of progress and any issues that had arisen.
- The project plan was formally reviewed each month and there was a good process for following up outstanding actions. This ensured that there was early warning of any problems that might cause slippage or affect the budget.

- There was a formal process of 'change control' for enhancements and other alterations. This was vital to ensure that both partners were clear about and agreed on any changes from the original plan.
- The importance of data conversion was identified at an early stage. It is important to consider how much of the existing data will be transferred, how to tackle issues of data cleansing (the process of ensuring that data that is transferred onto the new system is complete and accurate), how to set about bridging any data gaps, and so on.
- Appropriate learning interventions were organised at the appropriate time. (Often, the introduction of new systems is hampered by staff acquiring the necessary knowledge and skills either too late or too early. The latter problem happens surprisingly frequently, as learning programmes are organised to fit in with the original project timetable and when there is slippage the learning schedule is not readjusted.)
- There was a phased programme for the introduction of the new HR modules so as not to overload staff with too much change at one time.
- Parallel running of the old and the new systems ensured any teething problems could be sorted out without impacting adversely on the business. The increased workload of key staff during this period was recognised and planned for.
- There was robust and well-organised support in the early stages through a help desk and the use of local 'champions' of change who were specially trained to provide help and support to their colleagues.

PROJECT MANAGEMENT

A key factor in the successful delivery of a new or updated information system is good project management. This is a big area and one that is the subject of many books in its own right, including our own! Our intention here is to introduce you to a few of the key principles and tools.

The project team

Crucial to any project is the setting up the right project team and then ensuring that it operates as a high-performance team. This is a subject we tackle in some depth in our book *Project management: the people challenge* (Bee and Bee 1997). In it we include the following key issues:

- selecting a team that provides the necessary professional skills and experience but also takes into account the individual personal skills required to work effectively in a project environment
- taking time to turn a collection of individuals into an effective team, through running teambuilding activities, establishing team processes, etc
- clarifying roles and responsibilities
- providing relevant learning interventions in the project-specific areas and in the skills of project management
- ensuring the appropriate time commitment for project team members, with the right mix of full-time/part-time working on the project at its different stages
- establishing clear and reliable communication channels within the team, with those linked to the team and with the rest of the organisation.

Planning and controlling the project

At the heart of good project management is good project planning. You are probably familiar with the Gantt chart – see Figure 6.4 – which sets out the individual activities or tasks required to complete a project, and the timetable over which these will take place. This usually forms the basic working document for the project team.

There are three processes that lie behind the Gantt charts of most complex projects:

- The first process is preparing a *work breakdown structure*, which is a top-down approach for generating all the tasks associated with the project. The project is first broken down into its main areas, then each area is broken down again, and so on, and the result is presented rather like a hierarchical organisation chart.
- The second process is building a *project network*, which involves setting out the scheduling links between the tasks. In simple terms this is a diagram that sets out in graphical form which tasks have to be completed before others, which tasks can run in parallel, etc. It will consist of a network of paths through the project.
- The third process identifies the *critical path* through the project network, which is the longest path in time terms through the network. The critical path determines the duration of the whole project. Any delays on this path will delay the whole project and therefore particular attention has to be focused on the tasks along this path. Delays on the other paths may result in them in turn becoming the critical path.

There are several software packages that produce project planning charts – one of the most well known is Microsoft Project™. These packages enable the project team not only to schedule the timing of all the tasks, identifying the critical ones and the slack time associated with the others (that is, how long these can be delayed without affecting the overall project duration), but also to allocate responsibilities for tasks, and schedule resources and costs.

A particular project management methodology, PRINCE (Projects in Controlled Environments), has been developed to handle large ICT projects in the public sector and to be compatible with system development methodologies such as SSADM.

These planning tools can then be used to monitor and control the project. Effective monitoring ensures that problems with any part of the project – which include time slippage, overspends, resource issues – are identified at an early stage so that appropriate action can be taken to get the project back on schedule or to undertake any replanning necessary.

CONCLUSION

In this chapter we have covered the very important subject of developing an information system. Using the structure of the basic project model, we have discussed each of the stages from initiation of the project through to the final stage of evaluation. We have also explained some of the techniques used in the key stage of the requirements analysis. It is all too easy to take a mechanistic approach to the introduction of an information system, that is, to treat the exercise as simply reading items off a checklist. However, we cannot stress too strongly the need to be aware of both the technical and human implications, and of the possible range of responses and reactions of people to the new system. The success of an information system will depend entirely on the use to which all users put it. It can be technically the best system in the world, but if the users do not perceive it as such or understand how to get the best from it, it will be a failure. It is up to us, all of us, to play our part as appropriate in the design, development and use of our information systems.

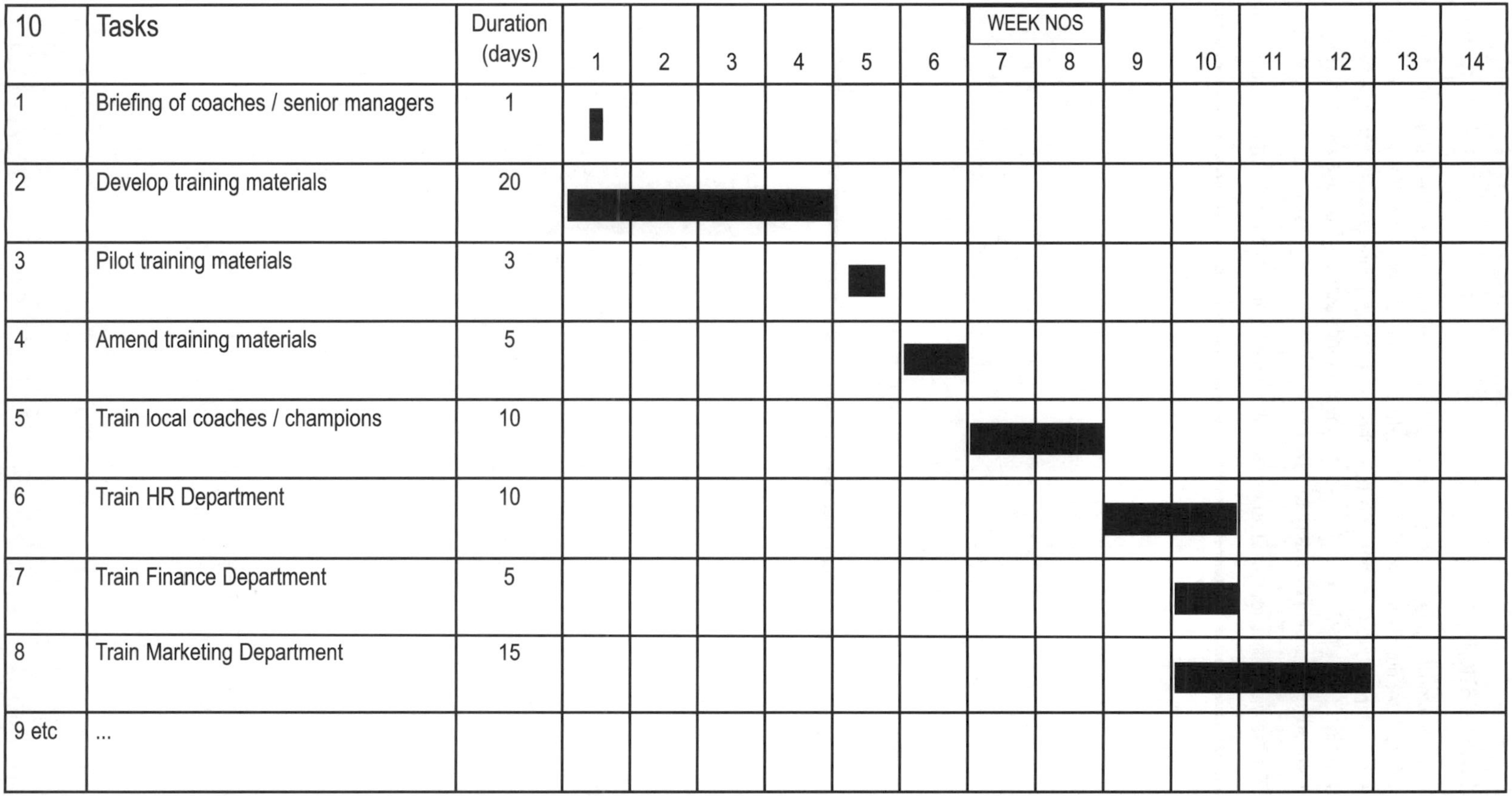

10	Tasks	Duration (days)	1	2	3	4	5	6	7	8	9	10	11	12	13	14
									WEEK NOS							
1	Briefing of coaches / senior managers	1	■													
2	Develop training materials	20	███	███	███	███										
3	Pilot training materials	3					■									
4	Amend training materials	5						■								
5	Train local coaches / champions	10							███	███						
6	Train HR Department	10									███	███				
7	Train Finance Department	5										■				
8	Train Marketing Department	15											███	███		
9 etc	…															

Figure 6.4 Gantt chart – example of training stage of an IS project

REVIEW QUESTIONS

1. Using the logical data modelling approach, list some attributes of the entity 'employee', and set out diagrammatically the nature of the relationship between employee and line manager. Comment on how this relationship might change with different organisational structures, such as a matrix organisation. What events might be included in the entity life history for an employee?

2. Discuss the benefits of including users in the development of information systems.

Data security

CHAPTER 7

CHAPTER OBJECTIVES

When you have studied this chapter, you will be able to:

- describe the main threats to data security
- outline the key approaches to dealing with these threats, including disaster recovery plans
- explain an organisation's legal responsibilities for data security.

INTRODUCTION

Organisations of every size, from small businesses to the major companies, are becoming more and more dependent on their information systems and the technologies that support them. Even the smallest organisation has become dependent on using computer systems for:

- simple things like producing a letter, an invoice or a cash flow forecast
- providing access to key data on suppliers, customers, financial position and the like
- manipulating this data into useful information for decision-making
- communicating with colleagues, customers, suppliers, etc near and far
- networking with customers and suppliers through electronic data interchange (EDI), partnership sourcing, etc
- providing Information to give it a competitive advantage.

Systems are also becoming increasingly global and more dependent on networks. The move towards providing access to information systems from wherever someone is working, through more powerful and sophisticated hand-held devices and different communication technologies, is both increasing our dependency on our information systems and at the same time making them more vulnerable. As individuals, we are also becoming more dependent on ICT to communicate with friends and families, access our bank accounts, do our shopping, run our diaries, hold key data on all aspects of our lives. Never has it been more important to protect our computer systems and data against a variety of threats. These include disasters both natural and malicious, various types of computer crime, computer viruses and/or combinations of these. Some religious and/or political terrorist groups are now described as being involved in 'cyber-terrorism'.

In this chapter we outline some of the main threats and a range of approaches to dealing with them. However, dealing with the burgeoning problems of computer crime/disasters/viruses, etc, is a very specialist and fast-moving arena and you will need to seek specialist advice to keep yourself up to date.

As organisations are required by law to keep their data confidential and accurate, and not misuse it, we also give an introduction to the relevant legislation.

Ward (1995) sets out three aspects to security:

- Protection: how confidential is the information? What steps need to be taken to control access? How secure is the system to outside attack?
- Recoverability: how vulnerable is the organisation to system or computer failure? How quickly does the system/computer have to be up and running again? How often should copies be made of data? How long do the copies need to be kept? Where should these copies be kept?
- The UK law relating to data security.

We shall look at each of these in turn.

PROTECTION

A whole industry has grown up of *hackers*: individuals and organisations, often operating internationally, who have become highly skilled in gaining unauthorised access to other people's ICT systems to cause chaos or to defraud, for example by gaining access to customers' bank account details. There are also so-called *ethical hackers* who try to break into systems – sometimes at the owner's request and sometimes on the basis of 'the public good' – to test their security.

One of the very common and disruptive threats comes through attack from computer viruses. Viruses can be described as 'infectious' computer programs that may self-replicate and spread quickly in the infected system, or from the infected computer device to another one. They threaten our systems by destroying data and/or interfering with processing and storage, and were originally introduced into systems when they were inadvertently (or maliciously) read into them from floppy disks. With the increasing inputting of programs and data into our systems electronically via the Internet (including e-mails), the virus problem has escalated.

There are several generic types of virus:

- The *link virus* attaches itself in a way that enables it to interfere with files and directories. It can be difficult to get rid of as the nature of the attachment (embeddedness) means that its removal can lead to the destruction of the data.
- The *worm virus* replicates itself within a computer/computer network using the resources of the new host, for instance to send e-mails to all the contacts in the computer's address book or to close down the system.
- The *parasite virus* copies itself into authentic programs, multiplying every time the program is run. In this way it will eventually overwhelm, slow down or even destroy programs, files or data. The parasite may stay hidden until activated by a particular event, such as the anniversary of the attack on the World Trade Center in New York.
- The *macro virus* is usually hidden in executable programs that are used in computing packages such as word processing, e-mail and browsers. Macro viruses are capable of very destructive activities.

Some of the hacking activities have become very sophisticated, for example replicating genuine web sites in order to steal access information and hijacking people's telephone connections onto premium rate lines, to name just a couple of the scams that are current as we write this edition.

So what can we do to protect ourselves? First, we can deny unauthorised people *physical* access. We can lock our doors and keep such people out of our buildings. We can put a physical lock on our computer that prevents either the keyboard or the disk drives from work-ing. Second, and more crucially these days, we can also provide a variety of *electronic* controls. With regard to the confidentiality and integrity of the stored information we can:

- assign passwords to allow entry to the system overall, or specific files, thus denying access to unauthorised users
- assign passwords for modifying files, which denies unauthorised users the ability to change the data
- assign passwords which allow access, but log or track any changes made and set up an audit trail of who has changed what, in what way and when, in your system
- use more sophisticated electronic controls such as hand, voice and retina print controls.

However, in these days of modems, satellite communication and other remote access, these measures are generally not enough and we often need to install:

- software barriers to the outside world (commonly known as *firewalls*) designed to prevent unauthorised access to or from a private computer/network)
- virus protection software.

Firewalls generally operate between an organisation's local area network (LAN) or wide area net-work (WAN) and external networks such as the Internet. They effectively behave like gatekeep-ers, and operate in a variety of ways similar to their physical equivalents, the security guards that police the entrances to our physical sites. For example, firewalls can stop incoming e-mails if the sender has not been authorised for access, or they can check with the member of staff to see if an e-mail is expected and wanted before letting it through.

Virus protection software automatically scans messages, programs, data and information being transferred either through the Internet or via external physical storage devices such as CDs, zip disks and USB ports. It also routinely scans the whole system for viruses. In this way viruses can be quarantined and treated, or sent to a virus checking company for analy-sis. As a result of the proliferation of viruses and their increasing variety and sophistication, anti-virus software has to be continually updated (usually through the Internet) to deal with the ever-changing threats.

A further weapon in the armoury is the use of *encryption* to protect sensitive data/files that are susceptible to electronic 'eavesdropping' while being transferred between different computer systems, for example by electronic data interchange (see Chapter 10). Encryption involves the conversion of the data into a secret code. The intended recipients (and only those recipients) have the key to this code, which allows them to decipher or decrypt it.

Electronic security in all its forms has become an industry in itself!

DISASTER RECOVERY

Many of us are familiar with the horror of finding that our computer systems are 'down', even temporarily. If this happens organisation-wide it can be disastrous – for our customers, our stocks, our finances and our corporate reputation. The potential natural threats include fires, floods, storm damage and water leaks, and the man-made threats include bombs, vandalism and viruses. In view of all these perils, it is imperative that we have plans and procedures in place to minimise the likelihood of such occurrences, and if they should happen despite our precautions, provide us with the means of recovering from these disasters quickly. These arrangements are often referred to as *business continuity plans*. Despite our ever-increasing reliance on our ICT systems, a recent article (Bisson 2004) reported that 97 per cent of organisations in Britain would not be able to carry on as normal after the event of a fire in their data centre. About half of those organisations had no idea how long it would take to get back to normal working. On the other hand there are organisations (see Case Study 7.1) that have to work to their customers' tight specifications for being back in business in days or even hours and, therefore, must have effective recovery measures in place.

Disaster recovery should be a matter of concern at the outset of the development of any information system. The main issues should be set out in the feasibility study (see Chapter 6) and then progressed so that the recovery processes are in place even before the system goes live. The idea is to have an effective action plan to cope with any disaster that might occur, whether natural or man-made. Such measures might include:

- setting up arrangements in alternative locations with compatible equipment and software
- making contingency arrangements with a commercial disaster recovery agency for support to be available if needed
- having temporary reciprocal arrangements with another organisation in your locality
- having comprehensive documentation of systems for back-up and recovery, and practising their use as regularly as we would practise fire drills
- ensuring all data, files, applications and operating systems are copied regularly and the copies placed in a secure, preferably remote location
- allocating responsibility for security and back-up in the organisation clearly to a specified individual in the same way as we would allocate responsibility for the management of health and safety, and ensuring top management support for the plan.

It is important that the plan is communicated to all those involved so that they are clear about the arrangements, and that the plans are reviewed regularly so that they take into account changes in business need or risk, and changes in ICT systems.

Case Study 7.1 sets out how one organisation has addressed this issue.

CASE STUDY 7.1

Cardiff County Council has pooled resources with two other Welsh councils, Carmarthenshire and Wrexham, to build a new disaster recovery centre in Cardiff. This went live at the end of 2004 and provides all three councils with the facilities to recover from a complete systems failure within a few hours. Cardiff had previously used a commercial disaster recovery service, but this had the disadvantages of providing only very limited back-up services and in a remote location away from the organisation's main customers (an aircraft hangar in Hertfordshire!). The shared approach has proved very cost-effective. The new system costs the same as the previous arrangement but provides a much wider range of back-up cover including social services, education, e-mail, people management and financial systems. The move made a great deal of sense as the three organisations were all running the same sort of systems and were linked through a high-speed network called the Wales Lifelong Learning Network which provided the infrastructure to support a shared disaster recovery centre.

THE UK LAW RELATING TO DATA SECURITY

The law relating to data security is developing all the time and you need to keep your environmental scan in action in this area. Here we look at three pieces of relevant legislation relating to data security and access: the Data Protection Act 1998, the Freedom of Information Act 2000 and the Computer Misuse Act 1990.

Data Protection Act (1998)

Let us look first at the legal framework for data protection. The *Data Protection Act 1998* (DPA), which came into effect on 1 March 2000 and replaced an earlier Act, regulates the use of personal data, defined as 'information about living, identifiable individuals'. The Act applies to all data held on computer and in paper format where it is organised into a 'relevant filing system'.

All organisations that hold or process such data must notify the Information Commissioner and comply with the eight data protection principles. The first five principles are to do with general standards of data holding and processing, and cover such issues as that the data must be:

- obtained fairly and lawfully
- processed only for specific and lawful processes
- be relevant, adequate and not excessive for those processes
- be accurate and kept up-to-date, and
- only kept for as long as needed.

The sixth principle relates to the rights of the data subjects and includes the right to request and be informed of all information held about them. It prevents the misuse of the information for direct marketing, gives rights to compensation and the removal and correction of inaccurate data.

The seventh principle requires organisations to ensure that 'they have adequate security precautions in place to prevent the loss, destruction or unauthorised disclosure of data'.

The eighth principle is concerned with transferring data out of the European Economic Area. Organisations are not allowed to do so unless they are satisfied that the country to which the data is being transferred can provide adequate levels of security or the data subject has given consent.

Of particular interest to HR professionals are the implications for the holding of employees' and others' data, and rights of access to it. There is now a code of practice aimed at employers – the *Employment Practices Data Protection Code* – which covers the following areas:

- recruitment and selection
- employment records
- monitoring at work, for example the use of telephones or e-mails
- medical information, such as occupational health, medical records, drug and genetic screening
- small businesses.

Details of the Data Protection Act and all the codes can be found on the website www.informationcommissioner.gov.uk.

Freedom of Information Act 2000

Another very important piece of legislation affecting public sector bodies in England, Wales and

Northern Ireland (Scotland has its own regime) is the *Freedom of Information Act 2000*. The Act applies to central and local government, the police, the NHS, schools, colleges, universities, and other public bodies such as the BBC and the Food Standards Agency.

The website cited in the previous section also provides detailed information about this Act, and states:

> *The Freedom of Information Act 2000 is intended to promote a culture of openness and accountability amongst public sector bodies by providing people with the right of access to the information held by them.*

> (www.informationcommissioner.gov.uk, 2004)

The Act enables people to gain access in two ways to information which is not covered under the Data Protection Act (which covers personal information about themselves) or by the Environmental Information Regulations 2004 (which covers environmental information):

- First, every public authority is required to make some of its information available through a publications scheme. This sets out what information will be routinely available, how it can be accessed and whether there is any charge. There was a phased programme of implementation of this stage, which started in 2002 and was completed in 2004.
- Second, from 1 January 2005 everyone the right to ask for specific information held by a public authority (although there are a number of exemptions), and the authority must comply as set out in the Act.

Computer Misuse Act 1990

The *Computer Misuse Act 1990* (CMA) provides powers to prosecute people who, deliberately and without authority, misuse computer systems. The CMA defines three offences:

- unauthorised access – this is commonly known as 'hacking' but also includes users who deliberately exceed their authority
- ulterior intent – unauthorised access with the intention of carrying out some serious crime, such as fraud or obtaining information for the purposes of blackmailing someone to whom the data relates
- unauthorised modifications in any form, including by computer viruses that are intended to impair the use of the computer system.

The focus of the Act is on protecting the computer systems rather than the data held on them. The law attempts to be comprehensive and all-embracing, but to a certain extent has been overtaken by events and does not, for example, cover electronic eavesdropping or the writing of viruses.

CONCLUSION

In this chapter we have introduced the very important subject of data security. Information is the lifeblood of most organisations. Failure to address the many and wide-ranging threats to our ICT systems can prove very costly in terms of recovery of the data, legal implications, lost business or organisational opportunities, and so on, and can ultimately jeopardise the very survival of the organisation. It is essential to take adequate routine precautions and also to plan for the worst scenario through a business continuity planning process. It is also important to be aware of the organisation's and individuals' responsibilities and rights as enshrined in legislation. It reinforces the need for us all to play our part in safeguarding the security and integrity of our ICT systems – at the design and development stages, in the maintenance of these systems, and in how we operate and use them.

REVIEW QUESTIONS

1. What sorts of issues would you consider in developing a disaster recovery plan for an organisation?

2. Data protection compliance should be an integral part of modern organisational practice. List some of the benefits that will accrue to those organisations that adopt effective data protection policies and procedures.

Human resource
information systems

CHAPTER OBJECTIVES

When you have studied this chapter, you will be able to:

■ list the core features of a human resource information system (HRIS)
■ describe some of the most common applications of an HRIS
■ explain the contribution that a well-designed HRIS can make to the work of the HR function and the organisation overall.

INTRODUCTION

We find it interesting, as we write this book on information systems (which are invariably computerised in some form these days), to look at some of the similarities between the two aids to achieving competitive advantage, information systems and human resource management (HRM). Both have struggled to be seen and used as a strategic, and in some cases even as a tactical resource.

Until relatively recently in many organisations HRM was seen as primarily an administrative function, keeping the personnel files and perhaps in some cases administering the wages, company cars, etc. It was not surprising that many HR departments in the 1990s, trying valiantly to cope with all the downsizing, resizing, right-sizing and so on of the time, were overwhelmed with their paperwork and far behind the strategic issues facing the business. It is salutary that 'almost half (of senior practitioners surveyed in 2003) felt that their strategic input was constrained by the time they were having to devote to administrative activities' (CIPD 2004). In the past the emphasis has been on coping with the present, but it is now moving gradually towards focusing on the future.

In the early days of computers the majority of the information systems to be computerised were the financial systems. For many organisations, introducing computers into HR departments used to be a low priority on the list of their ICT managers. Even when computerised HRISs did arrive they were largely an electronic version of what had gone before. Sadly, in many organisations updating and improving their HRISs often still falls well down the priority list behind the financial and operational systems of the business. Only recently we have seen this in two large organisations. One major European financial organisation which appeared to have state-of-the-art everything else was still operating with an antiquated set of dedicated HRISs which suffered from all the classic problems: inconsistent and poor-quality data, poor reporting systems, etc, and lack of compatibility. Another medium-sized public-sector organisation in this country was using a system that was over 10 years old and which was described as a 'pure record keeping database'. It was widely acknowledged as not meeting the needs of the HR function. A CIPD survey on *People and technology* (2003) found that satisfaction with HRISs was relatively low, with only a third of respondents thinking that their system met or mostly met their needs and with this figure dropping to 27 per cent for public sector organisations.

The same survey suggested that 40 per cent of the participants planned to change their system in the next three years. Things have clearly moved on from the early days, and relational databases are now the norm for new systems. It is impossible to imagine a system being installed without the facility for the users to be able easily to pull off their own customised reports. Intranets and the Internet have made it possible for the systems and their data to be distributed throughout the organisation. This can allow users to drill down to the level of detail they require to produce their own information and reports. As we show shortly, when used in multinational organisations these systems even allow the users to produce their reports in the language of their choice. There has also been an increasing emphasis on what are called self-service systems which, for example enable individuals to access their own records and make certain changes. Similarly managers, where authorised, are able to access and amend their own staff's records.

This chapter is about using information systems to support HR professionals in their roles. We start by looking at the core features of HRISs, then look at specific modules aimed at particular activities: for example, recruitment and learning and development. It is our intention not to present a complete review of what is available – a visit to the websites of the major players will provide that – but to try to set out the contribution a well designed and implemented HRIS can make to the work of the HR team and the organisation overall. We use case studies to illustrate that there is no 'one size fits all' approach – it is very much about deciding on the organisation's requirements and finding a system that meets those needs.

CORE FEATURES OF HR INFORMATION SYSTEMS

Whatever features are included, in overall terms the system should be simple to use, and be sufficiently flexible and intuitive for non-computer specialists to 'do it themselves'. Modern systems will generally use relational databases and offer powerful reporting tools enabling users to generate reports to answer almost any conceivable question. They will also incorporate or provide easy access to software packages that enables the data to be presented in user-friendly and eye-catching ways using a wide range of charting and graphical methods.

We can summarise the basic core features as follows. The system must:

- provide one source of all data on the people resources of the organisation, so that changes in data have only to be input once and all relevant files containing that data will automatically be updated
- enable users to generate reports to answer a wide range of questions and be flexible enough to answer questions not conceived of at the time of the design
- provide the facility for managers at all levels to drill down to the appropriate level of detail to produce information and reports to meet their needs
- be intuitive to use and user-friendly in all aspects of its operation
- be flexible enough to enable users to incorporate new types of data relatively easily, without requiring help from an ICT specialist
- be able to cope with growth/decline in staff numbers/records in a cost-effective way
- provide the facility to interface with other systems in the organisation
- if relevant, and increasingly it is in today's world of global organisations, handle data which may be organised and represented in different ways reflecting different countries' way of doing things.

At their most basic, HRISs are used to store data needed to support HR processes and to provide reports. However, most systems these days offer a wide range of additional features such as those set out below.

- The ability to automate time-consuming administrative processes such as those involved in recruitment and learning activities, using workflow approaches – see later in this chapter.
- The capability to access data and information across multi-site/multinational operations through the use of the organisation's intranet and/or the Internet.
- The opportunity for self-service for employees and managers, again using intranet/Internet technology. For employees this can range from simply providing access to information on HR policies, their holiday entitlement, etc, to the ability to change basic personal data on themselves such as their address, or put in requests for holidays or learning programmes, etc. The potential implications for line managers can be much greater in terms of updating employee records, accessing information and running reports on their teams, authorising absence, development activities and so on.
- Facilitate the use of modern HR tools such as competency frameworks, 360-degree feedback and development plans.

This discussion was all about features, but there are also some key issues in the approach to providing the system:

- A key issue is whether to use a single integrated system from one supplier. Some organisations have adopted enterprise planning resource (ERP) systems that integrate all the systems of the organisation – production, finance, HR and so on. The alternative approach – often referred to as 'best of breed' approach – is to select a specialist package for each use that interfaces with a corporate database. The arguments in favour of the first approach are the avoidance of any problems of integration, and the simplicity of dealing with only one supplier for maintenance and customer-support services. The advocates of the latter approach suggest that the main advantages are that it enables the best tool to be selected for the particular job and provides flexibility as it allows the different parts of the system to be upgraded as the need arises in that particular area.
- The move away from the traditional client/server architecture (where the data is held on a central server but the software for each application is held on the individual user's PC) to web-based models (where the applications are also hosted centrally) has opened up the opportunity for using an application service provider (ASP). This means the client effectively rents the applications as it needs them. The ASP is then responsible for the maintenance, upgrades, system security, etc. As we write this book, it is difficult to tell whether ASPs are likely to be a popular option in the future.

LEARNING FROM EXPERIENCE

We set out below two case studies describing the development of HRISs in two organisations. The first organisation is in the private sector, and the case study describes the planning of its first HRIS. The second organisation is in the public sector, and the case study describes the slightly chequered history of the development of its HRIS over the last five years. Both offer very valuable learning points.

CASE STUDY 8.1: LIFETIME GROUP LTD HUMAN RESOURCE INFORMATION SYSTEM

Company background

Lifetime Group Ltd was set up in 2002 to provide a computerised platform for portfolio management to independent financial advisers. The company started with two employees (the founding directors) in 2002, growing to 62 by mid-2004, and anticipated growing to about 300 in three years' time. The HR manager, Michaela Maycock, joined the staff in early 2004. She was recruited into a 'blank canvas' HR site and started all her systems and procedures from scratch. By mid-2004 it was very obvious that although it was a relatively small organisation, the operational requirements of this fast-growing business required an HR function that was both effective and efficient in producing HR information for top management and meeting the stringent standards of their regulator, the Financial Services Authority (FSA).

Justifying the system

With such a new company operating in the fast-moving arena of ICT and in a tightly regulated sector, the directors of Lifetime were very conscious of the following needs:

- to keep a tight control of staff numbers, so requiring quick and accurate headcount information
- to have accurate HR records and data on employees, and for these data and records to be quickly and easily amended
- for the data to blend seamlessly and accurately with its outsourced payroll provider
- to have accurate and up-to-date training and competency records, and evidence of continuing professional development – an important requirement of the FSA
- to provide the basis for an efficient HR administration function
- to support a busy recruitment function
- to minimise the work in updating records by making it necessary to input data only once
- to provide a reminder system, for example for training needs, the end of probationary periods, etc.
- to have high-quality management information on all parts of the business.

All these clear requirements helped Maycock produce a cost/benefit analysis to sell her case for the automation of her HR systems to the Executive Board. Maycock was keen to point out that her case was helped by the culture of the company, which was to be leading edge in all that it did, and to provide professional and supportive services to its employees to encourage trust and motivation.

She was also able to flag up further developments like the administration of the future flexible benefits scheme and the opportunity to provide some self-service features for managers and their staff. Maycock highlighted the importance of the latter feature to encourage managers to be proactive on, for example, absence management. There was also a particular FSA requirement to have, as part of a business continuity plan, a telephone contact trail of all employees in order to be able to tell them, in the event of a significant business stoppage out of hours, where to go to continue their work.

The critical success factors were identified as being:

- the ease of keeping the data up to date
- the ability to meet the need for a wide and varied range of management information accurately, quickly and easily – there was a high expectation of management information in the business.

Preparing the specification

Maycock successfully secured board agreement and went on to prepare a detailed specification of her requirements. In addition to calling on her own experience of using and developing HRISs, she used a variety of methods including:

- liaison with the top managers to understand their needs
- brainstorming within her small HR team
- networking with other HR professionals.

Maycock freely admits that she would have liked to involve her line managers more in the process. However, at that stage in the development of the business, line managers were focused very much on their own specific business issues and also lacked the experience of knowing their HR information needs in detail.

Selecting a supplier

From her previous experience, Maycock had a clear idea of the sort of supplier she was looking for. She wanted one that:

- was not too big – she did not want to use one of the really big players in the field such as Oracle or PeopleSoft
- had good experience of small and medium-sized customers
- offered the modules the company required now and in the future, such as self-service
- could provide a seamless link to the outsourced payroll system
- had low licensing costs to reflect the relatively small number of employees.

Maycock and her new assistant, Gemma Rayner, started with a website-based search for a suitable supplier. They soon identified, as readers of *Personnel Management* will testify, that there were a large number of potential suppliers that appeared to offer what was required. It was difficult to distinguish between them from their websites. Maycock and Rayner started with a long-list and whittled this down to a short-list of three based on a structured telephone interview. They ruled out one potential supplier because of its high initial quotation. There was not much difference between the remaining two, but the successful bidder gave a good demonstration of its system and unlike the other, included within its sales team the potential project manager who showed empathy with their needs.

The key features that attracted Maycock and Rayner to their supplier were:

- the flexibility offered by the system to make changes to the data fields and reports easily – these could be amended by the users without the intervention of an ICT specialist
- the system was intuitive in its operation and more user-friendly
- there was a good operator-training package on offer by the supplier on a cost per user requirement basis
- speedy implementation
- the relatively low licensing costs.

Implementation issues

Because Lifetime was such a new company its staff records at this time were very up to date and so data cleansing issues were likely to be limited. Also, because the existing systems were relatively unsophisticated, there was little 'tweaking' needed of the standard package, and the personnel data could simply be uploaded from existing spreadsheets. On this basis and the current number of existing employees, the supplier forecast a six-week installation process that would include operator training. The personnel records module would be implemented first, closely followed by the recruitment and training modules.

Next on the agenda would follow self-service, but Maycock was adamant that this feature would only be introduced when line managers had been convinced of the benefits to them. She had already experienced self-service applications that had effectively failed because of low take-up by managers and staff! Performance management was the next major application in her sights ... Watch this space, hopefully we can catch up with Maycock's progress and report back in our next edition.

CASE STUDY 8.2: MERSEYTRAVEL

Background

Merseytravel is the combined operating name used by two organisations, the Merseyside Passenger Transport Authority (MPTA) and the Merseyside Passenger Transport Executive (MPTE), which together provide the strategic overview and responsibility for travel and transport in the Merseyside area. The MPTE was set up under the Transport Act 1968 and the Authority was established on 1 April 1986 under the Local Government Act 1985. The MPTA comprises 18 local authority councillors representing the five local authorities of Merseyside. The MPTE advises and supports the Authority. As an organisation Merseytravel is committed to playing a major role in the continued regeneration of Merseyside, both economically and socially.

Merseytravel is composed of three 'business units', the MPTE employing 500 staff, Mersey Tunnels employing 350 staff and Mersey Ferries employing 120 staff; giving a total complement of 970 employees to be covered currently by the new HRIS.

Alastair Ramsay, the principal personnel officer in the executive section responsible for managing the current project, took up his job about five years ago. He inherited a situation of two HRISs each serving separate parts of the organisation. The need to up-grade the time and attendance system, and the problem that the system was not Year 2000 compliant, precipitated a move to provide one unified HRIS. This is the system currently in operation.

Ramsay honestly admits that the system, whilst an improvement on the previous set-up, turned out to be far from ideal. Its major problems are that it:

- is very labour-intensive, requiring 2.5 staff to service it
- is not user-friendly: for example, it is complex and difficult to update data and handle exceptions
- does not readily provide the quality of management information required
- has an interface with the supplier entirely through the IT department, which sometimes complicates and slows down the process of dealing with problems and making changes.

Ramsay explained that he learned a lot from this experience of implementing an HRIS, which is informing his approach to the new project. He summed up the improvements needed in the process:

- The new system needed to be HR-based, with the ability to add on other functions. The development of the first system had been focused too heavily on the time and attendance features.
- The project needed to be managed by the HR function as the users of the system. The previous system had been managed by the IT department, which had strong views about the type of software and hardware required.
- A much tighter specification, and one that took the user more into account, was required. The original specification was too simplistic, expected processing volumes were underestimated, and as a result financial considerations 'pushed the decision-making process into a corner' leading to a least-cost, low-quality solution.

Put simply, as summed up in their specification, Merseytravel wished to procure an HRIS:

> which will support the Personnel Division and the operational managers of a modern, diverse organisation in delivering its corporate objectives. The system will need to be flexible and responsive, providing information to support both the delivery of large-scale programmes and smaller routine day-to-day administrative tasks.
>
> (MTPE Invitation to Tender, July 2004)

Project initiation

In addition to the problems listed earlier, several other drivers emerged that led to the decision to go for a completely new HRIS. (The option to upgrade the existing system was explored but basically Merseytravel had lost confidence in the system and supplier, so it was decided not to take this route.) These new drivers were:

- The Race Relations Amendment Act 2000 required better monitoring information than could be provide by the existing system.
- District Audit was encouraging the greater use of information for capacity building and workforce planning.
- Line managers were asking for more and better information on their staff.
- There were major projects on the horizon that would require a range of different types of staff including temps and consultants, and a system was needed that could cope with a variety of terms and conditions.
- There was a range of new staffing initiatives in the pipeline. For example a competency framework was being developed and there was a new performance management system.

The process began in October 2003 when work was started to develop the business case to secure funding in the following year's budget. A project team, led by Ramsay, was set up. The team consisted of HR staff from the Executive and Tunnels Divisions, with administrative and clerical support that included expertise on the existing system. One support staff member worked on the project on a full-time basis, and the other members all worked part-time. IT, finance, legal, audit and committee-servicing support was provided as required. During January to April 2004 Ramsay obtained line manager and other specialist input into the system specification by running briefing sessions and workshops. He felt this not only provided a valuable contribution to the specification process, but was also an important ingredient in gaining management buy-in and ownership of the final system.

The specification

By June 2004 the specification was completed. It consisted of three elements:

- a general specification providing a description of the organisation, details of IT structure and technology, firewalls/system crash/backup facility, etc
- a functional specification
- a user specification that set out the 'soft elements', that is, the required user-friendliness.

The functional specification included the following basic requirements:

- general personnel administration – including absence monitoring, handling of grievance and disciplinary cases, and occupational health
- recruitment and selection administration
- workforce planning, including HR planning, career planning and performance management
- learning and development administration, including managing resources, learning plans, management of NVQs, and evaluation (at reaction and intermediate levels)
- time and attendance
- health and safety.

Ramsay felt that the third element, the user specification, was particularly important. It had been relatively straightforward to set out the functional elements. However, the team had learned from previous experience that although it was not easy to do, it was vital to try to set out the standards required for ease of use and general user-friendliness. We feel that this is a key issue and Ramsay is absolutely right to put the spotlight on it. The specification emphasises this perspective early on by stating:

> whilst basic core requirements are highlighted within the specification, it is more important to note that it is not intended that the specification details how facilities and features might be provided; **rather what the user expects to see**.
>
> (MTPE Invitation to Tender, July 2004, our bold)

So many systems founder because there is too much emphasis on facilities and features and too little on user-friendliness issues. Because of this, we thought readers would be interested to get a flavour of how Ramsay and his team approached this part of the specification:

> The 'system' should be 'user friendly' and allow:
>
> (a)   any authorised person who only occasionally uses a computer to be able to make simple enquiries of the system and produce reports;
> (b)   an occasional user to receive all necessary prompts from the system without needing to use a manual;
> (c)   all coding structures to be available, on screen, at data input stage, together with selection options;

(d)   all input codes to be automatically decoded so that the literal is understood;

(e)   the user to be able to link screens together as they wish at data input.

(MTPE Invitation to Tender, July 2004)

Ramsay saw the key success criteria for the new HRIS overall as:

- reduction in staff dedicated to running the system, allied to increased involvement in the routine updating and usage of the system by non-HR staff
- improvement in the quality of HR information for decision-making
- increased take-up of HR information by line managers and their greater involvement in HR issues
- a high level of user satisfaction in how the system operated.

Tender process

Expressions of interest were sought by mid-July 2004, and 12 suppliers made approaches. These were initially screened on the basis of financial status, organisational style and structure, client base, etc, which whittled the list down to eight that received the full tender pack. Full tenders were required within two months, with a deadline date of late September. Included in the tender pack was a self-scoring matrix devised by the project team – the suppliers had to rate themselves on a scale of 0 to 10 against a detailed set of requirement criteria. The team was not sure that the suppliers would provide an honest assessment of themselves but was pleasantly surprised at how useful this matrix was in selecting the short-list. A short-list of three tenderers was invited to the next stage. This stage consisted of a presentation and a half-day session where a range of users was invited to quiz the suppliers and 'play' with the proposed system.

There are now two suppliers left in the running. As part of the final decision-making process the project team is visiting their sites to:

- meet and get a feel for the staff they might be dealing with on a day-to-day basis
- look at the quality of their training facilities
- get hands-on experience of using the software with samples of Merseytravel's own data.

They will also be making visits to client sites of the potential suppliers, where the systems under offer are currently in use in situations similar to Merseytravel. We were impressed by the thoroughness of this stage of the process. Ramsay commented that his team was determined to get it right this time and recalled ruefully that the existing system was observed operating in a rope factory. A final decision was expected after Christmas 2004, and it was only at this stage that the cost was to be taken into account.

Next stages

Ramsay and his team went for an 'off-the-shelf' solution. However, the system will need to be tailored to ensure that it meets their specific requirements, and there will be extensive user-acceptance testing and training before final implementation and handover. The specification requires the chosen supplier to 'parachute in' one of its specialist staff to work alongside the HR staff during these stages. Given the attention that is being paid to seeking a supplier the team can work with, it will be interesting to see how well the relationship works. Ramsay is intending to include line managers in the project team during this final stage.

The original timetable gave the end of March 2005 for system implementation. New hardware was ordered to support the new system, and time was scheduled for training. However, the process is not being rushed. Bearing in mind that most of the participants are on the project part-time and their other work simply will not just go away, Ramsay is determined to allow sufficient time 'to get it right' even if it means accepting some slippage.

The future

As of writing (May 2005), we are hoping to keep in touch with Ramsay and his team and check back in about a year's time to see how the new HRIS is bedding down. You can look forward to an update in the third edition of this book! Although it is not part of the first phase of implementation, Ramsay is keen to introduce 'self-service' elements as soon as the system has proved itself and all the users are comfortable with its current functions. The specification set out that any system must be able to provide this capability. Like Ramsay, we are convinced that the move to 'self-service' is vital in order to free HR staff for more strategic tasks.

In discussion Ramsay explained that it was not intended that the HRIS would become part of a wider corporate information system. Nor, interestingly, did he expect that payroll would be run on the system, as Merseytravel has a very satisfactory arrangement with an outside agency.

In summary, the HR Division is seeking a straightforward, robust, user-friendly system capable of extension into the areas mentioned. We wish them all the best.

Both the case studies represent a familiar scenario for many readers – the implementation of an HRIS in a small or medium-sized enterprise (SME) environment. Both have adopted a best of breed approach rather than an ERP solution and both have gone for an 'off-the shelf' solution adapted to meet their needs. We have also had experience of the ERP approach used in a large organisation and shall draw out the learning points from this example as well. It is perhaps interesting that we have not had experience of an organisation choosing to develop the software for its HRIS from scratch. This probably reflects that the market for HRISs is now well developed, and there are a large number of companies offering comprehensive predesigned specialist solutions, as well as the major players in the ERP market offering specialist HR suites.

The major learning issues for developing an HRIS are:

- the importance of HR leading and driving the HRIS project
- establishing clear and measurable success criteria – which help focus on the key requirements and provide the basis of ensuring you get what you want
- having a clear, comprehensive and well-researched specification that sets out both 'content' and 'user-friendliness' requirements
- involving all users, including line managers, as much as possible in every stage of the project
- selecting a system that allows for additional data fields to be added easily and at low cost
- selecting a system that can be expanded to meet any forecast growth in the organisation

- selecting a system that can be expanded to take on additional functions or applications *post hoc*
- planning for, and not underestimating, the issue of data cleansing when transferring data from an existing system to the new system.

Most HRIS products are based on a modular approach. There is generally a core product that covers the basic personnel information on employees, with additional modules supporting specific HR functions. Two of the most frequently requested modules are the recruitment module and the learning and development module. We discuss these modules in more detail below.

RECRUITMENT MODULES

The bane of many HR professionals' lives is the mass of paperwork associated with recruitment. It is not unusual to have scores of applicants, even with the most tightly drawn personnel specification. All these applications need to be acknowledged and tracked through the process. At each stage there is usually the requirement for an appropriate letter to be generated and sent off to advise the applicant of the outcome. Most HRIS recruitment modules will do these chores automatically, thus saving an enormous amount of repetitive effort. What they do not do generally is make our selection decisions for us. However, we are beginning to see even this happening, with the introduction of some mechanistic sifting processes. This feature can be further developed where the organisation is using clearly defined competencies and/or behaviourally anchored ratings to differentiate between the candidates, and may go yet further with the development of recruitment applications incorporating expert systems.

Combined with intranet/Internet HR facilities, vacancies can also be posted automatically internally and on the organisation's website. Application forms can be either downloaded or filled in online. We discuss these features in more detail in the e-HR section in Chapter 10.

The system allows for the automatic collection of data and provision of reports on all aspects of the recruitment process. For example:

- it makes the systematic monitoring of equal opportunities in recruitment a reality, as reports on the breakdown of successful/unsuccessful candidates can be provided at every stage
- it enables automatic media analysis (to show which publication produced the best recruitment response)
- vacancy cost analysis (to show which media were the most cost-effective) is usually a standard feature
- important statistics such as the time taken to fill a vacancy and the overall costs can be produced.

Finally, the system will usually enable the successful applicant's details to be input automatically into the personnel records system.

LEARNING AND DEVELOPMENT MODULES

Like his or her recruitment colleagues, the learning professional will from time to time disappear into the paper quagmire. Records get out of date, and the administration associated with a single learning event can overwhelm even the most efficient members of staff, not to mention the perennial problems surrounding the allocation of rooms! Many organisations use outside facilities and contract with independent, freelance learning professionals to run their programmes, and the efficient professional will want to have the facts about these external resources immediately accessible. The learning and development module can automate and therefore simplify all these administrative functions. Case Study 8.3 describes the use of such a learning and development information system.

CASE STUDY 8.3

A major energy supplier needed to provide both a high volume and a wide range of learning programmes to ensure that its staff had the required skills to operate in this highly competitive, fast-moving and technically advanced industry. This vast amount of activity generated masses of paper and did not always work as efficiently as the organisation wished. It was decided to install a computerised information system to cope with the 'administration'. They looked for a system that effectively automated all parts of the process so that it was more efficient, less labour-intensive, involved less duplication of effort, was very customer-focused and was in line with the paper reduction policy. The users of the system were all the people in the learning and development chain – the participants, their managers, the administrators, the learning professionals, the print unit (which dealt with the handouts), the in-house learning centre staff and so on.

The system operates as follows:

1. All employees can access details of all learning events, including the learning objectives, competencies addressed, duration, locations, etc.
2. An employee can ask to attend a specific event using an online nomination form. This is forwarded automatically by the system to his/her line manager, who if appropriate will support the nomination and forward it to the Learning and Development department. Such nominations are often generated as a result of performance management interviews. The nominee then joins a waiting list.
3. As soon as there are enough people on the waiting list to make a programme viable, one is set up on the system.
4. People from the waiting list are then invited by a system-generated e-mail to confirm their commitment to attending a specific programme. If their reply is 'yes', their status is changed from applicant to participant.
5. Once all the replies are in, a standard e-mail confirmation message is sent to the Learning Centre advising that the programme will go ahead and automatically attaching the names of the participants. This confirms the booking of the rooms and learning facilitators involved.
6. Two weeks before the start of the programme the participants are e-mailed with their joining instructions, together with any pre-course work. An e-mail is sent to the print unit requesting that 'the attached inserts for the workbooks are copied'. It automatically specifies how many copies of the handouts and exercises are needed. The system takes the number of copies required from the participant list.
7. After the programme has taken place a reaction level evaluation form is automatically e-mailed to the participants. This is completed and returned online, with the system generating reminders if required.

Overall, the system uses a relational database with standard reports, for example on volumes of learning activity, whether it is classroom-based, distance learning or an outside programme, attendance rates, costs, etc. The system produces simple evaluation reports setting out the participants' satisfaction with the various programmes. There is also the opportunity for the system operators to produce their own ad hoc reports. Information is passed to the personnel records system that updates the learners' records. The system is password protected and has a built-in audit trail.

Examples of the benefits are:

- by making the current business processes more efficient it is possible to optimise the use of resources, such as the number of participants per course, utilisation of facilities, and enable learning needs to be met more quickly
- better productivity allows greater volumes of work to be achieved, faster and to higher levels of quality by existing resources
- by making the process more accessible to potential participants, it will encourage the take-up of learning and development opportunities
- there is complete auditability and reporting on all aspects of the process.

NB We were learning suppliers to this organisation. In terms of learning administration, it was the most efficient client organisation we have dealt with!

The identification and analysis of learning needs is another area where the power of IT can be harnessed to the advantage of the learning professional. It is particularly helpful where there are clearly defined competency levels specified for different jobs, and individuals can be assessed against these competency levels so that learning and development needs can be identified. Some systems also include details of specific learning interventions with the competencies they address, so that once a need has been identified an appropriate intervention can also be identified. The data on learning needs can be collected directly and relatively easily from potential participants and/or their managers using the intranet/Internet facility where this exists. Most modules also provide facilities such as development plans that can be accessed and updated by both the individual and his or her manager, to track progress in meeting the learning and development needs. The ability to model future organisational structures can make it possible to assess the volumes of learning activity (in different subject areas and at different levels) required in the future. In these ways, and probably others in the future, the technology provides the opportunity for learning professionals to be liberated from the present and to be able to cast their eyes into the future – to become more strategic!

Another area that has previously received little attention from ICT specialists is learning evaluation. Many packages now offer this capability in some form. Some are fairly limited and operate only at reaction level – the basic happy sheet – measuring participant satisfaction with the learning event by the use of simple questionnaires and analysis features. However, the use of intranet/Internet capability can allow data for intermediate evaluation (which assesses the impact of the learning on performance in the job) to be collected relatively easily from participants and other relevant parties such as their managers and colleagues, say three months and six months after the event.

OTHER MODULES

The range of add-ons to core HR systems is growing all the time. Health and safety, absence and leave management (often integrated with time and attendance systems) are now usually standard parts of the core module. The other common modules offered include payroll and pensions admin-istration and increasingly performance management, career planning and succession planning. It was interesting and encouraging to see that HR planning was part of the functionality specified by Merseytravel.

In our experience the development of modules to help with strategic HR planning has not kept pace with the more 'administrative' HR systems. However, a well designed and implemented HRIS will give the opportunity to the HR professional who wants to seize it – to be freed from the day-to-day routine chores and concentrate on making a real contribution to the business strategy of the organisation.

Useful further reading as an introduction to HRISs and including a range of case studies is the booklet *Human resource management systems* (IDS 2002). Also an all-round guide to products and services has been produced by *People Management* and is available on its website, www.softwaresource.co.uk.

CONCLUSION

In this chapter we have covered the key features of a HRIS and explained some of the most com-mon applications. We have seen how the development of relational databases combined with the ease of producing custom-made reports gives the HR professional the opportunity to access and make use of all the information needed for decision-making. The technology has also given the HR professional the opportunity to automate many of the administrative processes that previous-ly absorbed their energies in the day-to-day running of the function. The introduction of self-serv-ice approaches has further helped reduce some of the basic information-giving and data man-agement tasks. All these developments enable HR staff to tackle their operational and tactical roles more efficiently and effectively. The future lies in the extent to which HR professionals can now harness the power of information systems to develop their strategic role.

REVIEW QUESTIONS

1. What are the main benefits that might accrue from a well designed and implemented HRIS?

2. How might an HRIS help in managing performance?

Knowledge management systems

CHAPTER 9

CHAPTER OBJECTIVES

When you have studied this chapter, you will be able to:

- define the concepts of knowledge, knowledge management and knowledge management systems
- explain the importance of knowledge management to an organisation
- describe different approaches to the creation and distribution of knowledge
- analyse the factors that affect the success of knowledge management systems.

INTRODUCTION

So far in this book we have concentrated on information systems. However, as we set out in Chapter 1, the concept of knowledge management and its associated systems has become increasingly important as organisations seek to achieve competitive advantage. Peter Drucker in the early 1990s was already talking about knowledge becoming the basic economic resource, replacing the traditional concepts of capital, labour and natural resources. The late 1990s saw a burgeoning of interest in the key area of how this vital resource could be managed effectively. However, there remains much debate over exactly what is meant by the concept of knowledge and the accompanying concept of knowledge management. This is perhaps not surprising given that we are trying to capture something that is both so all pervasive and yet intangible!

On the other hand there is little debate about the importance of knowledge and knowledge management. Skapinker (2003) in his contribution to the CIPD's *Change agenda* identifies three main reasons:

- Knowledge has become a 'competitive weapon'. He describes the restructuring of economic activity in the developed economies away from manufacturing and towards services, and particularly professional and consulting services. It was Drucker who coined the phrase 'knowledge worker' to describe the increasing number of employees working in these areas. Even in the manufacturing industries that remain, the staff need to be highly skilled and knowledgeable to manage the sophisticated computer-controlled automated production processes. In today's world of rapid change, it can be argued that an organisation's knowledge base offers its best sustainable competitive advantage.
- Organisations have found out how easy it is to lose knowledge. In the early to mid-1990s many organisations downsized and found out to their cost that downsizing can have a very dramatic effect on their knowledge base. Many organisations failed to plan for the exodus of often their most experienced (and knowledgeable) employees.
- Advances in technology such as e-mail, organisational intranets, the Internet, more sophisticated databases and video conferencing have made it easier to access and share knowledge.

Beazley et al (2002) develop the theme of the implications for organisations of having knowledge workers:

- The emphasis is moving from being concerned about where people have worked and what they have done, to what they have learned and what they know.
- With the modern more organic structures, jobs and responsibilities are continually changing and evolving to reflect the changes in the environment. Rigid procedures and lengthy manuals are being replaced by more flexible systems which put a heavier emphasis on individuals' knowledge.
- The knowledge workers of today see their careers as spanning several organisations, and therefore knowledge is continually transferring in and out of organisations. It is probably fair to say that in most organisations this is happening in a fairly unmanaged way!
- The development of organisational models based on a core of key employees supported by a greater use of peripheral workers (Handy, 1989) again puts the spotlight on the problems of retaining knowledge.
- The concepts of continuous improvement require a knowledge continuum.

In this chapter we examine some of the different definitions of knowledge and knowledge management, look at the systems and infrastructure that underpin knowledge management, and finally discuss some of the approaches adopted in implementing knowledge management in organisations.

DEFINING KNOWLEDGE AND KNOWLEDGE MANAGEMENT

Knowledge

It is useful to review some of the various definitions put forward for the concept of knowledge. First is the definition and model we set out in Chapter 1, where Ward and Peppard (2002) describe it as 'information combined with experience, context, interpretation and reflection' and which sees knowledge as part of a continuum (the DIKAR model – see Figure 9.1.)

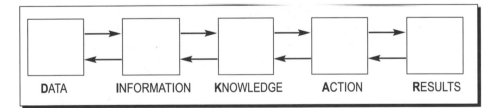

Figure 9.1 The DIKAR model
Source: Ward and Peppard (2002), reproduced with permission.

Beazley *et al* (2002) define knowledge as:

> *information organised into a framework, model, worldview, concept, principle, theory, hypothesis, or other basis of action that increases the understanding of a situation, improves problem-solving and decision making ...*

Both definitions emphasise that people act on the basis of knowledge, but Beazley *et al* add two different stages to the continuum:

Data → Information → Knowledge → Competency → Wisdom

They come to the debate from more of an HR perspective and see knowledge as contributing to the competency to do something. They use the example of a marketing executive who may have the knowledge to prepare a marketing plan but will need competency actually to implement it and achieve its objectives. They then take the concept a stage further, with wisdom defined as:

> competency refined by experience, practice, and maturity into above-average judgement, keen insight, and a holistic perspective that leads to sound decision making in highly complicated, rapidly changing situations ...

Nonaka and Takeuchi (in Henry, 2001) take a more philosophical approach, and contrast knowledge and information in these terms: 'knowledge, unlike information, is about *beliefs* and *commitment*. Knowledge is a function of a particular stance, perspective, or intention.' They too emphasise that unlike information, knowledge is always about action – it is always 'to some end'.

Knowledge is generally divided into two categories:

- *Explicit knowledge* – which can be found written down in official documents such as manuals, procedures, guides, etc.
- *Tacit knowledge* – which can roughly be described as the knowledge that is largely found inside employees' heads.

Tacit knowledge is unique and personal to the individual. It arises from people's experiences of doing their jobs, interrelating with their staff, managers, colleagues, customers, suppliers and so on. It includes an understanding of the context in which they are operating and is a mix of objective elements such as technical skills and detailed information about job-related tasks, and a subjective element which is all about intuition and judgement, etc. Often tacit knowledge can be such a natural and normal underpinning for what people do that they may not be aware of its extent, and have difficulty articulating it. *The challenge of knowledge management is to capture and make use of this tacit knowledge.*

Beazley et al (2002) then go on to talk of 'operational knowledge' which is critical and job specific, and is the subset of tacit knowledge that is required to perform well in a particular job. This can be a mixture of explicit knowledge, such as job descriptions and procedures, etc that have been 'tacitised', and what might be thought of as 'tacit-born' knowledge.

Knowledge management

So what do we mean by *knowledge management*? Skapinker (2003) uses a very simple definition to sum up knowledge management: it 'means using the ideas and experiences of employees, customers and suppliers to improve the organisation's processes'. What is very interesting and useful about this definition is that it embodies the purpose of knowledge management, ie to improve an organisation's performance, and also emphasises that it is about harnessing the knowledge of all the stakeholders in the organisation, not just the employees.

Laudon and Laudon (2003) describe it in terms of what is involved – as the 'set of processes developed in an organisation to create, store, transfer and apply knowledge'. Alavi (1997) helpfully describes the knowledge management process using a simple systems model – see Figure 9.2.

Although this diagram implies a linear sequence through the various stages, clearly this is not always the case. As Alavi and Leidner (2001) point out, individuals may create new knowledge (perhaps develop a new approach) and apply that knowledge without storing it (except in their

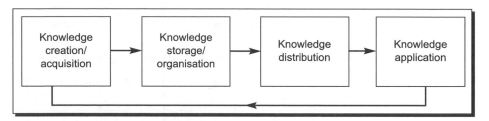

Figure 9.2 Alavi's systems model of knowledge
Source: Alavi (1997), reproduced with permission.

memories) or transferring it to others. It may be 'stored' at a later date through being incorporated as a new procedure or routine.

Alavi has also set out a framework for knowledge management which includes 'socio-cultural and organisational components' and technology. The first component recognises that successful knowledge management requires there to be a will within the organisation to both share knowledge and then also use it to good effect. Skapinker (2003) talks in terms of ensuring that all the organisation's systems are designed to support the goal of knowledge management: both the people management and development systems, and the organisation's ICT systems.

In this book we concentrate on the technology component. However we cannot emphasise enough the need to make sure that the organisation's culture, defined in the widest sense, encourages and rewards the sharing and application of knowledge. Although technology is very important, in some senses this is the easy bit. The hard bit is about harnessing the commitment and motivation of all those involved. A key starting point is that knowledge management must form part of the overall business strategy, and its role in the achievement of business objectives must be acknowledged and supported.

We shall look in more detail at the first stage in the process, which is widely regarded as both being the key, in that there can be no knowledge management system unless there is the ability to create and acquire the knowledge in the first place, and which is also the most demanding in both conceptual and practical terms.

Knowledge creation/acquisition

This is arguably one of the most difficult stages in the whole process. We need to return to the concept of the two types of knowledge: explicit knowledge, which is knowledge that can be codified and transmitted using formal language, and tacit knowledge, which is personal to individuals and based on their interaction with the world through experiences and therefore hard to formalise and communicate. Nonaka and Takeuchi (in Henry 2001) argue that human knowledge is created through the interaction between tacit and explicit knowledge, a process they refer to as 'knowledge conversion'. Their representation of this concept is shown in Figure 9.3.

They describe:

- *socialisation* – from tacit to tacit – as the process of creating tacit knowledge in the form of mental models and technical skills through sharing experiences
- *internalisation* – from explicit to tacit – as a process closely related to learning by doing, which involves individuals taking explicit knowledge, often in the form of procedures, diagrams or descriptions of experience, and converting it into their own mental maps

	Tacit knowledge	Explicit knowledge
		to
Tacit knowledge	Socialisation	Externalisation
from		
Explicit knowledge	Internalisation	Combination

Figure 9.3 Knowledge conversion
Source: Nonaka and Takeuchi (2001), reproduced with permission.

- *combination* – explicit to explicit – as the process of reconfiguring explicit knowledge through activities such as sorting and categorising existing explicit knowledge
- *externalisation* – tacit to explicit – as the process of articulating tacit knowledge in a form that can be readily understood and communicated to others as explicit knowledge.

Nonaka and Takeuchi take this a stage further with their concept of levels of 'knowledge creating entities' – ranging from individual, through group, organisational and interorganisational levels. Many writers on knowledge management stop at the organisational level, but increasingly competitive advantage is gained by creating, sharing and using knowledge at the interorganisational level, all the way through the supply chain. In Chapter 10 we discuss partnership sourcing and the implications for knowledge management of such approaches.

The part of this model on which knowledge management systems particularly focus is the conversion of tacit to explicit knowledge, which first happens at the individual level and then through a variety of processes takes place through the various knowledge-creating entity levels. We shall look at some examples of how organisations tackle this in the later section on approaches to knowledge management.

Some writers and practitioners in the field are expressing caution about some of the current approaches to knowledge management. They make the point that in our complex and fast-moving world, yesterday's knowledge may not always be helpful in enabling organisations to exploit tomorrow's opportunities and address tomorrow's problems. Anyone interested in exploring these thoughts will enjoy reading Maholtra (2004) on 'Why knowledge management systems fail?'.

SYSTEMS AND INFRASTRUCTURE FOR KNOWLEDGE MANAGEMENT

The purpose of a knowledge management system is to provide decision-makers/knowledge users in an organisation with the knowledge they require to make decisions and take action. Looking at it in terms of a simple systems model (see Figure 9.4).

In this section we focus on the sorts of systems and infrastructure that are used to implement a knowledge management strategy. Alavi and Leidner (2001) develops their earlier model to illustrate that a variety of IT tools can be used to support the different knowledge management processes in organisations – see Figure 9.5.

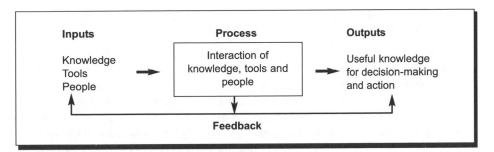

Figure 9.4 A simple model of a knowledge management system

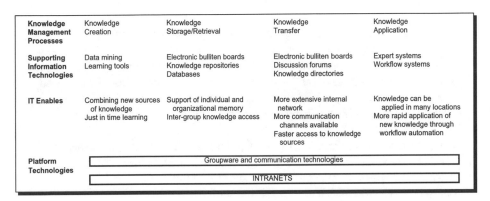

Figure 9.5 Knowledge management processes and the potential role of IT
Source: Alavi and Leidner (2001), reproduced with permission.

These are not intended to provide an exhaustive set of IT tools, but to emphasise the key role of IT in providing an infrastructure and environment that contributes to all stages of the knowledge management process in organisations.

SOME APPROACHES TO KNOWLEDGE MANAGEMENT

In this section we look at four approaches to knowledge management – knowledge communities, intranet/Internet-based information/knowledge centres, knowledge continuity management and expert systems.

Knowledge communities

An approach that has been developed by many organisations and in various formats involves setting up networks of people working in the same kinds of area and hence facing similar problems and challenges. Finneran (2004) offers a very clear definition of knowledge communities as:

> *Communities of interest that come together to share knowledge that affects performance. Knowledge Communities operate independent of traditional organisation structures to find common ground for their category of interest. They are virtual, global communities that are boundary-less and are not hindered by organisational or physical barriers.*

The key aspects of this definition are the emphasis on performance – the sharing of knowledge is towards the goal of action – and the fact that knowledge communities cut across traditional organisational boundaries. An interesting example is described in Case Study 9.1.

CASE STUDY 9.1

Carrington (2002) describes how a major international organisation, Shell International Exploration and Productions (SIEP), tackled knowledge management. SIEP is a very knowledge-intensive business – it is operating in a high-technology cutting-edge arena. Although there were many differences in the challenges faced by the different parts of the organisation in the various parts of the world, there were also many similarities. When a problem occurred in one part of the world it was likely that it had occurred before else-where and that a body of knowledge and expertise had been built up on how to deal with it. The example Carrington uses is retrieving broken tools from a borehole. The challenge was how to best capture this knowledge and share it.

SIEP's approach was to set up 11 global knowledge communities covering the core parts of the business and the support functions such as HR and procurement. Originally it set up over 100 smaller communities, but it found that people were having to belong to and tap into several communities to either find the expert they needed or assemble the information they required, so it moved to fewer but much larger communities. The advantages of the larger communities were that they generated more traffic and were more likely to survive.

Each new community starts with a small group of perhaps 10 to 25 people who are enthu-siastic and keen to share their knowledge and offer global representation. Once the group has got going, they invite others to join them and so the community develops upwards and outwards. Each community has a support structure:

- There is a moderator or co-ordinator who monitors and controls the content and traf-fic flow on the network. He or she encourages people to contribute and, if for exam-ple, there has been no response to a question posed, will search out appropriate experts and seek their views.
- On a regular basis, all new entries/materials are automatically compiled into an e-mail which is sent to all members – operating a bit like a 'community newspaper'.
- Each community has a 'regional ambassador' out in the operating companies who is called the hub co-ordinator. As the name suggests this person is responsible for generating and maintaining interest and contributions from his or her company.

SIEP is confident that it has already saved in excess of £134 million from knowledge sharing.

Nokia provides another interesting example of these types of networks or communities – this time working interorganisation and involving the supplier chain. Skapinker (2003) explains how Nokia has set up what it describes 'virtual companies' with 150 of its largest suppliers. Representatives from Nokia and its suppliers meet regularly to discuss how they can improve the way they work together. Although technology is important, Nokia emphasises that the key ingredient to the success of its knowledge management system is the continuous efforts to breakdown the traditional barriers – between departments such as marketing and manufacturing within the organisation, and between the different organisations in the company's supply chain. This is a good example of the type of activity and benefits to be derived form the partnership sourcing approach outlined in Chapter 10.

Intranet/Internet-based information/knowledge centres

Many organisations have harnessed the power of their intranets or the Internet to set up comprehensive repositories of information which can be accessed by individual employees wherever they are working. The sorts of information that are often included are:

- contact lists, telephone directories
- manuals, procedures, policy guidelines
- research papers, topic summaries
- news items
- committee/board papers
- best practice reports
- links to other relevant websites.

There are sophisticated search tools which enable the users to readily identify and extract the piece of information they require, or assemble all the information they need on a particular subject area.

There are also 'centres' set up to share knowledge between organisations. A good example is the one set up by the Improvement and Development Agency (IDeA) for sharing knowledge across all local authorities. It includes access to research and topic papers on areas of current interest, case studies, some very active discussion groups and access to online learning modules. There are also examples involving organisations in the same supply chain which have been set up under the partnership sourcing approach described in Chapter 10.

Knowledge continuity management

Beazley *et al* (2002) identify two processes that together form what they refer to as 'knowledge asset management'. These are the management of knowledge transfers within the same generation of employees and the management of knowledge transfers between successor generations of employees. What Beazley *et al* refer to as 'continuity management' is essentially concerned with the second:

> *a comprehensive, highly effective means for preserving corporate knowledge and productivity,* even when employees leave.

They describe *knowledge continuity management* as:

> *the efficient and effective transfer of critical operational knowledge – both explicit and tacit, both individual and institutional – from transferring, resigning, terminating, or retiring employees to their successors.*

It is all about having systems for ensuring the organisation harvests critical operational knowledge from employees, and then systems that transfer this knowledge to successor employees.

Beazley *et al* (2002) set out a process for both harvesting knowledge from existing employees and then transferring it to new employees. It consists of a number of stages:

- First, develop the business case for continuity management by looking at turnover rates, identifying those jobs that would merit continuity management, assessing the costs of losing knowledge/or having a slow build-up of knowledge by new employees, and looking at the extent to which the current organisational culture values and supports knowledge sharing.
- Develop a methodology for creating a knowledge profile for each job, which encapsulates

the operational knowledge required for that job. Then develop the knowledge profiles in appropriate levels of detail for relevant jobs in the organisation

■ Establish processes for transferring the operational knowledge to new employees.

Interweaving the various questionnaires, etc, that are used are processes that are much akin to more traditional knowledge management. For example, the process for developing and keeping up-to-date knowledge profiles involves setting up groups of employees doing the same job or type of job, who meet regularly to review the knowledge profiles and hence share knowledge. These are a good example of the communities of practice, ie small groups with common information needs and shared objectives, that underpin many knowledge management approaches.

Beazley *et al* (2002) also raise the very important issue that an organisation can have the best knowledge systems and databases in all the world, but that does not necessarily mean they will be accessed. Many of the early knowledge management systems have concentrated on making knowledge available (ie they are supply driven), but have not given the same thought to encouraging their use (ie by making them demand driven). Beazley *et al* advocate incorporating knowledge objectives and targets within the performance management system of the organisation, and reflecting effective knowledge sharing and use through the reward system. Clearly, HR professionals must play a key role in securing a knowledge-sharing culture and tackling the motivational issues. These are all exactly the same issues that need to be addressed for the successful introduction of an information system. However, it is even more important with knowledge systems because knowledge is a considerably more valuable asset to an individual than information. People need to be persuaded of the benefits to themselves as well as the organisation of sharing this very precious asset. As we discuss earlier, in many ways the technology is the easy bit; the people issues are the difficult ones!

Expert systems

Harry (1997) describes *expert systems* as 'attempts to model the human ability to use reasoning and acquire knowledge'. Similarly, Bocij *et al* (2003) describe expert systems as being:

> used to represent the knowledge and decision making skills of specialists so that non-specialists can take decisions. They encapsulate the knowledge of experts by providing the tools for the acquisition of knowledge and representation of rules and their enactment as decisions.

So an expert system is a computer system that can mimic the human ability to reason and acquire the knowledge people learn from doing something. It will follow the expert through a process using not only the knowledge of the expert (from a huge professional or technical database) but also the reasoning processes of the expert when converting this information into knowledge. This allows the non-expert operator to approximate to the performance of an expert in the particular specialism.

The list of applications is growing all the time and these are some examples:

■ medical diagnosis
■ credit decisions
■ insurance underwriting
■ product design
■ personal tax planning
■ investment decisions
■ fault finding in equipment.

Another interesting example developed as part of the e-government initiative was in the area of planning – see Case Study 9.2.

CASE STUDY 9.2

Waverley Borough Council has developed an 'expert system' to give its citizens a definitive answer on whether they need planning permission for their proposed development (for example, a new conservatory or loft extension). Appropriately called DINP (do I need permission), the web-based system takes users through a hierarchy of questions related to the actual building they are hoping to modify. It combines two underlying technologies – an electronic decision tree and a geographic information system that locates the specific property being developed. Applicants can see any constraints on the site (such as the building being listed or in a conservation area), and also details of the site's previous planning history. As the applicant answers the questions posed, the system automatically advises at any stage whether planning permission is required for that particular proposal on that specific site.

There are also artificial intelligence (AI)-type systems that have the ability to adapt and develop their decision-making ability as they expand their knowledge base. In other words, the system continues to learn the more it is used. Neural networks are an example of such systems. They try to model the way in which a neuron in the human brain holds and processes information. They use processes similar to those used in biological intelligence to learn problem-solving skills by increasing exposure to different and more complex problems. They are being applied in a wide range of areas including investment analysis (to predict the movements of shares and currencies), in marketing (to improve the effectiveness of mail shots), for process control, in credit rating, etc.

CONCLUSION

In this chapter we have introduced the very important and exciting world of knowledge management. Knowledge management has been around in some form or other for a long time. However, with the sophisticated ICT developments that have taken place over the last few years, we now have the tools to enable us to acquire, store, retrieve, share and apply knowledge for competitive advantage in a way we never had before.

REVIEW QUESTIONS

1. You work for a recently set-up organisation, a small but fast-expanding management consultancy. Most of the staff are young and ambitious, and the consultancy tends to work on leading-edge projects with a range of clients. Having read this book you are convinced of the need to introduce good knowledge management practices into the organisation. You now need to convince your MD. Write a brief summary setting out the key issues.

2. Your organisation is trying to introduce knowledge management practices. You have been working on an important project which has just been completed. How might you contribute?

The e-organisation

INTRODUCTION

Since we wrote the first edition of this book probably one of the most significant changes that we have seen is the impact of the Internet on the way we do business. Most organisations, to some extent or other, use the Internet to communicate with their customers and their suppliers, often creating electronic commercial networks that effectively replace or bypass the more traditional distribution channels. Here we have seen the burgeoning of e-commerce in the private sector and the e-government initiative in the public sector. In addition most organisations have harnessed the power of the Internet/intranet to streamline their business processes, giving rise to a plethora of e-business applications.

At the heart of all these developments and applications lies the concept of:

> integrating information across the enterprise creating an information technology infrastructure in which information can flow seamlessly from one part of the organisation to another and from the organisation to its customers, suppliers, and business partners.
>
> (Laudon and Laudon 2003)

The fascinating book *Blown to bits* (Evans and Wurster 2000) is about this 'information revolution', and describes with great clarity its far-reaching impact on all aspects of commercial and organisational life.

Evans and Wurster provide the startling statistic that:

> about one-third of the cost of health care in the United States – some $350bn – consists of the cost of capturing, storing, processing and retrieving information.

They argue cogently that information and the mechanisms for delivering it provide the fundamental 'glue' that holds together and defines the way organisations work both internally and externally throughout the value chain. There can be little doubt these days that information makes an enormous contribution to competitive advantage and it does so by impacting on every function of the business.

ELECTRONIC MAIL (E-MAIL) AND THE WORLD WIDE WEB (WWW)

The appropriate starting point for this chapter must be e-mail. It has revolutionised the way we communicate both within organisations, between organisations and in our personal lives. For most of us this form of communication is now far more commonplace than the traditional hard copy letters, memos, etc, sent through the physical post (either internal or external) or by fax, and it is easy to forget that this major change in the way we communicate has only developed over the last 10 years.

E-mail is a system that allows us to send and receive messages and images electronically using our computer terminals, and now increasingly our mobile phones and other hand-held devices. It provides almost instant communication both within organisations usually through an intranet and externally via a remote Internet service provider (ISP). This communication can be worldwide. Users can not only send memos, letters, etc, but also send large documents as attachments. For example, we sent the manuscript of this book via e-mail to our editor. It is also straightforward to send a wide range of other types of attachments, such as photographs and maps.

To many users the most important part of the Internet is the World Wide Web (WWW). The 'web' is the multimedia publishing side of the Internet. 'Pages' on websites are usually interactive documents using text, graphics (moving and still), pictures and sounds, which can be accessed using the web browsers on most computers. By using the unique website address enquirers can find out details about an organisation, its products, services and even its people. Many software providers now send their programs and updates via the web. It has opened up vast opportunities for searching for information – be it on holiday destinations, medical information or research on almost any business subject. There are now very powerful search engines, such as Google™ and Yahoo!™, which enable users to search very quickly and efficiently using key words or phrases.

A major innovation has been the move to broadband services which provide very high-speed data transfer. It allows users to remain connected to the Internet at all times and enables the transfers of very large amounts of data very quickly. We are also seeing the development of wireless technology in this area. Other systems such as Wi-Fi provide another advance in computer networking in the home or office. The system comprises a unit made up of a transmitter and broadband connection, which then allows Wi-Fi enabled computers to connect to the Internet and each other 'wirelessly', avoiding the need for cabling. This concept can be extended into geographical areas, so for example Westminster City Council uses a Wi-Fi system to communicate with its mobile workers.

It is perhaps not surprising that this revolution in communication has posed its own unique problems. It is not unusual for a busy manager to return to work after a couple of days away to find 100+ e-mails. There are concerns that people are using e-mail to avoid face-to-face communication – it is far easier, but rather less productive, to carry on a contentious debate by e-mail! It can often make someone feel more secure to copy their communication to anyone who might possibly have an interest, however minor. When the problems of spam (unwanted e-mail messages, usually advertisements, estimated by Email Systems Ltd (www.EmailSystems.com) to account for 83 per cent of all e-mails in November 2004) are added in, e-mail overload is the new time management issue of the twenty-first century.

As e-mail has developed as a major component of our communication systems, so has the need for users to be more efficient in the way they deal with e-mails. For example, there are now tools that make it possible to:

- file e-mails into appropriate folders
- search for e-mails with specific content
- match incoming e-mails to a database of contacts and so identify key or urgent communications, eg from customers
- monitor outgoing e-mails to avoid embarrassing mistakes, such as revealing you have been sent a blind copy by doing a Reply to All, or forgetting to attach an attachment
- use time management approaches with e-mails such as delegating them, but with a reminder that you are waiting for someone else to take action.

There are also concerns that staff may be sending personal e-mails in working time and using the Internet for inappropriate purposes. These range from personal activities such as researching holiday destinations and interrogating their bank accounts, to more serious abuses relating to accessing pornography and the like. This is all in addition to the ever-prevalent concern about the threat from viruses, etc (see Chapter 8).

Whole new businesses and specialist ICT applications have grown up to counter these problems. For example, it is possible to filter out spam and to monitor e-mail traffic and inappropriate use of the Internet. Practitioners need to be aware of the implications of the Human Rights legislation and particularly the Data Protection Act 1998 (see Chapter 7, which refers to a specific employment practices data protection code on an employer's rights to monitor staff). It is important for an organisation to set out its acceptable usage policy (AUP) in a clear and unambiguous way, and ensure that staff are aware of the policy's existence and the implications of not abiding by it.

E-BUSINESS AND E-COMMERCE

Two new terms that have entered the organisational dictionary are *e-business* and *e-commerce*. E-business is a very generic term and encapsulates the use of electronically mediated information exchanges to support the whole range of business processes, both within the organisation and with external stakeholders. Business processes can range from strategic planning to producing and delivering products and services, and encompass support processes such as the management of human resources, etc.

E-commerce is generally seen as a subset of e-business. There is a range of definitions in use for e-commerce. The narrowest definition sees it as simply concerning the process of buying and selling goods and services electronically (in other words, electronically mediated financial transactions). A more common definition suggests that it encompasses all electronically mediated transactions between an organisation and a third party, which would widen the definition to include the provision of information on all aspects of the relationship with third parties. The widest definition talks about the exchange of information across electronic networks at any stage in the supply chain, within the organisation, between the organisation and third parties, and including both financial and non-financial transactions.

E-commerce is commonly associated with consumer retail activities such as buying books from Amazon or groceries online, but it can be seen that in fact it has a much wider scope. It is helpful to consider the three categories of e-commerce (and at the same time understand another set of acronyms!) defined by Laudon and Laudon (2003):

- *business-to-consumer (B2C) e-commerce*, which involves providing products and services directly to individual end consumers, eg Waitrose-online grocery service and Amazon books

- *business-to-business (B2B) e-commerce*, which involves the provision of goods and services between businesses; this encompasses the whole arena of transactions up and down the supply chain
- *consumer-to-consumer (C2C) e-commerce*, which involves consumers providing goods and service directly to other consumers: perhaps the best of example of this is eBay, the massive web auction site which enables individual consumers to sell their goods to other consumers by auctioning them to the highest bidder.

Yet another distinction is in terms of how the Internet is accessed. With the advent of many mobile phones and other wireless hand-held appliances being Internet enabled, we are now seeing the rise of mobile commerce or *m-commerce*.

We look in detail at the two main areas of e-commerce, B2C and B2B, in the next two sections.

B2C E-COMMERCE

There can be little doubt that e-commerce has revolutionised the way many organisations do business. Particularly for small and medium-sized businesses, the Internet has opened up the opportunity to market on a much wider scale, selling anything from local organic food to oak water butts (see Case Study 10.1). As consumers we have become adept at buying almost anything online, running our bank accounts online, paying our bills online and so on.

CASE STUDY 10.1

A local small business is involved in selling oak water butts and garden accessories. The business is run from a house and garden in a small rural Suffolk village. Before the advent of e-commerce the business owner marketed these products by a range of methods including advertisements in a range of gardening magazines, and local papers. In order to have an impact and sell the product he needed to place several quite large, and therefore expensive, advertisements. Now he has a website and all he does is place very small adverts giving his website address. The website not only sets out a full range of products with up-to-date prices, it also shows pictures of the very attractive products. Customers can place orders online, and query the availability of different products online, with payment being made through traditional methods. The more sophisticated websites of the big players allow for purchasing online using credit cards, etc but given the issues around web security this is usually not worthwhile for a small business.

On a much wider scale the Web has enabled many organisations to fundamentally rethink the way they supply their goods to consumers. The 'traditional' model of

$$\text{manufacturer} \rightarrow \text{distributor} \rightarrow \text{retailer} \rightarrow \text{customer}$$

has effectively been 'blown to bits' and as you remove layers in the supply chain you reduce costs. It is now easy to buy plane tickets directly from airlines, leaving out travel agents. The ease and low cost of this approach is also encouraging people to go for bespoke holidays rather than package holidays, hence leaving out the intermediary package holiday companies. You can buy almost everything direct from the manufacturer/producer: computers, organic meat, binoculars, you name it. The removal of organisations or intermediary layers in the value chain is called *disintermediation*.

The Internet has also brought with it fundamental changes in the way information is provided to buyers. In the past, there was a trade-off for businesses between the *richness* and the *reach* of the information. Richness is about the depth and level of detail of the information. Reach is about how many people the business can provide with the information. For example, a sales-person can usually offer very rich information, but only to a small number of buyers. At the other end of the spectrum, advertising in newspapers, etc, provides rather summary and limited infor-mation, but to a very large audience. The Internet has revolutionised this trade-off. It is now possible to provide detailed information on products and services through a website which reaches a vast audience. However, from the consumer perspective it raises issues of how to search for the product or service you want.

Consumers may choose to use what are often referred to as *navigators*. Navigators that are based on maximising reach are typically those that purport to find the best deal on something. Examples are U-Switch and TheEnergyShop (on fuel prices) and sites such as Moneyfacts and Motley Fool (which compare saving rates and mortgage costs). However, these navigators are weak on depth and detail of the products/services compared with the navigators offered by indi-vidual suppliers. Rich navigational information from the supplier can also have the advantage over that provided by the retailer or generalist navigator when the product is continuously evolving – perhaps through technological developments – and the supplier provides the best state-of-the-art information, or where the supplier has very complex offerings which are continuously changing. A good example of the latter is telephone services.

B2B E-COMMERCE

Electronic data interchange (EDI) was an early example of B2B e-commerce. EDI enables com-puter-to-computer exchange of data electronically and automatically, without human intervention, and replaces activities involving the traditional paper-based exchange of information. EDI has been widely used in retailing, has spread rapidly (in one guise or another) in manufacturing, and is a perfect example of the use of ICT to gain competitive advantage.

In EDI, the systems can be supplier-focused or customer-focused. For example, in supplier-focused systems the supplier's computer regularly interrogates the buyer's inventory database(s) to determine whether stocks are at a pre-agreed reorder level. When they fall to this level, the sup-plier's computer automatically generates an order and arranges the delivery within the agreed timescale. In this way, EDI greatly reduces the administrative workload.

It is not only the transfer of physical goods that have benefited from EDI, it is also used widely for financial transactions. Most UK banks have been using the Bankers Automated Clearing System (BACS) since the early 1970s to settle regular payments. Another financial system that has gained wide acceptance is electronic funds transfer at point of sale (EFTPOS). With EFTPOS, customers have plastic cards containing details of their bank account encoded on a magnetic strip. The plas-tic card is 'swiped' through the retailer's card reader, the amounts and other transaction details are fed in via a small computer at the point of sale, and the details are automatically passed overnight to the purchaser's bank to effect the transfer of the funds.

The original EDIs were carried out using specialist EDI networks. A further development has been Internet EDI, which as the name suggests makes use of the public Internet. This reduces the cost of EDI significantly and hence has opened up opportunities for its use by a large number of smaller organisations. It is thus that e-procurement has really come of age.

Partnership sourcing

Another important development that has occurred in the procurement arena is *partnership sourcing*. At the core of partnership sourcing is a fundamental strategic re-think of the way businesses in the supply chain work together. During much of the twentieth century the prevailing B2B relationship in Western organisations was largely focused on:

- final invoice price (forced down by the power of the purchasers)
- a multiplicity of suppliers
- relatively short-term, arm's length contracts
- intense quality control of bought-in materials.

It was often characterised by an acute lack of trust between the parties. This was in stark contrast to the partnership approach adopted by successful Japanese manufacturers in the 1970s and 1980s, where supplier–purchaser relationships focused on maximising the efficiency of the whole value chain. Dyer and Ouchi (in Henry and Mayle 2002) contrasted American car manufacturers with their Japanese equivalents. Despite there being a far greater degree of vertical integration (ie more parts were produced internally), American companies were often dealing with as many as 10 times the number of suppliers as Japanese companies, and the costs of components were over 20 per cent higher than in the Japanese companies. In addition Japanese car manufacturers were able to develop new vehicles 30 per cent faster than US car companies.

Organisations in the West began to appreciate the competitive advantage of this approach and partnership sourcing is now actively pursued by a wide range of organisations. Lewis and Lytton define partnership sourcing as:

> *A commitment by both customers and suppliers, regardless of size, to a long-term relationship based on clear, mutually agreed objectives to strive for world-class capability and competitiveness ...*

> (in Henry and Mayle 2002)

For most organisations this has implied a major change in their business strategy. Instead of deals being done that 'force' suppliers to cut their profit margins to secure short-term business with major purchasers, suppliers and business customers openly discuss with each other their business objectives and long-term plans. They share technical and accounting information and financial details on their products, and jointly work to reduce costs to sustainable levels along the whole of the value chain. This style of working has represented a severe culture shock to many organisations. To 'open your books' to suppliers or customers was seen at the time to be almost committing business suicide. Research described by Rothwell (2002) showed that a number of factors needed to be present for this radical change to work. Among the more interesting for this book (aimed at HR professionals with an interest in ICT) are:

- culture change to remove resistance to the necessary business changes
- a substantial investment in intercompany training and development
- use of integrated cross-functional teams across internal departments and external business partners
- close linkages with a small number of primary suppliers
- information integration
- use of ICT for interfirm communication and data sharing

- linked CAM/CAD systems (see later in this chapter) along the supply/production chain (manufacturer, supplier, user)
- use of simulation modelling as a partial substitute for expensive prototyping of new designs
- use of shared expert systems as a design aid.

The advantages to the purchaser come from stripping out the indirect costs of procurement, by:

- having fewer direct suppliers to monitor, manage and pay
- reducing transaction costs, for example information gathering and analysis, negotiation, contract agreeing, ordering, billing and product movement
- reducing stock levels
- improving quality
- achieving faster and more efficient product development.

At the same time this creates conditions where the supplier is able to forward plan, make long-term investments with confidence and have greater financial stability. All parties benefit from sharing experience and expertise, thereby enabling them to develop and produce cheaper, higher quality products that sell – a true win–win situation!

High quality information systems and supporting ICT make a powerful contribution to the success of partnership sourcing. This approach to procurement is critically dependent on being able to share in-depth, accurate and up-to-date information on a regular and timely basis.

E-HR

E-HR has evolved as another sub-set of e-business and is set to influence dramatically the role of HR in many organisations. It encompasses such developments as self-service HRISs which enable authorised employees, line managers, etc to access a wide range of information on HR policies and procedures, personal information and HR management information. Authorised employees and line managers can also use the system to change specific data: for example to update personal information, book leave online, manage their own benefits packages, and arrange to attend learning events. HR professionals cease to be gatekeepers of HR information, and such initiatives provide the fundamental underpinning required to devolve the day-to-day HR role to line managers.

A major area of HR which has been affected by the e-business revolution is recruitment. Many large organisations now advertise their job vacancies on their websites, and a plethora of online recruitment agencies have grown up, including both specialists in particular sectors such as IT and engineering, and generalist ones that cover a wide range of jobs. Applicants can search for jobs online, be kept informed of vacancies, and apply using electronic application forms. At its most sophisticated a large part of the process can be carried out electronically – initial sifting, testing, the automatic setting-up of a database of applicants, generation of response letters, through to successful candidates' details being input onto the organisation's HRIS. The CIPD's annual survey on recruitment, retention and turnover showed that in 2003 about 70 per cent of organisations used their own websites to advertise vacancies, much the same as the previous year, but the number using commercial job sites had increased significantly, from 15 per cent to almost 40 per cent (CIPD 2004). However, the survey also showed that the move to make full use of electronic tools was quite slow, with only 24 per cent offering the facility for applications to be completed online, and only 4 per cent using any form of online testing.

The emergence of *e-learning* as a major new approach to the development of knowledge and skills is yet another facet of e-HR. It provides the learner with a direct link to learning resources, and passes a far greater degree of control to the learner than do traditional training courses. It is the next step on from the technology-based training (TBT) approaches developed in the 1990s, which involved learners working their way through predesigned programmes provided by disk or CD-ROM. Sloman (2001) defined e-learning as 'learning and training that takes advantage of connectivity'. At its most basic it is very similar to TBT, but the learning resources can be accessed through the intranet/Internet, which allows for ready access by the learner and for the packages to be up-dated regularly and easily. In our book *Learning needs analysis and evaluation* (Bee and Bee 2003), we comment:

> the real power and potential of e-learning comes from the ability for learners to interact with on-line tutors and other learners. This can happen asynchronously (ie not in real time) and involve the use of discussion groups, question-and-answer tutoring by e-mail, etc, or synchronously (ie the learner and tutor on-line at the same time) and involve virtual classrooms, audio-video conferencing, etc.

Another interesting example of e-HR is *e-mentoring*. By harnessing web technology, this extends traditional mentoring activities enabling mentoring to take place online at a time and place convenient to the participants. It can overcome geographic and time barriers and enable a wider range of people to get involved as both mentors and mentees. Typically it is used in addition to the traditional face-to-face meeting, but sometimes it can be the main channel of communication. Specialist software has been designed that combines mail, forum and evaluation capabilities, and addresses the key issues for managers of mentoring schemes of security, safety, confidentiality, management and measurement.

The implications of e-HR are potentially very great and very exciting. For the customer it provides a more efficient and effective service with more control. For the HR professional it gives the opportunity to take on a more strategic role, which can ensure HR really adds value to the organisation. The pace of the move towards e-HR, like all other e-business activities will vary with the organisation – the type of business it is in, the state of its ICT and information systems generally. However, there can be little doubt that e-business and all its ramifications will inevitably be the way forward for us all. For a good all-round introduction to the concept and issues involved with e-HR, try *eHR: an introduction* (Kettley and Reilly 2003).

Another term that is sometimes used in this context is *business-to-employee (B2E)*. This usually includes a wider range of activities than traditional HR management, such as the use of Internet technology for remote working, knowledge management, data mining, etc.

E-GOVERNMENT

Not surprisingly the public sector in the United Kingdom has not escaped the pressure to do business electronically. The government set a target of 2005 to have as many services as possible accessed electronically and the various public agencies able to talk to each other electronically. It talks about 'e-enabled' services and the need to integrate these with all the support services. (Needless to say this is a massive undertaking, and the government recently tempered its original target of having all services online by 2005!) For example, local authorities are being encouraged to set up portals for their areas which enable users to access the full range of services. This is a developing area, with the early systems consisting primarily of providing information: see Case Studies 10.2 and 10.3.

CASE STUDY 10.2

Rutland County Council was one of the early front runners in the field – see www.rutnet.co.uk. It provides information ranging from tourist accommodation and places to eat, through to details of the local planning process and job vacancies. However, there are few examples where it is actually possible to access a service online. For example, it is not possible to make a planning application online or comment on current planning applications. This is undoubtedly the next stage in the process.

CASE STUDY 10.3

East Riding unitary authority through its online service MyEastriding enables residents to log in securely to access personal information which enables them to pay council bills, track requests, find information out about their home and so on. East Riding's web portal www.eastriding.gov.uk is an impressive-looking site, but as we write much of the site is still under construction and its full potential is yet to be realised.

The results of a survey carried out in October 2004 by the Society of Information Technology Management (www.socitm.gov.uk) showed six million visitors to local council sites, which represented 20 per cent of UK internet users. Looking at job vacancies was by far the most popular activity, followed by searches for information on planning applications. The Society also reported that information gathering was proving more successful than online transactions, which supports our own experiences in this area.

The main central government site www.gov.uk is a mix of information and some online services. For example, users can apply online for a new passport or make an online tax return. It also provides a wide range of links into other public sector sites such as the main NHS portal, www.nhs.gov.uk. This site provides a helpful service that enables users to search for their nearest doctor or dentist by typing in their postcode. People can also check out the quality of their local hospital, and waiting times for different types of appointment. There are a number of exciting developments taking place in the NHS, including:

- the 'chooseandbook' system which will enable patients to choose a convenient place, date and time for hospital appointments, and book these online (see Chapter 6 for some of the early problems with its development)
- plans for all patient records to be held online so that they can be shared by GPs, hospitals, etc.
- electronic prescriptions which will mean that prescriptions no longer have to picked up from the GP but are sent online to the pharmacist.

The potential for improvements in many services is very great. For example, the e-Benefits project is about creating a suite of programs which will allow people to check their eligibility and apply for the many different state benefits available. The aim is to encourage more eligible people to take up benefits, and at the same time cut down the cost of administration and free up staff to deal with benefit fraud. Yet another example, still in its early stages as we write, is the ability to report crimes online to the police. Staying in the criminal justice area, the capability to streamline all parts of the justice system, allowing information to be passed electronically from one agency to another, is now on the horizon. There are some interesting experiments going on with e-democracy – to vote online in elections, to undertake consultation exercises online, facilitate online petitions, and so on.

The potential for cost savings too can be considerable. For example, the Improvement and Development agency (IDeA) has estimated that local authorities using e-procurement could reduce the price of goods and services by 8 per cent and reduce the costs of staff time and transaction costs by up to 70 per cent, resulting in total savings in the whole procurement process of as much as 15 per cent (www.nepp.org.uk).

OTHER APPLICATIONS

We focused in the first part of this chapter on the developments brought about by the Internet. However, it is worth remembering that the e(lectronic) organisation has been with us for some time and that there are a large number of e-applications that predate the Internet. There has been the developing trend over a number of years for users to be directly involved in their own computing rather than indirectly via computer professionals. This is generally referred to as *end-user computing*. At the first level it has been facilitated by the provision of user-friendly software for common tasks such as word processing, basic database manipulation and spreadsheet activities, all within the same 'environment', for example, the current industry standard Windows™ software. Once the busy manager has learned one computer application, all the others within the environment are relatively easy to use because of the common commands. There is a single learning curve, and each new application is a small increment in computing knowledge over the previous applications.

However, it is at the second level of end-user activities that the greatest strides have taken place, and this area will continue to develop. This list of end-user activities is already long, and growing all the time. Some of the current types of computer-assisted end-user activity are:

- computer-aided design (CAD), where computers are used to design products, buildings and components.
- computer-aided manufacture (CAM), where computers are used to assist in the control of the manufacturing process.
- computer-integrated manufacturing (CIM), a form of CAD/CAM where the entire industrial process from design to manufacture is controlled by computers.
- computer numerical control (CNC), where the process of resetting machines is controlled by computer, thereby making small batch manufacturing more economic.
- computer aided software engineering (CASE), used to automate many of the processes needed to analyse, design and build new systems.
- desktop publishing and text-handling (DTP), which provides the ability to create visually interesting and attractive documents containing both text and pictures, for example, for brochures and in advertisements.
- computer-based and multimedia training (CBT/MMT), in which the learners interact with the data stored on the computer to feel their way through the learning material at their own pace, receiving feedback visually and aurally as they go. (This was the precursor to e-learning described earlier.)
- decision support systems (DSSs), designed to support managers and specialists in their decision-making processes. The emphasis is on the word 'support', as the DSS does not take over the role of decision-making, but allows the manager/specialist to play 'what-if' games and use their judgement in deciding what to do next. DSSs assist the decision process best where there:

- is a large database
- is the need for a large amount of computer processing
- are complex relationships between the data
- is staged analysis of the problem requiring iteration between the human operator and the machine
- is a requirement for human judgement in the definition of the problem and in selecting between the range of acceptable solutions
- are several people involved in tackling the problem, and they all contribute their special expertise which can be co-ordinated by the computer.

Spreadsheets, modelling and simulation, sensitivity and risk analysis (see Chapter 3), and expert systems (described in Chapter 9) are all examples of decision support systems.

■ executive information systems (EISs), designed to provide a wide variety of summarised information that enables executives, usually top management, to plan strategically and monitor the strategic plan, drilling down only to the level of detail required. Typical information 'might relate to competitor performance, the legal context, the economic environment or market preferences' (Harry 1997).

Case Studies 10.4 and 10.5 give examples of some common end-user examples.

CASE STUDY 10.4

In a large organisation the central HR department was involved in a large number of projects, such as introducing major change initiatives. In order to manage these projects effectively all the project leaders were provided with a software application, MS Project™, to enable them to plan and manage their own projects. After two days of training all the project leaders were able to build network diagrams and Gantt charts (see Chapter 3), calculate the critical path and plan the use of resources. The package then enabled them to monitor progress and the use of resources throughout the life of the project. All the project leaders were HR professionals and had no specific IT specialist knowledge. The use of the package enabled them to undertake activities which previously would have been the province of the IT specialist.

CASE STUDY 10.5

As we discuss earlier in this section, the World Wide Web has provided the opportunity for many small organisations to market themselves through the Internet. Up until relatively recently, designing websites has been the province of the IT specialist. Now with software applications such as Microsoft FrontPage™, small business owners are able to design their own sites. For example, a local B&B owner has now designed a simple site setting out details of the facilities available, including photographs, costs, a location map and how to make contact, all after a small input of training. Nobody was more surprised than the owner herself at the ease at which this could be done. Her previous IT experience had been limited to word processing.

CONCLUSION

In this chapter we have tried to do justice to what is a major revolution in the way organisations use ICT in their business, whether they are public or private sector organisations and whatever their size. There can be little doubt that e-business in all its ramifications is dramatically changing how organisations interface with their customers, suppliers, employees and almost every other stakeholder. The potential for improving customer service and achieving significant cost reductions means that those organisations that are able to harness all these capabilities will discover substantial competitive advantage over those who trail behind.

REVIEW QUESTIONS

1. Give three examples of how you have used the Internet in the last month, and comment on its advantages and disadvantages.

2. Look at the website of your local authority and evaluate the extent to which it offers an improved service to you as a customer.

Looking ahead

CHAPTER 11

INTRODUCTION

And so, we arrive at the final chapter in this part of the book. Our purpose so far has been to introduce you to the concepts and applications of information systems. We have talked about the way in which technology now liberates us from the ICT specialist. (We mean no offence to ICT specialists – handing over the reins to the users can leave them free to use their abilities for creative and innovative developments.) We have distributed hardware, and dedicated professional software that is compatible with all our other business software. We have corporate databases where all the files have a relationship with other files, making it possible for users to access and update the data wherever it is filed. We can drill down and access the information at whatever level of detail we need. We have the facility to produce reports tailored to our needs and present them in exciting and eye-catching ways. We have the systems, processes and technology to harness and exploit our knowledge assets. Finally, our information systems and our administrative systems have been integrated, to take much of the drudgery out of them and free us up to use our time and creativity to the benefit of the organisation.

So, how will this affect the average manager/specialist? We would argue that through the combination of subjects covered in the two parts of this book – information systems and statistics – they can gain access to comprehensive, up-to-date data converted into the information, and then the knowledge that is needed to do their jobs effectively. Through the use of intranet/Internet/Wi-Fi type communications technology and the miniaturisation of our computing devices, we can access all our information resources from almost anywhere and at any time, freeing us from the physical boundaries of our offices and traditional 'office hours'. This is enabling global communication and access to information on a vast scale. The technology is not just transforming our working environment but is permeating through every aspect of our lives. It is transforming the way we shop, access our public services, communicate with our friends, listen to our music, drive our cars, etc, etc. Many of the developments are with us now, the potential of some of them is still to be realised, and there are some new, exciting developments which are on or just over the horizon. Perhaps we need a crystal ball to get an insight into these.

HOW WILL IT ALL WORK?

First, let us provide a few words on some of the relatively new electronic wizardry that is entering our worlds of work and home.

Personal digital assistants (PDAs)/XDAs

It is a rarity these days not to see people sitting in cafés and bars, or commuting on buses or trains, working on their laptop computers. These computers are getting ever smaller, to the extent that they sit not on our laps, but in the palms of our hands. The hand-held computer, known as the personal digital assistant (PDA), has arrived. With PDAs users can not only write, store and retrieve reports remotely from their desks, but use most of the other functions of computing – access databases, spreadsheets, e-mails, web surfing – and then synchronize the results on their desktop computers when they get back home or to their office. Many PDAs have integrated global positioning satellite

(GPS) receivers to guide people as they drive to appointments or walk to that city office block, and some are combined PDA and mobile telephones all in one (these are known as extensible digital assistants or XDAs).

Voice over Internet protocol (VoIP)

VoIP is an associated form of technology that is growing at a fast pace. A VoIP system converts ordinary voice calls into packets of data that can be sent from computer to computer over the Internet. The implications for organisations are potentially very great, ranging from the flexibility of moving extensions easily from desk to desk and taking work calls at home, to being able to dictate letters over the phone and have them arrive on the relevant person's PC ready for him or her to action. It is also easier and cheaper to set up a VoIP system than a traditional phone network, and cheaper to make calls at present.

Radio frequency identification (RFID)

RFID 'tags' are really small, pinhead-sized computer chips, which contain a code rather like a barcode, and a small antenna that is capable of receiving and transmitting data by radio waves. These devices have been around for some time, but it is only recently that their cost has reduced to a level which makes their widescale use a possibility. Their potential uses are almost endless:

- reducing shoplifting, by enabling goods to be traced after they have left the store, and thefts of items from homes and offices
- in manufacturing, by giving information on manufacturing, component by component, such as where the product was manufactured, stored, etc
- in logistics, locating an item for stocktaking or security purposes
- 'smart' domestic appliances that follow the instructions on the tag on how a product should be stored and/or cooked
- in the supermarket, a whole basket of goods can be scanned and priced in a single scan
- implants in people – for example, people could carry their medical records with them and have them accessed by a GP or hospital.

The potential uses for RFID chips are endless and we are only beginning to realise some of the benefits. As with many technological advances, there are also downsides. Might unscrupulous marketing professionals use the retail data for covert product/customer analysis? What are the invasion of privacy, human rights and data protection implications?

Virtual reality

Virtual reality is one form of technology that has been with us for some years now, although its full potential is still being realised. For example, when choosing a car from a catalogue, how nice it would be to go online and to be able to walk around the car and see it from all angles, to 'sit' in the car and see how good is the visibility, how easy it would be to reverse park, all without leaving home.

In the business context, why travel miles to a meeting? We already have the technology of the 'video conference'. Will this be replaced by the 'virtual reality conference' in the distant future? Science fiction writers might be able to beam us around their world, but this does not happen yet in the real world! However, it may soon be possible to beam our 'hologram' to a 3D screen. We will sit in a virtual reality 'hood' in company with holograms beamed in from all over the planet. Our voices will be transmitted along with our images, with simultaneous translations into selected languages. The 'voices' and 'ears' of our images will be two-way radios that convey our conversations. Just think, we would no longer have to endure many hours of travelling to cross the global village to meet our contacts. Just think also: if we can 'travel' on the Internet, what would this do for our regular commuting journeys? What effect would such changes have on business and HR systems? It will be as if we had actually made the journey although we had not stirred from our office or home workstation. In these days of global organisations and global markets, think of the time and energy saved for use on other creative tasks, as well as the reduction in carbon dioxide emissions.

Robotics

We have become accustomed to reading about the use of robotics in spacecraft, both manned or unmanned, and many of us will have benefited from the use of terrestrial robots in the manufacturing and warehousing environments. Robots are particularly useful in situations that are unfriendly or dangerous to humans, such as searching for landmines, or which require the repetitive but very accurate actions that robots are so good at, like many manufacturing processes. We have yet to see them move into the everyday life of the family home in any big way. For those who loathe cleaning, there are robotic vacuum cleaners now on the market ,and it is quite likely that the use of such robots will grow quite rapidly over the next few years. It is also possible that developments in neural networks type technology could revolutionise the science of robotics as we know it – bringing the design and development of robots that require little conventional programming but which learn experientially as they go along, like humans.

Transport

We have pondered on the technology of transport, and wondered why we have seen no really innovative new products recently that fundamentally change the way that we move around, as the development of the train, car and airplane have done in the past. Perhaps one of the answers is that the reasons for travelling may soon no longer be there. As we discussed earlier, the need to travel for work may be a thing of the past – as people no longer work in traditional offices, or physically come to meetings with colleagues or customers, etc. We have already described the impact the Internet and e-business in all its forms is having on our home life – the way we shop, bank and so on. Perhaps the only reason to travel in the future will be for pleasure.

However, we are seeing some developments that are improving the efficiency and effectiveness of current modes of transport. For example, the development and use of intelligent transport solutions (ITSs), which link intelligent information sensing points (roadside and satellite) with intelligent information devices in motor vehicles, will:

- be able provide 'controllers' with information on people's whereabouts and time of arrival at their destination
- give a wealth of information to the highway authorities and emergency services to enable them to decide whether to allow vehicles to join or exit motorway networks
- use automatic guidance systems in vehicles to allow for safe hands-free driving on motorways
- allow drivers to avoid congestion points and help them control the distance between their vehicle and the car in front, so reducing accidents, traffic jams and vehicle exhaust emissions
- charge vehicles automatically for travelling on some routes.

Similar developments, but far more advanced than we have described for motor transport, may soon revolutionise the way we travel by air. At present, airplanes fly along relatively tiny corridors called 'airways'. Ponder for a moment technology which might allow aircraft to fly directly from point to point in their own safe bit of airspace. Conflicting aircraft (and their pilots) would know when there are other aircraft potentially in the same airspace, and the automatic pilot systems would take appropriate collision avoidance action. These new information systems will:

- be more powerful than human pilots at spotting and resolving aircraft conflicts
- reduce nuisance alerts and allow more aircraft to be fitted safely into the same total airspace
- help aircraft to be flown more directly, therefore more quickly and cheaply, to their destination in their own safe 'cocoon' of airspace.

OUR ORGANISATIONS

Structures

There will be changes in the way organisations are structured. Traditionally, professionals in the same field were clustered on the same floor of an office block or in the same group of offices, because of the need for them to be physically close to their (paper) files and to communicate face to face. That tradition continues today, and there is still a tendency for finance staff, HR staff, the production team and so on all to be located in their own specific area. However, this will no longer be necessary as a result of distributed IT systems and the wide range of communication channels. Staff in the future will be located closer to their internal and external customers and suppliers. It may be that, on occasions, staff of a specific profession will need to be physically together to solve particular professional problems. However, for the majority of their time they will actually be solving problems with their customer and supplier colleagues.

Does this suggest the possibility of distributed professional staff as well as distributed information systems? When we think about this philosophy, there are no boundaries to this 'distribution', and the future may see much more physical integration of staff throughout the supply chain, with staff from purchasers and suppliers working together to mutual competitive advantage, as is seen in partnership sourcing arrangements (see Chapter 10). We have already begun to see this, as organisations adopt multidisciplinary project team or 'task team' working as it is sometimes known. These have taken over from single-function teams in tackling complex business problems in many organisations. Distributed information systems will accelerate this tendency.

All the pundits suggest that the move to flexible working will accelerate. Many people will be working from home with their VoIP, websites, e-mails and teleconferencing technology. Others will use their PDAs/XDAs from supplier/client/customer premises, or simply sitting somewhere nice, say sitting in the sunshine in the park or a neighbourhood café! Offices will be used for face-to-face meetings only when it is really helpful to get together in this way. As measures like partnership sourcing and outsourcing take off, organisational offices will become smaller, with perhaps an extension from 'hot-desking' (when employees no longer have their own personal desk) to the concept of 'hot-officing'!

Decision support systems (DSSs)

Perhaps some of the greatest changes in the future will come about as a result of developments in decision support systems (see Chapters 3, 9 and 10). One of the problems with DSSs has been that, because of their complexity, they have tended to take a long time to deliver benefits and have attracted the criticism that at best they give results that approximate to the real world at some time in the past. There is the criticism that the need constantly to feed them with copious amounts of day-to-day data renders them incapable of reaching the levels of responsiveness required by organisations operating at the forefront of competitiveness. The manager/specialist takes the decisions based on the 'support' given by the DSS and there are rarely arrangements for the DSS automatically to receive feedback on why option A was selected over option B. Therefore the DSS does not 'learn'. Also, there has rarely been any evaluation of the effectiveness of the 'support' in the fullness of time, presumably because DSSs tend to be used towards the strategic end of the decision-making chain and by the time the strategy is assessed the organisation has moved on.

Developments such as neural networks may have a lot to offer (see Chapter 9). When this almost human, or even superhuman, intelligence is applied to corporate database and knowledge management systems, it can become the dynamic centre of the decision-making process. It does not have to be told what to do, and it 'learns' by experience so that it will remember what has gone before and modify its 'support' in the light of current circumstances. It will contain the sum total experience of its organisation and it will truly support all decision-making aspects of the business it serves. In a future, where being able to act quickly in response to rapidly changing environmental factors matters, DSSs of this type will play a crucial role in enabling organisations to achieve competitive advantage.

SOME FUTURE DIRECTIONS FOR HR

Access to better information and the use of more sophisticated techniques for modelling an uncertain future may at last allow HR staff to get ahead of the game – by getting to grips with, say, HR planning. We foresee a far greater emphasis on HR planning in the future, as part of both organisational planning and planning on the wider social, political and economic front.

Developments in competency profiling, matching people to vacancies, now and for the future, and harnessing the power of expert systems, could see dramatic improvements in our ability systematically and without prejudice to produce short-lists for interview, leading to better and fairer selection decisions. Similar sorts of approach could revolutionise the way learning needs are identified and analysed.

Stuart (2004) states that employees in the flexible firm of the future will experience their 'flexibility' not only in the hours they work but also in the concept of having several jobs with the same employer and/or with several employers, at the same time. HR's role supporting these flexible arrangements will be crucial in terms of career planning, learning and development.

The advent of PDAs/VoIP, etc, etc has provided the opportunity for staff to remain accessible and in contact with their colleagues, customers and suppliers from almost anywhere and at any time. This raises important issues for how both staff and employers handle the work/life balance dilemma. There are already concerns about the culture of 'presenteeism' in many of our current workplaces. ICT developments may exacerbate these issues and HR will need to take a proactive role in addressing them.

Many of the developments in ICT raise ethical issues. The fact that RFID-type chips can be installed under people's skin, in components and finished goods does not mean that such developments will be always be used ethically. It is likely that business and personal ethics will need a higher profile to ensure that these new and powerful innovations are used to the general good.

CONCLUSION

ICT has moved so far and so fast in the last few years that the future can be bounded only by the limits of our imagination. Our ability to manage information and knowledge effectively is tomorrow's competitive advantage – if only we are able to harness it and make the conversion. We and our organisations cannot afford to ignore the technology – we would be abdicating our business and social responsibilities to the mercies of our competitors.

However, as we look into a future that appears to be dominated by technological advances, it is salutary to remember a forecast made by the Future Foundation (2004) that a substantial proportion of the population may be at 'risk of digital exclusion' if significant action is not taken to encourage everyone to engage with the Internet world.

It is with a certain humility that we write this chapter. Almost as the proverbial ink dries on the paper, it is likely that another technological breakthrough will have occurred. Our future will be both dominated and liberated by our abilities to handle the power of the ICT on offer.

Introduction to Statistics PART

NUMBERS INTO INFORMATION

Part 1 of this book is all about how we can use a systems approach to ensure that we have the right information, in the right form at the right time, to enable us to make the most effective decisions. Using statistics, which is essentially a collection of quantitative techniques, is an important part of this process – they can help us interpret and transform a mass of data into information to aid decision-making. They play a crucial role in enabling managers and specialists to *manage* their information. We have chosen those techniques that we feel will be most useful to the practitioner and tried to present them in a straightforward and understandable form.

In introducing you to the techniques we have tried to keep the theory to the minimum and concentrate on how they can be used. However, in order to use the techniques in the most effective way it is important to understand a little about the rationale and thinking behind them. The important step of translating our information into usable knowledge for decision-making requires us to use these techniques in a thoughtful way, understanding when it is appropriate to use a particular technique in a particular situation.

It is becoming increasingly important that we develop a wide understanding of all aspects of our organisations' work and do not become too insular within our own functions. So, we have used examples from across the organisation – from the world of marketing, production management, etc – as well as focusing on HR examples. We also include exercises for you to try (at the end of the chapters), but with answers provided as well (at the end of the book)!

The first chapters in this part of the book, Chapters 12, 13 and 14, cover what is known as descriptive statistics. These are techniques that can be used to help us present information to our bosses, staff, colleagues, customers, shareholders, etc, in ways that they will find most easy to understand. Chapter 15 covers probability and probability distributions, and contains some essential stepping stones to the next chapter. These may seem a little theoretical and, dare we say, heavy going! Please persevere because they are the gateway into the fascinating and very useful techniques of sampling and hypothesis testing, which are covered in Chapters 16 and 17 respectively.

Chapter 18 addresses the subjects of regression and correlation. Do not be put off by these technical terms – the techniques described in this chapter simply help us to identify and understand relationships in our data. The following chapter, Chapter 19, as its title (Forecasting and time series) suggests, is all about helping us to look into the future (the modern equivalent of the crystal ball!). Chapter 20 opens up the world of those peculiar numbers known as indices, and Chapter 21 introduces the fascinating world of decision-making. Finally, Chapter 22 harnesses the power of the computer, by using a typical spreadsheet package, to show you how to carry out all these useful statistical techniques without getting bogged down by the algebra and arithmetic.

We hope these chapters present the techniques in a way you will find easy to understand and absorb. However, if a particular section seems a little more difficult, please persevere. We promise you that none of it is too bad and we hope you will find some of it to be fun!

Tabulations

CHAPTER 12

CHAPTER OBJECTIVES

When you have studied this chapter, you will be able to:

- describe a range of ways for organising data in a tabular format
- set out data as an array, a frequency distribution, a relative frequency distribution and a cumulative frequency distribution.

INTRODUCTION

Data, in its raw form, often does not readily convey much information and, as managers/specialists, information is what we need to make decisions that are appropriate to the circumstances and produce the outcomes we require from our interventions. You will recall that in Chapter 1 we used the example of absence figures. In their raw form they did not convey much information. However once you started to manipulate them, by showing them as a percentage of working days, they started to provide useful information. In this chapter we shall look at a range of techniques that have as their basis organising the data into tabular format.

To illustrate what we mean, let us take a typical set of data (potential information) that you might come across. For ease of demonstration we have chosen a simple example, of the salaries of employees in a small firm (see Table 12.1).

Table 12.1 Salaries of employees in a small ICT firm (number of employees = 20)

Employee	Salary (£)
A	22,000
B	23,000
C	21,000
D	25,000
E	23,000
F	22,000
G	23,000
H	20,000
I	22,000
J	19.000
K	18,000
L	21,000
M	12,000
N	27.000
O	23,000
P	26,000
Q	24,000
R	24,000
S	19.000
T	20,000

What can we infer from this table? Not a lot, other than if we look hard, we see that the lowest salary is £18,000 and the highest is £27,000, and the other salaries are spread out randomly between the lowest and the highest in steps of £1000. Indeed, we might ask why we have bothered to set out data in this way anyway? Let us suppose that the aim is to establish whether the company is paying market rates to its employees. We might start by setting out the facts in some sort of table, probably in the order in which it has come from the salaries records. Table 12.1 actually sets out the salaries in alphabetical order of employee surname.

ARRAYS

One way in which we can start to get a feel for the information that is locked inside the data is to see how it is distributed or spread between the lowest and highest salaries. To do this we set out the salaries in ascending order of value – forming an *array in ascending order*. (see Table 12.2). (We could equally have set out the data in an *array of descending order*, by putting the highest salary first and the lowest salary last.)

Table 12.2 Salaries in an array of ascending order

Employee	Salary (£)
K	18,000
J	19.000
S	19,000
H	20,000
T	20,000
C	21,000
L	21,000
A	22,000
F	22,000
I	22,000
M	22,000
B	23,000
E	23,000
O	23,000
Q	24,000
R	24,000
D	25,000
G	25,000
P	26,000
N	27,000

Does this start to tell us anything more? Again, not a lot, except we can more easily see the range of salaries and, perhaps, that more people are paid at the £22,000 salary level than at any other. So, how can we summarise the data to give us more information?

FREQUENCY DISTRIBUTIONS

One way is to prepare it as a *frequency distribution*, that is, by showing the number of employees at each salary level (see Table 12.3).

This way of setting out the data is beginning to tell us, for example, how the most frequently occurring salaries 'bunch' around £22–23,000 and tail off towards the lower and higher salary levels. More people are paid £22,000 than any other salary and we could, if we wished, use this as a crude comparison with another employer to test the competitiveness of our pay rates. It would not

Table 12.3 Frequency distribution of salaries

Salary (£)	Frequency
18,000	1
19,000	2
20,000	2
21,000	2
22,000	4
23,000	3
24,000	2
25,000	2
26,000	1
27,000	1
Total	20

be a very efficient comparison because it would show the same result against an organisation that, for example, paid no salary over £22,000 provided its most common salary was £22,000.

Now, if there was a large number of salary points it might be helpful to group the salaries into salary bands, as shown in Table 12.4. It is important that there are no gaps between the bands or classes and that they do not overlap. The bands should always be the same size, unless this proves difficult as it sometimes will at the extreme ends of a widely spread distribution.

Table 12.4 Grouped salaries

Salary band (£)	Frequency
18,000–19,999	3
20,000–21,999	4
22,000–23,999	7
24,000–25,999	4
26,000–27,999	2
Total	20

Relative frequency distribution

Are we now at the stage where we can start to compare our salary levels with those of another organisation? We could lay out, or group, its salaries as we have our own. However, what happens if the other organisation, as is quite likely, has a different number of employees? The way to tackle this situation is to look at the percentages of the total number of employees in each organisation at certain salary points or in particular salary bands. In this way we create a *relative frequency distribution*. Taking Tables 12.3 and 12.4, we can now produce relative frequency distributions as shown in Table 12.5.

Table 12.5 Relative frequency distribution of salaries

Salary (£)	Frequency	%	Salary band (£)	Frequency	%
18,000	1	5	18,000–19,999	3	15
19,000	2	10	20,000–21,999	4	20
20,000	2	10	22,000–23,999	7	35
21,000	2	10	24,000–25,999	4	20
22,000	4	20	26,000–27,999	2	10
23,000	3	15	Total	20	100
24,000	2	10			
25,000	2	10			
26,000	1	5			
27,000	1	5			
Total	20	100			

If we look at the grouped data, that is in the salary bands, we can easily see that about one third of the employees (15% + 20% = 35%) are paid in the range £18,000–£21,999, about one third (35%) are paid in the range £22,000–£23,999, and about one third (20% + 10% = 30%) are paid in the range £24,000–£27,999. We can now quite readily make the comparison between our organisation and our competitor(s) in terms of what percentages of their employees fall into the various bands. The answer will give us some information on the competitiveness of our salaries.

Cumulative frequency distribution

Sometimes it may be helpful to know how many employees earn more than or less than a certain amount. In order to do this we would produce a *cumulative frequency distribution*, as shown in Table 12.6, for the grouped salaries used in our previous example.

Table 12.6 Cumulative frequency distribution of salaries

Salary band	Cumulative frequency	Cumulative %
Less than or equal to £19,999	3	15
Less than or equal to £21,999	7	35
Less than or equal to £23,999	14	70
Less than or equal to £25,999	18	90
Less than or equal to £27,999	20	100

Looking at our cumulative frequency distribution, we see that 15% of the employees earn less than £20,000, or alternately, 85% (100% – 15%) earn £20,000 or more. 35% earn less than £22,000, 70% earn less than £24,000 and so on. Now we have another good basis on which to make some sort of a comparison of this organisation's salary structure with that of other organisations. This is useful information, and for very little effort on our part – certainly no massive amount of number crunching, no complicated formulae around and not a single Greek letter in sight!

Before moving on, let us try the following example.

EXAMPLE

Set out below is some data on the ages of employees in a small organisation:

Ages of employees:

25	56	22	53	21	30	30	18	39	43
32	42	35	41	29	35	39	32	37	47
29	38	46	36	17	22	24	16	27	37
35	29	62	34						

What information can be drawn from this data? Where do we start? We could work out the average, but as yet we do not know what the average is (we cover averages in Chapter 13). For now we shall stay with the methods we have discussed already.

Our first approach, again, is to set out a table showing the ages in an array of ascending order of magnitude:

16	17	18	21	22	22	24	25	27	29
29	29	30	30	32	32	34	35	35	35
36	37	37	38	39	39	41	42	43	46
47	53	56	62						

We can then go on to group the data in age ranges, say with five-year intervals, and show the grouped frequency distribution, the relative frequency distribution and the cumulative frequency distribution – see Table 12.7.

Table 12.7 Employee ages: relative and cumulative frequency distributions

Age (years)	No. of employees in age group	Relative frequency %	Cumulative frequency %
Under 20	3	8.8	8.8
20–24	4	11.8	20.6
25–29	5	14.7	35.3
30–34	5	14.7	50.0
35–39	9	26.5	76.5
40–44	3	8.8	85.3
45–49	2	5.9	91.2
50–54	1	2.9	94.1
55–59	1	2.9	97.0
60–64	1	2.9	99.9*
Total	34	99.9*	

*varies from 100% due to rounding

Now we can begin to understand what the data might actually mean to the organisation. For example, we can see that only three of our staff are likely to retire during the next 15 years. If these are managers, what are the implications for the organisation's succession plan? We do not have the problem of a concentration of retirements, possibly leaving the organisation short of experienced people. Instead, we might have the problem, if the future management team is currently in the 30–34 and 35–39 age groups (some 40% of the employees fall in these groups), of employees finding their career advancement with us is restricted by this bottleneck. Unless something is done to prevent frustration driving these up-and-coming middle managers to seek advancement by moving to other organisations, we could experience high levels of staff turnover within these middle grades in the not too distant future. The intelligent analysis of the age profile may be the first early warning signals that this is about to occur. Here is an example of an opportunity for the HR professional to get in early to influence what is happening, rather than being left only to react to the crisis after the event.

Another interesting piece of information to come from the cumulative frequency table is that 35% of the staff are under 30 years of age, 50% under 35 and 77% under 40 – quite a young age profile. What implications might this have for, say, the development of a new benefits package? For example, the staff might be more interested in bonus payments than in pension provision. These issues would not have emerged from looking at the raw age data. We set off with a jumble of numbers and have transformed them into useful management information.

In Chapter 22 we describe how to use the spreadsheet package Microsoft Excel™ to produce frequency distributions.

CONCLUSION

In this chapter we have looked at ways in which raw data can be converted into meaningful information by setting it out in tabular form as arrays and frequency distributions. By using the relative and the cumulative forms of the distributions we continue this process of further refining our data. It is only when we have carried out this analysis that useful information is brought to light. In the next chapter we go on to look at other ways in which we can present our data so that it contributes to our decision-making process.

REVIEW QUESTIONS

1. The following table sets out productivity figures for operatives in a department manufacturing parts for a lighting system. The target levels for performance are 2,501 to 3,000 parts per day.

Parts/day	Frequency
2,001–2,250	8
2,251–2,500	2
2,501–2,750	20
2,751–3,000	25
3,001–3,250	3
3,251–3,500	2
Total	60

   Calculate the relative and cumulative frequency distributions and comment on the results.

2. A charity offers an advisory service with booked appointments. There have been complaints about waiting times at one of its two offices. The organisation has analysed the time that clients have to wait over a one-week period in both offices:

Time (mins)	Frequency Office 1	Frequency Office 2
<5	1	7
6–10	6	40
11–15	30	35
16–20	26	5
21–25	10	0
26–30	9	0
Total	82	87

   Comment on the results.

Diagrammatic methods

CHAPTER OBJECTIVES

When you have studied this chapter, you will be able to:

- describe a range of techniques for presenting data in a diagrammatic form and explain when to use them
- present data in the form of bar charts, pie charts, pictograms, frequency polygons, ogives, graphs and radar diagrams.

INTRODUCTION

So far, we have discussed organising the data into tabular form and seen the benefits of this type of presentation in helping us draw out some of the key information messages. However, some people find it easier to understand information displayed in diagrammatic form. This can be a particularly useful approach if the information is being presented to people who may not be used to dealing with and understanding figures, eg in a report aimed at general employees or shareholders. Information presented diagrammatically can also make a big impact, so diagrams are often used in presentations to groups of people. The saying 'a picture paints a thousand words' is particularly apt as a well chosen and presented diagram will often convey a complex message more simply and succinctly than a mass of figures. This chapter looks at a range of diagrammatic techniques.

BAR DIAGRAMS

The simplest technique is the *bar diagram* or *bar chart*. Let us look at an example of the use of a bar diagram in a sales situation. Suppose that there are three sales staff and the sales manager wants to keep a check on their progress. The sales manager can compile the monthly sales figures on a tabular basis, as shown in Table 13.1, setting out the actual sales per month and the relative sales of each member of the sales staff as a percentage of the monthly total sales.

What does this tell the sales manager? Sales are obviously rising sharply month by month, but who is actually scoring with the customers? Let us see what happens when we set out these figures in the form of a bar diagram – see Figure 13.1.

Table 13.1 Sales performance

	January sales £	%	February sales £	%	March sales £	%	Quarterly total £	%
Brown	10,000	32	12,000	24	18,000	17	40,000	21
Jones	9,000	29	18,000	36	50,000	46	77,000	41
Smith	12,000	39	20,000	40	40,000	37	72,000	38
Month total	31,000	100	50,000	100	108,000	100	189,000	100

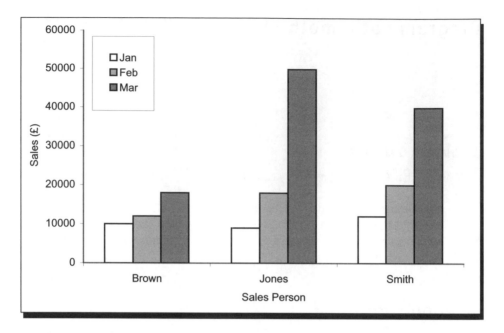

Figure 13.1 Bar diagram showing sales performance

From this picture we can see easily that Brown's progress is modest, Smith's results are very good, while Jones's results are quite spectacular, starting from the lowest base of £9,000 in January to achieving the highest sales total of £50,000 in March. Well done, Jones!

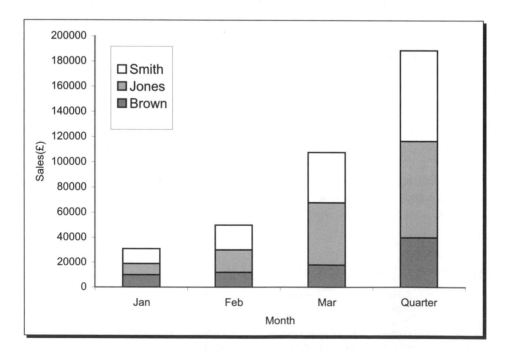

Figure 13.2 Stacked bar diagram showing sales performance

In a development of the bar diagram principle we could show the monthly sales total by way of a *stacked bar diagram*. In our example we have stacked the sales for each of the sales staff by month: that is, the monthly sales of Brown, Smith and Jones are added together and distinguished by colour or different shading, as shown in Figure 13.2. This has the advantage that it shows the growth in total sales very clearly. We have also shown a quarterly 'stack' as well.

PIE CHARTS

Another useful way of depicting this information in a relative sense, that is, to show pictorially the relative contributions made to total sales by Brown, Smith and Jones is to use a *pie chart*. As the name suggests, the total sales are shown as a circle with the sizes of the slices depicting the values of sales for the three staff, as shown in Figure 13.3.

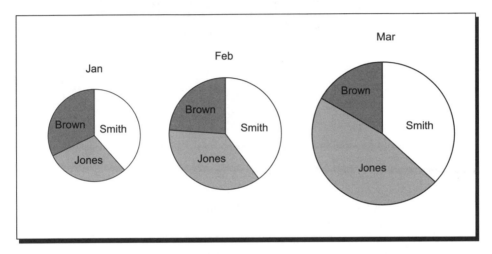

Figure 13.3 Pie charts showing monthly sales

Note how the area of the pie reflects the size of the total sales for the month, whereas the area/size of the slice equates to the proportion of total sales achieved by each sales person. In this way, we see at a glance that Jones is actually achieving a rising proportion of a growing monthly sales total.

Sometimes these diagrams are drawn as three-dimensional pies (or rather they look like the sort of whole cheeses you see in delicatessen counters!) rather than circles, and if you want to draw attention to a particular aspect that slice can be 'pulled out' – see Figure 13.4. We might want to emphasise in this case the member of the sales staff with the biggest share of sales, who is of course Jones.

PICTOGRAMS

One of the really eye-catching ways of presenting statistics is by using pictures instead of bars in our bar diagrams. This type of diagram is called a *pictogram*. Let us look at some examples:

■ A charity wants to show fund-raising in different regions of the country. It might use a pile of coins, or the '£' sign, or if it was concerned with looking after cats, it might use cats! (Using a cat as a symbol would be a particularly good way of showing the number of cats given new homes, etc.)

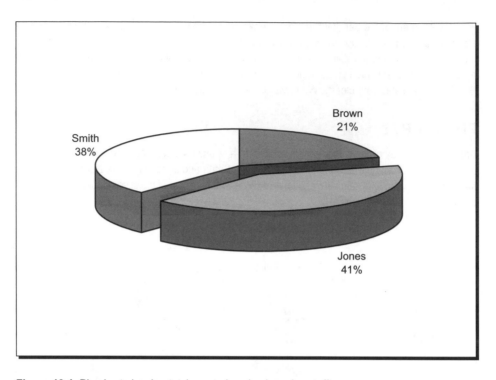

Figure 13.4 Pie chart showing total quarterly sales by sales staff

- An organisation wants to demonstrate the change in numbers of employees over a period of time: the pictogram might use stick-people.
- A supermarket wants to indicate increases in its bread sales over a period of time. Loaves of bread would make a good pictorial representation.

As you can see from Figures 13.5 and 13.6, the heights of the pictures represent the numbers involved and are equivalent to the heights of the bars in a bar diagram. In Figure 13.7 we have used a single loaf to represent a certain unit of sales, ie 1,000 loaves.

It is most important to ensure that the dimensions we have used for comparison are made clear to the reader. With pictograms, there is endless scope for us to use our imagination to provide good visuals to help get our message across to our audience – be they specialist and management colleagues or customers or members of the public, etc. Pictograms are of particular use when we are trying to communicate with a wider audience, some of whom may not have a good under-standing of the more sophisticated graphical and diagrammatic methods. A good example of the latter is the summary version of the annual report and accounts produced by large companies for their shareholders. They can also be very helpful in presentations, where using a pictogram can really grab an audience's attention, eg if you want to highlight an increase in accidents you could use the red cross symbol.

Pictograms work best when there is a very obvious symbol for the item of interest. Sometimes it is difficult to find an appropriate symbol – for example, to illustrate an increase in the number of training days. In all the workshops we have held on presenting information, no one has ever come up with a really good symbol! Also, when producing our pictograms it is important to take care in judging what the audience will find appropriate to their needs.

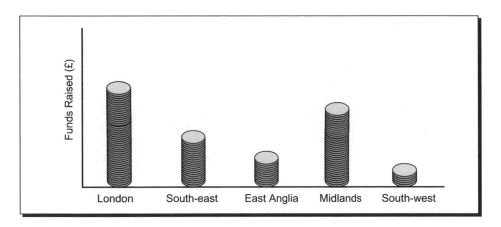

Figure 13.5 Pictogram of funds raised

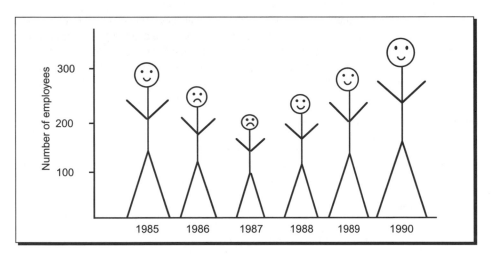

Figure 13.6 Pictogram showing changes in staffing

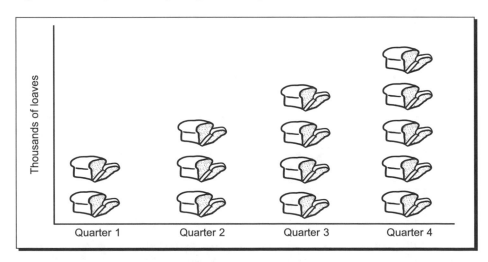

Figure 13.7 Pictogram showing bread sales

HISTOGRAMS

One of the best ways of representing a frequency distribution is by means of a *histogram*. Take the following set of data about calls to a switchboard - a sample of the number of calls per hour has been taken as a result of concerns about staffing levels – see Table 13.2.

Once again the raw data does not give us very much useful management information. In fact it is a quite meaningless jumble of figures in its present form. However, we can start to make sense of the data by going through the process described in Chapter 12 of setting out the data in an array of ascending order. From this we can produce a frequency distribution listing the number of occurrences when 65 calls were received in an hour (that is, 1), then the number of occurrences when 66 calls were received (3), then 67 (4), and so on to all the occurrences when '74' calls in an hour were received (3), as shown in Table 13.3.

By setting out the data in Table 13.3 in the form of a bar diagram of frequency against calls per hour, we get a histogram – see Figure 13.8. The difference between a bar diagram and a histogram is that the data for which frequencies are available is in a quantitative form and must be laid out in a fixed order, ie 65 is followed by 66 and so on. With bar diagrams, the order does not matter. In the example of sales staff performance it did not matter which order the salespeople were listed. We could have shown Jones first and Brown last (although clearly with time data, it is more helpful to show them in time order). Similarly, in the pictogram of fund-raising the order in which the regions are shown does not matter, although the organisation might have an order it commonly uses.

In the histogram in Figure 13.8 we can see that the tops of the columns form a sort of graph, rising in the middle and tailing off at both ends. Even now the information is still not leaping out of the page at us, although by inspection we can see that 70 calls per hour occurs more often than the other levels, and the level of calls per hour seem to be fairly evenly spread above and below the 70 figure.

Table 13.2 Calls per hour

69	70	73	70	71	71
67	72	71	71	68	73
67	70	74	68	70	70
66	68	67	70	69	69
68	70	72	73	72	71
70	69	69	72	70	73
66	70	72	73	74	68
70	70	73	68	66	67
71	65	68	70	72	70
70	70	68	74	72	71

Table 13.3 Frequency distribution of calls per hour

Calls/hour	Frequency of occurrence
65	1
66	3
67	4
68	8
69	5
70	16
71	7
72	7
73	6
74	3
Total	60

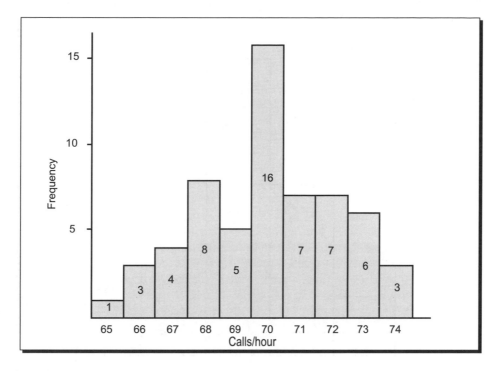

Figure 13.8 Histogram showing calls per hour

How can we take the presentation a step further? We can use the technique previously mentioned of grouping the data. Let us see what happens to our histogram when we group 65 calls per hour with 66, 67 with 68 and so on, and in addition present the information as relative frequencies, that is, percentages of the total. The information in tabular form is set out in Table 13.4.

We need to think a little at this stage about the group or class boundaries. Sometimes the real boundaries are the mid-point between the top of the previous class and the bottom of the next class. In Table13.4 the real boundaries are 64, 66, 68, 70, 72 and 74. When we come to draw the histogram it is easier sometimes just to show classes, and at other times to show the real boundaries. In the histogram in Figure 13.9 we have shown both to emphasise this point.

You may be forgiven at this stage for asking what practical significance all this has. Well, imagine you are the manager of the switchboard that is receiving the calls data that we have been working on. Assuming that your requirements for staff bear some relationship to the volumes of calls, this exercise could give you an indication of the 'right' level of staffing. From the grouped data histogram we can see that the 65 to 68 levels of calls occurred in 27% of the hours; 69 to 70 calls occurred in 35% of the hours; and 71 to 74 calls occurred in 38% of the hours. As it is often unpredictable which

Table 13.4 Relative frequency distribution of grouped calls per hour

Grouped calls/hour	Frequency	Relative frequency (%)
65–66	4	7
67–68	12	20
69–70	21	35
71–72	14	23
73–74	9	15
Total	60	100

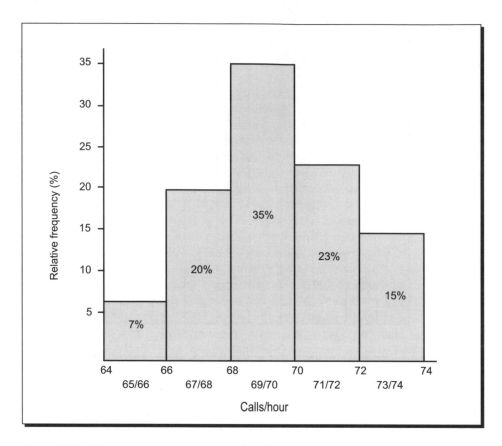

Figure 13.9 Histogram showing grouped calls per hour

will be the busy periods and which the quiet ones, and also unlikely that the manager will be able to deploy additional staff at short notice at the busy times, the grouped data histogram would be of some help. If the department were staffed up to a level that could handle 69 to 70 calls per hour, the staffing levels would be correct for 35% of the time. For 27% of the time the switchboard would be overstaffed and 38% of the time it would be understaffed, with very approximately one third of the hours falling into each category.

Incidentally, if the data in a graph or histogram rises to about the middle point then slopes off at about the same rate as it rose (as in the grouped data histogram) it is said to have a *symmetric distribution* and something approaching the celebrated *normal distribution*. Statisticians love a normal distribution because it allows them to make assumptions about the way the data will behave in their calculations. We look at the normal distribution in Chapter 15.

FREQUENCY POLYGONS

Another way of displaying the data from a histogram, which some people find more helpful, is to show it as a *frequency polygon*. Here, instead of using bars to show the frequency of events, we plot a graph of points at heights corresponding to the frequencies. Where the data is grouped, the points plotted are the group frequencies and the values are shown above the mid-point of the group intervals, as in Figure 13.10. In order for the frequency polygon to touch the horizontal (*x*) axis we have added groups of zero frequency at both ends of the graph.

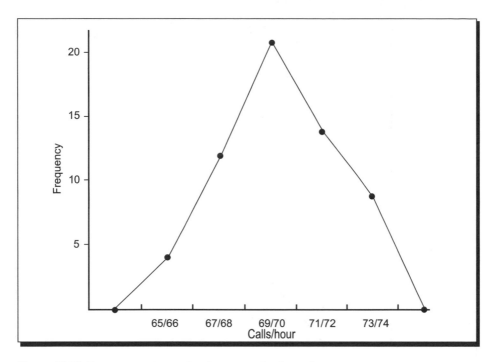

Figure 13.10 Frequency polygon showing grouped calls per hour

OGIVES

Sometimes it is helpful to plot a graph of the cumulative frequency distribution. This is called an *ogive,* and here the cumulative frequencies (of occurrences of calls per hour in the example) are plotted on the vertical (*y*) axis, and the levels of calls per hour along the horizontal (*x*) axis. The ogive can be particularly helpful to us where it is useful to know, for example in the switchboard situation above, the number of hours when the number of calls Is equal to or less than a specific number. We can easily draw up a table showing the cumulative frequencies from Table 13.4 – see Table 13.5.

To plot an ogive, the cumulative frequency is drawn against the upper boundary of each class. For example, 4 is plotted against 66 on the *x* axis, and 16 is plotted against 68 on the *x* axis, etc. The zero point of the ogive is shown at the lowest boundary, that is, 64. The ogive is shown as Figure 13.11.

If the manager of the switchboard knew that the staff could cope with up to 70 calls per hour, she or he could tell from the cumulative frequency table or the ogive that they would be able to answer all the calls on 37 out of the 60 hourly periods. The usefulness of the ogive is that it allows readings from intermediate points. For example, if the manager wanted enough staff to be able to cope with calls on half of the hourly periods, she or he could read across the ogive

Table 13.5 Cumulative frequency distribution of grouped calls per hour

Calls/hour	Cumulative frequency
Less than or equal to 66	4
Less than or equal to 68	16
Less than or equal to 70	37
Less than or equal to 72	51
Less than or equal to 74	60

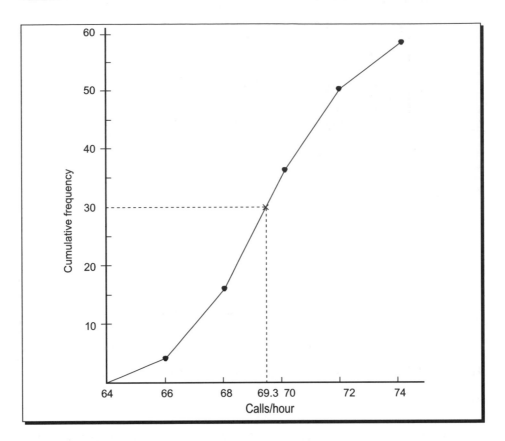

Figure 13.11 Ogive showing cumulative frequency of calls per hour

curve from the cumulative frequency of 30 to give a result of 69.3. Therefore if the switchboard was staffed up to deal with up to 69 calls per hour, it would be able to take all the incoming calls for about half the time. This is a particularly useful facility if the groupings are larger than those used in this example. Of course, the intermediate points could have been worked out from the table, but it is a lot easier to read them off from a graph, and certainly easier to communicate from this particular picture in, say, a presentation to colleagues.

GRAPHS

Next is the diagrammatic method that is probably most familiar to us, the *line graph*. These are most frequently used to show changes in data over time. Figure 13.12 shows the change in learning expenditure per employee. It shows very clearly that there was a steady growth in the early years, expenditure reached a plateau in Year 5 and then rose rapidly thereafter.

Line graphs can also be used to show relationships between variables. Continuing with the learning theme Figure 13.13 shows a *scatter diagram* plotting the scores of delegates in tests carried out in the learning session against their results in on-the-job performance tests. Each point represents a delegate. We are looking to see if there is a relationship between the two types of test – whether the learning test results are a good predictor of on-the-job performance. It is possible to fit a straight line through the scatter of points, called a *regression line*, which will give us information on the relationship. We discuss this approach in depth in Chapter 18.

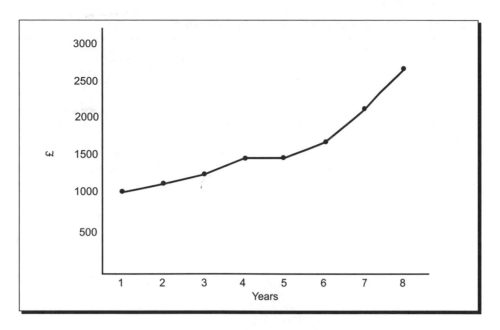

Figure 13.12 Graph of learning expenditure per employee over time

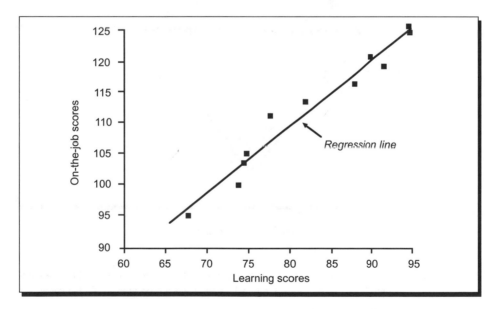

Figure 13.13 Scatter diagram and regression line of learning score versus on-the-job scores

RADAR DIAGRAMS

The *radar diagram* is a diagrammatic method that has become more popular in the last few years and is particularly well used in public sector organisations such as the police and the health service. It has come of age because these diagrams are so useful for displaying performance indicator information.

Take a simple example of a business selling a range of products and you want to compare actual sales performance with target performance over a period of a year (see Table 13.6).

Table 13.6 Comparison of actual sales with target performance

Product	Actual sales	Target	Performance indicator = Actual sales/Target
A	44,000	40,000 = 100	44,000/40,000 = 110
B	81,000	90,000 = 100	81,000/90,000 = 90
C	100,000	80,000 = 100	100,000/80,000 = 120
D	30,000	30,000 = 100	30,000/30,000 = 100

Performance indicators are then plotted relative to the target on the separate axes of the radar diagram, with the shaded area representing the target area and the outline area representing actual sales – see Figure 13.14.

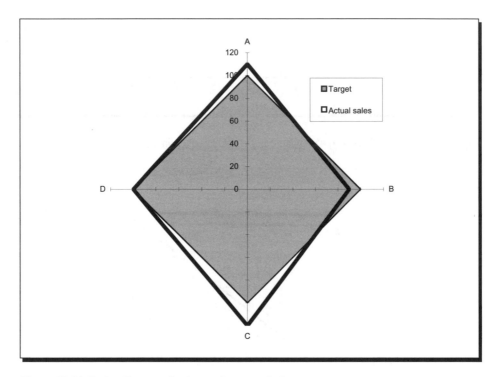

Figure 13.14 Radar diagram of sales performance indicators

From the diagram you can see quite easily which of the products have exceeded the sales targets – A and C; which have not met their target – B; and which are on target – D. However, the diagram does not display the detail.

The advantage of these diagrams is that they can show at a glance performance against a range of indicators on one diagram. In our example, they are all the performance indicators of the same type of data, that is, sales. However, they are particularly useful for showing performance indicators based on different types of data. They have been used in a variety of interesting ways:

■ comparing performance of individual police forces against the average performance of a group of similar forces on five main performance areas (which are themselves made up of a number of performance indicators) – see Figure 13.15

142

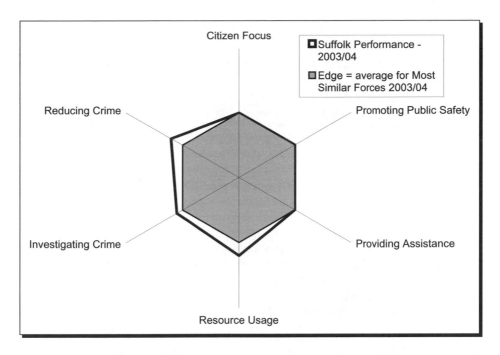

Figure 13.15 Radar diagram showing the performance of Suffolk Police in 2003/2004
Source: Police Performance Monitoring Report 2003/04, Police Standards Unit (2004)

- comparing the performance of individual strategic health authorities (SHAs) against the average performance of all SHAs
- as part of an educational needs analysis – to display actual knowledge against required knowledge for a number of indicators.
- comparing countries in the European Union on their innovation performance defined by a number of indicators
- as a self-evaluation technique – as part of a workshop session delegates are asked to compare the performance of their organisation against a range of thresholds – poor, average, good – in a range of performance areas in order to help define future strategy and priorities.

The diagrams are simple in concept but their effectiveness as a way of presenting information depends on the audience understanding how each performance indicator has been compiled and therefore what it means. Also, they can tend to imply that there is equal weight given to each performance indicator represented by each radial axis. This again reinforces the message that it is important that the audience understands what each performance indicator is measuring and therefore their relative importance.

CONCLUSION

We have demonstrated how the picture, by way of diagrammatic and graphical methods, can paint a thousand words. We have covered the bar diagram, pie chart, pictogram, histogram, frequency polygon, ogive, line graph and radar diagram for this purpose, hopefully showing how easy it is to present the data in these ways. In the next chapter we go on to look at the ways in which numerical methods can help provide management information for decision-makers.

REVIEW QUESTIONS

1. After a learning programme the 20 participants were asked to comment on the quality of the tutor, with the following results:

	Very good	Good	Fair	Poor	Total
Knowledgeable	15	5	0	0	20
Appropriate pace	0	4	12	4	20
Creates interest	10	5	4	1	20
Involves the group	1	8	7	4	20

Present the results diagrammatically and comment on them.

2. You have been asked to prepare an eye-catching presentation to staff. You have to convey the following information over a five-year period.
   - waiting times in a hospital A & E department
   - consumption of water
   - staff turnover.
   Explain briefly your choices for the presentation.

3. Currently all staff have their own desk in the sales department. The department is a mix of staff who spend much of their time out selling, and administration staff who are largely desk-bound. As pressure on space increases, the organisation decides to investigate the concept of 'hot desking', (staff sharing desk space in the department). It has conducted an initial survey of the time spent by staff at their desks during a day. The following data was collected:

Hours per day spent at their desks

1.3	4.6	2.0	0.8	7.5	2.6	6.2	7.8	2.8	5.3
8.4	1.5	3.5	7.0	2.6	9.3	1.9	3.9	6.3	1.1
7.2	0.9	2.8	6.6	3.3					

Summarise this data by producing:
   - a frequency distribution
   - a relative frequency distribution
   - a cumulative frequency distribution
   - a histogram.
   Comment on the results.

Numerical methods

CHAPTER OBJECTIVES

When you have studied this chapter, you will be able to:

- explain the use of measures of location and measures of dispersion
- calculate the mean (average), median, mode, lower and upper quartiles, range, interquartile range and standard deviation
- use these measures to summarise and compare sets of data.

INTRODUCTION

So far, so good, but what about all the figure work that statistics is supposed to be about? Where are all those calculations and formulae with all those funny Greek letters that are so confusing to the non-statistician? In Chapters 12 and 13 we covered ways of presenting and summarising data using tables and then diagrams and graphs. Both these methods are very useful to illustrate points in a report, or as visual aids in a presentation. However, numerical methods are sometimes very effective in summarising data and they become particularly valuable when the data are results from a survey – a sample, from which you wish to draw inferences about the overall population. We will come on to this very exciting subject of sampling in Chapter 16, but for the moment let us get back to our numerical methods.

There are usually two aspects of a data set which will interest us. The first aspect is concerned with the different sections of the data set, the most common being indications of the middle or average value. These are referred to as *measures of location*. The second aspect is concerned with the spread or variability of the data – referred to as *measures of dispersion*.

MEASURES OF LOCATION

There are three main measures of location with which you need to become familiar – the mean (sometimes called the arithmetic mean or average), the median and the mode. The first is probably the most widely used. They are all measures of the middle part of the data. In addition we shall also look at some other measure of location that tell us about different parts of our data set – quartiles, deciles and percentiles.

Mean

The *mean* (or *average*) is obtained by adding together all the individual items of data and then dividing by the number of items in the data set. Let us look at a simple extract from one of the earlier examples. Do you remember the monthly sales figures of Brown, Jones and Smith? Table 14.1 gives their January sales figures again to remind you.

Table 14.1 Sales performance for January

Sales staff	Sales (£)
Brown	10,000
Jones	9,000
Smith	12,000
Total	31,000

Some organisations measure the performance of their sales people by comparing individual monthly sales figures with the mean for all the sales staff. The mean of the January sales figures is obtained by adding up the sales for each sales person and dividing by the number of data items (in this case three – the number of sales staff) to get a mean of £10,333. The statisticians have a beautiful way of complicating this simple principle. They say, let x_1, x_2 ... x_n be the individual values of a data set with 'n' points in it, then the mean is calculated by the following formula:

$$\text{Mean} = \frac{x_1 + x_2 \dots + x_n}{n}$$

A mathematical notation which is commonly used by statisticians to indicate 'the sum of individual data items' is the Greek letter Σ (capital sigma), so, for example:

$$\sum_{i=1}^{5} x_i = x_1 + x_2 + x_3 + x_4 + x_5$$

x_i is a typical data item, and the terms '$i = 1$' and '5' below and above the Σ indicate the range of data items to be summed, in this case from 1 to 5. This formula can be generalised to any range of items, eg 'n':

$$\sum_{i=1}^{n} x_i = x_1 + x_2 \dots + x_n$$

and the mean, therefore =

$$\sum_{i=1}^{n} \frac{x_i}{n}$$

We now have a formula which we can use with any data set.

Let us take another example to reinforce the message. Table 14.2 sets out the sales figures for a company over a period of twelve years. What is the mean (average) sales for the period?

Substituting this data into our formula we have:

Table 14.2 Company sales

Year	Sales (£000)	Year	Sales (£000)
1	100	7	250
2	200	8	200
3	250	9	100
4	300	10	250
5	250	11	300
6	150	12	150

$$\text{Mean} = \sum_{i=1}^{12} \frac{x_i}{12}$$

$$= \frac{x_1 + x_2 + x_3 + x_4 + x_5 + x_6 + x_7 + x_8 + x_9 + x_{10} + x_{11} + x_{12}}{12 \text{ (the number of years)}}$$

$$= \frac{100 + 200 + 250 + 300 + 250 + 150 + 250 + 200 + 100 + 250 + 300 + 150}{12}$$

$$= \frac{2500}{12}$$

$$= 208.333$$

Therefore the average sales per year is £208,333.

The next issue is what happens if our data is presented in the form of a frequency distribution. For example, the visitors to a hotel were asked to rate the hotel on quality of service, on a scale of 1 (poor quality) to 6 (excellent quality) – see Table 14.3.

Using our previous formula:

$$\text{Mean} = \sum_{i=1}^{30} \frac{x_i}{30}$$

$$= \frac{2 + 2 + 3 + 3 + 3 + 4 + 4 + 4 + 4 + 4 + 4 + 4 + 4 + 4 + 4 \text{ and so on}}{30}$$

Table 14.3 Ratings for hotel

Rating	Number of visitors
1	0
2	2
3	3
4	10
5	12
6	3
Total	30

Clearly the quick way to calculate this is:

$$= \frac{0 \times 1 + 2 \times 2 + 3 \times 3 + 10 \times 4 + 12 \times 5 + 3 \times 6}{30}$$

$$= \frac{131}{30}$$

$$= 4.4$$

The formula we are using is:

$$\text{Mean} = \frac{n_1 \times x_1 + n_2 \times x_2 + n_3 \times x_3 + n_4 \times x_4 + n_5 \times x_5 + n_6 \times x_6}{n_1 + n_2 + n_3 + n_4 + n_5 + n_6}$$

where the n values are the frequencies and the x values are the ratings, so:

$$\text{Mean} = \sum_{i=1}^{6} \frac{n_i x_i}{\sum n_i}$$

This can be generalised to:

$$\text{Mean} = \sum_{i=1}^{n} \frac{n_i x_i}{\sum n_i}$$

where n_i is the frequency of that value of x_i summed over the range 1 to n.

The process is just the same when the data is grouped. For example, suppose the age distribution of purchasers of a particular product is as given in Table 14.4.

Table 14.4 Purchasers

Age category	Percentage of purchasers
20–29	15
30–39	60
40–49	25
Total	100

We can treat the percentages just like frequency data, with the total, n, as 100. The complication comes because we do not know how the ages are distributed through the categories. So, we make an assumption that they are distributed evenly through the categories, and take the midpoint as the x_i values. The midpoint of the 20–29 category is $(20 + 29) \div 2 = 24.5$, of the 30–39 category is 34.5, and so on. Therefore:

$$\text{Mean} = \frac{15 \times 24.5 + 60 \times 34.5 + 25 \times 44.5}{100}$$

$$= 35.5$$

Here we must pause for a moment and introduce the concept of a population and a sample. A *population* is defined as a collection of all the items in which we are interested. For example, if we were a marketing manager promoting the sales of cosmetics in the United Kingdom, the population of interest could be all women in the United Kingdom over the age of 14. Alternatively, the production manager in a factory making radios could be interested in quality control. His or her population here would be the total production of radios.

A *sample* is a portion of the population selected to represent the whole. Going back to our examples, we might choose a sample of, say, 500 women aged over 14 and find out what cosmetics they use. Our production manager might choose a sample of, say, 100 radios and test to see how many were defective. The results from our sample can then be used to provide information about the population as a whole.

We return to the fascinating subject of sampling in Chapter 16. However, it is useful to come to grips with some conventions at this stage. The mean of a population (with N values) is usually referred to by the Greek letter 'mu', written μ. The mean of a sample (with n values) is represented by the symbol $\bar{x}$ (called x bar). The means for both a population and sample are calculated using the same formula as shown earlier.

The average, or mean, is fairly familiar to most of us. We can use it, following on from our previous examples, to compare the sales of two or more different products over a period of time, or the effectiveness of different training programmes. The mean is a useful way of comparing two sets of data provided that the data has a symmetric distribution. If the distribution of the data is not symmetric but bunched up at one end or the other, it is said to be *skewed*. When data is skewed it is helpful to use another measure of location, the median, to help with our comparison.

Median

The *median* is probably the second most commonly used measure of location after the mean. It is the value falling in the middle when data items are arranged in an array of either ascending or descending order. If there is an odd number of items, the median is the value of the middle item. If there is an even number of items, the median is obtained by taking the mid-point of the two middle items, ie calculating the mean of the two middle points.

Let us look at an example. Suppose the results of a skills test for a group of engineering trainees are as shown in Table 14.5 (the trainees have been listed in order of lowest to highest results). We have calculated both the median and the mean.

If you look at the mean figure of 65.8, this suggests reasonable performance on the part of the trainees. However, if you scan the individual scores it is quite clear that the majority of trainees have in fact done very well, 11 out of 13 achieving scores of over 65 and over half achieving scores of 70 or above. The median score of 75 gives a much better indication of the overall performance. The mean score is being affected by two very low scores – the distribution of scores is skewed towards the top of the range.

Table 14.5 Test results

Trainee	Score on skills test out of 100	
1	10	
2	15	
3	65	
4	65	
5	70	
6	70	
7	75	← median
8	75	
9	75	
10	80	
11	80	
12	85	
13	90	
Total	855	
Mean	855÷13 = 65.8	

We can also use this method to compare the competitiveness of the salaries in different organisations. Let us set out the salary data for each organisation in an array of ascending order, as shown in Table 14.6.

Using the median as a way of comparing the competitiveness of salaries in the three organisations, Organisation 1 with a median of £22,400 ((21,800 + 23,000) ÷ 2) is the most attractive compared with £20,230 for Organisation 2 and £16,900 ((16,400 + 17,400) ÷ 2) for Organisation 3.

Table 14.6 Comparison of salary data

Organisation 1 £	Organisation 2 £	Organisation 3 £
12,000	14,290	6,520
12,950	14,600	6,730
13,800	14,930	7,408
14,250	15,066	11,406
14,872 ←Lower quartile 15,936	16,800	11,800
17,000	17,900 ←Lower quartile 17,900	12,208
19,272	18,208	12,472 ←Lower quartile 12,472
19,400	19,272	14,000
21,000	19,490	14,248
21,800 ←Median 22,400	19,600	14,472
23,000	20,230 ←Median 20,230	14,876
24,000	23,302	16,000
24,530	23,664	16,400 ←Median 16,900
25,000	24,028	17,400
25,200 ←Upper quartile 25,200	24,250	17,430
25,200	24,892 ←Upper quartile 24,892	18,600
26,000	25,216	19,632
27,400	26,064	20,460
29,000	27,000	22,726
34,686	27,400	24,280 ←Upper quartile 24,280
	27,900	25,000
		25,200
		25,432
		25,998
		26,400
		29,200

To refine this comparison further we can calculate the upper and lower *quartiles* and use these together with the medians to make further comparisons between the three organisations. The *upper quartile* is that value, in an array of numbers, above which one-quarter of the values fall and below which three-quarters fall. The *lower quartile* is the value, in an array, above which three-quarters of the values fall and below which one-quarter of the numbers fall. The upper and lower quartiles give us information about the upper and lower parts of the data, as opposed to the middle part. Using the median, the upper quartile and the lower quartile we get three benchmarks with which to compare the salaries (or any other data we wish to compare) in the three organisations. In our example, Table 14.7 summarises the information.

Table 14.7 Lower quartile, median and upper quartile

	Organisation 1 £	Organisation 2 £	Organisation 3 £
Lower quartile	15,936	17,900	12,472
Median	22,400	20,230	16,900
Upper quartile	25,200	24,892	24,280

Does this tell us anything more? What it does show is that the salaries of Organisation 2 are the best or most competitive at the lower levels (the lower quartile), with the salaries of Organisation 3 trailing well behind at that level. The salaries of Organisation 1 are the best at the middle levels and, while Organisation 1 and Organisation 2 are both more competitive than Organisation 3 at the upper levels, there is little to chose between them at this level. Published salary surveys use medians and quartiles to present their information.

We can if we wish take this measure of location further by looking at percentiles and deciles. *Percentiles* divide the range of data in the array into 100ths. Expressed in this way the median is the 50th percentile, the upper quartile in an ascending array is the 75th percentile and the lower quartile is the same as the 25th percentile. *Deciles* are simply percentiles ranged in groups of 10. The first decile in an ascending array has 10 per cent of the values below it and 90 per cent above it. The second decile has 20 per cent of the values below it and 80 per cent above it, and so on. Quartiles, deciles and percentiles are all measures of location that tell us about different parts of the data set, other than the middle area.

Mode

The final measure of location that we shall consider is the *mode*. This is another measure of the middle area of the data. The mode is the term given to the value that occurs with the greatest frequency in the data set. In the test example in Table 14.5, the most commonly occurring score is 75 with 3 occurrences, so this is the mode for that data set.

So, by using the mean (average), median, quartiles, percentiles, deciles and mode we can compare the data on different organisations, machines or anything else we care to choose, and locate the benchmarks for our comparisons with as much precision as we like. One final thing to remember about the mean, median and the mode is that, when the distribution of the data is symmetric, they are the same for all practical purposes. It is only when the distribution is skewed that they differ.

MEASURES OF DISPERSION

It is sometimes important to know how variable or dispersed data values are. To take a simple example, you are a manufacturer and have a machine that is vital to your production process. You have a choice of two service agents, both of which claim to repair a machine breakdown on average in four hours. You have been caught by these vague statements before so, with the benefit of having read this book, you ask for evidence of their actual repair times for, say, a sample of the most recent 20 call-outs. The data you receive is shown in Table 14.8.

Table 14.8 Repair times

Agent A	Repair time (hours)	5, 4, 3, 4, 3, 5, 4, 4, 4, 5, 3, 4, 3, 3, 4, 4, 4, 5, 5, 4.
Agent B	Repair time (hours)	3, 4, 5, 5, 2, 7, 5, 4, 3, 5, 4, 2, 6, 4, 4, 5, 3, 4, 3, 2.

By substituting these values in the formula we can calculate the mean for each data set:

$$\text{Mean, } \bar{x} \text{ for Agent A} = \sum_{i=1}^{n} \frac{x_i}{n} = \sum_{i=1}^{20} \frac{x_i}{20} = \frac{80}{20} = 4$$

(Remember Σx_i is simply the sum of all the 20 values of x_i (the repair times)).

Mean, $\bar{x}$ for Agent B is exactly the same.

So neither agent is breaking the trades description legislation and there is nothing to choose between them based on the mean. However, when we set out the data as histograms as shown in Figures 14.1 and 14.2, we now see two different pictures of the performance of the two repair agents. (Remember we describe histograms in Chapter 13.)

Now we can distinguish between the service provided by the two agents. If we look at Agent B, while it might be useful for the machine to be repaired in two hours on 15% of occasions, it might be totally unacceptable to have to wait for six hours for 5% of the time and seven hours for 5% of the time. So Agent A is the one for us. It is the dispersion of the data that has allowed us to differentiate between the two agencies.

Range

The simplest measure of dispersion is the range. The *range* for a set of data is the arithmetic difference between the highest and the lowest value. In the example above the range of repair times for Agent A is 5 – 3 = 2 hours. The range of repair times for Agent B is 7 – 2 = 5 hours. The data for Agent B is dispersed over a wider range than that of Agent A and, apart from providing a basis for deciding which service best suits our needs, the significance of a wide or narrow range of data will be discussed later. We come back to it in Chapter 16 when we cover sampling and the drawing of inferences.

Interquartile range

Another similar measure of dispersion is the *interquartile range*. This is the arithmetic difference between the upper and lower quartiles – which gives an indication of the spread of the mid-50% of the data set. So, looking back at the salary data, the interquartile range for Organisation 1 is £25,200 – £15,936 = £9,264.

Variance and standard deviation

The range is a good measure of dispersion for many purposes but it falls down as a vehicle for

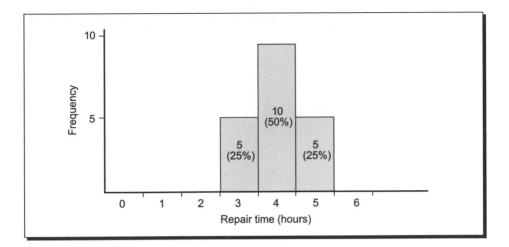

Figure 14.1 Histogram of repair times for Agent A

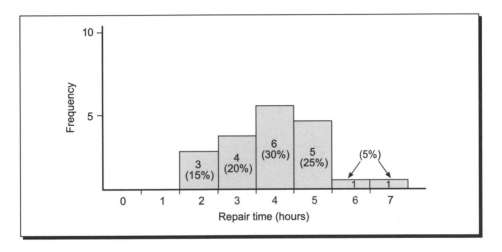

Figure 14.2 Histogram of repair times for Agent B

assessing data when, for example, there are rogue values at the top or bottom of the range which are some distance removed from the other values. In these cases the measures of dispersion called the *variance* and *standard deviation* are much more useful than the range. Both of these are measures of how dispersed the data is about the mean. To calculate them we work through the following steps:

1. First find the *mean* of the data set in the usual way by adding up all the values in the data set and dividing this by the number of values (N for a population and n for sample). For Agent A and Agent B above the mean is the same, $80 \div 20 = 4$.
2. Subtract each value from the mean to get the *deviation from the mean*.
3. Then *square the deviations* to get rid of the minus signs, as we are only interested in the size of the deviation and not whether it is positive or negative.
4. Add together the squares and divide the sum by the number of values in the case of a population (N) and by the number of values minus 1 for a sample ($n - 1$). We are finding the *average of the squared deviations*. In our example we divide the sum by $20 - 1 = 19$, as it is a sample. We now have the *variance* of the data.

5. As we had previously squared the deviations we now take the *square root* to obtain the *standard deviation*.

Expressed as a formula, where $x_1 \dots x_N$ are the values of the population and μ the population mean:

Variance of a population, usually referred to as σ^2,

$$= \sum_{i=1}^{N} \frac{(x_i - \mu)^2}{N}$$

Standard deviation of a population, referred to as σ,

$$= \sqrt{\sum_{i=1}^{N} \frac{(x_i - \mu)^2}{N}}$$

Similarly the formulae for a sample set, where $x_1 \dots x_n$ are the values of the sample and $\bar{x}$ the sample mean, are as follows:

Variance of a sample, usually referred to as s^2,

$$= \sum_{i=1}^{n} \frac{(x_i - \bar{x})^2}{n-1}$$

Standard deviation of a sample, referred to as s,

$$= \sqrt{\sum_{i=1}^{n} \frac{(x_i - \bar{x})^2}{n-1}}$$

These variances and standard deviations are not hard to calculate, but to do it by hand is rather time-consuming and tedious. However, you will pleased to hear that most well-known statistical packages will do the calculations for you, almost at a press of a button. In Chapter 22 we describe how you can use a spreadsheet package, Microsoft Excel™, to calculate a range of descriptive statistics including the mean, median, mode, variance and standard deviation for a data set.

Returning to the example of the two repair agents, the results look like this: the standard deviation for A is 0.73 and 1.34 for B. So we could say the data on Agent B is about twice as dispersed as that for Agent A. It was this difference in dispersion or variability of the data that made us favour Agent A over Agent B.

The standard deviation will be put to further practical use when we come to Chapters 15, 16 and 17 where we cover sampling and hypothesis testing. In the example above, we could have come to the conclusion that B is more dispersed than A simply by inspecting the data. However, when we have hundreds or thousands of items of data, or a large number of comparisons to be made, we need a calculation to reduce the problem to a single numerical value, hence the use of the standard deviation.

CONCLUSION

In this chapter we have started to get to grips with some of the number crunching. We have also met and mastered our first Greek letters! We have looked at measures of location (mean, median, mode, quartiles, deciles and percentiles) and measures of dispersion (range, interquartile range, variance and standard deviation) and seen how they can be used to summarise and compare different sets of data. We shall see that the standard deviation is very useful in many statistical techniques and shall return to it in several of the following chapters.

REVIEW QUESTIONS

1. An organisation has carried out an employee satisfaction survey. Staff were asked to rate their satisfaction on a scale of one to 100 on three aspects:
   - interesting and stimulating work
   - opportunities for learning and development
   - effectiveness of their manager.

   The results for two departments and the organisation as a whole are as follows:

	Department A	Department B	Whole Organisation
Interesting and stimulating work	Mean: 50 Standard deviation: 15	Mean: 75 Standard deviation: 4	Mean: 63 Standard deviation: 9
Opportunities for learning and development	Mean: 65 Standard deviation: 6	Mean: 60 Standard deviation: 11	Mean: 67 Standard deviation: 8
Effectiveness of their manager	Mean: 58 Standard deviation: 4	Mean: 68 Standard deviation: 5	Mean: 60 Standard deviation: 9

   Comment on the results.

2. A small chain of fashion shops has done a survey of its customers' incomes. The results for the three shops in the chain are set out below.

	Shop Suzi £	Shop Cecile £	Shop Marie £
Lower quartile	14,310	9,230	21,500
Median	18,990	18,830	26,250
Upper quartile	23,440	27,650	33,900

   Comment on the results and the implications for the business.

Introduction to probability and probability distributions

CHAPTER OBJECTIVES

When you have studied this chapter, you will be able to:

- explain what is meant by probability, random variables and probability distributions
- outline three ways of assessing probabilities
- set out the properties of a normal distribution.

INTRODUCTION

The word probability usually strikes fear into the hearts of the bravest non-mathematicians/statisticians. However, it is a concept of vital importance to managers and specialists and one they use, knowingly or unknowingly, almost every working day. We are faced all the time with the need to make decisions that involve uncertainty (see Chapter 1). Situations regularly crop up such as:

- Should we invest in a new factory, and what is the likely effect on profitability?
- What is the likelihood that our employees will settle for a 5% wage increase?
- What is the likelihood that a price decrease will boost sales?

Probability is a measure of uncertainty – a measure of the chance or likelihood that a particular event will occur. It is expressed on a scale of zero to one. If the probability is close to zero then the event is very unlikely to take place; if it is close to one then it is very likely to take place. If the probability is 0.5 then the event is equally likely or unlikely to take place.

We shall also talk about probability distributions. There are a range of probability distributions, but we focus primarily on the normal distribution, which is key to our understanding and ability to use sampling approaches.

EXPERIMENTS AND OUTCOMES

To get information on probabilities we carry out experiments, or in the business world, activities such as market research. Let us stay for a while with the concept of an experiment. An experiment will have outcomes and here are some examples:

Experiment	*Outcome*
Toss a coin	Head, tail
Throw a dice	1, 2, 3, 4, 5, 6
Make a sales call	Sale, no sale
Inspect a product	Perfect, imperfect

An outcome is often referred to as a *sample point* and all possible outcomes are the *sample space*. Take the example of tossing the coin:

Now consider a more complex example, where we toss a coin twice. A graphical way to help us think about this is a *tree diagram* (see Figure 15.1).

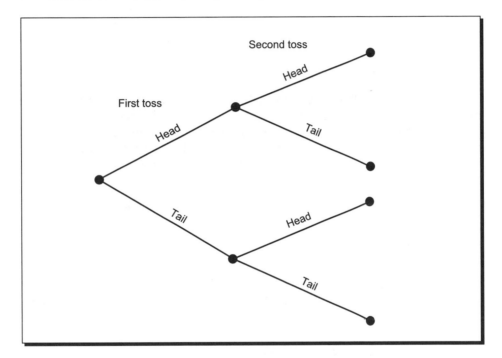

Figure 15.1 Tree diagram – tossing a coin twice

The outcomes, or sample points, of this experiment are:

> head, head
>
> head, tail
>
> tail, head
>
> tail, tail

These four sample points form the sample space.

The basic *rules of probability* are as follows:

- Probability values lie between zero and one.
- The sum of all the probability values associated with the outcomes of an experiment must be one.

EXPERIMENTAL OUTCOMES AND THEIR PROBABILITIES

Associated with each experimental outcome is the probability of it occurring. There are three basic methods of assigning a probability to an experimental outcome: the classical method, the relative frequency method and the subjective method.

The classical method

The *classical method* is based on the assumption that each outcome is equally likely. Good examples of this are tossing a coin and throwing a dice. When tossing a coin the probability of getting a head or tail is equally likely and as there are only two possible outcomes, the probability is 1/2 or 0.5 of getting a head or a tail. With the dice there are six outcomes, each equally likely. Therefore the probability of getting a particular number is 1/6 or 0.17. In our experiment of tossing a coin twice there are four outcomes and therefore the probability of getting a particular outcome is 1/4 or 0.25.

The relative frequency method

The *relative frequency* method is based on conducting an experiment or test to assess probable values. For example, suppose we are testing a product to see if it is perfect or defective. We take a sample, of say 100 items chosen at random, test them and find that 90 are perfect and 10 are defective. (By random, we mean chosen such that every member of the population is equally likely to be a member of the sample, independently of which other members of the population are chosen – more of this in Chapter 16.) The proportion of defective items in the sample is 10/100, or 0.1. If the ratio of defective to perfect items in the sample is the same as in the overall population then we could infer that the probability of finding defective items overall is 0.1.

The subjective method

The *subjective method* is, as the name suggests, where you make a best guess, based on examining the available information. Thus a horse might be assessed as having a probability of 0.5 of winning a race by one punter, but 0.4 by another reader of the form book. The subjective method reflects the individual's beliefs or expertise.

EVENTS AND THEIR PROBABILITIES

An *event* is a collection of outcomes or sample points. For example, one event is the probability of getting at least one head showing in two tosses of a coin. Looking back at the tree diagram in Figure 15.1, the event (obtaining at least one head) would include the following outcomes:

> head, head
>
> head, tail
>
> tail, head

but not tail, tail as this outcome contains no heads.

The probability of a particular event is equal to the sum of the probabilities of the sample points in the event. That is:

> the probability of getting at least one head in two tosses of the coin
>
> = the probability of getting head, head (that is, ¼)

+ the probability of getting head, tail (that is, ¼)

+ the probability of getting tail, head (that is, ¼)

= ¼ + ¼ + ¼

= ¾ or 0.75.

So, if we toss a single coin there is the probability of 0.5 that it will come down heads. By doubling our chances, that is, by tossing the coin twice, we increase the probability of achieving one head to 0.75. In other words, doubling the chance only increases the probability by 50%. Can you think of a practical example of this principle?

What about having a night watchman whose two states are to be awake or asleep and these are equally likely. If we need to have a watchman awake more than 50% of the time, then employing two watchmen each night would give us the probability of a watchman being awake for 75% of the time. (There are undoubtedly better ways of ensuring an awake watchman but we won't go into them just now!) Let's look at a more realistic example. Suppose as a company we have a 50% chance of winning any contract – perhaps we have only one other competitor which is of similar capability to ourselves. If we tender for two contracts we would have a 75% chance of winning one.

RANDOM VARIABLES

A *random variable* is a numerical description that defines the outcome of an experiment or test. For any experiment, a random variable can be defined such that each possible outcome generates one, and only one, value of the random variable. Examples of random variables are shown in Table 15.1.

Table 15.1 Random variables

Experiment	Random variable	Possible values of random variable
Test a production run of 100 cars	Number of defective cars found	0, 1, 2, ... 100
Observe length of a queue	Number of people in the queue	0, 1, 2, etc
Measure times of a production activity	Length of time taken to carry out production activity	2 mins 50 secs, 3 mins, 4 mins, etc

A random variable can be described as discrete or continuous depending on the sort of numerical values it takes on. A *discrete random variable* is one that takes on a finite number of values (say, 1 to 5) or an infinite sequence (say, 1, 2, 3, etc). Examples are number of units sold, numbers of customers, etc. A *continuous random variable* can take on an infinite number of values in an interval, for example percentages, time, weight or distance. Take for example the random variable of employees' heights. An interval could be defined as all heights between 200 and 220 cm. As an individual's height can theoretically be measured to a very high degree of accuracy, for example, 210.679438 ... cm, then you can see (we hope) that there is an infinite number of values in this interval.

PROBABILITY DISTRIBUTIONS

A *probability distribution* for a random variable describes how the probabilities are distributed or spread over the various values that the random variable can assume. Probability distributions provide the bedrock to the theory and understanding of the vitally useful process known as *statistical inference*, and in particular estimation and significance testing. These are covered in the next two chapters.

Let us take a simple example to help you understand what a probability distribution is. Suppose you are contemplating opening a restaurant and your bank manager wants some evidence on local trade before giving you a bank loan. So you are interested in information on the number of times per month people in the area eat out. You select 200 people at random and interview them to obtain this data. The results of the survey are set out in Table 15.2.

Table 15.2 Probability distribution for eating out

Random variable (No. of times eaten out in a restaurant during last month)	Frequency (no. of people who ate out this number of times)	Probability (of people eating out this number of times)
0	20	20/200 = 0.10
1	80	80/200 = 0.40
2	50	50/200 = 0.25
3	40	40/200 = 0.20
4	10	10/200 = 0.05
	200	1.00

This table describes a probability distribution of a discrete random variable – in other words, a discrete probability distribution – and it can be shown diagrammatically, as in Figure 15.2.

It is quite straightforward to calculate measures of location and dispersion of random variables. It is very similar to the work we did in Chapter 14 on numerical methods, where we were manipulating data. If we take the values of a random variable as $x_1, x_2, x_3...x_n$, with the associated probabilities as $p(x_1), p(x_2), p(x_3)...p(x_n)$, then:

Mean of a random variable x (often referred to as the *expected value*)

$$= x_1 p(x_1) + x_2 p(x_2)...x_n p(x_n)$$

$$= \sum_{i=1}^{n} x_i p(x_i)$$

Variance of a random variable x

$$= (x_1 - mean)^2 p(x_1) + (x_2 - mean)^2 p(x_2)... (x_n - mean)^2 p(x_n)$$

$$= \sum_{i=1}^{n} (x_i - mean)^2 p(x_i)$$

which can be simplified to:

$$= \sum_{i=1}^{n} x_i^2 p(x_i) - mean^2$$

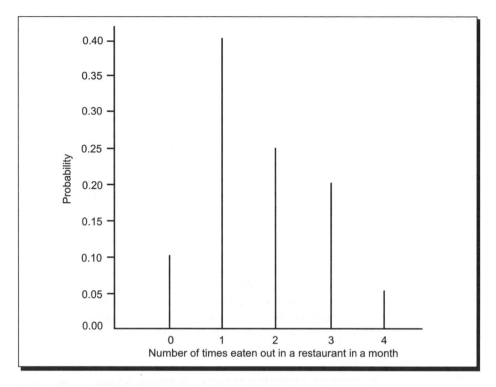

Figure 15.2 Probability distribution for dining out in a restaurant in a month

The standard deviation = $\sqrt{\text{variance}}$

Using our previous example:

Mean value of the random variable, *the number of times people eat out each month* (from Table 15.2)

$$= (0 \times 0.10) + (1 \times 0.40) + (2 \times 0.25) + (3 \times 0.20) + (4 \times 0.05)$$

$$= 0.4 + 0.5 + 0.6 + 0.2$$

$$= 1.7$$

In other words, on average people eat out 1.7 times each month. However, eating out is a discrete random variable as people cannot actually eat out 0.7 or 1.7 times per month. The people in the sample actually eat out on average between once and twice per month.

Using the earlier example again and the simplified formula:

The variance of the random variable, *the number of times people eat out each month*:

$$= (0^2 \times 0.10) + (1^2 \times 0.40) + (2^2 \times 0.25) + (3^2 \times 0.20) + (4^2 \times 0.05) - 1.7^2$$

(Take note of where the figures in the above equation have come from. The probabilities p came from the Table 15.2, and the mean 1.7 came from the earlier calculation.)

Continuing with the calculation:

Variance = 0 + 0.4 + 1.0 + 1.8 + 0.8 − 2.89

= 1.11

Standard deviation = $\sqrt{\text{variance}}$

= $\sqrt{1.11}$

= 1.054

There are a number of discrete probability distributions, for example the binomial distribution. However, we shall not cover these here but move on to the next type of probability distributions – those for continuous random variables.

Continuous probability distributions

A *continuous random variable* may assume any value in an interval, for example, weight, distance, time, etc. All of these can take on values of infinite numbers of decimal points, depending on how accurately they are measured. When we talked about a discrete random variable we defined the probability distribution as something that gave the probability of the random variable assuming a particular value. The equivalent expression for a continuous random variable is a *probability density function*, for reasons which will become clear later in this section.

In order to illustrate the concept of a continuous probability distribution, we shall use the simple example of a *uniform distribution*. A delivery lorry travels from London to Cardiff, and the journey time can take any value between 150 minutes and 200 minutes. If the probability of a journey time falling in any one-minute interval is the same – that is, it is equally likely to fall between 160 and 161 minutes as between 174 and 175 minutes, and so on – then it is said to have a uniform distribution. Since there are 50 one-minute intervals, all of which are equally likely, the probability of the journey time falling in any one-minute interval is 1/50. Now let us look at this distribution in graphical form as shown in Figure 15.3.

What is the probability of the journey time falling between 150 and 175 minutes? Intuitively, since this falls halfway along the total range, we feel that the probability might be 1/2. Alternatively, as budding statisticians we can use the probability formula from page 158:

The probability of an event = the sum of the probabilities of the constituent outcomes

Probability of a journey time between 150 and 175 minutes, p(150 – 175)

= p(150 – 151) + p(151 – 152) + p(152 – 153) ... + p(174 – 175)

= 25 × 1/50

= 1/2 (just as our intuition suggested).

Another approach is to take the area of the graph contained within the interval 150 and 175.

Here, area = height × width

= 1/50 × 25

= 1/2 or 0.5

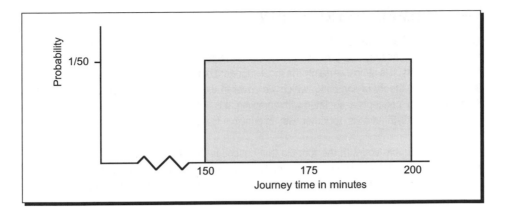

Figure 15.3 Uniform probability density function for journey times

Similarly, let us work out the probability of the journey time falling between 160 and 180 minutes. Look at the graph in Figure 15.4.

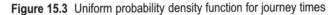

Area   = height × width

       = 1/50 × 20

       = 2/5 or 0.4

Therefore, to find the probability of the journey time falling between 160 and 180 minutes we take the area of the graph bounded by the interval 160 to 180 minutes. Hence, we calculate the probability of the random variable falling in a particular interval by calculating the area bounded by the density curve over that interval. That is why the distribution of a continuous random variable is called a probability density function.

We now move on to the very important continuous distribution, the normal distribution.

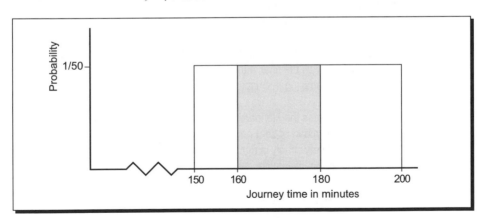

Figure 15.4 Shaded area gives the probability of journey time falling between 160 and 180 minutes

THE NORMAL DISTRIBUTION

We mentioned the normal distribution in Chapter 13. We said then that statisticians love the normal distribution because it allows them to make assumptions about the way data will behave in their calculations. It is almost certainly the most important of the distributions you will come across. It is vital to the theory of sampling, which we cover in the next chapter. In order to understand some of the key concepts associated with sampling, it is important to make sure you understand what a normal distribution is, together with its principal features.

We shall not trouble you with the formula that describes the normal curve, the graphical representation of the density function of the normal distribution. It is sufficient for our purposes to know that it is bell-shaped (see Figure 15.5) and has the principal features set out below.

The principal features of a normal distribution are as follows:

- The highest point of the normal curve occurs at the mean. The mean is also the mode and the median for the normal curve (see Chapter 14).
- The mean of the distribution can be any value – positive, negative or zero.
- The curve is symmetrical about the mean, with tails extending infinitely in both directions, and theoretically never touching the horizontal (x) axis.
- The spread of the curve determines the standard deviation: that is, the flatter the curve, the larger the standard deviation for the same mean (see Figure 15.6).
- The total area under the curve is 1. (This is true for all continuous probability distributions.)
- It has the very important feature that applies to all normal distributions, whatever their mean (μ) or standard deviation (σ), that:

  68.26% of the time, a normal random variable assumes a value within plus or minus one standard deviation of its mean, that is between $\mu \pm 1\sigma$.

  95.44% of the time, a normal random variable assumes a value within plus or minus two standard deviations of its mean, that is $\mu \pm 2\sigma$

  99.72% of the time, a normal random variable assumes a value within plus or minus three standard deviations of its mean, that is $\mu \pm 3\sigma$.

In other words, a random variable with a normal distribution falls in the interval of $\mu \pm 1\sigma$. for about two-thirds of the time, and nearly all time in the interval of $\mu \pm 3\sigma$. We shall make good use of this feature when we come to sampling in Chapter 16.

You may at some time come across the *standard normal distribution*. This is a normal distribution with the particular features of a mean of zero and a standard deviation of one. In fact all normal distributions can be expressed very simply in terms of the standard distribution. Tables have been developed for the standard normal distribution which statisticians find very useful.

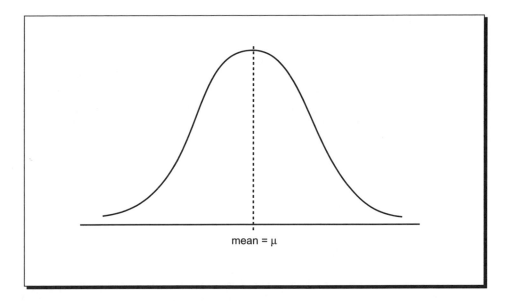

Figure 15.5 A typical normal probability distribution

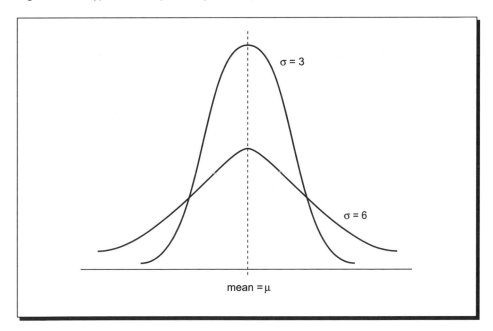

Figure 15.6 Two normal distributions with mean μ, but different standard deviations

CONCLUSION

We hope that you now understand what a random variable is and that you feel at home with the concepts of probability and probability distributions. We have introduced the fascinating and very important normal distribution. The next two chapters go on to show how we can apply all that we have learned so far to a subject close to the hearts of all statisticians and very useful in the business world – sampling and hypothesis testing.

REVIEW QUESTIONS

1. An engineering company is considering expanding its factory, which will enable it to manufacture a new range of products. The MD must decide whether to go for a small-scale or large-scale project. There is uncertainty about the likely level of demand for the new range of products, which has been categorised as low, medium and high. It has been estimated that the probability for each level of demand is 0.2, 0.6 and 0.2 respectively. The finance director has developed a series of profit forecasts for both options:

Demand	Small-scale project (£000s)	Large-scale project (£000s)
Low	100	0
Medium	300	250
High	500	800

    Which option should the MD choose to maximise the expected value of profit?
    Which option might be chosen to minimise risk or uncertainty?

2. A railway company states in its printed timetable that the journey time from Atown to Btown is 2 hours 10 minutes. Since the timetable was printed, problems with the track have caused journey times to be uniformly distributed between 2 hours 15 minutes and 2 hours 30 minutes.

    What is the probability that the train will be not more than 10 minutes late?
    What is the probability that the train will be more than 20 minutes late?

Sampling, estimation and inference

INTRODUCTION

In this chapter we describe the statistical technique of sampling, and the part it can play in providing information for management decision-making. You may first want to ask, 'Why take samples at all?' Well, the purpose of sampling is to produce information about a large *population* from a small portion of that population – a *sample*. When the sample is chosen using statistically correct methods it is possible to draw valid conclusions about the larger population by the process of *statistical inference*. Being able to draw these conclusions from a smaller sample than the whole population generally ensures the process will be quicker and less costly than if the whole population were to be surveyed. Approaching the sampling exercise correctly produces early, less costly results without compromising the accuracy too much. However, it is not always helpful to take a sample. If the population is relatively small in size or the list of the population, the *sampling frame,* and the data on it are readily accessible, for example, the pay of employees from the payroll file on the computer, it may be easier to work with the population as a whole.

One of the most frequent and well-known statistical sampling exercises takes place before British General Elections, and predicts how people are going to vote on the day. Other sampling exercises conducted on a regular basis indicate which of the political parties has the strongest support from the voters at that time, and even give us details about the popularity of the various party leaders. They are often used to seek views on controversial issues such as the wind farm debate. Clearly, the pollsters do not interview the whole population of Great Britain to give us these eye-catching results; they interview a small, statistically valid sample of the population. Most respectable polls give an indication of the size of their sample and sometimes how those people interviewed were selected. The figures can be quite dramatically small. A sample of just over 1,000 people, properly selected, can give a good indication of how the rest of us 26 million voters intend to vote!

Examples of sampling in the business world are:

- In market research, to find out information about, for example, peoples' attitudes or their purchasing habits. Many organisations carry out employee satisfaction surveys to

> gauge staff's views on a wide range of topics, such as the availability and quality of learning and development opportunities, the quality of management, pay and conditions and ICT provision.

- In manufacturing, to test the life of, say, batteries. A sample of 100 batteries is taken from production and tested to see how long, on average, they last. (This is an example where there is no alternative to sampling, since it would not be realistic to use up all the products in the tests!)

- In retailing, to try out and test shoppers' reaction to a new product. A chain of 1,000 stores might be interested in seeing how well an exotic fruit, for example, will sell. It could try it in a small sample of the stores, say 20. If it tried the product out in all the stores and it failed, it would have the expense and embarrassment of a lot of rotting exotic fruit!

The sample results provide *estimates* of what the results might be if the whole population was surveyed. The estimate is unlikely to be exactly the same as the true value for the population as a whole and one of the things we will want to know is how good our estimate is: that is, how close it is to the true value for the population.

We first look at how we choose a sample, then go on to discuss point estimates. To help us answer the question of how good our estimate is, we need to understand a little about sampling distributions. We examine in detail the sampling distributions of two important types of estimate – the sample mean and the sample proportion. From these sampling distributions, we are then able to define confidence limits for these estimates. Finally, we explain how to calculate sample size and talk briefly about how to cope with small samples.

HOW TO CHOOSE A SAMPLE

There are several different methods we can use to select a sample, and our choice between these methods will depend on a number of factors as we shall explain later in this chapter. We start with the most common method, simple random sampling, then go on to discuss systematic sampling, stratified random sampling and cluster sampling. All of these are known as *probabilistic methods*, because the sample members have a known probability of being selected for the sample. This enables us to make statements about sampling errors – about how 'close' the sample estimates are to the true population characteristics. There are a number of other methods which are described as non-probabilistic. They are often created either to mimic a random method, such as quota sampling, or for 'convenience'. We discuss a range of *non-probabilistic methods* – quota sampling, focus groups, convenience sampling and snowball sampling. With all non-probabilistic methods it is difficult to comment on the accuracy of the estimates, etc.

Simple random sampling

First let us consider the case where there is a finite population, that is, the size of the total population is known. A *simple random sample* of size n from a population of size N is selected in such a way that every sample of size n has the same probability of being selected.

Let us consider a simple example. Suppose we are a small business with six vans and we want to know their petrol consumption figures with a reasonable degree of accuracy. We do not have the resources to monitor all six vans and decide to monitor two of them. How many different pairs of vans (samples) could we pick from the six vans (the population)? Let us set out all the possibilities, labelling the vans A to F:

AB, AC, AD, AE, AF

BC, BD, BE, BF

CD, CE, CF

DE, DF

EF

There are 15 different samples that could be chosen.

One option would be to write the names of each of the 15 samples on a card, put them in a large hat and pull out a card. Since each card has an equal probability of being picked, that is, 1 in 15, it is a random sample. Clearly if the population size was very large, then the number of potential samples would also be very large, and this method would be too laborious. A good alternative is to use random number tables prepared by statisticians. A section of one is given as Table 16.1.

Suppose we wanted to pick a sample of, say, 40 cars from a production run of 3,000 cars for testing. We would start by numbering all the cars from 0001 to 3000. Then, using the line in the table marked with *, we choose numbers in groups of four digits (as there are four digits in the number '3000'), discarding the numbers over 3000: 1058, 1301, (4389 – discarded), 2145, 2134, and so on until we have 40 appropriate numbers.

We can start anywhere in the table and go up, down or across to get our random numbers. The tables are designed in such a way that there is no bias in the selections: for example, the numbers within the range 2001 to 3000 have no better or worse chance of being selected than any other range of numbers. Using the random number tables gives us confidence that the 40 numbers are

Table 16.1 Extract from a random numbers table

98554	52502	11780	04060	56634	58077	02005	80217	65893	78381
89725	00679	28401	79434	00909	22989	31446	76251	17061	66680
49221	37750	26367	44817	09214	02074	65641	14332	58221	49564
31783	96028	69352	78426	94411	38335	22540	37881	10784	34658
51025	72770	13689	21456	48391	00157	61957	11262	12640	17228
*10581	30143	89214	52134	76280	77823	61674	96898	90487	43998
51753	56087	71524	64913	81706	33984	90919	86969	75553	87375
96050	08123	28557	04240	33606	10776	64239	81900	74880	92654
93998	95705	73353	26933	66089	25177	62387	34932	62021	34044
70974	45757	31830	09589	31037	91886	51780	21912	16444	52881
25833	71286	76375	43640	92551	46510	68950	60168	26399	04599
55060	28982	92650	71622	36740	05869	17828	29377	01020	90851
29436	79967	34383	85646	04715	80695	39283	50543	26875	94047
80180	08706	17875	72123	69723	52846	71310	72507	25702	33449
40842	32742	44671	72953	54811	39495	05023	61569	60805	26580
31481	16208	60372	94367	88977	35393	08681	53325	92547	31622
06045	35097	38319	17264	40640	63022	01496	28439	04197	63858
41446	12336	54072	47198	56085	25215	89943	41153	18496	76869
22301	07404	60943	75921	02932	50090	51949	86415	51919	98125
38199	09042	26771	15881	80204	61281	61610	24501	01935	33256
06273	93282	55034	79777	75241	11762	11274	41685	24117	98311
92201	02587	31599	27987	25678	69736	94487	41653	79550	92949
70782	80894	95413	36338	04237	19954	71137	23584	87069	10407
05245	40934	96832	33415	62058	87179	31542	18174	54711	21882
85607	45719	65640	33241	04852	87636	43840	42242	22092	28975

selected totally randomly. To a large extent, the advent of computers has overtaken the need for random number tables, as simple spreadsheet packages such as Microsoft Excel™ can readily generate random numbers.

Systematic sampling

If the sample is to be taken from a very large population, it may be too laborious or impractical to go through and number every item in order to identify the sample members using random numbers. A much simpler alternative is to use *systematic sampling*.

Let us suppose there is a population of 10,000 from which a sample of 500 is needed – that is, a ratio of one sample member for every 20 population members. We choose the first sample member randomly from the first 20 members of the population and then take every twentieth population member thereafter until we have our sample of 500.

Stratified random sampling

This is a complicated name for quite a simple but very useful concept. With *stratified random sampling*, the population is divided into strata and a random sample is chosen from each stratum. Examples of such strata are geographical locations, age groups and factories. This method has the advantage of ensuring that there are sufficient sample members in each stratum (for example, in each age group) to ensure information can be obtained on each stratum, as well as providing a basis for overall estimates for the whole sample.

Cluster sampling

Getting our data by taking a simple random sample of the population is much cheaper than carrying out a comprehensive survey of the whole population. However, random sampling and systematic sampling can be very expensive on occasions, and *cluster sampling* is sometimes used to reduce sampling costs by concentrating the sampling in a small area. For example, let us say that we are interested in finding out the electorate's view of a particular policy which is due to be implemented by the local authority. The voting population could be over 100,000 and we might be seeking a sample of 500. It could be very expensive to go and interview every 2,000th person on the electoral register as these individuals would probably live miles apart. Instead we might randomly select several clusters of voters – perhaps by postal districts – and then all the voters within the clusters would form our sample.

Another example is that you might be interested in seeking teachers' views on a new aspect of the curriculum. Schools would be the clusters and you would randomly select a number of schools and then survey all the teachers in each one. *Multi-stage sampling* is an extension of cluster sampling in which the sample is drawn randomly from within the clusters, instead of the whole cluster being sampled. Cluster sampling is often used for very large surveys.

Quota sampling

Quota sampling is a method often used for consumer market research. Typically, interviewers are given quotas for the people they must interview, to represent a typical cross-section of the population. Then, the interviewers might stand in a shopping centre and stop people 'randomly', until they have fulfilled their quotas. There are sometimes concerns that bias can creep in with this method, as the interviewer might either consciously or subconsciously seek out or avoid some individuals – for example, those dressed scruffily. It will depend on the purpose of the survey whether such a bias is important.

Focus groups

Focus groups are another method often used in consumer market research. They usually consist of groups of 8 to 12 people who are brought together to discuss a particular topic, such as features sought in new cars, or attitudes to health provision. They provide more in-depth information on expectations, needs, etc.

Convenience sampling

Convenience sampling is as the name suggests, a sample that is chosen for its convenience. For example, volunteers might be sought to participate in research on access for disabled people, or a professor might use his lecture class for some research.

Snowball sampling

Snowball sampling relies on existing sample members identifying other sample members. This is sometimes used when it is difficult to get a reliable population list, eg in research on street gangs or animal rights activists. Also, it may be helpful when it is difficult to persuade participants to take part in a survey and it is necessary to use the knowledge and contacts of existing sample members, eg in research on MPs, hospital consultants, etc.

POINT ESTIMATES

We explained at the beginning of this chapter that the purpose of sampling is to provide information about a population of interest from a small sample of that population. The types of information about the population that we are interested in might be the average value, the proportion or the standard deviation.

For example, suppose as part of a review of a new benefits package, we want information on the profile of employees who use the staff restaurant. Aspects of interest might be their age profile, salary profile, type of work, as well as information on the usage such as level of spend and preference for different types of food. The age profile could be used to provide information on the targeting and costs of different benefits packages. We might want to know, for example:

- the average age of all the employees using the staff restaurant
- the proportion of users who are under 30
- the variation in ages of users, measured by the standard deviation.

We would choose a sample using one of the (probabilistic) methods discussed earlier in this chapter and then work out from that sample the following statistics:

- the sample mean
- the sample proportions
- the sample standard deviation.

These sample statistics will be *point estimates* of the population statistics, that is of:

- the population mean
- the population proportion
- the population standard deviation.

It should be obvious that the information gained from the sample is unlikely to give an exact estimate, and a different sample would probably give slightly different results. To illustrate this point let us take a simple example, again based on employees who use the staff restaurant and their age – see Table 16.2.

We shall take two samples of 20 employees from the population of 100 employees, using the systematic sampling method. For the first sample we shall use as the starting point, employee number 4, and for the second sample, employee number 1. We pick every fifth employee for our samples, as shown in Table 16.3.

We can now calculate the following:

Population mean	=	39.9 years (by adding all the ages in the population and dividing by 100)
Sample mean from sample 1	=	39.5 years (by adding all the ages from sample 1 and dividing by 20)
Sample mean from sample 2	=	41.9 years (by adding all the ages from sample 2 and dividing by 20)

As you can see, the sample means give different estimates of the population mean. Usually, of course, we take only one sample and use it to calculate estimates of the population characteristics of interest. Then, what we need to know is how close our estimate is likely to be to the population characteristic we are trying to measure. To find this out we must understand a little about sampling distributions. We covered the groundwork in Chapter 15 when we introduced probability distributions, so persevere and you will be delighted with the simplicity of the technique.

Table 16.2 Ages of employees

17	42	23	48	29	52	31	59	38	62
63	39	34	57	54	27	23	46	44	19
45	16	22	49	27	54	34	57	62	37
19	45	50	21	27	52	57	34	39	64
62	37	59	33	27	53	47	23	16	43
62	59	54	49	44	19	24	29	34	39
20	45	25	50	30	55	35	60	40	65
26	34	37	42	44	37	33	27	25	28
52	48	47	43	41	40	37	29	29	32
31	34	37	46	44	51	47	33	24	54

Table 16.3 Two samples from a population of 100

Sample 1		Sample 2	
48	38	17	52
57	44	63	27
49	62	45	54
21	39	19	52
33	16	62	53
49	34	62	19
50	40	20	55
42	25	26	37
43	29	52	40
46	24	31	51

SAMPLING DISTRIBUTIONS AND CONFIDENCE LIMITS

As usual, it is easier to understand a concept by looking at an example. Suppose we are a mail order firm and we want to know more about our customers so that we can make our advertising more cost-effective. Suppose their income is of particular interest and we want to know:

- the average income of our customers
- the proportion of customers with incomes in excess of £25,000
- the range, or variation, in income.

Clearly the population of interest is all our customers who could number 10,000, 100,000 or even more. How best to go about the exercise? The first step would be to choose a sample of say 100 customers, and obtain data on their incomes. As we have explained before, it would be possible to go on choosing different samples of 100 customers, and each time get slightly different values for:

- the sample mean
- the sample proportion
- the sample standard deviation.

Let us suppose the sampling exercise is carried out four times, using the same sampling method, and we find that the sample means (in this case, average income) are as shown in Table 16.4.

Table 16.4 Sample means from sampling exercises

Sample number	Sample mean (average salary)
1	£15,014
2	£15,450
3	£14,995
4	£15,222

If we took, say 200 of these samples, we would find that we could prepare a frequency distribution, as we did in Chapter 12 – see Table 16.5.

Table 16.5 Frequency distribution of sample means

Mean income (£)	Frequency	Relative frequency	
14,801–14,900	10	0.05	5%
14,901–15,000	22	0.11	11%
15,001–15,100	38	0.19	19%
15,101–15,200	50	0.25	25%
15,201–15,300	44	0.22	22%
15,301–15,400	24	0.12	12%
15,401–15,500	12	0.06	6%
Total	200	1.00	100%

We could then go on to draw a histogram as we did in Chapter 13 (see Figure 16.1). This histogram gives the *sampling distribution* of the sample mean. In other words it describes the way in which the average income, calculated from the 200 different samples of 100 customers, varies because of variations in the different samples. Using a sample proportion would give a similarly shaped distribution. Each in turn would be the sampling distribution of that sample statistic.

Let us continue with our example of average customer income. Each time we take another sample we get another outcome (as explained in Chapter 15) of the sample income. Thus the

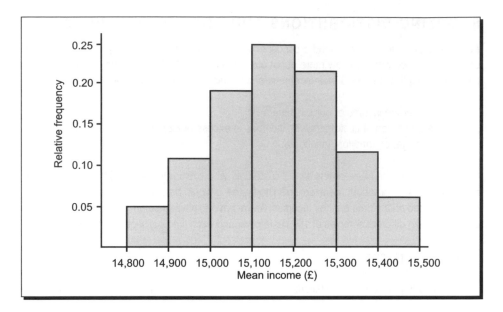

Figure 16.1 Relative frequency histogram of values of mean income from 200 samples

average income statistic is a random variable (another term from Chapter 15) with a distribution, and it is possible to work out the mean and the standard deviation of the sampling distribution of the random variable average income. So, how does this help us to answer the question 'How good is our estimate?'

A very useful and important theorem in statistics is the *central limit theorem.* This tells us that:

> *If simple random samples of size n are drawn from a population with mean μ and standard deviation σ, the sampling distribution of the sample mean, $\bar{x}$,approaches a normal distribution with mean μ and standard deviation $\sigma/\sqrt{n}$ as the sample size becomes large.*
> (Based on Anderson et al 2001)

This is important because it means that we can apply the very useful properties of the normal distribution that we discussed in Chapter 15 to the distribution of the sample mean. In practice, for any sample of 30 or more, the central limit theorem can apply. If the population distribution itself is known to be normal, then the sampling distribution of the sample mean can also be assumed to be normal for sample sizes below 30 as well.

Now, you will recall from Chapter 15 the very useful characteristics of a normal distribution that:

1. 68.26% of the time, a normal random variable assumes a value within plus or minus one standard deviation of its mean, that is, 68.26% of the time $\bar{x}$ falls in the range:

$$\mu \pm \frac{\sigma}{\sqrt{n}}$$

2. 95.44% of the time, a normal random variable assumes a value within plus or minus two standard deviations of its mean, that is, 95.44% of the time $\bar{x}$ falls in the range:

$$\mu \pm \frac{2\sigma}{\sqrt{n}}$$

3. 99.72% of the time, a normal random variable assumes a value within plus or minus three standard deviations of its mean, that is, 99.72% of the time $\bar{x}$ falls in the range:

$$\mu \pm \frac{3\sigma}{\sqrt{n}}$$

Let us look rather more closely at case 2. This can be expressed a little differently as: there is a 95.44% chance, or 0.9544 probability, that $\bar{x}$ falls in the range:

$$\mu \pm \frac{2\sigma}{\sqrt{n}}$$

It is shown by the shaded area in Figure 16.2. Rather than a 95.44% chance, it is more convenient to talk in terms of a 95% chance, or 0.95 probability, of $\bar{x}$ falling in a particular interval. It can be shown that there is a 95% chance (rather than 95.44%) or a 0.95 probability of the sample mean $\bar{x}$ falling in the range:

$$\mu \pm \frac{1.96\sigma}{\sqrt{n}} \quad \text{(1.96 rather than 2)}$$

Similarly, there is a 99% chance or a 0.99 probability of the sample mean $\bar{x}$ falling in the range:

$$\mu \pm \frac{2.58\sigma}{\sqrt{n}} \quad \text{(2.58 rather than 3)}$$

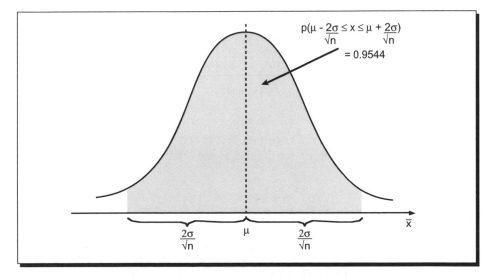

Figure 16.2 Normal distribution of $\bar{x}$ with mean μ and standard deviation $\sigma / \sqrt{n}$

In most cases the population standard deviation σ is not known and the sample standard deviation s is used to estimate it. (This may be seen as a bit of a fiddle, but please accept that it is quite all right!) Then it can be seen from the above that there is a 95% chance, or a 0.95 probability that x̄ will fall in the range:

$$\mu \pm \frac{1.96s}{\sqrt{n}}$$

Intuitively, we can rewrite this relationship as there being a 95% chance, or a 0.95 probability, that μ will fall in the range:

$$\bar{x} \pm \frac{1.96s}{\sqrt{n}}$$

(In repeated sampling, each sample generating its own confidence limits, 95% will include μ. Don't worry if you can't see this – just accept our word for it.)

These are known as the *95% confidence limits* (or *confidence interval*) for the population mean, μ.

Similarly $\bar{x} \pm \dfrac{2.58s}{\sqrt{n}}$ are the *99% confidence limits* (or *confidence interval*) for the population mean, μ.

Enough of all this theory, let us look at an example. An organisation sends out a large number of small packages, and an important part of its costs relates to the courier service it uses for distribution. It needs to negotiate terms with the courier service, and to do this it needs to establish the average weight of its parcels and the range of confidence limits, be they 95%, 99% or whatever. Assume a random sample of 30 packages is chosen, with the weights set out in Table 16.6.

Table 16.6 Average package weights (grams)

160	179	188	180	188	195
185	190	162	165	183	199
167	192	186	181	194	172
182	166	187	172	168	181
175	176	195	161	184	172

The sample mean x̄ = $\dfrac{\text{sum of the weights}}{30}$ = 179.5

We are now going to work out the confidence limits. First we work out the sample standard deviation, either manually or using the computer (see Chapters 14 and 22):

$$\text{Sample variance } s^2 = \sum_{i=1}^{n} \frac{(x_i - \bar{x})^2}{n-1}$$

$$= 122.9$$

Sample standard $= \sqrt{122.9}$
deviation s

$= 11.1$

Therefore, we can be 95% confident that the population mean lies within the range:

$$\bar{x} \pm \frac{1.96s}{\sqrt{n}}$$

$$= 179.5 \pm \frac{1.96 \times 11.1}{\sqrt{30}}$$

$$= 179.5 \pm 4.0$$

$$= 175.5 \text{ to } 183.5$$

In other words we can be 95% confident that the average package weight will fall within the range 175.5 to 183.5 grams (see Figure 16.3).

Now, after all that theory, we begin to see the usefulness of understanding the sampling distribution of the sample mean. It enables us to give, with confidence, a range around our estimate within which the population mean will fall.

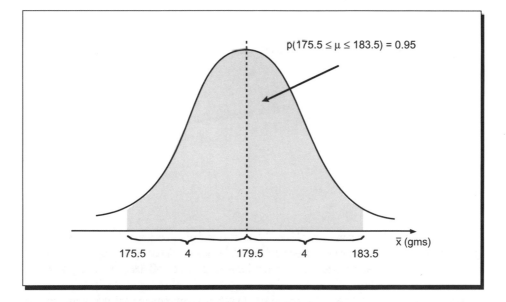

Figure 16.3 95% confidence limits for mean package weights

Similarly we can go through exactly the same process for the population proportion p. The 95% confidence limits for the population proportion p are:

$$\bar{p} \pm 1.96 \sqrt{\frac{\bar{p}(1-\bar{p})}{n}} \quad \text{where } \bar{p} \text{ is the sample proportion}$$

The formula can also be used for $\bar{p}$ expressed in the form of a percentage as follows:

$$\bar{p} \pm 1.96 \sqrt{\frac{\bar{p}(100-\bar{p})}{n}}$$

CALCULATING SAMPLE SIZE

Now that we have some measure of the accuracy or *precision* of the estimate of our population mean, we can go on to look at another very important decision in sampling, the sample size. *We can calculate the sample size that is required to give a certain width of confidence limit.*

In the package weight example, we calculated with 95% confidence that the population mean lay within plus or minus 4 grams of the sample mean of 179.5. Suppose now we decide that we want to be 95% confident that the population mean lies within a range of plus or minus 3 grams of the sample mean, ie giving a *sampling error* of 3 grams. We can calculate the required sample size as follows:

$$3 = \frac{1.96s}{\sqrt{n}} \quad \text{(see page 176)}$$

We can manipulate this equation to isolate n by multiplying each side by $\sqrt{n}$ and dividing each side by 3, as follows:

$$\sqrt{n} = \frac{1.96 \times 11.1}{3} \quad \text{(s = 11.1 from page 176)}$$

$$= 7.252$$

Squaring both sides gives:

$$n = 7.252^2$$

$$= 52.6$$

Rounding this up, it means that we would need a sample size of 53 packages to be 95% sure of this greater precision that the population mean will fall within plus or minus 3 grams of the new sample mean (rather than the sample size of 30, which achieved a precision of plus or minus 4 grams).

Similarly, we can go on to work out a sample size to achieve a maximum particular sampling error at the 95% confidence level, for a population proportion, as follows:

$$n = \frac{1.96^2 \times \overline{p}(1 - \overline{p})}{(\text{sampling error})^2}$$

Note that:

1. All the above formulae for confidence limits and sample sizes depend on calculating the value of the sample standard deviation. The formulae used for these are based on the sample being selected by simple random sampling. If you are using a different method, such as stratified random sampling, the sample standard deviation is calculated differently – seek advice from a friendly statistician!

2. Also, where there is a finite population and the sample size is more than 5% of that population, it is necessary to make what is known an a finite population adjustment, when calculating confidence limits and sample sizes. It involves applying the factor:

$$\sqrt{\frac{N - n}{N - 1}}$$

to the standard deviations of $\overline{x}$ and $\overline{p}$.

All the examples in this book assume that it is not necessary to make a finite population adjustment.

CONCLUSION

We hope that you now have a good understanding of the basic concepts of sampling. Sampling is a vital tool for gathering information. It has enormous power, but must be used with care and understanding. In the next chapter we go on to look at significance and hypothesis tests, which test the significance of our sample results.

REVIEW QUESTIONS

1. A survey of student loans based on a sample of 100 final-year students at a particular university showed an average loan of £8,540 and a sample standard deviation of £1,400.
   a. Calculate 95% and 99% confidence limits for the population average and comment on the results.
   b. What sample size would you need to achieve a confidence interval of ± £150 at the 95% confidence level? Explain your result.

2. An organisation has surveyed 150 of its customers to find out their views on customer service. 66% commented that the quality of service at the point of sale was excellent and 48% commented that the quality of after-sales care was excellent. You need to report the results back to the MD. The MD may ask for details of how the precision of the results could be improved in later surveys. (This issue is less straightforward than for a sample mean; think about it and then read the answer!)

Hypothesis testing

CHAPTER OBJECTIVES

When you have studied this chapter, you will be able to:

- explain the purpose of hypothesis testing
- define the different types of error
- use a range of hypothesis tests including chi-squared tests
- explain the application of statistical process control.

INTRODUCTION

In the previous chapter we saw how we could draw conclusions about a population from a sample using the technique of statistical inference. We focused our attention on the use of samples for estimating such measures of the population as its mean and proportions of the population possessing a given characteristic. Another major use of sampling is to test hypotheses about the population itself. This technique is frequently adopted in scientific work – for example, testing drugs in pharmaceutical research.

However, hypothesis testing is also of value in the business world, particularly for quality control. Suppose a firm makes components – in this case, bolts. It is very important that these bolts are of a particular size or very close to it, let us say 3 cm in length, or they will be rejected by the customer. Let us use again the Greek letter μ to define the mean or average size for the population of all bolts manufactured.

If $\mu = 3$ cm, there is no problem.

If $\mu \neq 3$ cm, there is a problem which the firm will have to address.

NULL AND ALTERNATIVE HYPOTHESES

We tackle this exercise by first defining the *null hypothesis* and the *alternative hypothesis*. The null hypothesis (referred to as H_0) is the tentative assumption about the population characteristic to be tested. The alternative hypothesis (usually referred to as H_1) covers all other plausible states of the population characteristic. In the example:

H_0: $\mu = 3$ cm

H_1: $\mu \neq 3$ cm

The next step is to choose a sample of, say, 50 bolts and measure them. If the sample results are consistent with the null hypothesis, then we are said to *accept* H_0. However, if the sample results differ significantly from the null hypothesis then we reject H_0 and conclude that H_1, the alternative hypothesis, is true. But what do we mean by the interesting phrase 'differ significantly'?

Before we discuss the interesting and key concept of significance, we need to explain about the different hypothesis tests. There are three types:

1. One type is that already covered in the earlier example, where the item either is the correct size or it is not, ie both oversized and undersized bolts will be rejected by the customer. This type of test is expressed as:

    $H_0: \mu = \mu_v$

    $H_1: \mu \neq \mu_v$

    where μ is the mean of the population as a whole and μ_v is the specific value being tested.

2. Another type is where the acceptable limit is greater than or equal to a certain specification and the customer will reject an item that is less than the specification. This type of test is expressed as:

    $H_0: \mu \geq \mu_v$

    $H_1: \mu < \mu_v$

    An example of this type is a firm making light bulbs which are guaranteed to give 100 hours of life. In order to meet the specification, and not contravene the Trade Descriptions Act, it is important that the light bulbs have an average life of 100 hours or more, that is $\mu \geq 100$. The test is then expressed as:

    $H_0: \mu \geq 100$

    $H_1: \mu < 100$

3. The third type is where to meet a specification, an item must not be greater than a certain level. This type of test is expressed as:

    $H_0: \mu \leq \mu_v$

    $H_1: \mu > \mu_v$

    An example of this is in food manufacturing, where the level of a certain chemical additive in the product must not be greater than, say, 25 parts per million, that is $\mu \leq 25$ ppm. The test is then expressed as:

    $H_0: \mu \leq 25$

    $H_1: \mu > 25$

The first type of test (number 1) is called a *two-tailed test*, and the other two types of test (numbers 2 and 3) are called *one-tailed tests*. This is another set of curious terms, you may think, but in fact they refer to the 'tails' of our old friend the normal distribution. The tails are the sections at either end of the distribution covering those extreme values that are distant from the mean. More of this later because we now need to say a few words about the errors involved in hypothesis testing.

TYPES OF ERROR

We would like to think that the test of bolts, light bulbs or whatever would always lead us to accept the null hypothesis, H_0, when it is true and reject it when it is false. However, as we are sure you now appreciate, sampling is not an exact science and there are errors involved. The possible situations that can occur are shown in Table 17.1.

Table 17.1 Types of error

	Accept H_0	Reject H_0
H_0 true	Correct decision	Type 1 error
H_0 false	Type 2 error	Correct decision

As you can see from this simple table, there are two possible types of error:

- Type 1 error – which occurs when we reject H_0 even when it is true.
- Type 2 error – which occurs when we accept H_0 even when it is false.

In a sense, hypothesis testing is rather similar to the situation in a criminal court where:

H_0: the defendant is innocent
H_1: the defendant is guilty.

The defendant is considered innocent until proven guilty, and the jury is most concerned to ensure it does not find an innocent person guilty, that is, does not make a Type 1 error. In fact, it is the Type 1 errors that establish the significance level of the test.

Traditionally, and we shall follow this convention in this chapter:

α is defined as the probability of making a Type 1 error.

β is defined as the probability of making a Type 2 error.

TWO-TAILED HYPOTHESIS TESTING

Let us go back to the example of the firm manufacturing and testing bolts. Our hypothesis test is expressed as follows:

H_0: $\mu = 3$ cm

H_1: $\mu \neq 3$ cm

We take a sample size of 50 bolts, and let us assume the sample average $\bar{x}$ is 2.95 cm and the sample standard deviation s is 0.25 cm. We decide to set the Type 1 error, α, at 0.05: that is, we are content with a 5% chance of accepting H_0 when it is false. As the sample size is over 30 units, we can assume that the sample mean has a normal distribution and test whether this sample mean comes from a population with the characteristic $\mu = 3$ cm.

We want the confidence interval (recall the discussion in Chapter 16) to be such that there is only a 0.05 probability that it will not include the population mean. Look at Figure 17.1.

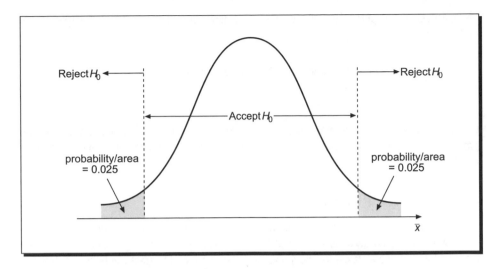

Figure 17.1 Two-tailed hypothesis test, with Type 1 error, $\alpha = 0.05$

We reject H_0 if the population mean μ falls in the shaded areas, that is, in either of the two tails which each have a probability of 0.025 and which together give a total Type 1 error of 0.05. In other words, we accept H_0 if μ falls in the range:

$$\bar{x} \pm \frac{1.96s}{\sqrt{n}} \quad \text{(95\% confidence interval from page 176)}$$

$$= 2.95 \pm \frac{1.96 \times 0.25}{\sqrt{50}}$$

$$= 2.95 \pm \frac{0.49}{7.071}$$

$$= 2.95 \pm 0.07$$

$$= 2.88 \text{ to } 3.02$$

Since the hypothesised population mean of 3 cm lies within this interval, we accept H_0: that is, we accept the null hypothesis. If, on the other hand the sample mean had been 2.9 cm, the confidence interval would have been 2.83 to 2.97 (2.9 ± 0.07) and we would have rejected the null hypothesis, as the hypothesised population mean of 3 cm lies outside this confidence interval of the sample. From Figure 17.1 you will readily see why this is called a two-tailed test! (NB In practice μ is fixed, and the confidence interval changes from sample to sample.)

The same principles and approach apply if you want to carry out a hypothesis test on a population proportion. For example, if we set out the test as follows:

H_0: $p = p_v$ where p_v = the particular population proportion we want to test

H_1: $p \neq p_v$

Then, we would accept H_0 at the 95% confidence or significance level, that is with a Type 1 error of 0.05, if p_V falls in the range:

$$\overline{p} \pm 1.96 \sqrt{\frac{\overline{p}(1-\overline{p})}{n}} \quad \text{where } \overline{p} \text{ is the sample proportion and } n \text{ the sample size}$$

We have concentrated on the most useful type of hypothesis test, the two-tailed test. Very similar procedures apply to the one-tailed test, but in this case we are only concerned about one tail of the distribution.

STATISTICAL PROCESS CONTROL

The statistical technique described earlier has been developed to provide a very useful mechanism for monitoring quality control – the *statistical process control chart*. This is simply a chart (see Figure 17.2) that has at its centre line the value of the variable of interest when the process is in control. In the example discussed earlier, the process is making bolts and when it is in control the length of the bolt is 3 cm – so the centre line would be set at 3 cm. The two lines labelled UCL (upper control limit) and LCL (lower control limit) set the limits for deciding when the process is out of control.

As samples are taken, the average value of the bolts is calculated and logged on the chart. As long as the results are within the limits, there is no need for action. However, if a value falls outside the limits, the process must be examined and adjusted – perhaps the machines reset. As you may have guessed, the limits are our old friends the confidence limits of the sample mean and are usually set at the 99.72% level, that is, $\pm 3s / \sqrt{n}$ (where s is the sample standard deviation and n the sample size). There are variations on this approach which focus on the range rather than the standard deviation, and also where the range of the sample rather than the sample mean is used as the measure of interest.

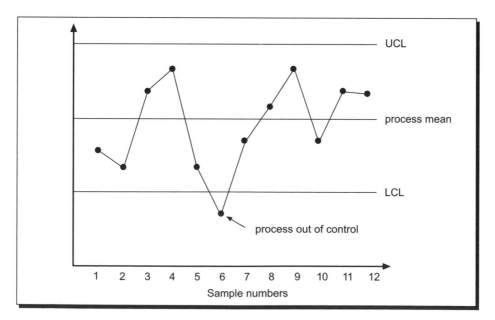

Figure 17.2 Statistical process control chart

TWO-POPULATION INFERENCE (INDEPENDENT SAMPLES)

Up until now we have considered only situations which involve one population – in the above examples, the population of all bolts manufactured by the firm. However, in many practical decision-making situations we are dealing with two different populations – usually because we want to compare them with each other. For example, we might want to compare the mean salary for female employees with the mean salary for male employees to test how well our equal opportunities policy is working.

Basically we follow exactly the same procedure as before. However this time we are interested in the difference between the two sample means. Taking the equal pay example, our hypothesis is that there is no difference in male or female salaries and can be expressed as:

$$H_0: \mu_1 - \mu_2 = 0$$ where μ_1 and μ_2 are the population means of the male

$$H_1: \mu_1 - \mu_2 \neq 0$$ and female employees

This is a two-tailed test.

Let us suppose the test is carried out by randomly sampling the male and female populations of employees, and gives the results in Table 17.2.

Table 17.2 Results of a two-population test

Male employees	Female employees
$n_1 = 70$	$n_2 = 80$
$\overline{X}_1 = £15,800$	$\overline{X}_2 = £15,200$
$s_1 = £1250$	$s_2 = £1000$

This time we shall set the probability of a Type 1 error as 0.01. This means that we are willing to accept a 1% chance of rejecting the null hypothesis even when it is true.

It can be shown (please simply accept our word for this!) that the 99% confidence interval for $\overline{X}_1 - \overline{X}_2$ is

$$(\overline{X}_1 - \overline{X}_2) \pm 2.58 \sqrt{ \frac{s_1^2}{n_1} + \frac{s_2^2}{n_2} }$$

$$= (15,800 - 15,200) \pm 2.58 \sqrt{ \frac{1250^2}{70} + \frac{1000^2}{80} }$$

$$= 600 \pm 2.58 \times 187$$

$$= 600 \pm 482$$

$$= 118 \text{ to } 1082$$

Our null hypothesis, H_0, is $\mu_1 - \mu_2 = 0$. As the value of $\mu_1 - \mu_2$ under our null hypothesis (that is, zero) falls outside the range 118 to 1082 calculated above, we reject the null hypothesis. Given the results of the sample, we cannot be sure that our equal opportunities policy is effective at this point in time. Such policies can often take time to show their effects, so one possible conclusion is that the equal opportunities policy has not yet worked and the organisation still has some way to go on this issue.

Pragmatists among us might ask what is the point of all these calculations when we can see from the results of the samples (mean salaries for men and women of £15,800 and £15,200 respectively) that men are better paid than women? What we, as statisticians, are interested in is whether the difference between the two sample means is *significant*. By significant we mean: is the difference between the means likely to represent an actual difference in salaries between the populations of male and female employees, or is the difference simply a result of errors due to sampling?

Exactly the same procedure can be followed in one-tailed tests: for example, to test whether the average profit per acre for wheat on organic farms is greater than for wheat grown on farms using pesticides. Similarly we could use these approaches when dealing with proportions rather than means. For example, continuing the equal opportunities policy example, it could be used to compare the proportions of males and females at different managerial levels.

So far we have discussed how to set up a hypothesis test by defining null and alternative hypotheses. We discussed the two types of error that can occur, but concentrated on the most important error, the Type 1 error, which is the error of rejecting H_0 when it is true. We have shown how to carry out a hypothesis test using the confidence limit approach, and discussed the two different types of tests – two-tailed and one-tailed. Finally, we looked at the situation where two populations were involved.

All the hypothesis tests covered so far involved testing means and proportions. We shall now look at two rather different types of hypothesis test.

CHI-SQUARED TESTS

These hypothesis tests are as straightforward as the ones we discussed earlier, but they are used in different situations. We shall look at two types of test – *goodness of fit* and *independence tests* – and because they are based on a probability distribution called a chi-squared (χ^2) distribution, they are called *chi-squared tests*.

Goodness of fit

There are various 'goodness of fit' tests for different types of populations. However, the most commonly used is the test for what is known as a *multinomial population*. This is a population where each member of the population is assigned to one, and only one, of several classes or categories.

Let us take an example of where a goodness of fit test might be used for a multinomial population. Suppose you are a company that sells a cat food called Paws. You are about to embark on a major advertising campaign and will want to know whether it has a significant effect on your market share. Suppose there are three other major brands of cat food product and the market shares before the advertising campaign are as follows:

Your brand	Competitors' brands		
Paws	Yummy	Furries	Cat-eats
30%	15%	40%	15%

Following the advertising campaign you commission a survey of 200 cat owners, who are asked which cat food they buy. The results are as follows:

Your brand	Competitors' brands		
Paws	Yummy	Furries	Cat-eats
80	20	70	30

The null hypothesis is that the advertising campaign has had no effect and therefore:

$$H_0: p_{PAWS} = 0.3, p_{YUMMY} = 0.15, p_{FURRIES} = 0.4, p_{CAT\text{-}EATS} = 0.15$$

The alternative hypothesis is that the population has been affected by the advertising campaign and therefore:

$$H_0: p_{PAWS} \neq 0.3, p_{YUMMY} \neq 0.15, p_{FURRIES} \neq 0.4, p_{CAT\text{-}EATS} \neq 0.15$$

The test looks at differences between the observed results or frequencies from the sample and the expected results or frequencies if the null hypothesis is true, ie if the market shares are unchanged. The expected results are calculated by applying the original market share proportions to the sample of 200 cat owners. This gives the following expected results:

Your brand	Competitors' brands		
Paws	Yummy	Furries	Cat-eats
200×0.3	200×0.15	200×0.4	200×0.15
= 60	= 30	= 80	= 30

It follows that the bigger the differences between the observed and the expected results, the less likely it is that the null hypothesis is true. The statistic χ^2 is computed using the formula:

$$\chi^2 = \sum_{i=1}^{k} \frac{(o_i - e_i)^2}{e_i}$$

where
o_i = observed frequencies for class i
e_i = expected frequency for class i
k = number of classes

In our example there are four classes (the four brands) and we work out the statistic as follows:

$$\chi^2 = \frac{(80-60)^2}{60} + \frac{(20-30)^2}{30} + \frac{(70-80)^2}{80} + \frac{(30-30)^2}{30}$$

$$= \frac{400}{60} + \frac{100}{30} + \frac{100}{80} + \frac{0}{30}$$

$$= 6.7 + 3.3 + 1.3$$
$$= 11.3$$

If we took lots of samples and calculated their χ^2 values by comparing their observed results with their expected results as above, the statistic would be shown to have a χ^2 distribution with what is known as $k-1$ degrees of freedom. In our case $k = 4$, so the number of degrees of freedom is 3. The only requirement is that generally the minimum size of a class/category is 5. Table 17.3 sets out the χ^2 distribution.

Table 17.3 Chi-squared (χ^2) distribution

α = area or probability

d.f./α	0.250	0.100	0.050	0.025	0.010	0.005	0.001
1	1.32	2.71	3.84	5.02	6.63	7.88	10.8
2	2.77	4.61	5.99	7.38	9.21	10.6	13.8
3	4.11	6.25	7.81	9.35	11.3	12.8	16.3
4	5.39	7.78	9.49	11.1	13.3	14.9	18.5
5	6.63	9.24	11.1	12.8	15.1	16.7	20.5
6	7.84	10.6	12.6	14.4	16.8	18.5	22.5
7	9.04	12.0	14.1	16.0	18.5	20.3	24.3
8	10.2	13.4	15.5	17.5	20.1	22.0	26.1
9	11.4	14.7	16.9	19.0	21.7	23.6	27.9
10	12.5	16.0	18.3	20.5	23.2	25.2	29.6
11	13.7	17.3	19.7	21.9	24.7	26.8	31.3
12	14.8	18.5	21.0	23.3	26.2	28.3	32.9
13	16.0	19.8	22.4	24.7	27.7	29.8	34.5
14	17.1	21.1	23.7	26.1	29.1	31.3	36.1
15	18.2	22.3	25.0	27.5	30.6	32.8	37.7
16	19.4	23.5	26.3	28.8	32.0	34.3	39.3
17	20.5	24.8	27.6	30.2	33.4	35.7	40.8
18	21.6	26.0	28.9	31.5	34.8	37.2	42.3
19	22.7	27.2	30.1	32.9	36.2	38.6	43.8
20	23.8	28.4	31.4	34.2	37.6	40.0	45.3
21	24.9	29.6	32.7	35.5	38.9	41.4	46.8
22	26.0	30.8	33.9	36.8	40.3	42.8	48.3
23	27.1	32.0	35.2	38.1	41.6	44.2	49.7
24	28.2	33.2	36.4	39.4	43.0	45.6	51.2
25	29.3	34.4	37.7	40.6	44.3	46.9	52.6
26	30.4	35.6	38.9	41.9	45.6	48.3	54.1
27	31.5	36.7	40.1	43.2	47.0	49.6	55.5
28	32.6	37.9	41.3	44.5	48.3	51.0	56.9
29	33.7	39.1	42.6	45.7	49.6	52.3	58.3
30	34.8	40.3	43.8	47.0	50.9	53.7	59.7
40	45.6	51.8	55.8	59.3	63.7	66.8	73.4
50	56.3	63.2	67.5	71.4	76.2	79.5	86.7
60	67.0	74.4	79.1	83.3	88.4	92.0	99.6
70	77.6	85.5	90.5	95.0	100.0	104.0	112.0
80	88.1	96.6	102.0	107.0	112.0	116.0	125.0
90	98.6	108.0	113.0	118.0	124.0	128.0	137.0
100	109.0	118.0	124.0	130.0	136.0	140.0	149.0

The χ^2 distribution is a family of distributions where each is distinguished by a single parameter, its degree(s) of freedom. Entries in the table give χ^2_α values, where α is the Type 1 error or the area/probability in the upper tail of the χ^2 distribution. For example, for $\alpha = 0.050$ and with 8 degrees of freedom $\chi^2_{0.05} = 15.5$

Let us see how we use the table. First, as for the earlier hypothesis tests, we must choose our significance level (Type 1 error): let us choose α = 0.05. We reject the null hypothesis if the differences between observed and expected frequencies are large, that is, when the value of χ^2 is large. Therefore our rejection area of 0.05 is the upper tail of the distribution. In our case there are four classes (k = 4) and therefore there are three degrees of freedom. From the table we look across row 3 and down column 0.050 and we find:

$$\chi^2_{0.05} = 7.81$$

As the value of χ^2 in the cat food example, 11.3, is greater than the value of 7.81 from the table, it falls in the shaded area of the χ^2 distribution shown in Table 17.3, and therefore we reject the null hypothesis. This tells us that the market structure has changed, but not how or why. However, from looking at the results, it can be seen that the Paws brand has gained at the expense of both the Yummies and Furries brands, with the Cat-eats share being unaffected. Therefore, it would be reasonable to conclude that the advertising campaign has been a success.

'Well', says the cynic, 'we could have told you that by simple observation of the sample results.' 'Possibly', says the statistician, 'but you do not know whether the differences observed in the sample results are merely caused by chance errors resulting from the sampling process. This test enables us to say that the result is significant at the 5% level.' Hence these tests are often referred to as *significance tests* – they are testing the significance of the results. You can see where the name 'goodness of fit' comes from as well – because what we are testing is whether our observed (from the sample) results are a good fit with the results we would expect if our null hypothesis is true.

We now go on to look at another application of the χ^2 test, the test of independence.

Test of independence

As the name suggests, a *test of independence* is a test for checking the independence of two variables. For example, you might want to see whether salary or career progression was independent of the gender of employees. You might wish to find out whether consumer preference for free-range eggs was independent of age, or whether production was independent of the day of the week, etc. Let us take a very simple example. Suppose you want to determine whether or not there are differences in preference for full-cream milk, semi-skimmed milk and skimmed milk between the under-25 and 25-and-over age groups.

Our hypotheses are as follows:

H_0: milk preference is independent of whether the milk consumer is under 25 or 25 and over

H_1: milk preference is not independent of whether the milk consumer is under 25 or 25 and over

The next step is to carry out a survey of, say, 300 milk drinkers. The results are shown in Table 17.4.

Table 17.4 Results of a survey of milk drinkers

Consumer	Full cream	Semi-skimmed	Skimmed	Total
Under 25	20	30	50	100
25 and over	50	80	70	200
Total	70	110	120	300

These are the observed results. Just as in the test for goodness of fit, we need to work out the expected results if the null hypothesis is true. If there are no preference differences between the two age groups, then we could work out the expected proportions from the total results as follows:

proportion preference for full cream	= 70/300	= 0.23
proportion preference for semi-skimmed	= 110/300	= 0.37
proportion preference for skimmed	= 120/300	= 0.4

If we then apply these proportions to the totals for each age group, we arrive at the expected frequencies in Table 17.5.

Table 17.5 Expected frequencies for milk drinkers

Consumer	Full cream	Semi-skimmed	Skimmed	Total
Under 25	23	37	40	100
25 and over	46	74	80	200
Total	69*	109*	120	300

*due to rounding errors.

It is helpful for the arithmetic to combine the observed results and the expected results into one table (see Table 17.6). (A table such as this which combines observed and expected frequencies is called a *contingency table*.)

Table 17.6 Combined observed and expected results

Consumer	Full cream	Semi-skimmed	Skimmed
Under 25	20 (23)	30 (37)	50 (40)
25 and over	50 (46)	80 (74)	70 (80)

(observed values shown first, expected values in brackets)

We then compute a similar statistic as before using the formula:

$$\chi^2 = \sum_i \sum_j \frac{(o_{ij} - e_{ij})^2}{e_{ij}}$$

where o_{ij} = observed result for row i and column j in the contingency table, eg o_{11} = 20
        e_{ij} = expected result for row i and column j in the contingency table, eg e_{11} = 23

This looks very complicated, but all it means is that we are working out the formula:

$$\frac{(\text{observed} - \text{expected})^2}{\text{expected}}$$

and summing over all the classes or entries in the table.

In our example:

$$\chi^2 = \frac{(20-23)^2}{20} + \frac{(30-37)^2}{37} + \frac{(50-40)^2}{40} + \frac{(50-46)^2}{46} + \frac{(80-74)^2}{74} + \frac{(70-80)^2}{80}$$

$$= \frac{9}{23} + \frac{49}{37} + \frac{100}{40} + \frac{16}{46} + \frac{36}{74} + \frac{100}{80}$$

$$= 6.30$$

This statistic can again be shown to have the χ^2 distribution if the null hypothesis is true. The number of degrees of freedom are worked out as follows:

(number of rows − 1) × (number of columns − 1)

In our example:

$$1 \times 2 = 2$$

We are now ready to test for independence, and we again decide to choose the 5% significance level. As before, we will reject the null hypothesis for large values of χ^2. From Table 17.3, looking along row 2 and down column 0.050:

$$\chi^2_{0.05} = 5.99$$

As our computed χ^2, 6.3, is greater than 5.99 we reject the null hypothesis and conclude that the preference for different types of milk is not independent of whether the consumer is under 25 years or over 25 years of age. Again, strictly speaking, we can draw no further conclusions about the relationship. However, observation of the contingency table shows us that a greater proportion of the older age group appears to have a preference for the full cream and semi-skimmed milks, whereas a greater proportion of the younger age group has a preference for skimmed milk.

This is another simple but useful test. The only rules that we have to remember are that the observed results are always expressed as whole numbers – they are frequencies of occurrence – and that the size of each class (for example under-25, 25-and-over) should generally be greater than 5. When dealing with a large number of classes and approaching this minimum class size, a good option is to combine some of the classes. Also, we must remember that the test only indicates whether there is independence or not between classes. It cannot and does not tell us anything about the nature or causes of the relationship. However, it is usually quite easy to deduce some simple conclusions about the relationship by looking at the contingency table.

CONCLUSION

We have covered a range of different hypothesis and significance tests to suit quite a wide variety of situations. Although they sound rather daunting at first, we hope we have shown that once you understand the principles, they are in fact very easy and straightforward to carry out.

REVIEW QUESTIONS

1. A study of the mean parking times in a multi-storey car park showed that the mean length of stay was 175 minutes. The car park was subsequently refurbished and the charges increased. The owner would like to find out whether these changes have had any impact on the mean parking time. A random sample of 100 cars shows a mean parking time of 160 minutes and sample standard deviation of 55 minutes. Set up the appropriate hypothesis test using a 5% significance level, and comment on the results.

2. A kitchen retailer claims that the mean time from placing an order to completion of the kitchen is 7.8 weeks. An independent researcher wants to check this claim. Set up the appropriate hypothesis test and explain how it can be used to comment on the retailer's claim.

3. A survey of employees carried out a year ago showed overall satisfaction levels with the service offered by the HR department as follows:

Very good	Good	Poor	Very poor
21%	45%	30%	4%

In this year's survey of 250 employees the results were as follows:

Very good	Good	Poor	Very poor
55	135	52	8

Use a goodness of fit test to see whether opinions have changed and comment on the results. (Use a significance level of 1%.)

4. Three suppliers provide the following data on defective parts:

Supplier	Good	Minor defect	Major defect
A	90	3	7
B	170	18	7
C	135	6	9

Test for independence and comment on the results.

Regression and correlation

CHAPTER OBJECTIVES

When you have studied this chapter, you will be able to:

- explain the use of regression analysis and correlation
- interpret the output from simple linear regression analysis
- explain how the use of this technique can be extended to more complex problems.

INTRODUCTION

'Oh dear', we hear you say, 'not another set of incomprehensible terms!' However, they are easily explained and provide very useful tools for the decision-maker. As a manager/specialist you may often find yourself faced with drawing conclusions or making recommendations based on the relationship between different variables. For example, as an HR manager you might be interested in looking at whether absenteeism is related to a factor such as age, hours worked, distance from home to work, etc and therefore decide on appropriate measures to tackle the issue. As a marketing manager, you might be interested to see the extent to which sales are related to expenditure on advertising, and use this information to make decisions on the advertising budget, and so on. Regression analysis and correlation are techniques which can help us all in this area of decision-making.

REGRESSION ANALYSIS

Regression analysis is a technique that enables us to describe the relationship between variables using a mathematical equation. In regression analysis there are two types of variables, described as dependent and independent:

- The *dependent variable* is the variable being predicted by the relationship; in the above examples, absenteeism and sales are dependent variables.
- The *independent variable* is the variable which is being used to predict the dependent variable. For example, age, hours worked and distance from home to work are independent variables used to predict absenteeism, and money spent on advertising is an independent variable used to predict sales.

In the first section we are going to look at the simplest form of regression analysis, *simple linear regression*. This is used in situations where there are only two variables – the dependent variable and one independent variable – and the relationship between them can be described as a straight line. Situations involving two or more independent variables are analysed by using *multiple regression* techniques, and these are described briefly in the third section. Before that, in the second section, we look at *correlation*. Whereas with regression analysis we are interested in finding a mathematical equation relating two variables, with correlation we are interested in determining the extent to which the variables are related, or the strength of the relationship.

SIMPLE LINEAR REGRESSION

Let us take our usual simple example. Suppose you are a haulier. Up until now, for each tender you have submitted you have prepared detailed figures on the cost of the work. You are now expanding and you want a simple way to work out a cost for a job. You suspect that the most important influence on the cost of the job is the distance to be travelled. You want to test whether or not this is the case, and so look back at the last eight jobs and obtain the data shown in Table 18.1.

Table 18.1 Comparison of haulage cost against distance

Job	Distance (miles)	Cost (£)
1	20	200
2	25	250
3	35	275
4	37	300
5	48	400
6	60	450
7	75	500
8	80	600

The first step is to present the information graphically, by plotting the jobs on a graph of cost against distance. Traditionally, as we are trying to predict cost, (ie it is the dependent variable), we put cost on the vertical axis (the *y* axis) and the independent variable, distance, on the horizontal axis (the *x* axis). The graph, shown as Figure 18.1, is known as a *scatter diagram*.

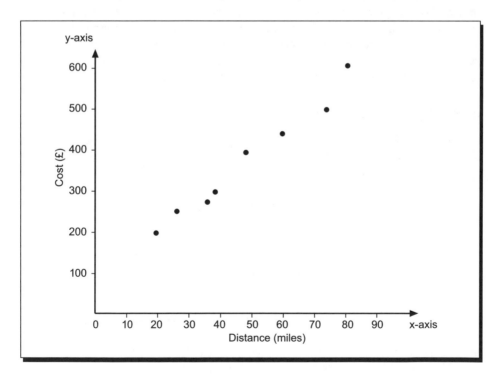

Figure 18.1 Scatter diagram of cost/job against distance travelled

The scatter diagram indicates that there does appear to be a linear relationship: in other words, the pattern of the dots is roughly in a straight line. A graph showing a straight line or linear relationship between two sets of data can be expressed in the form of a mathematical equation:

$y = a + bx$

where:

a   is the intercept where the graph intersects the y axis (that is, the value of y when $x = 0$).
b   is the slope of the line. (The bigger the value of b the greater the slope, in other words the greater the increase in y for a unit increase in x. b can be negative which means that y decreases as x increases.)

The aim is to find the straight line which best fits the points in the scatter diagram. Suppose we define the line of best fit as:

$y = a_0 + b_0 x$

(where a_0 and b_0 are the values of a and b associated with the specific straight line.)

Then for a value of $x = x_i$, the predicted value of y_i would be $a_0 + b_0 x_i$.

We define the *prediction error* as:

actual value – predicted value

$y - (a_0 + b_0 x_i)$

We define the *line of best fit* as one for which:

■   the sum of errors is zero (that is the sum of the differences of the points above and below the line, the positive and negative errors, cancel out).
■   the sum of these errors squared is minimised; the errors are squared to remove the effect of the negative and positive signs.

This is known as the *least squares method*, and it can be shown that the line of best fit, $y = a_0 + b_0 x$, is when:

$$a_0 = \frac{\Sigma y}{n} - b_0 \frac{\Sigma x}{n}$$

$$b_0 = \frac{\Sigma xy - \dfrac{\Sigma x \Sigma y}{n}}{\Sigma x^2 - \dfrac{(\Sigma x)^2}{n}}$$

where n is the number of observations or points on the scatter diagram.

We can calculate the values of a_0 and b_0 manually. Going back to the example, it is helpful to set out a table with the following computations – see Table 18.2.

Table 18.2 Comparison of haulage cost against distance – useful tabulations

Job	Distance	Cost			
	x	y	xy	x^2	y^2
1	20	200	4,000	400	40,000
2	25	250	6,250	625	62,500
3	35	275	9,625	1,225	75,625
4	37	300	11,100	1,369	90,000
5	48	400	19,200	2,304	160,000
6	60	450	27,000	3,600	202,500
7	75	500	37,500	5,625	250,000
8	80	600	48,000	6,400	360,000
Total	380	2,975	162,675	21,548	1,240,625
	Σx	Σy	Σxy	Σx^2	Σy^2

Note: The y^2 column is not required to calculate the regression line, but is included as it will be used in a later calculation.

Substituting the values from the table into the formulae above we get:

$$b_0 = \frac{\Sigma xy - \dfrac{\Sigma x \Sigma y}{n}}{\Sigma x^2 - \dfrac{(\Sigma x)^2}{n}}$$

$$= \frac{162,675 - \dfrac{(380 \times 2,975)}{8}}{21,548 - \dfrac{(380 \times 380)}{8}}$$

1130.5

14(3125

$$= \frac{21,362.5}{3,498}$$

$$= 6.1$$

(We calculate b_0 first because we need to use the value in the calculation of a_0.)

$$a_0 = \frac{\Sigma y}{n} - b_0 \frac{\Sigma x}{n}$$

$$= \frac{2,975}{8} - \frac{6.1 \times 380}{8}$$

$$= 371.9 - 289.8$$

$$= 82.1$$

Therefore the estimated regression equation is:

$$y = 82.1 + 6.1x$$

This shows that there is a positive intercept on the y axis (at £82.10), and that the slope is such that cost increases with distance at a rate of 6.1:1. Figure 18.2 shows the regression line.

How would we use this equation? Suppose we want to tender, and therefore estimate the cost, for a job which involves a distance of 40 miles? Using the regression equation we get:

$$y = 82.1 + 6.1x$$
$$= 82.1 + (6.1 \times 40)$$
$$= 82.1 + 244$$
$$= 326.1$$

That is, the cost for a journey of 40 miles would be £326.10. We can only be really confident about using the regression equation for predictions of values of x, in this case distance, within the data set that has been used to estimate the equation (in this case 20 to 80 miles). If we use it to predict values outside this range then we are making the assumption that the data will continue to behave in the same way. This will not always be the case. For example, a farmer might find that there is a good linear relationship between his yield of potatoes and rainfall – as the rainfall increases so does the yield. However, after a certain level of rainfall the relationship might change significantly – perhaps with the yield even decreasing.

The arithmetic gets somewhat tedious for situations with lots of observations and in practice, you would use a computer package (see Chapter 22). Nevertheless, it is useful to understand what the computer is doing for you. However, the most important thing to know is when and how to use regression analysis.

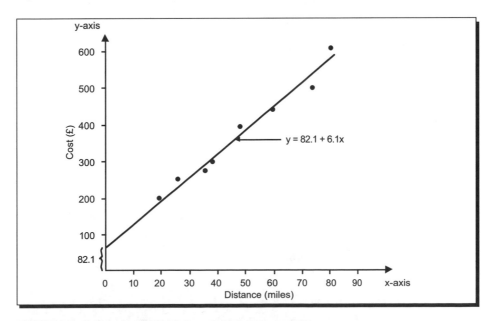

Figure 18.2 Estimated regression line of cost/job against distance

Therefore, it might also be useful to get some idea of how good a fit the regression line is to the raw data. The measure used is called the *coefficient of determination* and is usually denoted by the symbol r^2. It calculates how much of the error $(y - y_0)$ has been reduced by finding the regression line. The coefficient of determination is, in fact, the proportion of the total sum of squares (without using regression) that can be explained using the estimated regression equation, that is:

$$r^2 = \frac{\text{sum of squares explained by regression}}{\text{total sum of squares (before regression)}}$$

The coefficient of determination can be computed using the following formulae:

Sum of squares explained by regression

$$= \frac{\left(\Sigma xy - \dfrac{\Sigma x \Sigma y}{n}\right)^2}{\Sigma x^2 - \dfrac{(\Sigma x)^2}{n}}$$

Total sum of squares before regression

$$= \Sigma y^2 - \frac{(\Sigma y)^2}{n}$$

You will recognise the same arithmetic terms as were used before. So, using the totals from Table 18.2:

Sum of squares explained by regression

$$= \frac{\left(162{,}675 - \dfrac{(380 \times 2{,}975)}{8}\right)^2}{21{,}548 - \dfrac{(380 \times 380)}{8}}$$

$$= \frac{456{,}356{,}406}{3{,}498}$$

$$= 130{,}462$$

Total sum of squares before regression

$$= 1{,}240{,}625 - \frac{(2{,}975 \times 2{,}975)}{8}$$

$$= 1{,}240{,}625 - 1{,}106{,}328$$

$$= 134{,}296$$

Therefore

r^2 $= \dfrac{130,462}{134,296}$

     $= 0.97$

The estimated regression equation has accounted for 0.97 or 97% of the total sum of squares. We would be delighted with a result as high as this in practice, as the closer r^2 is to 1 (or in explaining 100% of the total sum of squares), the better is the fit of the regression line.

Again in practice a suitable computer package is normally used to calculate the coefficient of determination (see Chapter 22) – you do not need to be able to do the calculations. However, you do need to understand what the results tell you.

CORRELATION

There will be many decision-making situations where we are primarily interested in finding out the extent to which two variables are related, rather than calculating a linear equation. We use a statistic, the *correlation coefficient,* to establish the strength of the relationship between two variables. The features of the correlation coefficient are:

- The value lies between −1 and +1.
- A value of +1 means that the two variables are perfectly related in a positive sense, that is, as one increases so does the other. Positive values close to +1 show a strong (though not perfect) positive relationship – see the scatter diagram (Figure 18.3).
- A value of −1 means that the two variables are perfectly related in a negative sense, that is, as one increases the other one decreases. Negative values close to −1 show a strong (though not perfect) negative relationship – see the scatter diagram (Figure 18.4).
- Values close to zero show that there is no linear relationship – see the scatter diagram (Figure 18.5.)

As a simple exercise you might like to consider in which of the following HR examples (assuming there is a relationship) the variables might be positively or negatively correlated:

- labour turnover and unemployment rates
- absence rates and stress
- accidents and H&S training.

If there is a relationship, it is likely that:

- labour turnover and unemployment rates are negatively correlated – as unemployment rates go up, people are less likely to change jobs and therefore labour turnover will go down
- absence rates and stress are positively correlated – as stress goes up, it is likely that so will absence rates
- accidents and H&S training are negatively correlated – as health and safety training increases, you would hope that accidents will come down.

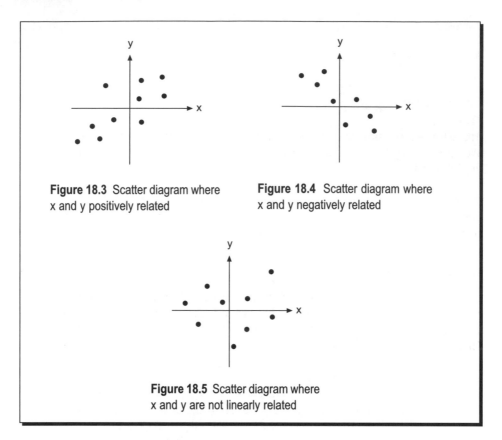

Figure 18.3 Scatter diagram where x and y positively related

Figure 18.4 Scatter diagram where x and y negatively related

Figure 18.5 Scatter diagram where x and y are not linearly related

The correlation coefficient, usually denoted by r, is defined by:

$$r = \pm \sqrt{\text{coefficient of determination}}$$

In the example on haulage costs, $r^2 = 0.97$, therefore:

$$r = \pm \sqrt{0.97}$$

$$= \pm 0.985$$

This shows a strong correlation between distance in miles and the cost in £s. From the scatter diagram, Figure 18.1, it is clear that the relationship is positive.

There are some very important points that need to be borne in mind when using correlation analysis. In fact caution is the order of the day in interpreting the results. It is essential to be aware that the result on its own tells us little or nothing about the meaning or implications of the relationship, other than whether it is strong or not. To explain this point we can use the example of the relationship between cigarette smoking and lung cancer. Originally, the statistical evidence was available before the medical evidence. The high correlation suggested that there was a link between the two, but the physical evidence between the two was not available, and until scientists identified the physiological link, a causal relationship could not be confirmed.

The reason for caution is that it is quite easy to find examples where two variables are correlated, but where it is obvious that changes in the one are not *caused* by changes in the other. Let us take three kinds of example:

- Each variable may be quite independently related to another third variable. For example, there can be quite a high correlation between the price of washing machines and the price of cars, merely because both are related to a third variable, time.
- The variables may be related via another, intermediate variable. For example, it is likely that there is a high positive relationship between the size of a child's hand and the quality of handwriting. However, there is no direct causal relationship: this is the effect of a third variable (age) at work.
- The variables might be linked by sheer chance, sometimes called a nonsense correlation. For example, in the 1930s a statistical link was noted between the number of radios in use and the number of suicides. It is possible to test for this chance relationship, but we shall not cover it in this book. Readers should simply be aware that the possibility exists.

The final point to be borne in mind is that this chapter has been about testing for a *linear*, that is a straight line, relationship. The two variables could be related in other ways that we do not cover. Examples of non-linear relationships are curvilinear and exponential relationships, as shown in Figures 18.6 and 18.7:

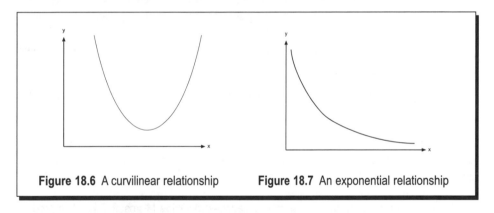

Figure 18.6 A curvilinear relationship   **Figure 18.7** An exponential relationship

MULTIPLE REGRESSION

Multiple regression sounds a rather grand term for what is really a very simple extension of linear regression. Instead of having only one independent variable, we have two or more. In the real world of business, this is very useful as, by and large, business situations are complex and there may be a number of factors affecting a particular result. For example, if we are a company launching a new product we might well advertise in newspapers, on television, local radio, etc, and wish to know the impact of each of these forms of advertising on the sales results. Alternatively, we might need to understand what led to a good performance in our sales force – considering factors such as age, years of experience, training, gender, etc.

Explaining how to carry out a multiple regression is beyond the scope of this book. However, we want to tell you enough to recognise when it would be helpful to use this technique and to make you aware of some of the difficulties. There are several computer packages available which will do all the hard work of the calculations – you just need to be aware when the technique might be useful.

First, we must explain the basic concept. Suppose you are trying to examine a particular variable, for example, the sales of a new product and you suspect it is dependent on a number of other variables, x_1, x_2, x_3 and so on. In our earlier example, the variables would be the different types of advertising. To start, we set up an equation similarly to the way we did in the simple linear case:

$$y = a + b_1x_1 + b_2x_2 + b_3x_3 + b_4x_4 \ldots + b_nx_n$$

where y is the dependent variable and x_1, x_2 ... x_n are the independent variables.

Now, from this base we can carry out all sorts of interesting tasks:

- We can calculate the values of b_1 to b_n and hence use the equation to predict values of y from different values of x_1 to x_n. As with the simple linear situation, we can only be confident about such predictions within the respective ranges of each of the variables x_1 to x_n.
- We can find out how good a fit the equation is to the data using r^2, the coefficient of determination.
- We can test whether there is a significant relationship between the dependent variable and independent variables. We can do this as a total and also test each independent variable. Often the so-called independent variables are not independent of each other. In our example of the sales force performance, age and years of experience might well be related. We might find that years of experience is not a significant factor when age appears in the equation, although it might be if age was not included. If age proved to be the more powerful influence, we would not bother with years of experience in the equation. As far as is possible, it is best to avoid including variables that are highly correlated, as it is difficult to separate out the effect of the individual independent variables on the dependent variable.
- We can calculate the importance of each independent variable in explaining the differences in the values of the dependent variable.

It is important to remember again that this technique is again based on *linear* relationships. There are lots of other relationships, for example those that are curvilinear, but here the mathematics becomes a bit more tricky!

In Chapter 22 we describe how to use the spreadsheet package Microsoft Excel™ to produce scatter diagrams, simple linear regression lines and calculate correlation coefficients.

CONCLUSION

We hope we hear you say, 'that wasn't too bad at all'. Regression and correlation techniques are simple but very powerful statistical tools. However, as we have tried to emphasise, the user must beware of trying to draw too many conclusions. We set off with simple linear regression and correlation, which are both quite easy to understand, but in practice it is multiple regression which enables us to cope with more complex situations, and which will prove most useful in the business world.

REVIEW QUESTIONS

1. A temp agency specialising in clerical staff regularly seeks staff by placing advertisements in the local newspaper. It has been experimenting with the size of the advertisement. The following data shows the number of responses resulting from each advertisement:

Size of advert (column ins)	Responses
1	30
2	42
3	60
4	56
5	82
6	76

    A friendly statistician offers to carry out a regression analysis and comes up with the following information:

    $y = 23 + 9.9x$, where y = no. of responses and x = size of advert; $r^2 = 0.88$

    The agency wants to increase its response to 100 and wants to know what size of advert to select.

    Explain with the use of a diagram what this information means and the implication for the business.

2. The reservations manager of a major airline wants to estimate the relationship between the number of reservations and the actual numbers of passengers showing up for a specific flight. The manager wishes to use the information to estimate what size of airplane should be used for different reservation levels. For example, what would be the number of passengers expected from 350 reservations and from 575 reservations? Data is gathered over a random sample of 12 different days:

Days	Reservations	Passengers
1	150	210
2	548	405
3	156	120
4	121	89
5	416	304
6	450	320
7	462	319
8	508	410
9	307	275
10	311	289
11	265	236
12	189	170

    The research department at the airline supplies the reservations manager with the following information that:

    $y = 55 + 0.64x$, where y = no. of passengers and x = no. of reservations; $r^2 = 0.90$

    Explain with the use of a diagram what this information means and the implications for the business.

Forecasting and
time series

CHAPTER OBJECTIVES

When you have studied this chapter, you will be able to:

- describe the contribution of forecasting to achieving organisational objectives
- outline a range of different approaches to forecasting, both quantitative and qualitative
- explain how forecasting techniques might be used in a range of situations
- interpret the output from a time series analysis.

INTRODUCTION

This chapter looks at the very useful technique of forecasting. It is useful in the sense that it can help managers from all professions to focus on what is likely to happen in the future. To be able to predict the future accurately is to be rich beyond comparison, and if we were capable of doing this we would need no other business skills at all and most of us would be redundant!

For any organisation, whatever its size, it is vital to plan ahead. Depending on the size and nature of the business, a manager may be required to plan a year ahead or perhaps even 20 years ahead. If you are an operational manager in a manufacturing business you will need to forecast production levels in order to plan orders for raw materials, schedule production lines and assess labour requirements, etc. If you are in retail you will need quite detailed sales forecasts in order to prepare buying plans, assess inventory levels and so on. Many large-scale businesses plan at least five years ahead, and sometimes more, in order to forecast their requirements for new factories, shops or warehouses and hence their requirements for capital investment.

In the HR function, the ability to be able to forecast the numbers of staff with the right skills required to implement the organisation's strategic plans is an important role for the HR planning specialist. Following on from this, the ability to forecast the implications for recruitment and learning and development activities to achieve the forecast staffing requirement is vital to enable HR to contribute fully to organisational success.

In Chapter 3 we discussed how information systems can be used to help in the planning process. This chapter explains some of the statistical techniques we can use to help us with our planning. However, we must remember that our results will only be as good as the data we use to make the predictions and, very importantly, the extent to which the future is likely to continue along the same lines as the past. Our fallibility in this latter area means that there is a vital role for managers and specialists to exercise their judgement in pursuit of business objectives.

As you will readily appreciate, managers could spend quite a lot of time trying to forecast the future. How is it done? Do they use a crystal ball or perhaps the modern equivalent, the computerised information system? In fact there are various ways to approach the challenge of forecasting the future, and these fall into two main types: quantitative methods and qualitative methods.

QUANTITATIVE METHODS

Quantitative methods use statistical techniques to analyse the historical data in order to predict the future.

Time series approach

If we use only historical data relating to the particular item we are trying to forecast, then the forecasting technique is called a *time series* method. For example, if we are a retailer of prams and are trying to forecast sales of prams, then a time series approach would analyse the historical data on pram sales.

Causal approach

If, however, we are going to use historical data relating to other variables, then we use what is known as a *causal* approach. A causal approach to forecasting pram sales might involve looking at the pattern of births to predict the demand for prams. Linear or multiple regression techniques can be used for this purpose – see Chapter 18.

In this chapter we concentrate on the time series approach.

QUALITATIVE METHODS

Qualitative methods usually involve using the judgements of experts on what the future will hold for us. This is a particularly useful approach if, for some reason, there is no historical data, for example on the launch of a new product. It is also useful if it is known that something has happened which makes the historical data a poor guide to the future. Examples could be when there has been an advance in technology and the cost of the product drops dramatically, or which affects the demand for a product, or the need for people to produce it. Good examples are the dramatic increase in home computers and the use of the Internet, the growth and development of mobile phones with their myriad features, and the radical change in food-buying habits from home-prepared to convenience foods, etc.

There may be sudden discontinuities caused by new legislation, perhaps on food safety, or unexpected events such as the BSE scare, the 9/11 terrorist disaster, and as we write the devastating natural tsunami disaster. We are living in a time of great change, when increasingly perhaps the one certainty is that the future, particularly in the longer term, is unlikely to be the same as the past in many areas. This puts particular emphasis on qualitative approaches.

Delphi approach

One particular qualitative method used is the *Delphi approach*, which was developed by the Rand Corporation. A panel of experts are each asked to fill in a questionnaire giving their view of the future for, say, the sales of a product. From the results of the first questionnaire a second is produced which includes the range of opinions of the group. Members of the panel are asked to reconsider their views in the light of the new information from the group. The process goes on until a measure of consensus is reached. The full Delphi approach is a fairly sophisticated technique, and it is likely that in many organisations the qualitative method will simply involve a group of people, experts in their areas, sitting around a table thrashing out what appears to be the best forecast for the future.

Other qualitative methods often used, particularly for short-term forecasting, are bottom-up or top-down forecasting (which are in essence the same type of approach).

Bottom-up approach

In the *bottom-up approach*, managers at the lowest hierarchical level are asked to make a judgement on what, for example, their sales are going to be, then these forecasts are combined. Take for example a large retail chain of several stores, each store consisting of many departments. In the first instance all the department managers in all the stores are asked to estimate their sales increase for the next year, based on their specialist local knowledge. These departmental estimates are combined to give the forecast increase for each store, and when the store increases are combined, this produces the forecast increase in sales for the whole chain. Top management then considers the overall result in the light of their knowledge of the wider environment, such as the economic situation, and might accept the overall forecast or vary it according to their assessment.

Top-down approach

The *top-down approach* works in the reverse order. Top management lay down their view of the likely change in sales overall. This sales forecast is then allocated across individual stores, and the head of each store allocates the forecast change across departments.

There are advantages and disadvantages to both approaches. The bottom-up approach is useful where local conditions can have a significant effect. For example, the sales increase for a store in a rapidly expanding new town is likely to be considerably greater than that for a store in an established area. Also, the approach is considered to be more motivational because those who have to achieve the target forecast have actually been involved in the decision-making for the forecast. The top-down approach is useful where there are few local variations and the expertise to make the forecasts is concentrated in the head office.

Although qualitative approaches are widely used, we believe that particularly for more short-term forecasting, where it is appropriate and possible to use it, quantitative approaches can make a greater contribution than is currently the case. We are going to concentrate on the quantitative methods for the rest of this chapter and, in particular, on the time series approach. However, often a combination of approaches is appropriate – a time series approach to explore the outcomes based on the assumption that the future will continue to be like the past, combined with other more qualitative approaches to look at 'what if' scenarios, such as what would be the implications of a more rapid increase in demand than the past, what would be the implications of change in leisure habits, and so on.

It is interesting that in the realms of academia there has been a shift away from relying primarily on quantitative approaches in research, to taking a pluralistic approach embracing a wide range of qualitative methods as well. In the increasingly complex world in which organisations operate the need for a pluralistic approach also becomes ever greater. The ability of organisations to harness the power of both the quantitative and qualitative approaches will give significant competitive advantage.

STRUCTURE OF A TIME SERIES

A *time series* is simply a set of results for a particular variable of interest, for example sales or births, taken over a period of time. In order to try to understand the pattern in a time series of data, it is helpful to consider what is known as the *structure* of the time series. There are four separate elements to consider:

- trend
- cyclical

- seasonal
- irregular.

It all sounds a bit technical, but don't worry, it is really very straightforward. Stay with us while we explore each of the above elements in turn.

Trend element

In a set of time series data, the measurements are taken at regular intervals, possibly hourly, daily, weekly, monthly, quarterly, yearly, etc. There will almost certainly be random fluctuations in the data, but in some cases the data will exhibit a shift to either lower or higher values over the time period in question. This movement is called the *trend* in the time series, and is usually the result of some long-term factors such as changes in consumer expenditure, changes in technology, demographic trends, etc.

There are various trend patterns. Set out in Figures 19.1 to 19.4 are some examples comparing sales over time. In a time series graph, time is always along the *x* axis and the variable being measured along the *y* axis. Suppose these are sales of consumer products.

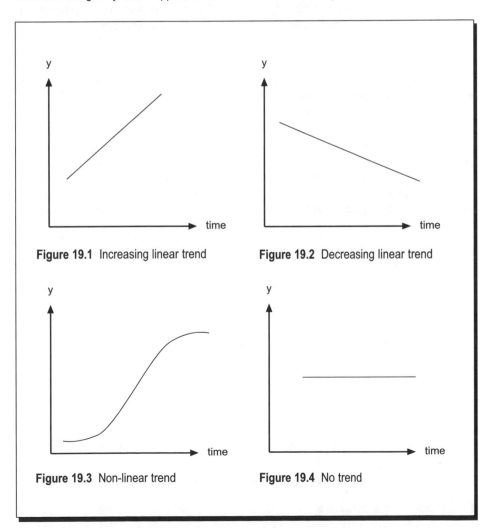

Figure 19.1 Increasing linear trend

Figure 19.2 Decreasing linear trend

Figure 19.3 Non-linear trend

Figure 19.4 No trend

Figure 19.1 shows that sales are increasing steadily over time, and could represent, say, DVD players where the market is steadily expanding. Figure 19.2 shows that sales are decreasing steadily over time. Perhaps this could represent the sales of stand-alone cookers as there is a move to fitted hobs and built-in ovens. Figure 19.3 shows a very interesting pattern, a non-linear trend, where sales set off slowly, then show a period of rapid growth, and finally level off. Students of marketing will recognise this graph as the very common product life cycle, where sales of the product are measured from the date of product launch, through its growth period, until saturation point is reached and its sales remain steady. Figure 19.4 shows no trend in sales over time, neither increases nor decreases. This could represent the sales of a basic commodity such as potatoes, where if there is no change in the size of the population, sales might remain quite steady over a long period of time. There could be an occasional blip as a result of, say, a health scare or, alternatively, the promotion of high-fibre jacket potatoes, but there is no overall trend.

Cyclical element

Sometimes a time series displays a trend of some sort but in addition shows a cyclical pattern, of alternative sequences of observation above and below the trend line. Any regular pattern of observations of this type which lasts longer than a year is called the *cyclical element* of the time series. The graph in Figure 19.5 displays a cyclical pattern of sales. This is, in fact, a very common occurrence, representing cyclical fluctuations in the economy as evidenced, say, by retail sales.

Seasonal element

Whereas the cyclical pattern is displayed over a number of years, there may be a pattern of variability within one-year periods. For example, the sales of lawnmowers are likely to peak in the second or third quarters of the year, whereas the sales of toys will peak in the pre-Christmas period. The element of the time series which represents variability due to seasonal influences is called, not surprisingly, the *seasonal element*. However, while it normally refers to movements over a one-year period, it can also refer to any repeating pattern of less than a year's duration. For example, daily passenger figures on the London Underground show clear seasonal movements within the day, with peaks around the rush-hour periods of 7.30 am to 9.00 am and 4.30 pm to 6.30 pm, moderate levels during the remainder of the day, and a tailing-off in travel during the evening.

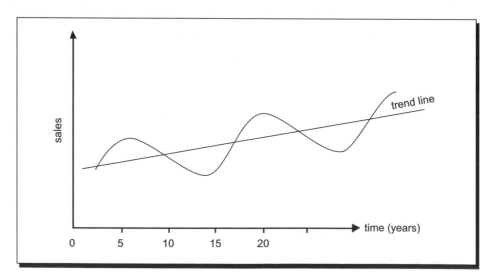

Figure 19.5 Cyclical fluctuations

Irregular element

Finally we come to the *irregular element*, which is the element that cannot be explained by the trend, the cyclical and/or the seasonal elements. It represents the random variability in the time series, caused by unanticipated and non-recurring factors which, by their very nature, are unpredictable.

Let us recap briefly. A time series can show:

■ a trend – a long-term shift in the data
■ a cyclical pattern – where the measurements show alternate sequences above and below the trend line over periods greater than a year
■ a seasonal pattern of movements within a year
■ an irregular element which is the random variability in the data.

In the next section we look first at one of the forecasting techniques called *smoothing methods*, appropriate for fairly stable time series, where there are no significant trends, cyclical or seasonal patterns. We then go on to look at how to forecast from a time series with a long-term linear trend, and finally how to deal with seasonal elements.

SMOOTHING METHODS

Smoothing methods are used to *smooth* out the irregular element of time series where there are no significant trends, cyclical or seasonal patterns. There are two commonly used smoothing methods:

■ moving average
■ exponential smoothing.

We shall discuss only the *moving average* method in detail as, by and large, it meets most needs. Exponential smoothing is an alternative method, which is a little more complex to calculate, but has the advantage that it requires very little historical data to put it into use. The moving average method involves using the average of the most recent data values to forecast the next period. The number of data values used to compile the average can be selected in order to minimise the forecasting error – more of this in later in the section.

Let us take a simple example of the weekly sales of flour from a supermarket. Some sample data is given in Table 19.1.

Let us choose to use four data values, that is, base our forecast on a four-week moving average.

Table 19.1 Weekly flour sales from a supermarket

Week	Sales (kg)	Week	Sales (kg)
1	30	9	31
2	33	10	28
3	29	11	32
4	32	12	35
5	30	13	32
6	32	14	29
7	34	15	31
8	30	16	28

Forecast for week 5   = moving average of weeks 1 to 4

$$= \frac{30 + 33 + 29 + 32}{4}$$

$$= 31$$

Since the actual value for week five is 30, the forecast error is said to be 30 − 31, that is, −1.

We go on with the forecast for week six, dropping the first week's results and including the results for the fifth week as follows.

Forecast for week 6   = moving average of weeks 2 to 5

$$= \frac{33 + 29 + 32 + 30}{4}$$

$$= 31$$

The forecast error is 32 − 31 = +1.

We go on repeating the calculation and the results are set out in Table 19.2. The forecast error has been squared to get rid of the minus signs.

The results, shown graphically in Figure 19.6, demonstrate how the moving average *smooths* out the fluctuations in the original series.

We mentioned forecasting error earlier, and it might be thought that the simple way to work out the overall forecasting error for the series of data is to take the average of the individual forecasting errors. However, you will see that as some of them are positive and some are negative,

Table 19.2 Weekly flour sales, four-week moving average forecast

Time	Time series	Moving average forecast	Forecast error	Forecast error squared
1	30			
2	33			
3	29			
4	32			
5	30	31.00	−1.00	1.00
6	32	31.00	+1.00	1.00
7	34	30.75	+3.25	10.56
8	30	32.00	−2.00	4.00
9	31	31.50	−0.50	0.25
10	28	31.75	−3.75	14.06
11	32	30.75	+1.25	1.56
12	35	30.25	+4.75	22.56
13	32	31.50	+0.50	0.25
14	29	31.75	−2.75	7.56
15	31	32.00	−1.00	1.00
16	28	31.75	−3.75	14.06
		Totals	−4.00	77.86

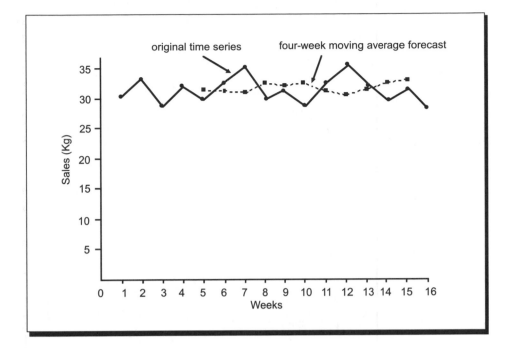

Figure 19.6 Flour sales time series and four-week moving average forecast]

they tend to cancel each other out. So, instead, we use the average of the squared errors, some-times referred to as the *mean squared error*. The mean squared error in the example is:

$$\frac{77.86}{12} = 6.49$$

Now, you will remember we mentioned earlier that it is possible to choose the number of data points to use in the moving average in order to minimise the forecasting error. So we could repeat the previous calculations for perhaps a three-week or a five-week moving average, and see which gives the smallest forecast error. We shall not do that here! However, it is very easy to set up the calculations in Microsoft Excel™ (see Chapter 22).

TREND PROJECTIONS

In this section we look at how to forecast from a time series that shows a long-term linear trend. In fact we use a technique you are already familiar with – linear regression. Let us consider some of the historical data for the production of toasters set out in Table 19.3 and shown graphically in Figure 19.7.

Table 19.3 Toaster production

Year	Units (000s)	Year	Units (000s)
1	50	6	54
2	52	7	57
3	56	8	60
4	51	9	62
5	48	10	58

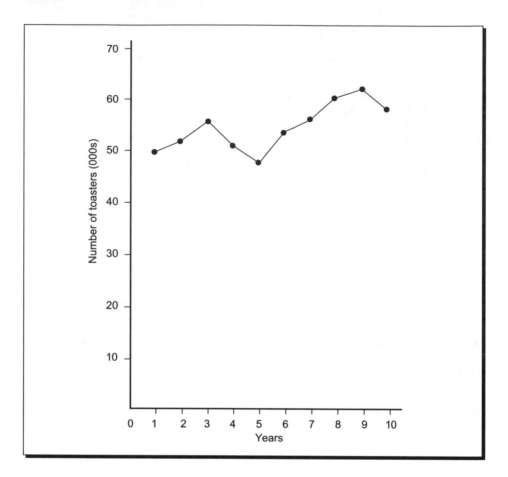

Figure 19.7 Time series of the production of toasters

You will recall from Chapter 18 that the linear regression equation linking a dependent variable y and an independent variable x is:

$$y = a_0 + b_0 x$$

In order to emphasise that the independent variable is 'time', we express the equation as follows:

$$y_t = a_0 + b_0 t$$

where

y_t = forecast value of time series in time t
a_0 = intercept of the trend line
b_0 = slope of the trend line
t = time point.

We can calculate the values of a_0 and b_0 in exactly the same way as we did in Chapter 18 – either manually using the formulae for a_0 and b_0, or using a suitable computer package such as Microsoft Excel™ (see Chapter 22).

We get values of a_0 = 48.58 and b_0 = 1.13 and therefore the equation can be written:

$$y_t = 48.58 + 1.13t$$

The slope indicates that over the past 10 years there has been an increase in production of about 1,130 toasters each year. Figure 19.8 shows the trend line.

If we wanted to forecast production in years 11 and 12 we would calculate it as follows:

y_{11} = 48.58 + 1.13 × 11

         = 48.58 + 12.43

         = 61.01 (or 61,010 toasters)

and

y_{12} = 48.58 + 1.13 × 12

         = 48.58 + 13.56

         = 62.14 (or 62,140 toasters)

and so we could go on.

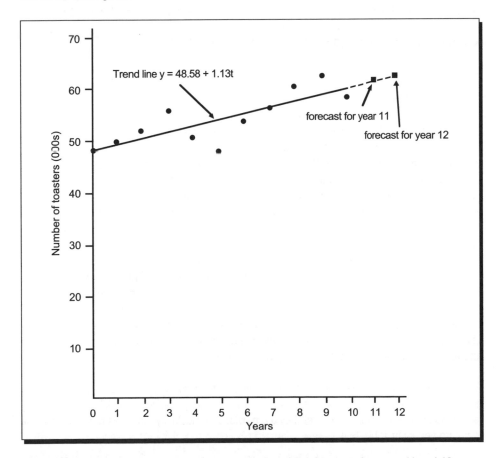

Figure 19.8 Trend line of the production of toasters – giving forecasts for years 11 and 12

Remember, this method assumes that there is a linear (straight line) trend, and crucially the future will be like the past. As you will remember from our introduction to trends, there are several different types of trend, but it is beyond the scope of this book to explain how to deal with non-linear trends.

FORECASTING WITH SEASONAL ELEMENTS

So far we have covered how to forecast a time series where there are no significant trends, cyclical or seasonal elements, using the moving averages smoothing method. Then we looked at how to forecast a time series which displays a long-term linear trend, using linear regression techniques. Now we shall explain how to tackle a time series which has both a trend and a seasonal element. (We shall not look at cyclical elements, as seasonal effects are far more common.) We shall use what is known, for reasons that will become obvious shortly, as the *multiplicative model*. There is an alternative approach, the additive model, which we do not pursue here.

The multiplicative approach assumes that the time series value (Y), can be formed by multiplying the trend element (T), the seasonal element (S) and the irregular element (I) as follows:

$$Y = T \times S \times I$$

T is expressed in units of the item being forecast. However, the S $\times$ I factor, referred to as the seasonal factor, is measured in relative terms, with values above 1 showing a seasonal and irregular effect above the trend, and values below 1 showing a seasonal and irregular effect below the trend. For example, assume we have a trend forecast of 100 units for a particular time period, and values of S $\times$ I equal to 1.08. Then, the value of the time series for that period is:

$$Y = 100 \times 1.08$$

$$= 108$$

The first stage in the forecasting procedure is to calculate the seasonal factors. This is a straightforward if lengthy process manually (although very easy to set up on computer using a package such as Microsoft Excel™). It involves smoothing out the time series using the moving averages method described earlier in this chapter. If we assume the seasonal factors are quarterly, then we would calculate the moving averages based on groups of four data points. When we are dealing with seasonal elements such as quarters, we need an added step – to work out what are known as *centred moving averages*, which are simply averages of the moving averages. (This is because the calculated quarterly average, say for the first year, is in effect a figure representing the mid-point of the year, ie between the second and third quarters. The next moving average will represent a point between the third and fourth quarters. If we average these two, a centred moving average, we obtain a point against the third quarter.) Dividing the original observations by the equivalent centred moving averages gives a seasonal factor for each observation. We then take all the seasonal factors shown against the first quarter observations and take an average to obtain the first quarter seasonal factor, and so on for the remaining three quarters. (In this way we average out the I effect.)

Let us look at a specific example in an area of interest to many organisations, energy consumption. It is measured in gigajoules (a term which allows all energy requirements to be expressed by a common unit regardless of whether they are provided by electricity, coal, gas or whatever). The data are set out in Table 19.4.

Table 19.4 Energy consumption of an organisation

Year	Quarter	Energy consumption (000 Gigajoules)	Year	Quarter	Energy consumption (000 Gigajoules)
1	1	100	4	1	120
	2	80		2	111
	3	70		3	100
	4	90		4	115
2	1	110	5	1	130
	2	93		2	120
	3	98		3	108
	4	100		4	122
3	1	115			
	2	100			
	3	90			
	4	110			

The time series graph of the original observations together with the centred moving averages we have calculated is set out in Figure 19.9. It shows a clear seasonal influence, with energy consumption being (as we would expect) lowest in the second and third quarters, and highest in the first and fourth quarters.

Using the process described earlier we obtain the following seasonal factors:

1st quarter	1.145
2nd quarter	0.983
3rd quarter	0.845
4th quarter	1.027

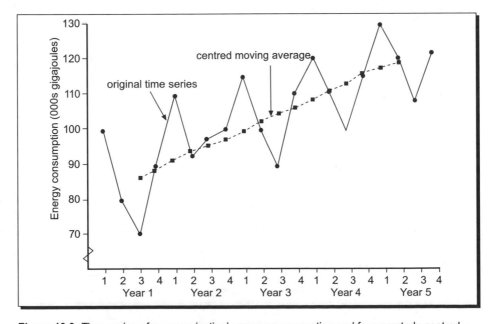

Figure 19.9 Time series of an organisation's energy consumption and four-quarterly centred moving average

This shows us, as expected from the graph, that the highest consumption is in the first quarter and is about 15% above the average quarterly value. The lowest level of consumption is in the third quarter and is nearly 16% below the quarterly average. The second and fourth quarters show consumption very close (within 2–3 %) to the quarterly average.

We are now ready to go on to the next stage and identify the trend. Let us go back to the model:

$$Y = T \times S \times I$$

This can be rewritten as:

$$T = \frac{Y}{S \times I}$$

Therefore, it can be seen that the trend element (T) can be calculated by dividing each observation by the appropriate seasonal factor. This process is called *deseasonalising* the time series. We can now plot the deseasonalised trend line, using the deseasonalised figures rather than using the original observations. Note the difference between Figure 19.9 and Figure 19.10.

Now, although the graph has some fluctuations, there is a discernible trend which we can go on to calculate as we did in the previous section, using linear regression. This time, however, we are using the deseasonalised results rather than the original observations. The trend equation can be calculated to give the following:

$$T_t = 80.4 + 2.2t$$

and is shown in Figure 19.11.

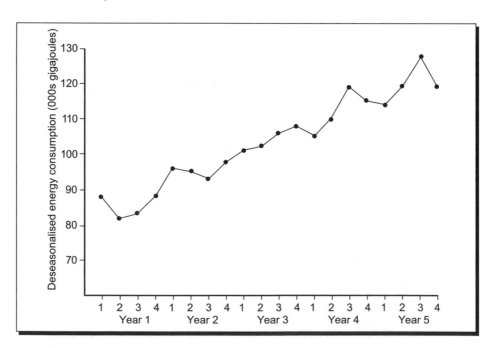

Figure 19.10 Deseasonalised energy consumption

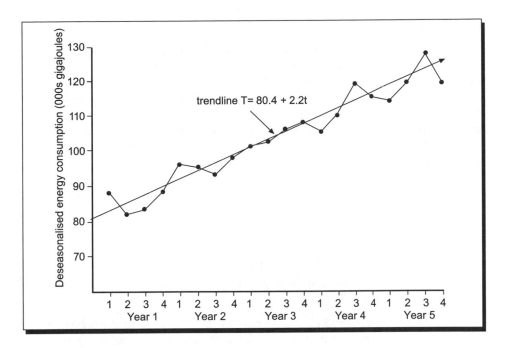

Figure 19.11 Trend line of deseasonalised energy consumption

The slope of 2.2 indicates that over the past five years, or 20 quarters, the company has experienced an average deseasonalised increase in energy consumption of 2,200 gigajoules per quarter.

So, to forecast the trend element for the first quarter of year six, that is the twenty-first quarter, we use the trend equation:

$$T_{21} = 80.4 + 2.2 \times 21$$

$$= 126.6$$

We then apply the seasonal factor for the first quarter to get the forecast:

$$Y = 126.6 \times 1.145$$

$$= 145.0$$

In the same way, we can go on to forecast other future quarters.

This might seem a rather complex set of calculations. However, it is quite straightforward really: you just need to follow it step by step. First we smoothed the data to identify the seasonal elements for each quarter. We then went on to identify the trend by working out the linear regression equation for the deseasonalised results. We use this trend equation to forecast the trend element and then apply the appropriate quarterly seasonal factor to arrive at the final forecast.

So far we have discussed quarterly data; however we might have data for a different time interval, where the seasonal effect is, say, monthly. The approach is identical except that a 12-month moving average replaces the quarterly moving average, and we go on to identify 12 seasonal factors.

CONCLUSION

So there you have it – time series analysis and forecasting – all quite straightforward, as we promised. However, all the quantitative methods described are critically dependent on the belief that the future will be an extension of the past. Unfortunately this is not always the case, and we must constantly bear this assumption in mind. The further ahead we try to forecast, the less relevant can be the past trends and the greater the importance of incorporating qualitative approaches, simulation models, etc. As ever, in pursuing the statistical technique we must never suspend our professional judgement about the meaningfulness of the results of our calculations and therefore, in the ultimate, the use to which these results can be put.

REVIEW QUESTIONS

1. You work for a train operator and are responsible for the HR function supporting the train driver section. You have been given a forecast of the staffing requirements for train drivers for the next 5 years which have been based on an annual increase of 10% each year. Explain how you might set about using these figures to plan ahead for the work of the HR function.

2. You work for a company that produces lawnmowers and you want to predict the workforce it will require over the next year. You have compiled the following time series data:

Number of people employed

Year	Quarter 1	Quarter 2	Quarter 3	Quarter 4
1	600	1,500	1,000	400
2	1,000	1,800	1,500	700
3	1,400	2,600	2,300	1,200
4	1,900	2,800	2,500	1,800
5	2,200	3,400	2,800	2,100
6	2,400	3,600	3,000	2,000
7	2,800	4,000	3,500	2,700

You handed over the figures to the company's statistician who provided the following further results and says, mysteriously, that she has used the multiplicative time series model.

The seasonal factors are:

Quarter 1 = 0.899

Quarter 2 = 1.362

Quarter 3 = 1.118

Quarter 4 = 0.621

and the trend equation is:

$T_t = 633 + 106t$

Using diagrams, explain the results and their implications for the company. Comment on the method used.

Index numbers, published indices and sources of data

CHAPTER OBJECTIVES

When you have studied this chapter, you will be able to:

- use index numbers to analyse and present data
- explain the purpose of the Retail Prices Index (RPI) and how it is measured
- make price adjustments
- define the difference between primary and secondary data
- identify appropriate sources of data.

INTRODUCTION

Index numbers simply present data as a proportion or percentage of some base value. They can be used for a variety of purposes. Perhaps the most common use is to measure changes in data over time. Rather than simply presenting the data as a series of observations measured over the time period, it is often clearer and more useful to present them in index number form. For example, let us take two factories producing radios. Their performance, as measured by the number of radios manufactured, is shown in Table 20.1.

Table 20.1 Manufacture of radios by two factories:

	2001	2002	2003	2004
Factory A	1,500	1,600	1,800	2,200
Factory B	4,000	4,500	4,600	5,000

It is difficult to see which factory has improved its performance most. So we shall express these results as index numbers, using 2001 as the base year. To do this we divide each result by the result for 2001 as shown in Table 20.2. (Alternatively, the index numbers can be presented in percentage form, by multiplying by 100.)

Table 20.2 Indexed performance of radio manufacturers

	2001	2002	2003	2004
Factory A	$\frac{1,500}{1,500}$ $= 1.00$	$\frac{1,600}{1,500}$ $= 1.067$	$\frac{1,800}{1,500}$ $= 1.200$	$\frac{2,200}{1,500}$ $= 1.467$
Factory B	$\frac{4,000}{4,000}$ $= 1.00$	$\frac{4,500}{4,000}$ $= 1.125$	$\frac{4,600}{4,000}$ $= 1.150$	$\frac{5,000}{4,000}$ $= 1.250$

Although Factory B is making 1,000 more radios in 2004 than in 2001 whereas Factory A is making only 700 more, it is clear from using index numbers that Factory A's increase in performance, at 46.7%, is superior to Factory B where performance has increased by only 25%.

The usefulness of index numbers becomes even more marked when we try to compare unlike items. For example, suppose Factory A makes bottles and Factory B makes cars, and production is as shown in Table 20.3.

Table 20.3 Bottle and car production

	2001	2002	2003	2004
Factory A (bottles)	10,000	12,000	13,000	16,000
Factory B (cars)	500	650	800	900

It is clearly meaningless to try to compare the actual increase in bottles with the actual increase in cars, so how *do* you judge an increase of 6,000 bottles against an increase of 400 cars? One option is to turn them into common units, for example, the money value of production. This could help, but this approach could cause as many problems as it solves! We look at this suggestion shortly, but first let us look at the increases in terms of an index of units based on 2001. The results are shown in Table 20.4.

Table 20.4 Indexed performance of manufacturers

	2001	2002	2003	2004
Factory A (bottles)	1.0	1.2	1.3	1.6
Factory B (cars)	1.0	1.3	1.6	1.8

Clearly Factory B is increasing production at a faster rate than Factory A.

Another useful advantage of index numbers is that they make it possible readily to produce graphs showing trends in different types of data sets – see Figure 20.1.

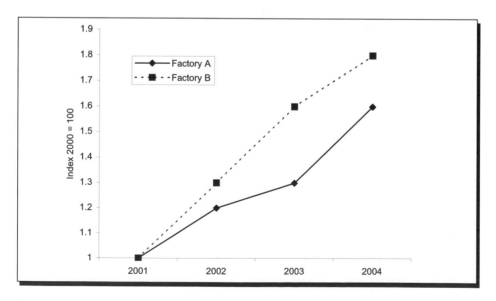

Figure 20.1 Graph of increase in production in Factories A and B

Let us now look at the example in terms of the value of production, as we suggested earlier. Suppose that the value of a bottle is 25p and the value of a car is £10,000, and these values remain constant over time. The results are shown in Table 20.5.

Table 20.5 Value of production

| | Value of production (£) | | | |
	2001	2002	2003	2004
Factory A (bottles)	2,500	3,000	3,250	4,000
Factory B (cars)	5,000,000	6,500,000	8,000,000	9,000,000

We can express this increase in value of production as an index based on 2001. The results are in Table 20.6.

Table 20.6 Value of production expressed as an index

	2001	2002	2003	2004
Factory A (bottles)	1.0	1.2	1.3	1.6
Factory B (cars)	1.0	1.3	1.6	1.8

Yes, the index numbers are the same as we obtained previously. However, let us suppose the unit value of the bottle increases as follows:

2001	2002	2003	2004
25p	30p	40p	50p

and the unit value of the car increases as follows:

2001	2002	2003	2004
10,000	11,000	12,000	13,000

Now the value of production (£) is shown in Table 20.7.

Table 20.7 Revised values of production

	2001	2002	2003	2004
Factory A (bottles)	2,500	3,600	5,200	8,000
Factory B (cars)	5,000,000	7,150,000	9,600,000	11,700,000

Expressing these results as index numbers with 2001 as the base year, we get the values in Table 20.8.

Table 20.8 Revised values of production expressed as an index

	2001	2002	2003	2004
Factory A (bottles)	1.00	1.44	2.08	3.20
Factory B (cars)	1.00	1.43	1.92	2.34

The picture has changed: Factory A appears to be performing better, but is it? No, the answer has been clouded by the price increase. Factory A has not increased its productivity more than Factory B, it has merely benefited from a steeper price increase. So it is necessary to be very careful, when making such comparisons, to ensure that you understand what is being compared and what conclusions can be drawn. In the next section we consider this issue of the changing value of money as we look at one of the most well-known and useful indices, the Retail Price Index (RPI).

So far we have discussed the use of index numbers to measure trends over time. Another important use of index numbers is to measure performance against targets. In Chapter 13 we discussed how index numbers could be used to compare sales performance against targets, and then shown diagrammatically using a radar diagram. Similarly, how they could also be used very powerfully to compare performance data against some sort of average performance, for example in police performance monitoring reports (Police Standards Unit 2004), which compared individual police forces' performance against an 'average of similar forces'.

THE RETAIL PRICE INDEX (RPI) AND CONSUMER PRICE INDEX (CPI)

The *Retail Price Index (RPI)* is probably one of the most important and useful published sets of indices. It sets out to measure the change in the price of goods and services bought for consumption by households in the United Kingdom. It is one of the most familiar measures of inflation, and is probably the only economic indicator that is readily understood and appreciated by non-economists, as people can see the direct impact on their financial well-being.

The base year is revised at regular intervals to maintain it as a readily understood set of indices. It was revised in January 1974 and again in January 1987. These months then became the base points for subsequent years. (Incidentally, the RPI is presented in the percentage form of the index, ie with 100 as the value for the base period.) The RPI is designed to try to measure changes in prices in an average or representative basket of goods and services. The main categories in the current basket, and for which separate indices are published, are:

- food
- catering
- alcoholic drink
- tobacco
- housing
- fuel and lighting
- household goods
- household services
- clothing and footwear
- personal goods and services
- motoring expenditure
- fares and other travel costs
- leisure goods
- leisure services.

Within each category there is a vast range of individual items. Basically a sample of prices is taken from different areas and different types of stores on a monthly basis. In all over 110,000 prices per month are collected. In addition 10,000 further prices are collected to reflect the prices of items sold in other ways, such as through catalogues, and items which will not be picked up through the main sample, such as utility prices. From these it is possible to estimate individual indices.

How then is it possible to arrive at one figure – one index number? A simple way would be to take a straight average, that is, take all the different index numbers based on the same year, add them together and divide by the number of categories.

Let us take a simplified example. Suppose the indices for January 2004 based on January 2001 for three items (A, B and C) are:

$I_A = 110$

$I_B = 130$

$I_C = 140$

Simple average $= \dfrac{110 + 130 + 140}{3}$

$= \dfrac{380}{3}$

$= 126.7$

This would only be appropriate if each of the separate indices was equally important. However, it is quite obvious that changes in electricity prices will have a much greater impact on the population at large than, say, changes in one specific food product, because people spend much more on electricity than on that one food item. Therefore, in order to arrive at a true average, it is necessary to weight the different components. Let us suppose that the average family spends 50% of its income on item A, 30% on item B and 20% on item C.

Weighted average $= \dfrac{110 \times 50}{100} + \dfrac{130 \times 30}{100} + \dfrac{140 \times 20}{100}$

$= (110 \times 0.5) + (130 \times 0.3) + (140 \times 0.2)$

$= 55 + 39 + 28$

$= 122$

The weighted average, 122, is less than the simple average, 126.7, reflecting the fact that the price increase in the most important item – Item A – is rather less than for the other two items. Government statisticians use the results of another survey, the Expenditure and Food Survey (previously the Family Expenditure Survey), to arrive at the different weighting factors to apply. This survey examines expenditure patterns of a sample of households.

Set out in Table 20.9 is the Retail Price Index (all items) from 1984 to the end of 2004. It can be seen that it provides monthly indices and average annual indices between 1984 and 2004, and that it has been rebased in 1987.

Table 20.9 Retail prices index (all items)

January 1974 = 100

	Annual average	Jan	Feb	Mar	Apr	May	June	July	Aug	Sept	Oct	Nov	Dec
1984	351.8	342.6	344.0	345.1	349.7	351.0	351.9	351.5	354.8	355.5	357.7	358.8	358.5
1985	373.2	359.8	362.7	366.1	373.9	375.6	376.4	375.7	376.7	376.5	377.1	378.4	378.9
1986	385.9	397.7	381.1	381.6	385.3	386.0	385.8	384.7	385.9	387.8	388.4	391.7	393.0
1987		394.5											

January 1987 = 100

	Annual average	Jan	Feb	Mar	Apr	May	June	July	Aug	Sept	Oct	Nov	Dec
1987	101.9	100.0	100.4	100.6	101.8	101.9	101.9	101.8	102.1	102.4	102.9	103.4	103.3
1988	106.9	103.3	103.7	104.1	105.8	106.2	106.6	106.7	107.9	108.4	109.5	110.0	110.3
1989	115.2	111.0	111.8	112.3	114.3	115.0	115.4	115.5	115.8	116.6	117.5	118.5	118.8
1990	126.1	119.5	120.2	121.4	125.1	126.2	126.7	126.8	128.1	129.3	130.3	130.0	129.9
1991	133.5	130.2	130.9	131.4	133.1	133.5	134.1	133.8	134.1	134.6	135.1	135.6	135.7
1992	138.5	135.6	136.3	136.7	138.8	139.3	139.3	138.8	138.9	139.4	139.9	139.7	139.2
1993	140.7	137.9	138.8	139.3	140.6	141.1	141.0	140.7	141.3	141.9	141.8	141.6	141.9
1994	144.1	141.3	142.1	142.5	144.2	144.7	144.7	144.0	144.7	145.0	145.2	145.3	146.0
1995	149.1	146.0	146.9	147.5	149.0	149.6	149.8	149.1	149.9	150.6	149.8	149.8	150.7
1996	152.7	150.2	150.9	151.5	152.6	152.9	153.0	152.4	153.1	153.8	153.8	153.9	154.4
1997	157.5	154.4	155.0	155.4	156.3	156.9	157.5	157.5	158.5	159.3	159.5	159.6	160.0
1998	162.9	159.5	160.3	160.8	162.6	163.5	163.4	163.0	163.7	164.4	164.5	164.4	164.4
1999	165.4	163.4	163.7	164.1	165.2	165.6	165.6	165.1	165.5	166.2	166.5	166.7	167.3
2000	170.3	166.6	167.5	168.4	170.1	170.7	171.1	170.5	170.5	171.7	171.6	172.1	172.2
2001	173.3	171.1	172.0	172.2	173.1	174.2	174.4	173.3	174.0	174.6	174.3	173.6	173.4
2002	176.2	173.3	173.8	174.5	175.7	176.2	176.2	175.9	176.4	177.6	177.9	178.2	178.5
2003	181.3	178.4	179.3	179.9	181.2	181.5	181.3	181.3	181.6	182.5	182.6	182.7	183.5
2004	186.7	183.1	183.8	184.6	185.7	186.5	186.8	186.8	187.4	188.1	188.6	189.0	189.9

Source: *Monthly Digest of Statistics, Office for National Statistics* © Crown Copyright 2005.

Since December 2003, the Consumer Price Index (CPI) has been used as the basis for the government's inflation target. (This was previously called the UK Harmonised Index of Consumer Prices (HCIP), and was developed to provide a measure that could be used to make reliable comparisons of inflation rates across EU countries.) It differs from the RPI in that it excludes a number of items, mainly related to housing, that are included in the full RPI and it covers all private households whereas the RPI excludes certain types of household which are felt to have atypical spending patterns (for example, very high-income households). The CPI is available from January 1996 onwards. Prior to that date there are estimates and indicative figures going back to 1975.

Using the RPI

The RPI continues to be used for a wide range of purposes, such as for the indexation of pensions and state benefits, in wage agreements, and in imposing restrictions on utility prices. It also has a major advantage at present because of its familiarity and credibility based on its longer history. Hence, we have continued to use the RPI as the basis for calculating the impact of price changes in this edition.

So, how do we work out a particular increase in prices? Let us look at some examples.

- What is the price increase between January 1995 and July 2003?

    Index for January 1995   = 146.0

    Index for July 2003   = 181.3

    We want the July 2003 index based on January 1995, that is, rebasing the index on January 1995 = 100, so we divide each index by 1.46:

    Index for January 1995 $= \dfrac{146.0}{1.46} = 100.0$
    (Based on January 1995 = 100)

    Index for July 2003 $= \dfrac{181.3}{1.46} = 124.2$
    (Based on January 1995 = 100)

    Therefore prices increased by 24.2% over the period January 1995 to July 2003.

- What is the price increase between 1990 and 2000? Here we use the annual averages, and in fact these are probably the ones most frequently used and quoted. The calculations are just the same as before.

    Average index for 1990   = 126.1

    Average index for 2000   = 170.3

    Again, we want the 2000 index based on 1990, that is, when the index in 1990 = 100, so we divide each index by 1.261:

    Index for 1990 $= \dfrac{126.1}{1.261} = 100.0$
    (Based on 1990 = 100)

    Index for 2000 $= \dfrac{170.3}{1.261} = 135.1$
    (Based on 1990 = 100)

    Therefore prices increased by 35.1% between 1990 and 2000.

- What is the price increase between March 1986 and December 1995? This is a little trickier as the index was rebased in 1987. The index number for January 1987, with January 1974 as the base year, is 394.5. To get index numbers based on January 1987 as 100 we therefore divide by 3.945. To go the other way, that is, from an index based on January 1987 = 100 to January 1974 = 100, we multiply the index number by 3.945 as follows:

Index for December 1995   = 150.7
(Based on January 1987 = 100)

Index for December 1995   = 150.7 × 3.945 = 594.5
(Based on January 1974 = 100)

Index for March 1986   = 381.6
(Based on January 1974 = 100)

We now have both the indices on the same base, ie January 1974 = 100. Next we calculate March 1986 as the new base point, converting it to 100 by dividing by 3.816:

Index for March 1986 $= \dfrac{381.6}{3.816} = 100.0$
(Based on March 1986 = 100)

Index for December 1995 $= \dfrac{594.5}{3.816} = 155.8$
(Based on March 1986 = 100)

Therefore prices increased by 55.8% over the period March 1986 to December 1995.

- What is the price increase between 1984 and 1997? Again we are covering a period with a change of base year, so we proceed as in the previous example.

Average index for 1997   = 157.5
(Based on January 1987 = 100)

Average index for 1997   = 157.5 × 3.945 = 621.3
(Based on January 1974 = 100)

Average index for 1984   = 351.8
(Based on January 1974 = 100)

As we want the 1997 index to be based on 1984, we divide each index by 3.518.

Index for 1984 $= \dfrac{351.8}{3.518} = 100.0$
(Based on 1984 = 100)

Index for 1997 $= \dfrac{621.3}{3.518} = 176.6$
(Based on 1984 5 100)

Therefore prices increased by 76.6% between 1984 and 1997.

As these examples show it is quite simple to manipulate the indices to get the information we want, but how might we use this information?

The RPI is a vital tool when we want to look at the trend in data over time which is affected by price increases. An obvious example is earnings. Suppose you want to look at how the earnings of your organisation's workforce have increased after allowing for inflation, or increased *in real terms*, which is the phrase commonly used. Suppose average earnings have moved in actual terms as shown in Table 20. and expressed as an index based on 1997 = 100.

Table 20.10 Average earnings for the organisation

Year	Earnings (£)	Index (based on 1997=100)
1997	12,000	100
1998	12,600	105
1999	14,100	118
2000	14,600	122
2001	15,800	132
2002	17,100	143
2003	17,700	148
2004	18,500	154

Over the whole period, earnings have apparently increased in money terms (that is, not adjusted for price inflation) by 54%.

Now let us adjust for price inflation using the RPI. There are two ways of doing this, both basically the same: express all the earnings either at 1997 prices or at 2004 prices. In fact we could express them in any price year, as long as we are consistent. Let us do it in terms of 1997 prices, and choose June 1997 as the base period, as June is the month of the organisation's pay settlements. We multiply each year's earnings by:

$$\frac{\text{RPI June 1997}}{\text{RPI in June of that year}}$$

The results are shown in Table 20.11.

Table 20.11 Earnings adjusted for price inflation

Year	Actual earnings (£)	RPI June	Earnings at 1997 prices (£)	Index (based on 1997=100)
1997	12,000	157.5	12,000 × 157.5 ÷ 157.5 = 12,000	100
1998	12,600	163.4	12,600 × 157.5 ÷ 163.4 = 12,145	101
1999	14,100	165.6	14,100 × 157.5 ÷ 165.6 = 13,410	112
2000	14,600	171.1	14,600 × 157.5 ÷ 171.1 = 13,440	112
2001	15,800	174.4	15,800 × 157.5 ÷ 174.4 = 14,269	119
2002	17,100	176.2	17,100 × 157.5 ÷ 176.2 = 15,285	127
2003	17,700	181.3	17,700 × 157.5 ÷ 181.3 = 15,376	128
2004	18,500	186.8	18,500 × 157.5 ÷ 186.8 = 15,598	130

Using the RPI gives quite a different picture. Overall real earnings have increased by only 30% in the seven years. Between 1999 and 2000 in real terms, earnings were virtually static. This was because although earnings rose by 3.5%, inflation rose by almost the same amount (171.1 ÷ 165.6, ie 3.3%). As you will appreciate, we feel sure, the trade unions will be far keener to talk about real earnings than actual earnings!

Clearly, when you look at earnings over a very long period, for example in social research, taking account of price inflation becomes essential. This is well demonstrated in this extract from the *Independent* reporting on a survey of the lives of children and young people:

> When teenagers started work in 1949, they were paid relatively low wages. On average a man aged under 21 earned 58 shillings and sixpence (£2.92) a week (or £152 per year), which, taking account of inflation, would be an annual wage of £2,872 today. Girls under 18 earned the equivalent of £2,460. The report said: 'Even the lowest paid just-out of-school workers would get at least £5,000 a year.'

> *(Independent*, January 1999)

Let us take another example. Suppose you are the manager of a department store and you measure your performance by sales. However, you are really interested to know how your sales have increased in real terms after taking out the effects of inflation, or what the *volume sales* increase is (as opposed to the sales value increase in actual money terms). This time we will express our sales in terms of the latest year, 2004, (and use the average annual indices), which we get by multiplying the sales figures by:

$$\frac{\text{RPI in 2004}}{\text{RPI in that year}}$$

Table 20.12 Sales volumes

Year	Actual sales (£m)	RPI (annual average)	Sales at 2004 prices (£m)	Index (based on 2000=100)
2000	20	170.3	20 × 186.7 ÷ 170.3 = 21.9	100
2001	25	173.3	25 × 186.7 ÷ 173.3 = 26.9	123
2002	27	176.2	27 × 186.7 ÷ 176.2 = 28.6	131
2003	30	181.3	30 × 186.7 ÷ 181.3 = 30.9	141
2004	36	186.7	36 × 186.7 ÷ 186.7 = 36.0	164

Therefore, over the period 2000 to 2004, sales increased by volume by some 64%.

We hope you have begun to see just how useful is the RPI. The most commonly available source is the *Monthly Digest of Statistics* which, as the name suggests, is published monthly by the government. There are other price indices available, geared towards particular sectors. For example, producer price indices measure the prices that producers have to pay for inputs such as raw materials and fuel. This is a producers' price index rather than a consumers' price index like the RPI. As the price of inputs eventually feed through to the finished product and consumer prices, the producer price indices are often seen as an early warning of changes in inflation levels.

STOCK MARKET INDICES

Another set of well-known and regularly quoted indices are those applying to the stock market. Stock market indices tell us the movement over time in aggregate share prices, or the prices of other listed securities such as bonds. In Great Britain the most widely used and best known are those published in the *Financial Times* (*FT*). Some of these are calculated by the *FT* itself, but the indices in most common use nowadays are those with FTSE in the title. They were formerly a joint enterprise between the *FT* and the London Stock Exchange but are now calculated and updated by an independent company, FTSE Group.

The most commonly quoted index of the London market nowadays is the FTSE 100 or 'Footsie 100'. As its name suggests it comprises 100 shares, representing the largest and most active shares in the market. It is calculated continuously throughout the day. The base level was set at 1,000 at the end of business on 30 December 1983. The next 250 companies in terms of importance comprise the FTSE 250 index which, taken together with the FTSE 100, gives the FTSE 350 index. Smaller companies are represented by the FTSE Small Cap index.

The widest index is the FTSE All-Share index, which includes all the companies in the above indices, and represents over 98% of the value of UK companies listed on the London market. This is broken down into numerous sub-sectors according to industry and type of business. Investors thus have benchmarks against which to compare the performance of specific parts of their portfolios.

In addition there are separate indices of particular sectors of the market, such as technology stocks (which may cross several industrial categories).

The *FT*'s own FT30 index is a much older yardstick. It is a price index of the shares of 30 premier industrial, commercial and financial companies in the United Kingdom. Started in 1935, it is not now very representative of the importance of different sectors of the market and is comparatively rarely quoted. It serves mainly as a very long-run measure of the performance of the UK market and as a measure of market mood on any particular day. The *FT* also publishes its own long-running indices of government bonds.

Other indices published daily in the *FT* cover the performance of stocks in a particular overseas country or geographic region. In addition, the *FT* quotes published indices like the Dow Jones Industrial Average for Wall Street or the Nikkei for Tokyo which are produced in other countries for their own markets. Overseas indices should be used with caution because (you will appreciate this as a student of statistics) they are not all calculated in the same way.

SOURCES OF DATA

Sources of data are categorised into two main types – *primary data* and *secondary data*. Primary data is data that you collect specifically for your own purpose(s), eg carrying out a survey of staff attitudes to the staff restaurant or asking managers to monitor timekeeping over a period of time. Secondary data is data that has been collected for another purpose which you then go on to use for your analysis. In simplistic terms there are three types of secondary data:

- Information from within your own organisation. Most organisations maintain a wide range of information, eg sales information, information on employees, such as numbers, ages, salary levels, absence data, etc. This information will probably have been collected to monitor the performance of the organisation, or for payroll or pension purposes, etc. However, you may want to go on and use it to analyse productivity, or to explore absence rates and their relationship to other variables such as age, salary level, etc, ie use it for your own specific purpose. The advantage of this type of secondary data is that it is usually readily available (assuming the organisation has a well designed and developed information system – see Part 1). There may be problems of confidentiality, and perhaps issues such as the data not quite being in the form that is required. For example, a reorganisation might make it difficult to track sales and workforce information for a specific department over time, or data from the performance management system might be kept as individual records on a manual system, and it would be a major collation job to look at average performance grades, etc.

- Information that is in the public domain. In the next section we discuss some of the most useful sources from government statistical publications. The government amasses and publishes information on a wide range of areas, usually in very summary form, for the United Kingdom as a whole or on a regional basis, or particular sectors of industry. There are also sources of published information on individual organisations.
- Private market research information, which is available at a cost, perhaps through membership of a particular group of organisations or simply by purchasing the results.

Information from within your organisation is essentially the subject of Part 1 of this book. We go on here to look at the other areas.

GOVERNMENT STATISTICAL PUBLICATIONS

Some of the most commonly used sources are set out below and categorised by type of data. All are available from The Stationery Office, tel: 0870 600 5522. The government website www.statistics.gov.uk is also a valuable source of online government data.

General information

General information is set out in the following publications:

- *Monthly Digest of Statistics*, a collection of the main sources of statistics from all government departments.
- *Annual Abstract of Statistics*, which contains more series of data than the *Monthly Digest* and a greater run of years.
- *Social Trends*, which draws together key social and economic data to show trends in society (annual).
- *Regional Trends*, which includes a wide range of demographic, social, industrial and economic statistics at a regional level (annual).

Population and households

Population and household information is available from:

- *Census*: a full census is carried out every 10 years. The last one was in 2001, giving information across a whole range of subjects, for example, household composition, income, transport to work, etc.
- *Expenditure and Food Survey*, a continuous survey of household expenditure, food consumption and income (annual).
- *General Household Survey*, a continuous sample survey of households covering a wide range of social and economic policy areas (annual).

Employment/earnings/retail prices

Details on employment, earnings and retail prices are set out in:

- *Labour Market Trends*, which includes information on employment and unemployment, earnings, labour costs, retail prices and so on (monthly).

- *New Earnings Survey*, which relates to earnings from employment by industry category, at April each year.

General economy

General economic statistics are set out in:

- *Economic Trends*, a useful selection of tables and charts on the United Kingdom economy (monthly).
- The *United Kingdom National Accounts* – the *Blue Book* – gives detailed estimates of the national accounts (annual). It is a bit heavy going for most people but beloved by economists.

A useful reference tool is the *Guide to Official Statistics* which provides a comprehensive list of official statistics with a brief description of the data and their availability.

PRIVATE MARKET RESEARCH

There are numerous surveys carried out regularly by private agencies. Some of the ones with which we are most familiar are:

- income and earnings surveys
- public opinion surveys on such topics as the state of the UK political parties, people's views on the environment, etc
- surveys aimed at particular industries or products, for example, the *Which?* consumer surveys on cars, and market reports produced by such organisations as the Economist Intelligence Unit.

ORGANISATION INFORMATION

There are four excellent sources of information on individual organisations:

- The annual report and accounts published by all stock market-quoted companies. Often these are in the form of glossy brochures and, apart from giving the financial information on the company, they give background information on the company's products, its workforce, markets, expansion plans and so on.
- Stockbroker bulletins – city brokers regularly produce bulletins on companies for their investors. Again, although biased towards the investor, they usually provide a very useful appraisal of the company.
- Newspaper articles – particularly from the *Financial Times*, and other quality newspapers – often provide an easy-to-read, potted summary of the company's characteristics. They are usually published when annual or interim results are announced, or when there is some particular interest in a company – perhaps a takeover bid, or the company has diversified in some way. Some large libraries carry a very useful reference set of such articles, called McCarthy cards, indexed by company name.
- Companies House holds information concerning live companies in England and Wales and brief details on dissolved ones, eg annual accounts and lists of directors. Its website, www.companieshouse.gov.uk, provides free access to basic company information. Similar information is available for companies registered in Scotland and Northern Ireland.

A growing trend for information in the public domain is to be able to obtain access to it through the Internet.

Finally, a word of caution about all sources of secondary data. It is very important to read the small print, and ask questions such as: does the data refer to the United Kingdom or Great Britain? How does workforce data deal with part-time workers? Does salary information include bonuses? Have there been any changes in the way the data has been collected over time?

The great advantage of secondary data is that it is usually much cheaper than collecting your own primary data and often immediately available. Its great downfall is that you need to be sure that it does in fact provide you with the information you need.

CONCLUSION

We hope that our discussion of index numbers has given you a feel for this very useful topic. Together with the rich and varied sources of information detailed above, it should help you to get to grips with analysing and understanding organisations and their happenings. If you are in doubt about sources of information, a good place to start is the research library or knowledge website of your own organisation, if such a facility exists. The CIPD's own library and website is another useful source, and of course, increasingly such information is available generally through the Internet. Otherwise a local college/university library, or the local public library, will contain a surprising amount of information, and have very helpful staff who know where to find it for you.

REVIEW QUESTIONS

1. You work for an organisation that makes components for cars. You want to know how productivity has changed over the last five years in a factory which makes a specific component. There was a major upgrade of the machines in Year 4. You have assembled the following information:

Year	Production (000s)	Workforce
1	323	165
2	350	173
3	363	175
4	405	200
5	455	200

Comment on the results.

2. The Learning and Development department has been set some performance targets. The results for the year 2004 are set out below.

Performance indicator	Target	Actual
Learning days/employee (days)	4	4.4
Satisfaction score (out of 6)	5	4.5
Utilisation of learning facilitators (%)	75	81
Utilisation of learning accommodation (%)	90	70

Present the results in a simple visual way and comment briefly on them.

3. There have been a number of complaints from members of staff that prices in the staff canteen having been rising very fast. You have been asked by your MD to investigate and have come up with following information covering the last five years.

Year	Average earnings in the organisation	Average price of lunch	RPI (all items)	RPI canteen meals
2000	12450	4.40	170.3	233.8
2001	13000	4.70	173.3	245.9
2002	13600	4.90	176.2	260.3
2003	14756	5.00	181.3	271.2
2004	16000	5.50	186.7	280.7

Comment on the results.

Decision theory

CHAPTER OBJECTIVES

When you have studied this chapter, you will be able to:

- explain the use of pay-off tables and the maximin/minimax/maximax/minimin criteria in structured decision-making situations
- use expected monetary values to make decisions
- use decision trees to structure and make decisions
- explain the concepts of risk and utility.

INTRODUCTION

In Part 1 we discussed the main purpose of information systems as being to provide information for our decision-making, and discussed the decision-making process itself. *Decision theory* is a rather grand name for what is quite a straightforward approach to structured decision-making. Decision theory, or as it is sometimes called *decision analysis*, is used to arrive at an optimal (best) strategy when faced with a number of alternative strategies or decisions and an uncertain future situation.

To take a very simple example, suppose we are a buyer for a clothes shop and we need to decide in the autumn how much rainwear to buy for the spring. Clearly if there is a wet spring and summer, demand will be great, but if the sun shines a lot, the demand will be limited. On the one hand we want to buy enough to meet demand and gain maximum profits, but on the other hand we do not want to buy too much and end up having stock on our hands at the end of the season, which the shop will have to reduce in price to sell. How do we decide what to buy so far in advance, when nobody can know for certain what the weather is going to be like?

We look first at a very simple way of structuring such decisions using the technique of pay-off tables and then applying some simple decision criteria. We then go on to discuss the technique of expected monetary value, and the concepts of risk and utility.

PAY-OFF TABLES

The best way to explain decision theory is to use an example. Suppose we are furniture manufacturers and we want to build a new factory. We have the choice between building either a small, medium or large factory. We therefore have three decision choices which we shall call d_1, d_2 and d_3:

d_1 = build a small factory

d_2 = build a medium-size factory

d_3 = build a large factory

Our decision will be based on how we see the future market for our product. In this simple example, suppose there are two possible outcomes – a high demand or a low demand. If we build our factory too small and demand is high, we will lose sales and profit. However, if we build our factory too large and demand is low, we will have expensive spare capacity on our hands and potential losses. Let us label the two outcomes O_1 and O_2:

O_1 = low demand

O_2 = high demand

The next step is to estimate the pay-offs for each combination of decision and outcome. In this case the pay-off is measured in terms of profit, and we can construct a *pay-off table* for this decision-making problem as shown in Table 21.1.

Table 21.1 Pay-off table

Decision choice	Outcome	
	Low demand O_1	High demand O_2
Build a small factory d_1	£20,000	£50,000
Build a medium factory d_2	£10,000	£80,000
Build a large factory d_3	–£10,000	£100,000

The figures in this table are best estimates of what the profit might be under the different circumstances. In a commercial situation we probably would have a good idea what the demand might be, but let us assume that we have no confidence in our view of the future. In this case, we will need some criteria or some basis on which to make our decision. Let us look at two of these – the *maximin/minimax* criterion and the *maximax/minimin* criterion.

Maximin/minimax

The *maximin* decision criterion is the pessimistic, or conservative, approach to arriving at a decision. As the name suggests, the aim is to maximise the minimum possible pay-offs, or in this case profits. From Table 21.1, the minimum pay-offs for each decision are:

Decision choice	Minimum pay-off
Build a small factory d_1	£20,000
Build a medium factory d_2	£10,000
Build a large factory d_3	–£10,000

We then choose the decision which gives us the maximum of the minimum pay-offs. In this example we would choose d_1: to build a small factory.

If the pay-off table was constructed on the basis of costs rather than profit, we would reverse the criterion to *minimax*: that is, we would choose the minimum from the list of the maximum costs related to each decision.

Maximax/minimin

While maximin and minimax offers a pessimistic decision criterion, *maximax* does quite the opposite – it is an optimistic criterion. This time we list the maximum pay-offs for each decision:

Decision choice	Maximum pay-off
Build a small factory d_1	£50,000
Build a medium factory d_2	£80,000
Build a large factory d_3	£100,000

Then we select the decision that gives the maximum pay-off – in this case, to build a large factory. Again, if we are dealing with a pay-off table of costs, we would reverse the criterion and use a *minimin* criterion.

EXPECTED MONETARY VALUE

We now go on to look at a slightly more complex, but more useful technique, for making decisions where you have some expectation, or can apply some probability to the outcomes. Suppose we have a number 'n' of decision alternatives:

$$d_1 \, d_2 \, ... \, d_n$$

and a number N of outcomes

$$O_1 \, O_2 \, ... \, O_N$$

Suppose also:

p_1 = probability of outcome O_1 occurring
p_2 = probability of outcome O_2 occurring
.
.
.
p_N = probability of outcome O_N occurring

You will recall from the discussion on probability in Chapter 15 that:

$p_i \geq 0$ for all outcomes, and

$p_1 + p_2 + ... p_N = 1$

The *expected monetary value* (EMV) of a decision is the sum of the weighted pay-offs for each outcome, with the weights being the probability of that pay-off or outcome occurring. Therefore the EMV of a particular decision d_i

= $p_1 \times$ pay-off for decision i and outcome 1
  + $p_2 \times$ pay-off for decision i and outcome 2
   .
   .
   .
  + $p_N \times$ pay-off for decision i and outcome N

Using this formula and the factory example, let us assume that there is a probability of 0.4 that low demand will be the outcome, and a probability of 0.6 that high demand will be the outcome. Then:

EMV of decision d_1 = (0.4 × 20,000) + (0.6 × 50,000) = £38,000

EMV of decision d_2 = (0.4 × 10,000) + (0.6 × 80,000) = £52,000

EMV of decision d_3 = (0.4 × −10,000)+ (0.6 × 100,000) = £56,000

The criterion for selection is the decision with the highest expected monetary value – in this case, d_3.

If the probabilities are reversed (that is, the probability for low demand is 0.6 and for high demand is 0.4) then the calculation produces the following EMVs:

EMV of decision d_1 = (0.6 × 20,000) + (0.4 × 50,000) = £32,000

EMV of decision d_2 = (0.6 × 10,000) + (0.4 × 80,000) = £38,000

EMV of decision d_3 = (0.6 × −10,000) + (0.4 × 100,000) = £34,000

Now the decision to be taken is d_2 – to build a medium-size factory.

So, it can be seen that the choice of decision is critically dependent on the probabilities of the different outcomes occurring. More about this later, but let us now take a look at a way of analysing decision-making problems graphically using a decision tree.

DECISION TREES

You will remember that in Chapter 15 we used a tree diagram to visualise a multi-step experiment of tossing a coin twice. We use a similar diagram here to help in the solution of decision-making problems. We can re-express the furniture factory problem, using a *decision tree*, as shown in Figure 21.1.

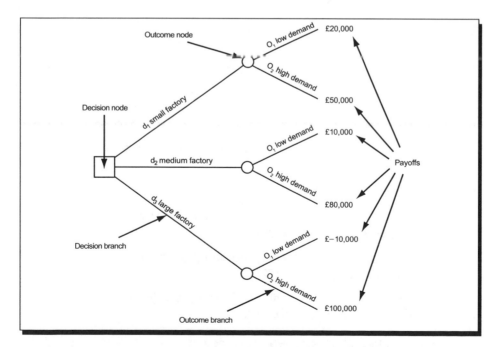

Figure 21.1 Decision tree of factory problem

237

The tree is made up of nodes:

■ decision nodes
■ outcome nodes.

and branches:

■ decision branches
■ outcome branches.

If we now add in the probabilities of the outcomes occurring, for example 0.4 for low demand and 0.6 for high demand, the tree looks like Figure 21.2.

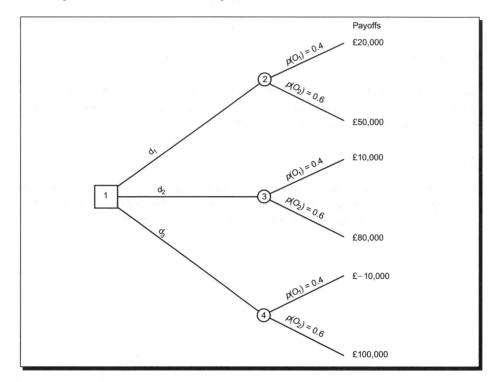

Figure 21.2 Decision tree of factory problem showing probabilities of outcomes

We work backwards through the tree shown in Figure 21.2.

EMV of node 2	$= (0.4 \times 20{,}000) + (0.6 \times 50{,}000)$
(Same as EMV of d_1)	$= £38{,}000$
EMV of node 3	$= (0.4 \times 10{,}000) + (0.6 \times 80{,}000)$
(Same as EMV of d_2)	$= £52{,}000$
EMV of node 4	$= (0.4 \times -10{,}000) + (0.6 \times 100{,}000)$
(Same as EMV of d_3)	$= £56{,}000$

We now have a decision tree which looks like Figure 21.3.

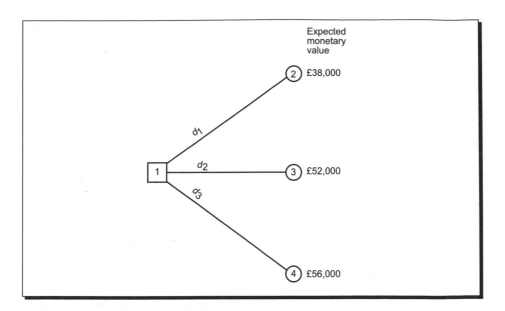

Figure 21.3 Decision tree of factory problem showing expected monetary values of the decisions

It can be seen that the best decision is again d_3, exactly the same as using the expected monetary value criteria and the pay-off table. The decision tree is really just a graphical representation of the pay-off table.

We have noted the importance of the probabilities of the outcomes. How do we arrive at them? Well, there are several ways – for example, we might look at what has happened in similar circumstances in the past, or carry out a market research survey, or use a qualitative technique such as the Delphi approach of asking experts for their views (see Chapter 19). It is even possible to work out how much it is worth paying for information on probabilities.

RISK AND UTILITY

Another area of decision-making concerns the decision-maker's attitude to *risk*. Suppose we are faced with the choice of two investments – investment X will provide us with a definite return of £10,000, while investment Y will provide us with a 50:50 chance of £30,000 or nothing:

EMV (X) = £10,000

EMV (Y) = $(0.5 \times 30,000) + (0.5 \times 0) = £15,000$

Based on the earlier criterion we should choose investment Y. However, it is quite likely that the investor would choose investment X. We see creeping in here the preference of the decision-maker. Investment X is said to have a higher *utility* – utility being a measure of the decision-maker's preference which takes into account not just the expected monetary value but the risks involved.

The concept of utility is particularly useful where there is no strict money value, like profits or costs, associated with an outcome. There are some interesting examples of this in the field of medicine, and to demonstrate the contribution that decision theory can make to dealing with such problems, let us look at the very difficult decision which faces some people of whether to have an operation.

There are probabilities associated with the outcomes: the operation might be a success or it might not. So here we have a classic decision-making situation with known probabilities of the risks. However, it is not possible to set monetary values on the outcomes. Each patient will have his or her own set of utilities, which take into account what it would mean to him or her either to live with an unsuccessful outcome to the operation, or to live with not having the operation. It can be a very difficult decision, but it is one that can sometimes be helped by using a decision-analysis technique.

CONCLUSION

So as you have seen, decision theory is quite easy. Although we have tackled it at a simple level, the concepts can be applied widely and to more complex situations. In essence, it is a way of approaching and structuring the decision-making process in a logical and systematic way, using some predetermined criteria. Try using the techniques in some of your everyday situations and see which criterion suits you, what is your attitude to risk, and what are your utilities.

REVIEW QUESTIONS

1. A company has produced an innovative gadget for cleaning shoes called ShoePerfect. The initial market research has suggested that if the company decides to manufacture and sell the product itself, there are two possible scenarios: high demand, which would result in profits of £300,000, and low demand, resulting in a profit of £50,000. Alternatively, the company has been made an offer of £150,000 to buy out the patent. Given the innovative nature of the project, there is little information on the likelihood of the different scenarios occurring. Structure the problem to help the company in its decision-making.

2. You are working in the HR department of a medium-sized organisation and currently your information costs per employee are £150. You are considering investing in a state-of-the-art HR information system (HRIS). There is every likelihood that the organisation will undergo a major expansion. If this expansion goes ahead and you purchase the system, the cost per employee will be £100. If you do not purchase the HRIS, you are likely to have to subcontract a lot of the information processing work at a cost of £175 per employee. There is a small chance, estimated at around 20% that the expansion will not take place, in which case the system would result in a cost per employee of £200. Structure the problem so as to help in the discussion with the management team – you have found in the past that a visual approach is useful.

Using a computer package for statistical analysis

CHAPTER OBJECTIVES

When you have studied this chapter, you will be able to:

■ use a typical spreadsheet package, Microsoft Excel™, to undertake a selection of the statistical processes described in this book.

INTRODUCTION

Computers can play a very important role in helping managers, administrators and HR professionals understand, explore, analyse and present data – transforming it into information that will be useful to the organisation. Once the province of the professional statistician, many software packages used for statistical analysis are both relatively inexpensive and also accessible to the layperson. This has provided the layperson with the ability to carry out quite sophisticated statistical processes relatively easily. However, herein lies the potential dual danger, of using an inappropriate statistical approach and of misinterpreting the outcomes of the analysis. That is why in this book we have tried to give you an understanding of:

■ what the different techniques can be used for
■ the logic and rationale behind the techniques – without overwhelming you with too much statistical theory (we hope!) – because we believe that if you understand some of the theory you will be able to make better use of the technique
■ some of the pitfalls to watch out for.

There are a number of statistical packages available, ranging from sophisticated packages such as SPSS™ and Minitab™, through smaller packages designed for specific purposes, eg learning evaluation, manipulating competency data etc, to general purpose spreadsheets such as Microsoft Excel™, which have basic statistical capabilities. If you want to analyse the results of a survey, then a package such as SPSS™ is designed to handle the quantitative outcomes from questionnaires and produce tabulations and charts, as well as carry out more complex statistical techniques. If you want to analyse general data such as sales information and absence rates, the facilities offered by a package such as Microsoft Excel™ will meet the majority of needs. Such packages also usually have very good facilities for producing a wide range of charts quickly and easily.

As many readers will have access to a spreadsheet package, in this chapter we concentrate on the facilities offered by a typical package, Microsoft Excel™. We describe how to use it to undertake a selection of the statistical processes described in this book. Our aim is not to provide a comprehensive guide, but to demonstrate how straightforward it is to undertake simple statistical analyses using such packages.

Please note that we are not trying to teach you how to use Microsoft Excel™, and in fact assume that you have some knowledge of the basic commands, such as how to open worksheets, save worksheets, move and copy data, etc. Also bear in mind that the rate of change and improvement of all software packages is so great that by the time you come to read this book, it is possible that some of the details will have changed.

As a starting point remember that, like all spreadsheet packages, the basic working document in Microsoft Excel™ is the *worksheet*, which consists of rows and columns which can be used to enter and store data.

FREQUENCY DISTRIBUTIONS

Aim: To produce a frequency distribution, a cumulative frequency distribution and a histogram.

Example: Ages of employees from Chapter 12.

Process
Step 1   Input the data - see Figure 22.1, as rows 4 to 37 of column A.

Step 2   Identify bins (an Excel term) for the upper limit of the classes, < 20, 20–24, 25–29, etc, that you wish to use for grouping the data, eg 19, 24, 29 as rows 4 to 13 of column C.

Step 3   Select *tools* from menu.

Step 4   Select *data analysis* option.

Step 5   Select *histogram*.

Step 6   In the dialogue box, enter:

input range: A4:A37

bin range: C4:C13

Select *output range* and enter *E4* (this identifies the upper left-hand corner of the area in the worksheet where the frequency distribution will appear). Select *chart output*. Select *ok*.

Note
If the data analysis facility is not available in the tools menu, it is usually possible to install it by selecting *add-ins* from the *tools* menu, then selecting *data analysis toolpak* and entering *ok*.

The frequency distribution and accompanying histogram produced by this process is shown on Figure 22.1. To obtain the cumulative frequency distribution, follow the above steps, but select *cumulative percentage* instead of *chart output*.

	A	B	C	D	E	F	G	H
1								
2								
3	AGES		BINS					
4	25		19		Bin	Frequency		
5	56		24		19	3		
6	22		29		24	4		
7	53		34		29	5		
8	21		39		34	5		
9	30		44		39	9		
10	30		49		44	3		
11	18		54		49	2		
12	39		59		54	1		
13	43		64		59	1		
14	32				64	1		
15	42				More	0		
16	35							
17	41				Bin	Frequency	Cumulative %	
18	29				19	3	8.8%	
19	35				24	4	20.6%	
20	39				29	5	35.3%	
21	32				34	5	50.0%	
22	37				39	9	76.5%	
23	47				44	3	85.3%	
24	29				49	2	91.2%	
25	38				54	1	94.1%	
26	46				59	1	97.1%	
27	36				64	1	100.0%	
28	17				More	0	100.0%	
29	22							
30	24							
31	16							
32	27							
33	37							
34	35							
35	29							
36	62							
37	34							
38								
39								
40								
41								
42								
43								

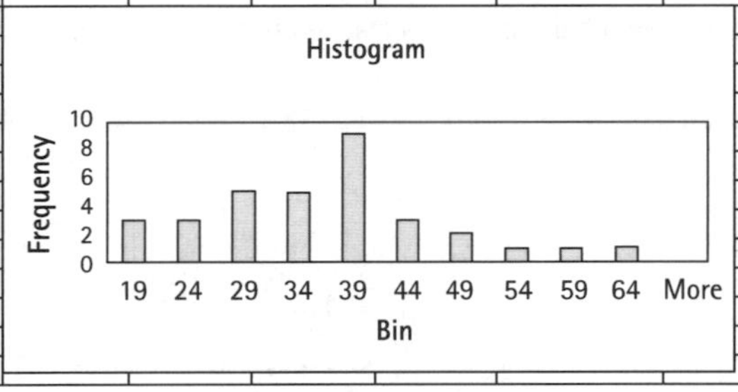

Histogram

Figure 22.1 Frequency distribution, cumulative frequency distribution and histogram

Once you have produced the histogram it is possible to improve its presentation by resizing, better labelling and scaling of axes and so on using the various chart facilities offered by Microsoft Excel™ (see under the section on Diagrammatic methods).

DIAGRAMMATIC METHODS

Microsoft Excel™ is excellent at producing all sorts of diagrams and charts.

Aim: To produce a bar diagram, stacked bar diagram and pie chart.

Example: Sales performance from Chapter 13.

Process
Step 1 Input data on sales performance – see Figure 22.2. Select the data by highlighting it, including the row and column labels.

Step 2	On the toolbar, select the *chart wizard* icon (looks like a bar chart).
Step 3	You will be offered a range of types of charts. Select the appropriate type, eg *column, pie chart,* etc. Select the appropriate sub-type by highlighting the appropriate chart. Enter *next.*
Step 4	The dialogue box will show the highlighted table in the *data range* box.
	Select the row or column option. Choosing the row option for our bar chart would give months along the *x* axis; choosing the column option would give sales persons along the *x* axis. Enter *next.*
Step 5	Enter the chart title and axes labels in *category x axis* and *value y axis* boxes. Enter *next.*
Step 6	Select whether you wish the chart to be shown as *new sheet*, ie as a separate worksheet, or *object in*, ie embedded in the existing worksheet with the data set (as shown in Figure 22.2). Enter *finish.*

Figure 22.2 shows a bar diagram, a stacked bar diagram and a pie chart for January sales.

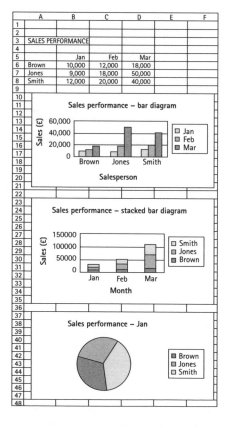

Figure 22.2 Bar diagram, stacked bar diagram and pie chart

The chart wizard facility offers the opportunity to produce a wide range of different diagrams in all sorts of different formats. For example, the bar charts and pie charts can be shown three-dimensionally. It also offers the facility to produce graphs, scatter diagrams and radar diagrams as well as some more unusual charts.

It is very easy to customise the presentation, for example choosing the font size of the chart titles and axes labels, the scale of the axes, and the colour and patterns used for the bars.

NUMERICAL METHODS

Microsoft Excel™ has a very useful facility for producing a range of descriptive statistics through operating one function.

Aim: To produce the mean, median, mode, range, standard deviation and variance.

Example: Repair times from Chapter 14.

Process
Step 1   Input data on repair times for Machine A – see Figure 22.3.

Step 2   Select *tools* from menu.

Step 3   Select *data analysis* option.

Step 4   Select *descriptive statistics*.

Step 5   In the dialogue box, enter:

input range: A5:A24 for Machine A.

Select *output range* and enter: *D3* (this identifies the upper left-hand corner of the area in the worksheet where the descriptive statistics will appear).

Select *summary statistics*. Select *ok.*

Step 6   Repeat above steps for Machine B.

	A	B	C	D	E
1					
2					
3	REPAIR TIMES			Machine A	
4	Machine A	Machine B			
5	5	3		Mean	4.00
6	4	4		Standard Error	0.16
7	3	5		Median	4.00
8	4	5		Mode	4.00
9	3	2		Standard Deviation	0.73
10	5	7		Sample Variance	0.53
11	4	5		Kurtosis	-0.93
12	4	4		Skewness	0.00
13	4	3		Range	2.00
14	5	5		Minimum	3.00
15	3	4		Maximum	5.00
16	4	2		Sum	80.00
17	3	6		Count	20
18	3	4			
19	4	4		Machine B	
20	4	5			
21	4	3		Mean	4.00
22	5	4		Standard Error	0.30
23	5	3		Median	4.00
24	4	2		Mode	4.00
25				Standard Deviation	1.34
26				Sample Variance	1.79
27				Kurtosis	-0.07
28				Skewness	0.29
29				Range	5.00
30				Minimum	2.00
31				Maximum	7.00
32				Sum	80.00
33				Count	20.00

Figure 22.3 Descriptive statistics

As you can see from Figure 22.3, it is possible to obtain a wide range of descriptive statistics. We have highlighted the statistics of greatest interest. Some of the others are familiar, eg minimum and maximum values of the data set, the sum of all the data values, the number of data values. Some of the other items, eg standard error, kurtosis and skewness, are beyond the scope of this book.

SAMPLING

Aim: To produce confidence intervals for the sample mean.

Example: Package weights from Chapter 16.

Process
This is a two-stage process:

1. Calculate the sample mean and sample standard deviation.
2. Calculate the confidence limits.

The first stage is accomplished by the process described in the previous section on descriptive statistics.

Step 1 Input data on journey times – see Figure 22.4.

Step 2   Calculate the sample mean and sample deviation as in previous section.

Step 3   Choose an empty set of cells to record the result.

Step 4   Select *insert* from menu.

Step 5   Select *functions* option.

Step 6   Select function category: *statistical.*
Select function name: *confidence.* Select *ok.*

Step 7   In the dialogue box, enter:
alpha: 0.05 (for 95% confidence limits, alpha = 1 − 0.95).
standard dev: 11.1 (from Descriptive Statistics).
size: 30 (size of sample).
Select *finish.*

Notes
1   Instead of using *insert* and *functions*, you can use the *functions wizard* f_x.
2   It is possible to calculate the sample mean and standard deviation through using the *functions wizard* – using *average* and *stdev.*
3   Within the *descriptive statistics* option is the facility to calculate the confidence level of the mean. However, this is for small sample sizes, ie less than 30.

	A	B	C	D	E	F	G	H
1								
2								
3	AVERAGE PACKAGE WEIGHTS							
4	160			Descriptive statistics				
5	179							
6	188			Mean	170.5			
7	180			St. error	2.0			
8	188			Median	181.0			
9	195			Mode	172.0			
10	185			St. dev	11.1			
11	190			Sample V	122.9			
12	162			Kurtosis	−1.0			
13	165			Skewness	−0.2			
14	183			Range	39.0			
15	199			Maximum	160.0			
16	167			Minimum	199.0			
17	192			Sum	5385.0			
18	186			Count	30.0			
19	181							
20	194			Interval		4.0		
21	172			Confidence interval		175.5	to	183.5
22	182							
23	166							
24	187							
25	172							
26	168							
27	181							
28	175							
29	176							
30	195							
31	161							
32	184							
33	172							

Figure 22.4 Confidence interval for a sample mean

REGRESSION AND CORRELATION

Aim: To produce the regression equation, coefficient of determination and chart showing the regression line on the scatter diagram.

Example: Haulage costs from Chapter 18.

Process

Step 1   Input the data on haulage costs and distance in Figure 22.5. Select the data, ie columns *B7:B14* and *C7:C14*, and make sure the x values (distance data) are in the first column.

Step 2   On the toolbar, select the *chart wizard* icon (looks like a bar chart).

Step 3   You will be offered a range of types of charts – select the appropriate type, ie *XY (scatter)*.
Select the appropriate sub-type by highlighting the appropriate chart.
Enter *next*.

Step 4   The dialogue box will show the highlighted data in the *data range* box.
Enter *next*.

Step 5   Enter the *chart title* and axes labels in *category x axis* and *value y axis* boxes.
Enter *next*.

Step 6   Select whether you wish the chart to be shown as *new sheet*, ie as a separate worksheet, or *object in*, ie imbedded embedded in the existing worksheet with the data set (as shown in Figure 22.5).
Enter *finish*.

Step 7   Select *chart* on the toolbar.
Select *add trendline* (to add the regression line to the chart).

Step 8   In the dialogue box, select type by highlighting the appropriate chart.
Select *options*.
Select *display equation on chart*.
Select *display R^2 value on chart*.
Enter *ok*.

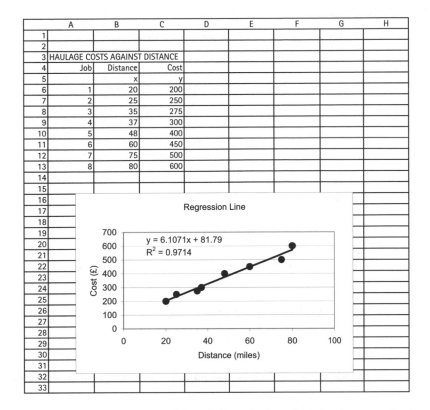

Figure 22.5 Regression equation, coefficient of determination, chart showing regression line on the scatter diagram

As you can see from Figure 22.5, the process described above first plots the data on a chart, then draws the regression line on the chart, and finally prints out the equation for the regression line and the coefficient of determination (R^2) on the chart. To calculate the correlation coefficient, you simply take the square root of the coefficient of determination. You can also calculate the correlation coefficient using f_x, the *statistical* category and choosing the *correl* option.

An alternative process using *tools* from the menu, the *data analysis wizard*, followed by the *regression* option, provides output in tabular form but in a more complex format. This output also includes information which allows you to test that the relationship between the two variables is significant, and provides confidence limits for the parameters in the regression line – both of which are beyond the scope of this book.

FORECASTING

We cover two of the key techniques, moving average forecast and trend projections.

Aim: To produce a moving average forecast of a set of data.

Example: Flour sales from Chapter 19.

Process

Step 1 Input data on flour sales – see Figure 22.6.

Step 2 Select *tools* from menu.

Step 3 Select *data analysis* option.

Step 4 Select *moving average*.

Step 5 In the dialogue box, enter:
input range: B7:B22 for flour sales
interval: 4 (for a four-weekly moving average)
output range: D7 (this identifies the upper left-hand corner of the area in the worksheet where the descriptive statistics will appear). It is helpful to choose the appropriate cell which places the forecasts against the correct period.

Select *chart output*. Select *ok*.

The process described above produces a four-weekly moving average forecast and a chart showing the original data set and the moving average. (The presentation of the chart can be customised in terms of labelling the axes, adjusting the title, scale, etc). Using the basic spreadsheet facilities, we have gone on to calculate the mean squared error (MSE) of the forecast (Σ(forecast error)^2 /12) as a measure of the accuracy of the forecast (see Figure 22.6).

You will recall from Chapter 19 how we commented that you could vary the interval for the moving average in order to minimise the forecasting error. We repeated the process to produce a three-weekly moving average forecast, just altering the input for the interval to three instead of four, and again calculated the MSE. You will see that in fact a three-weekly moving average is a slightly better approach to smoothing the data.

Aim: To produce trend projections.

Example: Toaster production from Chapter 19.

Process

If we just want to produce the forecasts, then the following process does this very simply.

Step 1 Input data on toaster production in Figure 22.7.

Step 2 Choose an empty cell to record the output, ie the forecast.

Step 3 Select *insert* from menu.

Step 4 Select *functions* option.

Step 5 Select function category: *statistical.*
Select function name: *forecast.*
Select *ok.*

Step 6 In the dialogue box, enter:
X: 11 (the year for which you want your forecast).
Known Ys: B7:B16 (toaster production data – see Figure 22.7).
Known Xs: A7:A16 (years data – see Figure 22.7).
Select *ok.*

	A	B	C	D	E	F	G	H
1								
2								
3	FLOUR SALES							
4	Week	Flour	4-week	Forecast	Error	3-week	Forecast	Error
5		sales	moving	error	squared	moving	error	squared
6			average	B–C	$(B-C)^2$	average	B–F	$(B-F)^2$
7	1	30						
8	2	33						
9	3	29						
10	4	32				30.67	1.33	1.78
11	5	30	31	-1	1.00	31.33	-1.33	1.78
12	6	32	31	1	1.00	30.33	1.67	2.78
13	7	34	30.75	3.25	10.56	31.33	2.67	7.11
14	8	30	32	-2	4.00	32.00	-2.00	4.00
15	9	31	31.5	-0.5	0.25	32.00	-1.00	1.00
16	10	28	31.75	-3.75	14.06	31.67	-3.67	13.44
17	11	32	30.75	1.25	1.56	29.67	2.33	5.44
18	12	35	30.25	4.75	22.56	30.33	4.67	21.78
19	13	32	31.5	0.5	0.25	31.67	0.33	0.11
20	14	29	31.75	-2.75	7.56	33.00	-4.00	16.00
21	15	31	32	-1	1.00	32.00	-1.00	1.00
22	16	28	31.75	-3.75	14.06	30.67	-2.67	7.13
23				Total	77.88		Total	83.33
24				MSE	6.49		MSE	6.41
25								

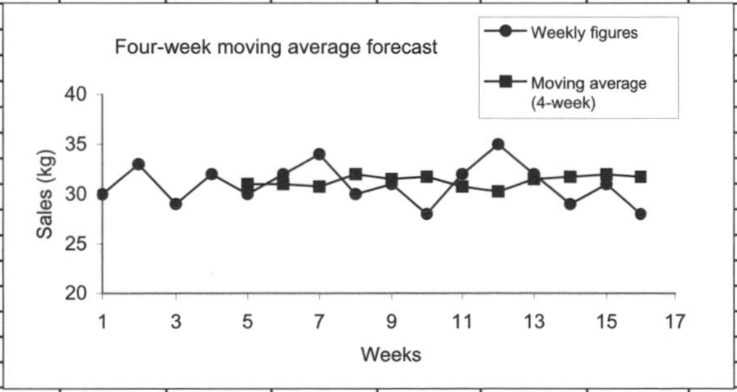

Figure 22.6 Moving average forecasts

	A	B	C	D	E
1					
2					
3	TOASTER PRODUCTION				
4	Year	Toaster		Forecast	Forecast
5		production		Year 11	Year 12
6		(000s)			
7	1	50		61.00	62.13
8	2	52			
9	3	56			
10	4	51			
11	5	48			
12	6	54			
13	7	57			
14	8	60			
15	9	62			
16	10	58			

Figure 22.7 Trend projections

To produce the forecast for any other year, just input the year number into the X box, eg 12..

If you want to display the regression equation that is the basis for the forecast, the easiest route is the process described under the section on regression and correlation.

Now is the time to go out and 'experiment' with your own data sets – have fun!

CONCLUSION

We hope the description of how to use a typical spreadsheet package for some of the most common statistical activities will encourage you to explore and experiment with the facilities offered by such a package. These enable us quickly and easily to analyse our data and present the results as useful information. No longer do we have to struggle with the sometimes quite complex arithmetic and algebra, but instead we can concentrate on deciding what is the appropriate technique to use, and what might be the most helpful way to present the information. We hope that you will find using the computer both an exciting and liberating experience.

This concludes Part 2, our journey through statistical techniques. We hope you will find them useful in your quest to turn 'numbers into information'. These techniques, together with an understanding of the concepts and applications of information systems covered in Part 1, provide you with the key to managing your information effectively – which in our view is crucial to both individual and organisational success in today's world of accelerating change and ever-increasing technological advances.

Appendix
Answers to review questions

CHAPTER 1

Question 1

The key issues concerning content, presentation and timeliness of providing information on leavers are set out below:

Content

Given the administration involved with someone leaving the organisation, it is likely that the data will be reasonably accurate. Whether someone has left the organisation is fairly clear-cut – however one possible issue is whether information on all leavers is of interest. For example, should those on short-term contracts that have been completed, or secondees returning to their organisation, or those retiring, be included? It is important to focus on the purpose of providing the information.

The area of interest will often be the 'voluntary leavers' and it may be worth considering whether information should be provided separately on this group. Another issue is whether information on *why* staff are leaving is required. It is difficult to take action to reduce the numbers of leavers, assuming this is desired, unless the reasons are known, such as uncompetitive salaries, poor management or personal development concerns.

Presentation

The first key issue to consider is who will want the information. For example, individual line managers will want to know detailed information on leavers in their areas of responsibility. The chief executive will be interested in organisation-wide figures, but also perhaps areas where there have been an 'exceptionally' high level of leavers. The HR manager might want summary figures by department or division and an analysis of the 'voluntary' leavers by the reasons for leaving.

Depending on the business of the organisation, the chief executive may be particularly interested in specific types of staff that might critically affect the performance of the organisation, such as ICT staff, specialist finance staff or particular trades.

The numbers of leavers (however defined – see earlier) is not a particularly useful piece of information. It would be more helpful to relate the number of leavers to the size of the unit, department, whatever. The most commonly used statistic is the 'turnover rate':

$$\frac{\text{No. of leavers in a certain period}}{\text{Average number of staff in the period}} \times 100\%$$

Timeliness

An interesting issue is over what period of time it is helpful to have this information. If turnover is considered a problem, monthly figures may be appropriate for all levels of user. The HR manager may be wish to keep a close eye on this indicator as it will have a double interest – it directly impacts on the level of recruitment activity and also can sometimes be used to provide an indicator of problems such as low morale in specific areas. If turnover rates are low then quarterly or even six-monthly information may be adequate.

Question 2

It should be possible to estimate the ongoing savings of the move in terms of reduced rent and business rates with some certainty. If the move is to a new purpose-built HQ, there may be some risks in terms of the final development costs. These can be minimised by good planning information at the outset, and then good project monitoring information during the development process. If the organisation needs to sell its existing building, again there will be an element of risk associated with the final price received. If the sale/move takes longer than expected, uncertainty creeps in, in terms of the state of the market for commercial properties.

If the staff have been surveyed to ascertain their willingness to move (a sensible idea!), it will usually be possible to obtain information that will enable you to categorise staff into: those who will definitely move, those who are likely to move but where there is a small element of risk, and those who are uncertain (possibly involving partners with jobs, or other family commitments). The costs of redundancy, recruitment and training of new staff, and removal expenses for those that are moving will depend on the decisions of these staff. The degree of certainty of the information will depend on what proportion of staff fall into each category. Information will be needed on the availability of staff with specific skills in the area where the new HQ will be based to enable the risk of being able to recruit to be assessed.

Other areas of uncertainty will be the impact of the move on the motivation of the staff, and how future customers may be affected by a different location. (It should be possible to get information on existing customers' reactions if handled with care.)

CHAPTER 2

Question 1

a A human being

A human being is a very complex system and there are numerous examples of different inputs, processes and outputs:

air   →   **PROCESS**   → continuing life of the human being

                → water vapour and carbon dioxide

Respiratory process

learning programme→   **PROCESS**   → new knowledge, skills, behaviours
existing knowledge,   → job results
skills, behaviours →   → job satisfaction
motivation →

Learning process

b A photocopier

A photocopier in comparison is a relatively simple system:

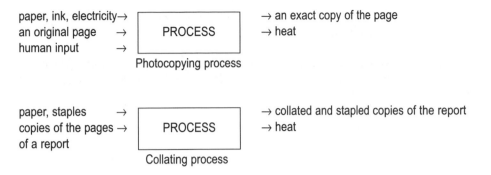

paper, ink, electricity→
an original page → | PROCESS | → an exact copy of the page
human input → | | → heat
Photocopying process

paper, staples → | PROCESS | → collated and stapled copies of the report
copies of the pages → | | → heat
of a report
Collating process

Question 2

a An HR performance management information system

Examples of hard properties are – length of time in the job, salary
Examples of soft properties are – performance grading by the manager, development needs.

An HR performance management system provides many examples of both hard and soft properties. The length of time in a job, level of salary can be assessed by precise measurement. However, a manager's grading of a member of staff by definition requires judgement and reflects the views and values of the manager. Similarly, an assessment of the development needs requires both the manager and member of staff to make judgements on gaps in performance and the reasons for these.

b A stock control system

Examples of hard properties are – stock levels of particular products, total wastage
Examples of soft properties are – forecasts of stock required, wastage due to staff dishonesty

With accurate counting processes, it should be possible to count precisely how many items of stock there are. Similarly, if the administrative systems are sound, it should be possible to assess precisely how much stock there should be and therefore the difference between the two gives the total wastage.

However, the forecast of stock required depends on judgements to be made about the demand for particular products and the lead times for deliveries, etc. Although it should be possible to measure overall losses precisely, it is unlikely, for example in a retail setting, to be able to assess precisely and without using judgement whether losses are attributable to customer theft or internal theft.

CHAPTER 3

Question 1

The example of a house move is used here. Set out below are the decisions required and the types of information needed to support them at the three levels: strategic, tactical and operational.

Strategic level

Do we want to move? Information on household objectives, views of members of the household.

How much space do we want/need – more, less, the same as existing? Information on existing space and projected space needs.

What sort of area(s) do we want to live in, eg urban or rural, proximity to public transport, closeness to work, schools etc, general environment? Information on household objectives, views of members of the household.

What do we want to pay/can we afford? Information on household finances now and projected.

What other factors would affect our decision, eg quiet neighbours, low crime, low council tax? Information on household objectives, views of members of the household, household financial information.

Tactical level

How will we finance the purchase, eg mortgage, savings, other loans? Information on savings, income, mortgage rates, etc.

Which estate agents shall we use? Information on estate agents in areas of choice to determine which cover the sorts of property being sought.

Who will we use for the legal work, eg local solicitor, online legal service, friend? Information on costs, recommendations.

How will we organise our viewing, eg weekends, evenings, a week's intensive looking? Information on household's schedule of activities.

How quickly do we need to move? Information on any constraints, eg school term dates, starting date of new job.

Operational level

What properties shall we view? Information on houses for sale.

How much will we pay for our chosen property? Information on similar properties in the area, household financial planning information.

What furniture and belongings do we take, eg what will we leave behind, throw away, sell? Information on existing furniture and belongings – quantity, size, colour, etc. Information on new property – what is being left behind such as carpets and curtains, size of rooms, colour schemes.

How will we move our furniture and belongings, eg use a removal firm, hire a van, use friends' help and vehicles? Information on costs, availability of services.

What is the exact date will we move on? Information on how long the purchase is likely to take, etc.

How long will it take to prepare, eg pack up, clean the our existing house? Information on belongings being taken, amount of cleaning required.

Are all the legal and financial issues dealt with, eg searches completed, documentation signed, mortgage in place, etc? Documentary information confirming these.

Have all the services been informed – to terminate contracts on existing property and start contracts on new property? Checklist of activities.

Question 2

Examples of internal and external information, their sources and how the information is used is set out below:

External Information

Information	Sources	Purpose
Salary surveys	Commercial organisations produce these surveys on a regular basis	To review salary levels in order to make decisions on salary changes
Unemployment forecasts	Government reports	To predict future wastage rates
Market research on a new product	Specially commissioned report from a market research company	To estimate the demand for the new product

Internal information

Information	Sources	Purpose
Sales of a particular product over the last five years	Sales information system	To forecast demand over the next two years
Number of staff reaching retirement age	HR information system	To predict known wastage due to retirements
Customer satisfaction with the level of a particular service	Survey of customers	To identify changes in service required

CHAPTER 4

Question 1

Authors' note: A useful approach to this question is to use the structure provided by the elements of a control system (see pages 42–43) and then to consider the questions posed in respect of your organisation's performance management system.

Elements	Performance management system
Some form of performance standard or target that has resulted from our planning process	Do all staff have clear performance standards and targets which have been agreed with them? Does the planning process set out how organisational objectives can be cascaded down to individual objectives? Is this process transparent to all involved?
A measure of the level of performance achieved	How well does the system record the level of performance? To what extent is performance capable of being measured objectively, ie there is no element of judgement? Where performance is subjective, eg a manager's assessment perhaps using a rating scale: • how good is the evidence supplied to back up the assessment? • how consistent are assessments across individuals and managers?
The calculation of the effect of environmental disturbances, variance or performance gap between expected and actual results	This is critically dependent on the quality of the information to support the first two elements. How well does the system allow for the performance gap to be identified and specified?
The feedback of these variances to the control system	How well do managers provide feedback on the performance gap to the individual? Is the feedback accurate, honest and constructive?
Action by the control system to return to the plan	How well does the system enable the appropriate action, eg coaching, learning programmes, change of job, to be identified to meet the performance gap? How well is the action implemented?
The opportunity to feedback to a higher control unit if the environmental disturbances are so great that the original plan and/or objectives are no longer appropriate	How does the system deal with serious variances in performance, eg where disciplinary action may be required? How does the system deal with changes in targets and objectives?

The other issue that should be considered is: how timely is the information provided by the control system?

- Does the system allow for feedback at frequent enough intervals? Some performance management systems are very rigid, involving feedback interviews only once a year or at most twice a year. Modern performance management systems encourage managers and staff to meet more frequently on an informal basis to encourage timely feedback.
- How quickly is action taken to address any performance gap? Sometimes, it can take a long time to arrange for learning interventions to take place and even longer to implement more serious action, eg a job change or disciplinary action.

Question 2

Authors' note: There are many areas from which you might provide examples of control systems. The two examples used here are budgetary control and the monitoring of performance indicators. In addition, there are numerous examples associated with production control where sophisticated computer control systems are constantly monitoring all aspects of the production process and are programed to make minor adjustments to settings of machines, etc, to ensure the final product conforms to its specification. They often use statistical process control charts – see Chapter 17. These will be double-loop systems allowing for a higher level of control to take place if the deviations from the specification become too great.

Two examples are:

- An important area common to all organisations is budgetary control. Mostly such systems operate as open systems (*much like the absence control example in Case Study 4.2*). Management information reports are produced at regular intervals: weekly, monthly, etc. These set out the budget amount (the target comparator) and then the actual amount that has been recorded by the system, and the difference between the two figures represents the variance. Many budgetary systems use exception reporting, which highlights only those variances of a certain size, eg more than plus or minus 5% away from the target. Exception reporting allows a supervisor responsible for many cost codes to focus on the ones that may be causing concern, and decide the appropriate action to stay within budget. At this point the system is operating as a single-loop system. However, if the supervisor decides that it is either not possible or perhaps not desirable to stay within budget, then s/he may seek agreement from a more senior manager to change the budget level. At this stage the system is operating as a double-loop system.
- Another important area, in the public sector particularly, concerns the control systems associated with monitoring performance indicators. Again these will be open-loop systems where performance against target is reported in regular performance reports. To take the example of police forces, they are statutorily required to monitor performance against a set of national performance indicators. A local police authority will set the targets each year. The indicators include levels of overall crime, level of types of crime (eg violent crime), detection rates, etc. If there are deviations from the target, action may need to be taken by the appropriate police officers to try to bring performance back on target. At this point the system is operating as a single-loop system. If a decision is required to perhaps change the target, or perhaps there are concerns about the way the performance indicator is being measured, the matter would be referred to the police authority (a higher-level authority) and the system operates as a double-loop system.

CHAPTER 5

Question 1

Three examples of how the miniaturisation of storage devices have affected organisations are:

- the use of RFID tags in retail environments to prevent shoplifting, to monitor goods in the supply chain, etc
- enabling staff who are visiting clients and suppliers to carry around small devices that allow them to access all the information they need relating to that client/supplier, and which could include sophisticated software for fault diagnosis, a database of spare parts, etc

- making it easy to communicate with mobile workers – sending and receiving data, eg updated specifications, parts lists, detailed reports, e-mails.

Question 2

Authors' note: There are many types of database you might wish to use as an example. We shall use the example of an HR information system (HRIS). If it is a relatively modern HRIS it is likely to have a relational database structure. You might wish to comment on how easy it is to access data at different levels of detail, provide information over different time periods, produce tables and charts, etc.

Examples of the types of information you might extract and for what purpose are shown below:

Type of information	Purpose
Breakdown of staff by gender and ethnic origin	To review the organisation's progress against diversity objectives
Trends in labour turnover	To identify if there are changes in labour turnover in specific areas of the organisation which might require action
Median and quartile salary levels for different categories of staff	To make comparisons with industry-wide salary levels (using salary survey data) to investigate whether the organisation remains competitive in salary terms
Learning days/employee by department	To review the learning activities in the organisation – there may be a target set for this indicator

CHAPTER 6

Question 1

There are potentially a large number of attributes that might be associated with an entity of an employee. These could include:

- name
- address
- date of birth
- length of service
- department
- job title
- salary
- holiday entitlement.

The employee will traditionally have one manager, and a manager usually will have many employees. Hence the traditional relationship between an manager and employee is a one-to-many as shown below.

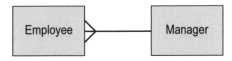

In other organisational structures such as a matrix structure, an employee might have more than one manager, so the relationship becomes many-to-many as shown below:

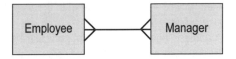

Typical events in the entity life history of an employee would be:

- joining the organisation
- completing the probation period
- getting promoted
- leaving the organisation.

Question 2

The benefits of including the users in the development of information systems are:

- First and perhaps most obviously, the users of a system are arguably in the best position to know what information the system needs to produce. They will know what frustrates them about the current method of working: information is not currently available, some task are very time-consuming, it is difficult to produce information in a user-friendly format, information arrives too late for it to be useful, etc. Key to the process of requirements analysis is helping the users articulate exactly what they need from the system now and in the future – to think beyond the current constraints and explore the potential of how the system could help them do their jobs and meet organisational objectives.
- Key to the success of an information system is persuading *all* the users that it is worth all the input of time, effort and resources, and that it will make a real difference to their ability to do their jobs and achieve their targets. You will need their help at all stages, and it is worthwhile making considerable effort to gain their *buy-in*. There are a number of ways of doing this – by organising demonstrations of the potential of the system tailored to the audience at an early stage, by involving key users in the project team, by ensuring good communication throughout the project.
- The more the users have been involved in the development in a constructive and productive way, the more they will understand the potential of the system, how it works, and any issues surrounding the implementation. This knowledge will be invaluable at the stage of training the users in the new system and then in supporting them during the implementation phase. It will also help in the design of the training and follow-up support required, as the suppliers will have a greater understanding of the existing knowledge and skills of the users.
- Involving the users throughout the process enables (hopefully!) a good working relationship to be developed between them and the ICT specialists. Having such a relationship can help ensure that any problems are approached constructively, with all sides trying to find answers rather than apportion blame. Users will also be encouraged continuously to seek ways to improve the performance of the system rather than find fault. With most new systems there will be teething problems – a good team approach will ensure that these are dealt with quickly and the system is implemented efficiently and effectively.

CHAPTER 7

Question 1

I would consider the following issues in developing a disaster recovery plan for an organisation:

- Identifying the organisation's most critical business systems, and determining the impact on the organisation of a major failure of these systems. How long can the organisation survive with a system down? For example, what is the maximum time the organisation can survive without a properly functioning HRIS?
- Carrying out a risk analysis and identifying what particular risks the organisation is likely to experience. Will the risks be from fire, flood, power supply interruptions, malicious damage or terrorism? Then drawing up a matrix with axes showing the degree of the risk against the severity of the likely damage caused. Clearly the most important threats to plan for are the high-probability, high-impact ones.
- Investigating the procedures for providing back-up data and systems. Where are all the back-up data and system discs? Are these in safe locations? When were they last saved? How quickly can they be retrieved?
- Developing action plans for manual operation (or alternative site operation) for the most critical systems. These should allocate responsibilities for key activities to individual staff members, and include a communication plan.
- Securing senior management support for both maintaining adequate back-up procedures and for the action plans to be followed in the event of a disaster.
- Communicating relevant details of the disaster recovery plan to all members of staff.
- Testing the disaster recovery plan at regular intervals. Colleagues would be asked to complete learning logs of their experience in the practice drills for feeding back in post-exercise review sessions. Depending on the lessons learned, the disaster recovery plan would be amended where necessary.
- Regularly updating the plans to reflect changing business priorities, systems and risks.

Question 2

Authors' note: Look on the relevant website!
Organisations that adopt effective data protection policies and procedures will find the following benefits:

- Protection from legal action against challenges to their data protection practices.
- Increased trust and openness in the workplace, as employees and job applicants will have confidence in the employment practices relating to the way information about them is held and used.
- Employees will be encouraged to respect the personal data of customers and others through their greater level of awareness of personal data.
- Better housekeeping – weeding out out-of-date records will make valuable information easier to retrieve, and will free up space in filing systems, both paper-based and computerised.
- Systems will more easily meet various other legal requirements, as the DPA is intended to be consistent with other pieces of UK legislation such as the Human Rights Act (1998).
- Global businesses will be helped in complying with similar legislation in other countries, as the DPA is in line with legal requirements in other European Union member states on data protection.
- Improved performance management, as issues relating to the misuse of information will be clarified by informing workers of the principles of data protection and the consequences of not complying with the DPA.

CHAPTER 8

Question 1

Benefits that can result from a well designed and implemented HRIS include:

- Improved access to HR data. Not only will HR staff be able to access data at the level of detail and in the form they require, but the opportunities of self-service options mean that the data is also accessible to those who directly need it. For example line managers could have access to absence data relating to their teams, which will help them manage absence in a more proactive way. Individual employees could have direct access to information useful to themselves, eg holiday entitlement, HR policies and guidelines, vacancies, learning and development information. Not only does this provide a better service for the employees and line managers, it reduces the administrative burden on HR staff in supplying this information.
- Better quality HR data and information. Use of relational databases helps to ensure that data is consistent and easily updated. Allowing for the easy updating of data by those directly involved, eg employees for their own personal details, line managers providing absence figures, should also help in maintaining the quality of the basic data. The powerful reporting systems then enable relevant and useful HR information to be produced from that data. The ability of users – HR professionals, line managers, directors, etc – to produce reports that really address their needs means that there will be better quality and more timely information available for decision-making. This should result in a better quality of HR management.
- More efficient and effective HR processes. The use of workflow techniques means that many of the time and labour-consuming administrative processes can be automated. The obvious example is recruitment, where filling a vacancy can be a massive administrative exercise involving hundreds of letters and pieces of paper flying around. The system largely replaces all the basic administrative human effort, and can go some way to automating the early selection stages by sifting applications. Similarly with organising a learning programme. Not only do these facilities potentially save resources, they can also provide a better level of service. They can make processes quicker and will have built-in follow-up systems which should reduce the potential for errors and omissions. They can also help ensure standardised approaches and processes.
- A more effective HR function. Because they reduce the administrative burden, HR staff will have the time to focus on the more proactive activities which can help add value to the organisation. Together with the improved information, it will enable HR professionals to identify and tackle problems in their early stages, for example turnover hotspots, to forecast the HR implications of business decisions and generally take a more strategic role in the organisation. This in turn will raise the profile of HR and allow it to make a more effective contribution to organisational success.

Question 2

The ways in which a well designed and implemented HRIS might help in managing performance are by:

- Having good quality information about performance which can be accessed at various levels, eg team and individual (this is a fundamental requirement).
- Having the facility to enable 360 degree feedback to be produced against competency profiles easily and simply online, which can then be summarised for use in a performance management interview.

- Including competency frameworks and helping ensure that there are consistent job profiles across the organisation.
- Having a workflow system that reminds managers and staff of the need to carry out performance management interviews and supplies the relevant paperwork, eg forms and guidance, online, with built-in checks to ensure that the interview and relevant paperwork have been completed, and a system to issue reminders.
- Producing statistics monitoring the performance management system, eg the number/proportion of performance management interviews completed on time, one month late, three months late.
- Producing development plans that can be accessed by the individual, manager and HR professional, thus enabling all concerned to use the development plans as a proactive tool to improve performance and develop new competencies.
- Being able to carry out basic performance management interviews to be carried out online, which may benefit remote and home-working employees. (However, there may well be concern that these will not be as effective as those carried out face-to-face, which allow for a more in-depth and constructive dialogue than may be possible online.)

CHAPTER 9

Question 1

My response to the MD would be:

I believe that there is considerable competitive advantage in introducing sound knowledge management practices into our organisation. My reasons for this are as follows:

- Our business is primarily based on the knowledge and skills of our staff. Our staff are archetypal 'knowledge' workers. Although we have guidance and procedures on how to work with clients and approach projects, every project is unique and we rely heavily on the experience and judgement that they bring to each piece of work. Our main asset is our staff.
- As staff work on new projects they are continuously expanding their knowledge base of:
  - our client organisations (their business issues, culture, staff contacts)
  - how to handle projects
  - which techniques work well and which do not
  - how to work with other members of the team, etc.
- At the moment, when a member of staff leaves we lose this accumulated knowledge.
- Most of our staff are young and ambitious. As a small organisation we will only be able to offer limited promotion prospects. My experience of similar organisations suggests that staff are likely to move on after two/three years. If we do not address the issue of knowledge management we will be losing the vital commodity on which the success of our organisation is based.

Question 2

The contribution I could make is as follows:

I am conscious that I have learned a lot from working on the project and that other members of the project team will have done so as well. It would be valuable if we were able to capture this learning and share it with others who might face the same sorts of issues in the future. My proposals are:

- We set up a project review session with all members of the project team. The objective of the session will be to capture the learning from the project – both what we did well and what we could have done better. It may be helpful if we use a facilitator who is not a member of the team so that we can all participate.
- Based on this review session, we produce a short summary of the learning points and make it available through the intranet-based knowledge centre that has been established.
- The process outlined above is used after all projects and it may be helpful
  - for individual team members to keep learning logs to capture points of interest as they occur
  - if there is a standard format for post-project review summaries.

CHAPTER 10

Question 1

Authors' note: There are many examples you might use. We have used the Internet in the following ways during the past month:

- We live in a very rural part of Suffolk and our nearest library is half an hour's drive away. A really useful service for us is the ability to renew our library books over the Internet. Not only does it save us the trouble of driving to the library (thereby making savings costs in terms of time, petrol costs and environmental pollution), we are able to do this at any time day or night (very useful for busy professionals such as ourselves). Initially this service was rather slow as you had to renew one book at a time and there was not the opportunity to do a 'renew all'. This has now changed, all the books on loan are displayed on screen at the same time and you simply indicate which you want to renew. The only problem with this very useful service is if a book has been requested by another user you cannot renew it, and therefore will clock up fines until it has been physically returned. It is also very helpful to be able to search for books and request books online.
- We have been running some learning programmes in mainland Europe. Some of these have been arranged at short notice. We like to send out pre-programme questionnaires to establish individual needs and issues. We were able to send these out by e-mail and have them returned online within a few days. The advantage was speed of interaction and ease of completion by the learners. It was also very easy to chase the non-returns, so we achieved a higher than usual return rate.
- We have been carrying out research on a company to which we were submitting a business proposal. Its website provided very useful information on business and financial performance (from looking at its annual report and accounts), on the structure of the organisation, the aims and objectives, etc. It was also interesting to see how well designed the website was technically and for ease of use, and how the company was using it, eg for marketing purposes and recruitment.

Question 2

Authors' note: We looked at the following areas on our local authority site: planning, refuse collection, jobs and general information. Our evaluation of them as customers is set out below.

Planning

We tried to check what planning applications had been submitted for our village. This was not as easy as it could have been. All the applications are listed by week of receipt and then ordered alphabetically under each date, so we had to search within each weekly list. It would have been helpful to use a search facility to pick up any applications in our village. It is even more difficult to find out what has happened to a planning application. These are listed by reference number.

The site is particularly poor for anyone intending to put in a planning application. It is not possible to apply online, or download any forms, nor was there any advice offered on how to apply. All that was given was an e-mail address for enquiries! However, there was a link to the national Planning portal which had a lot of helpful information and the capability to make a planning application online for certain local authorities – but not ours!

Refuse collection

This is a subject close to our hearts as we are keen on recycling. Our council has recently moved to a two-bin system, black bins for 'dirty' rubbish and blue bins for recyclable rubbish. Blue and black bins are collected on alternate weeks. It is easy to forget which week is for which type of bin. It would have been helpful to have the schedule on the website – it is not. However, there was a useful list of recycling sites by village/area, although the accompanying map was useless.

Jobs

Vacancies are listed and job descriptions are provided. It is not possible to apply online, but an application form can be downloaded and printed out for manual completion.

General information

It was useful to find the name of our local councillor, his address and e-mail address. However, users have to know the name of the ward that they live in. The site provides contact numbers and e-mail addresses for most services. It is very much geared to providing `information and not for online transactions. It was quite difficult to find our way through to the information we wanted – better search facilities would help.

CHAPTER 12

Question 1

The relative and cumulative frequency distributions for the productivity figures are set out below:

Parts/day	Frequency	Relative frequency distribution %	Cumulative frequency distribution %
2,001–2,250	8	13	13
2,251–2,500	2	3	16
2,501–2,750	20	33	49
2,751–3,000	25	42	91
3,001–3,250	3	5	9
3,251–3,500	2	3	99*
	60	99*	

*Due to rounding

75% of the operatives are achieving a productivity level of 2,500–3,000 parts/day. However, a size-able minority, 16%, are below this level and 13% are in the 2,001–2,250 band. This might suggest that some operatives are newly trained and are building up their productivity levels, or that there is some other reason for their below-standard performance. If the training records suggest that this group have not recently been trained, then the following options might need investigating:

- whether some form of retraining is required – particularly if the initial training took place some time ago, or there have been any changes in the process since training
- whether there are any differences in the machinery that is being used by this group or any other external factors, eg closeness to stores for picking up raw materials, that might affect productivity levels
- motivational factors, eg quality of supervision, absence/sickness records.

8% of the operatives are achieving above-standard performances. It may be useful to look in detail at this group and identify possible reasons for this. Also, this group may provide useful coaches for those staff who are underachieving.

Question 2

The relative and cumulative frequency distributions for both offices are set out below:

Time (mins)	Frequency Office 1	Relative Frequency Office 1 %	Cumulative Frequency Office 1 %	Frequency Office 2	Relative Frequency Office 2 %	Cumulative Frequency Office 2 %
<5	1	1	1	7	8	8
6–10	6	7	8	40	46	54
11–15	30	37	45	35	40	94
16–20	26	32	77	5	6	100
21–25	10	12	89	0	0	
26–30	9	11	100	0	0	
	82	100		87	100	

There is a marked difference in waiting times between the two offices. In Office 2 most people, 94%, wait 15 minutes or less, whereas in Office 1 less than half, 45%, are seen within 15 minutes. Just over half, 55%, have to wait more than 15 minutes in Office 1 compared with only 6% in Office 2. The sorts of issues that may need to be investigated are:

- how the booking system is arranged, eg the time allowed for appointments, catch-up gaps between groups of appointments
- experience and training of staff – in getting at the information on the client problem, discussing and agreeing solutions, handling the paperwork, time management
- whether there is a difference in the types of client problem being dealt with at the two offices, eg more complex, unusual problems at Office 1.

CHAPTER 13

Question 1

Authors' note: You could use bar diagrams, pie charts or pictograms to answer this question. Most commonly, bar diagrams are used for this type of data. Also, you could either present the frequency data (ie the number of delegates commenting in each quality category), the raw data in the table, or the relative frequencies (ie the percentage of delegates commenting in each quality category). If you wanted to compare two tutors, or the same tutor over two programmes, and there were different numbers of delegates commenting, it would make sense to use relative frequencies so that the results can be compared directly. Also, it is usually more powerful to comment in terms of percentages, ie to say 75% of delegates, rather than 15 out of 20.

Answers to review questions

Knowledgeable

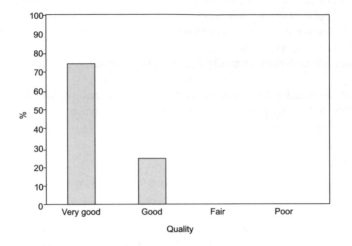

Appropriate pace

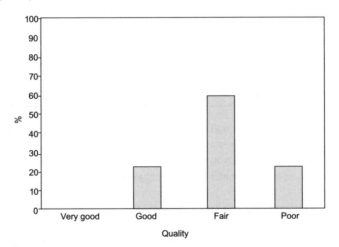

Creates interest

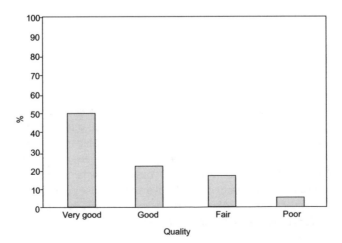

Involves group

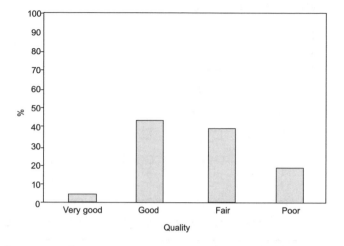

The delegates rated the tutor highly on her knowledge, with 100% rating the tutor very good or good. 75% of delegates commented favourably on the tutor's ability to create interest. The delegates were more mixed on the question of the tutor's ability to involve the group. The weakest area was whether the pace of the course was appropriate, with only 20% of the delegates rating this aspect good, the vast majority, 60% rating it fair and 20% as poor.

Question 2

Authors' note: The most eye-catching methods of presentation are pictograms. Be creative. Here are some examples:

Pictogram of waiting times

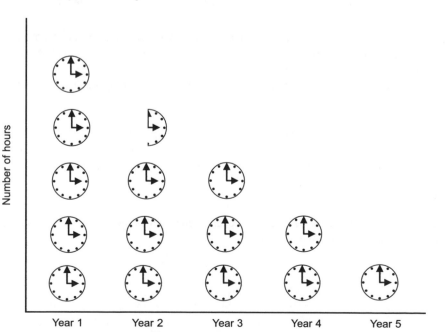

Pictogram of water consumption

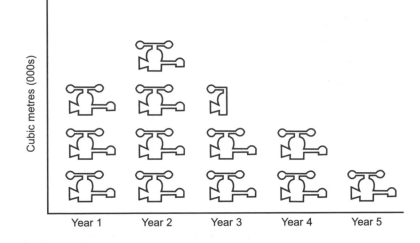

Pictogram of staff turnover

- Waiting times in a hospital A & E department. The clock is a well-known symbol of time.
- Water consumption. We have used the symbol of a tap, which is readily understood as the medium for supplying water.
- Staff turnover. This is not an easy one for which to identify an appropriate symbol. We have used the idea of people running away (from the organisation!).

In the first and second of these examples, each symbol represents a unit of data, ie minutes of time or thousands of cubic metres of water consumption. In the third example, the height of the symbol or picture represents the numbers involved and provides the relative scale.

Question 3

Set out below are the frequency, relative frequency and cumulative frequency data on the number of hours staff spend at their desks:

Hours at desk	Frequency	Relative frequency %	Cumulative frequency %
< 2	6	24	24
2 < 4	8	32	56
4 < 6	2	8	64
6 < 8	7	28	92
8 < 10	2	8	100
Total	25	100	

Note: the symbol < means less than but not equal to the number following it, so that 2 < 4, includes the values of 2 and 3.

Histogram of hours spent at desk

Just over half of the staff spend half their time or less at their desks, and nearly a quarter spend less than two hours. 36% of staff spend the greater part of each day at their desk. This suggests that there is the opportunity for 'hot desking' for at least half the staff. Allowing two desks for the six staff who spend less than two hours in this office, and four desks for those who spend between two and four hours at their desks, would give a saving of eight desks overall. Although this would suggest a saving of nearly a third in terms of space, this will partially be offset by the need for the staff sharing desks to have some form of personal space for diaries, pending trays, filing drawers, etc.

CHAPTER 14

Question 1

Department B had a considerably higher than average score for interesting and stimulating work than the organisation as a whole. Also, the small standard deviation shows a consistency of views amongst those responding. In contrast Department A scored relatively low in this area and showed a very wide variation in results. Department B fared well in terms of the effectiveness of its manager, again with a consistency of results. Department A was close to the organisational average, with again only relatively little spread in the results. Interestingly Department B's staff were on average less satisfied than the organisation as a whole with the opportunities for learning and development, but there was quite a wide spread of results. This was the best result for Department A – an average close to the organisational average with a consistency of approach.

Particular attention needs to be paid to the nature and content of the work in Department A. Perhaps initiatives such as job rotation or job enrichment might be considered. In Department B, there needs to be a greater focus on learning and development. Given the wide range of views, attention may need to be given to the systems and procedures for identifying learning needs. Generally, the scores for the effectiveness of line management look disappointing across the organisation, and these were consistent, suggesting that the problem is widespread. There may be a need to carry out a programme of management development.

Question 2

The interquartile ranges for the three shops are set out below:

	Shop Suzi £	Shop Cecile £	Shop Marie £
Lower quartile	14,310	9,230	21,500
Median	18,990	18,830	26,250
Upper quartile	23,440	27,650	33,900
Interquartile range	9,130	18,420	12,400

Shop Suzi has the smallest interquartile range, with 50% of customers with incomes between about £14,300 and £23,500. Although Shop Cecile has about the same median customer income as Shop Suzi, there is a much wider interquartile range, with the lower quartile well below and the upper quartile well above those of Shop Suzi. Shop Marie has quite a different customer income profile from the other two shops, with 75% of customers' incomes above £21,500 and 25% above £33,900.

The results suggest that Shop Marie would benefit from a good range of higher-priced merchandise. Shop Cecile has a very diverse customer income profile, and would best be served by a cross-section of the ranges. Shop Suzi's customer profile is clustered closely around the median income of £18,990, and the best approach would be to concentrate on the mid-priced ranges.

CHAPTER 15

Question 1

These are two discrete probability distributions, with the values of the random variable, x and y, being the different profit forecasts associated with each of the three demand options:

Demand	Small-scale project		Large-scale project	
	x (£000)	Probability p(x)	y (£000)	Probability p(y)
Low	100	0.2	0	0.2
Medium	300	0.6	250	0.6
High	500	0.2	800	0.2

The expected value of profits for the small-scale project:

$$= \sum_{i=1}^{n} x_i \, p(x_i)$$

$$= (100 \times 0.2) + (300 \times 0.6) + (500 \times 0.2)$$

$$= 20 + 180 + 100$$

$$= 300$$

ie the expected value of profits for the small-scale project is £300,000.

The expected value of profits for the large-scale project:

$$= \sum_{i=1}^{n} y_i \, p(y_i)$$

$$= (0 \times 0.2) + (250 \times 0.6) + (800 \times 0.2)$$

$$= 150 + 160$$

$$= 310$$

ie the expected value of profits for the large-scale project is £310,000.

The standard deviation in expected profits for the small-scale project:

$$= \sqrt{\sum_{i=1}^{n} x_i{}^2 \, p(x_i) - \text{mean}^2}$$

$$= \sqrt{(10,000 \times 0.2) + (90,000 \times 0.6) + (250,000 \times 0.2) - 300^2}$$

$$= \sqrt{2,000 + 54,000 + 50,000 - 90,000}$$

$$= \sqrt{16,000}$$

$$= 126.5$$

ie the standard deviation in expected profits for the small-scale project is £126,500.

The standard deviation in expected profits for the large-scale project:

$$= \sqrt{\sum_{i=1}^{n} y_i{}^2 \, p(y_i) - \text{mean}^2}$$

$$= \sqrt{(0 \times 0.2) + (62,500 \times 0.6) + (640,000 \times 0.2) - 310^2}$$

$$= \sqrt{37,500 + 128,000 - 96,100}$$

273

$$= \sqrt{69{,}400}$$

$$= 263.4$$

ie the standard deviation in expected profits for the large scale project is £263,400.

Based on the expected value of the profit, the MD might be tempted to go for the large-scale project, as it offers £10,000 additional profits. However, the standard deviation for the large-scale project is more than double that for the small-scale project, suggesting that this is the riskier option.

Question 2

As the journey times are uniformly distributed between 2 hrs 15 mins and 2 hrs 30 mins, ie over a 15-minute interval, the probability of the journey time falling in a particular one-minute interval is 1/15. The probability of the train not being more than 10 mins late is represented by the shaded area for the interval 2 hrs 15 mins and 2 hrs 20 mins – see the figure below for a diagrammatic representation of the problem.

Shaded area gives the probability of journey time falling between 2 hrs 15 mins and 2 hrs 20 mins

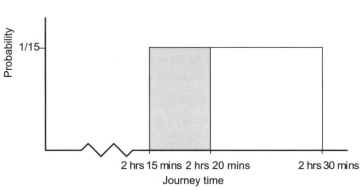

The probability the train being no more than 10 mins late:

$= p$ (2hrs 15mins – 2hrs 16mins) + p (2hrs 16mins – 2hrs 17mins) ... + p (2hrs 19mins – 2hrs 20mins)

$= 5 \times 1/15$

$= 1/3$

The probability the train being more than 20 mins late:

$= p$ (2hrs 30mins – 2hrs 31mins) + ...

$= 0$

Therefore on one-third of occasions it is likely that the train will be 10 mins or less late. On two-thirds of occasions the train will be between 10 and 20 mins late.

CHAPTER 16

Question 1

a

The 95% confidence limits for the population average student loan:

$$= \bar{x} \pm \frac{1.96s}{\sqrt{n}}$$

$$= 8{,}540 \pm \frac{1.96 \times 1{,}400}{\sqrt{100}}$$

$$= 8{,}540 \pm 274$$

$$= 8{,}266 \text{ to } 8{,}814$$

The 99% confidence limits for the population average student loan:

$$= \bar{x} \pm \frac{2.58s}{\sqrt{n}}$$

$$= 8{,}540 \pm \frac{2.58 \times 1{,}400}{\sqrt{100}}$$

$$= 8{,}540 \pm 361$$

$$= 8{,}179 \text{ to } 8{,}901$$

We can be 95% confident that the average loan for final-year students falls in the interval £8,266 to £8,814. To increase our level of confidence to 99% widens the interval to £8,179 – £8,901.

b

To achieve a confidence interval at the 95% level of ± £150, the sample size would need to be:

$$= \frac{(1.96s)^2}{(\text{sampling error})^2}$$

$$= \frac{(1.96 \times 1{,}400)^2}{(150)^2}$$

$$= 335$$

To achieve an almost halving of the confidence interval, reducing it from ± £274 to ± £150, would require an increase in sample size of over three times. Given the costs of surveying, it will be important to decide how precise an estimate of the average loan is required.

Question 2

It is important to indicate to the MD how precise the results are. I feel that he or she would be comfortable with a 95% level of confidence, and so decide to report back with 95% confidence limits.

The 95% confidence limits for the point-of-sales proportion are:

$$\bar{p} \pm 1.96 \sqrt{\frac{\bar{p}(100 - \bar{p})}{n}}$$

$$= 66 \pm 1.96 \sqrt{\frac{66(100 - 66)}{150}}$$

$$= 66 \pm 1.96 \times \sqrt{14.96}$$

$$= 66 \pm 7.6$$

$$= 58.4\% \text{ to } 73.6\%$$

The 95% confidence limits for the after-sales proportion are:

$$\bar{p} \pm 1.96 \sqrt{\frac{\bar{p}(100 - \bar{p})}{n}}$$

$$= 48 \pm 1.96 \sqrt{\frac{48(100 - 48)}{150}}$$

$$= 48 \pm 1.96 \times \sqrt{16.6}$$

$$= 48 \pm 8.0$$

$$= 40\% \text{ to } 56\%$$

Between 58% and 74% of customers felt the customer service at point-of-sale was excellent. However, only between 40% to 56% expressed the same view about the quality of the after-sales service.

The confidence interval varies with the proportion likely to occur. For example, it was greater for the 48% statistic than with the 66% statistic. It is at its highest at 50%. (If you look at the formula, the variation comes from the $\bar{p}(100 - \bar{p})$ part – this is greatest at $50 \times 50 = 2,500$, and lowest at the low/high proportions eg $99 \times 1 = 99$.) To improve the precision of the results to a maximum of $\pm 5\%$ would require a sample size of:

$$= \frac{1.96^2 \times \bar{p}(100 - \bar{p})}{5^2}$$

$$= \frac{1.96^2 \times 50 \times 50}{5^2} \quad \text{(worst case option)}$$

$$= \frac{9,600}{25}$$

$$= 384$$

CHAPTER 17

Question 1

As the owner is interested in whether there has been any change in mean parking time, the appropriate hypothesis test would be:

$H_0: \mu = 175$ mins

$H_1: \mu \neq 175$ mins

We will reject H_0 if the population mean μ falls in the shaded areas of the figure below, that is, in either of the two tails which each have a probability of 0.025 and which together give a total Type 1 error of 0.05. In other words, we will accept H_0 at the 5% significance level if μ falls in the range:

$$= \bar{x} \pm \frac{1.96s}{\sqrt{n}}$$

$$= 160 \pm \frac{1.96 \times 55}{\sqrt{100}}$$

$$= 160 \pm \frac{107.8}{10}$$

$$= 160 \pm 10.8$$
$$= 149.2 \text{ to } 170.8$$

Two-tailed hypothesis test for mean packing times, type 1 error, $\alpha = 0.05$

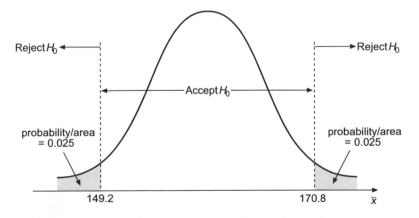

The population mean of 175 falls outside this range, therefore we reject the null hypothesis and conclude that there has been a change in the mean parking time. We are confident that there is only a 5% probability of rejecting the null hypothesis if it is true.

Question 2

The researcher is interested only in whether the average time from order to completion of a kitchen is longer than that claimed, 7.8 weeks, so he or she will be setting up a one-tailed test, with the following hypotheses:

H_0: $\mu \leq 7.8$ weeks

H_1: $\mu > 7.8$ weeks

The researcher will take a sample of kitchen fittings and reject the null hypothesis, H_0, if μ falls in the shaded area in the figure below, that is in the upper tail. If s/he is using a 5% significance level, the probability/area of the tail will be 0.05.

One-tailed hypothesis test for kitchen-order completion times, type 1 error, $\alpha = 0.05$

Question 3

As the issue of interest is whether there has been a change in opinion, the null hypothesis is that there has been no change:

H_0: $p_{VG} = 0.21$, $p_G = 0.45$, $p_P = 0.3$, $p_{VP} = 0.04$

Then the alternative hypothesis is:

H_1: $p_{VG} \neq 0.21$, $p_G \neq 0.45$, $p_P \neq 0.3$, $p_{VP} \neq 0.04$

The expected results of this year's survey based on the null hypothesis being true would be:

Very good	Good	Poor	Very poor
52.5	112.5	75	10

The observed results of this year's survey are:

Very good	Good	Poor	Very poor
55	135	52	8

$$\chi^2 = \sum_{i=1}^{k} \frac{(o_i - e_i)^2}{e_i}$$

$$= \frac{(55 - 52.5)^2}{52.5} + \frac{(135 - 112.5)^2}{112.5} + \frac{(52 - 75)^2}{75} + \frac{(8 - 10)^2}{10}$$

$$= \frac{6.25}{52.5} + \frac{506.25}{112.5} + \frac{529}{75} + \frac{4}{10}$$

$$= 0.12 + 4.5 + 7.05 + 0.4$$

$$= 12.07$$

The χ^2 distribution has three degrees of freedom (no. of classes − 1).

$$\chi^2_{0.01} = 11.3 \text{ (from Table 17.3)}$$

As the value of χ^2, 12.07, is greater than the value of 11.3 from the table, it falls in the shaded area of the distribution as shown in Table 17.3, and therefore we reject the null hypothesis. This tells us that the employees' opinions have changed, and looking at the results suggests that employees' perceptions of the service offered by the HR Department have shifted upwards – they feel that the service has improved.

Question 4

The null hypothesis is that there is no difference between the profile of defects between the suppliers:

H_0: the proportion of defects is independent of the supplier

And the alternative hypothesis is that the proportion of defects varies with supplier:

H_1: the proportion of defects is not independent of the supplier

The observed results are:

Supplier	Good	Minor defect	Major defect	Total
A	90	3	7	100
B	170	18	7	195
C	135	6	9	150
Total	395	27	23	445
Proportion of total	$\frac{395}{445} = 0.89$	$\frac{27}{445} = 0.06$	$\frac{23}{445} = 0.05$	

The expected results if the null hypothesis is true are derived by applying the overall proportions for each state of defect to the totals of parts from each supplier, eg 0.89 (proportion of good parts) × 100 (total of parts for supplier A) = 89† (providing the first entry in the first column in the next table):

Supplier	Good	Minor defect	Major defect	Total
A	89†	6	5	100
B	174	12	10	196*
C	134	9	8	151*

*rounding errors

It is now possible to calculate:

$$\chi^2 = \sum_i \sum_j \frac{(o_{ij} - e_{ij})^2}{e_{ij}}$$

$$= \frac{(90-89)^2}{89} + \frac{(3-6)^2}{6} + \frac{(7-5)^2}{5} + \frac{(170-174)^2}{174} + \frac{(18-12)^2}{12} + \frac{(7-10)^2}{10}$$

$$+ \frac{(135-134)^2}{134} + \frac{(6-9)^2}{9} + \frac{(9-8)^2}{8}$$

$$= 0.01 + 1.5 + 0.8 + 0.09 + 3 + 0.9 + 0.01 + 1 + 0.13$$

$$= 7.44$$

This χ^2 distribution has 4 degrees of freedom (2×2), ie (number of rows − 1) × (number of columns − 1).

$$\chi^2_{0.050} = 9.49 \text{ (from Table 17.3)}$$

As the value of χ^2, 7.44, is less than the value of 9.49 from the table, it falls in the non-shaded area of the distribution as shown in Table 17.3, and therefore we accept the null hypothesis. This tells us that there is no significant difference between the suppliers in terms of defective parts provided.

CHAPTER 18

Question 1

The business is interested to find out whether and to what extent the response rate to its adverts is affected by the size of advert. The scatter diagram and regression line shown in the figure below indicate that there is a linear relationship with a positive trend, ie as advert size increases so does the response.

Scatter diagram and regression line of responses against advertisement size

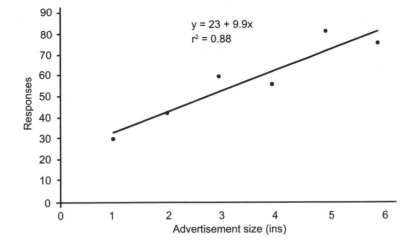

The equation of the regression line tells us:

- that the line of best fit crosses the y axis at the value of y of 23, ie when x = 0, y = 23
- the slope of the line is 9.9, ie for every increase of one column inch, the response increases by 9.9.

The coefficient of determination r^2 indicates how well the regression line fits the data: r^2 can vary between 0 and 1, the closer to 1 the better the fit. An r^2 value of 0.88 indicates that the regression line reduces the error by 88%, suggesting a strong relationship between the two variables, advert size and level of response, and therefore that the regression line would provide a good means for predicting response levels from the size of the advert.

If the agency wishes to achieve a response level of 100, the advert size is calculated by putting y = 100 in the regression equation:

$$y = 23 + 9.9x$$
$$100 = 23 + 9.9x$$
$$100 - 23 = 9.9x$$
$$\text{or } 9.9x = 77$$
$$x = \frac{77}{9.9}$$
$$= 7.8$$

The agency would need an advert of 8 column inches to achieve a response level of 100. It is important to emphasise that the regression line is reliable for predicting values within the data set of 1 to 6 inches. However, there are no particular grounds for thinking that the relationship would change greatly for values of x above 6 inches in this example.

Question 2

The reservations manager wants to find a way of predicting the number of passengers from the reservations made. This is to try to ensure optimal take-up of seats on the airplane, and avoidance of disappointed customers who cannot get a seat on the flight they want. The scatter diagram and regression line shown in the figure below indicate that there is a linear relation with a positive trend, ie as reservations increase, so does the actual number of passengers.

Scatter diagram and regression line of passengers against reservations

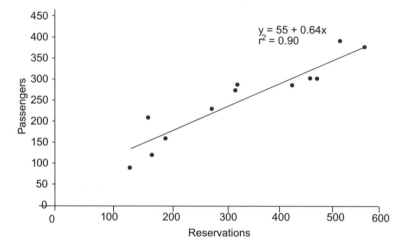

The equation of the regression line tells us that:

- the line of best fit crosses the y axis at the value of y of 55, ie when $x = 0$, $y = 55$
- the slope of the line is 0.64, ie for every increase of one reservation, the actual number of passengers increases by 0.64.

The coefficient of determination r^2 indicates how well the regression line fits the data: r^2 can vary between 0 and 1, and the closer to 1, the better the fit. An r^2 value of 0.90 indicates that the regression line reduces the error by 90%, suggesting a strong linear relationship between the number of reservations and passengers, and therefore that the regression line would provide a good means for predicting the number of passengers from reservations made.

To predict the number of passengers from a reservation level of 350, put $x = 350$ in the regression equation:

$y = 55 + 0.64x$

$y = 55 + (0.64 \times 350)$

$y = 55 + 224$

$y = 279$

With 350 reservations, the airline should expect 279 passengers actually to show up for that specific flight. As the value of $x = 350$ lies within the range of data used to calculate the regression line, we can be confident in the result.

To predict the number of passengers from a reservation level of 575, put x = 575 in the regression equation:

$$y = 55 + 0.64x$$
$$y = 55 + (0.64 \times 575)$$
$$y = 55 + 368$$
$$y = 423$$

With 575 reservations, the airline should expect 423 passengers actually to show up for that specific flight. As the value of x = 575 lies outside the range of data used to calculate the regression line, we need to be cautious in using the result – we are assuming that the relationship is maintained beyond the range. In this case the value of x = 575 is quite close to the end of the data range, and there are no grounds for thinking that the relationship might change greatly.

CHAPTER 19

Question 1

The forecast suggests a significant increase in the number of train drivers employed. They key issue is to estimate the recruitment and training activity that is likely to result from such an increase. In order to forecast the number of train drivers to be recruited, in addition to the forecast increase, the likely wastage rates will need to be estimated. It is relatively straightforward to predict the number of train drivers who are retiring by looking at the age distribution of existing drivers. However, a forecast of the voluntary leavers will also be required. It would be helpful to look at the past history of wastage rates for voluntary leavers, and identify whether there has been any trend in wastage rates, or whether there appear to be any links with, say, levels of unemployment in the area.

As train driving is a highly skilled job, there may be a considerable amount of training required before a new recruit becomes operational. It may be helpful to look back at the past history of new recruits in terms of the mix between:

- fully trained recruits who may just need induction training
- recruits who are partially trained – perhaps their experience is on a different type of train and they will need familiarisation training
- recruits who are unskilled and will need a full programme of training.

This may help to predict the level and type of training activity required. It will also be useful to research the failure rates of new recruits, to build this into the recruitment forecast.

With the sorts of increase in numbers forecast, additional recruitment and training staff might be needed, or it might be necessary to make arrangements to outsource the additional activity in some way, eg using recruitment agencies or employing training consultants.

Question 2

The figure below shows a plot of the original observations and the trend line. From the diagram, it can be seen that there is both an upward trend, ie the workforce is gradually increasing over the years, and a strong seasonal effect, ie the results vary considerably but in a consistent manner between the four quarters.

Time series of workforce and trend line

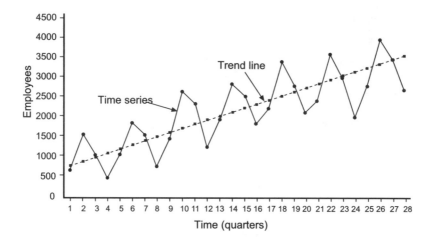

The statistician had analysed the time series using the following model:

Y = T × S × I, where T is the trend element, S the seasonal element and I the irregular element.

S/he has calculated the seasonal factors, the S × I element, using this model. The seasonal factors support the visual information from the graph, in that the workforce peaks in the second quarter of the year when it is on average about 36% higher than the quarterly average. It remains above average in the third quarter, at 12% above the quarterly average. It falls significantly in the fourth quarter, when it is 38% below the quarterly average, and is still well below the quarterly average in the first quarter. These results also make common sense given the nature of the product: the demand for lawnmowers is likely to be highest in the summer quarters, particularly in the early summer, and tail off significantly in the first winter quarter. Sales and hence production needs will begin to pick up in the first quarter as customers think about their grass-cutting requirements prior to the main grass-cutting season in spring. The workforce is likely to mirror this demand.

The results have then been deseasonalised by dividing the original observations by the respective seasonal factors, and linear regression analysis carried out on these deseasonalised results. The equation of the trend line has been calculated as:

$T_t = 633 + 106t$, where t is the time period expressed in quarters

The trend line demonstrates that there has been a steady increase in workforce over the seven years, at an average of 106 employees per quarter.

To predict next year's workforce, first the trend element is calculated from the trend line.

Year 8, Quarter 1, $t = 29$

$T_{29} = 633 + 106 \times 29$

$T_{29} = 633 + 3,074$

$T_{29} = 3,707$

The seasonal factor is then applied, $(S \times I)$ for Quarter 1, ie 0.899.

Predicted workforce in Year 8, Quarter 1 = $3,707 \times 0.899 = 3,323$.

In a similar way, the other three quarters can be predicted as follows:

Year 8, Quarter 2, $t = 30$

$T_{30} = 633 + 106 \times 30$

$T_{30} = 633 + 3,180$

$T_{30} = 3,813$

The seasonal factor is then applied, $(S \times I)$ for Quarter 2, ie 1.362.

Predicted workforce in Year 8, Quarter 2 = $3,813 \times 1.362 = 5,193$.

Year 8, Quarter 3, $t = 31$

$T_{31} = 633 + 106 \times 31$

$T_{31} = 633 + 3,286$

$T_{31} = 3,919$

The seasonal factor is then applied, $(S \times I)$ for Quarter 3, ie 1.118.

Predicted workforce in Year 8, Quarter 3 = $3,919 \times 1.118 = 4,381$.

Year 8, Quarter 4, $t = 32$

$T_{32} = 633 + 106 \times 32$

$T_{32} = 633 + 3,286$

$T_{32} = 3,919$

The seasonal factor is then applied, $(S \times I)$ for Quarter 4, ie 0.621.

Predicted workforce in Year 8, Quarter 4 = $4,025 \times 0.621 = 2,500$.

These predictions are based on the assumption that the future will continue like the past. Given that we are only predicting one year ahead and there are no reasons to believe that there are major changes on the short-term horizon that might affect the results, the predictions for the workforce should provide a reasonable basis for the company's staffing plan.

In the longer term technological advances, for example the concept of robot mowers, may have a significant effect on demand for this type of product. Another possible long-term factor that could affect demand is changes in climate, eg global warming.

CHAPTER 20

Question 1

Authors' note: The productivity figures for each year can be calculated by dividing the production level by the workforce for that year. We then suggest that you present the data as an index based on year 1.

Year	Productivity components/ employee (000s)	Index based on Year 1 = 100
1	323/165 = 1.958	100
2	350/173 = 2.023	103
3	363/175 = 2.074	106
4	405/200 = 2.025	103
5	455/200 = 2.275	116

Productivity increased steadily, but at a low level, for the first three years. However, in Year 4 there was a downturn and productivity dropped back to about the level in Year 2. This was at a time when production levels were increasing and so was the workforce. Then productivity recovered significantly in Year 5. This suggests that the upgrade in machinery caused some disruption in the production schedules during the year of implementation; however, there was a significant productivity gain in the following year suggesting that the new machinery was having an impact.

Question 2

Authors' note: We suggest you first present the information in the form of index numbers, with the target as the base figure for each performance indicator. There are then two ways to present the information visually: using a radar diagram (see the first figure below) or using a bar chart (see the second figure below).

Performance against target in 2004 (based on target = 100)

Performance indicator	Target	Actual	Actual performance*
Learning days/employee (days)	4	4.4	$(4.4/4) \times 100 = 110$
Satisfaction score (out of 6)	5	4.5	$(4.5/5) \times 100 = 90$
Utlisation of learning facilitators (%)	75	81	$(81/75) \times 100 = 116$
Utlisation of learning accommodation (%)	90	70	$(70/90) \times 100 = 78$

* based on target = 100.

Radar diagram comparing actual performance with target

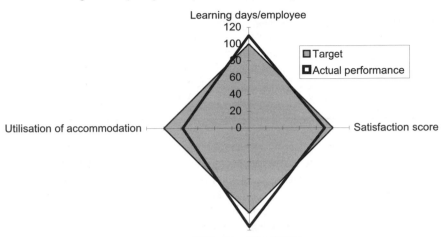

Bar chart showing performance indicators

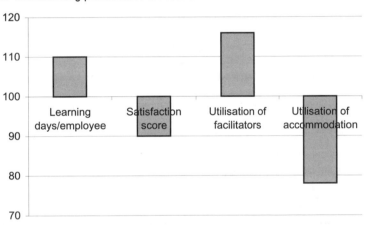

Both diagrams clearly show that the Learning and Development department has improved on its target in the terms of learning days/employee and in the utilisation of learning facilitators. However, participants' satisfaction with their learning experience is below target, and the utilisation of learning accommodation is well below target.

Question 3

Authors' note. We suggest that you compare how fast prices have risen in the canteen with average earnings in the organisation, the general RPI and the specialist relevant RPI, by preparing index numbers based on the earliest year's figures.

Year	Average earnings in the organisation	Average price of lunch	RPI (all items)	RPI canteen meals
2000	100	100	100	100
2001	104	107	102	105
2002	109	111	103	111
2003	119	114	106	116
2004	129	125	110	120

Index based on Year 2000 = 100

The RPI results indicate that canteen prices have been rising faster than general prices – over the five-year period, at double the rate. However, prices in the organisation's canteen have risen even faster, with a particularly large increase in 2004. It will be worth investigating the reasons for this and whether this sort of price increase is justified. For example, has there been a change in terms of the quality of food offered? It will be useful to point out to staff that overall canteen prices have risen less fast than average earnings in the organisation during the last five years.

CHAPTER 21

Question 1

A helpful way to set out the problem is in the form of a pay-off table:

	Outcomes	
Decision choices	Low demand O_1	High demand O_2
Manufacture and sell the product d_1	£50,000	£300,000
Sell the patent d_2	£150,000	£150,000

If the company adopts a pessimistic or conservative approach, it would use the maximin criterion, which maximises the minimum possible pay-offs.

The minimum pay-offs for each decision are:

Decision choices	Minimum pay-off
Manufacture and sell the product	£50,000
Sell the patent	£150,000

The company would then choose the decision that gives it the maximum of the minimum pay-offs, ie the company would choose to sell the patent.

If the company adopts a more optimistic approach, it would use the maximax criterion, which seeks to maximise the maximum pay-offs:

Decision choices	Minimum pay-off
Manufacture and sell the product	£300,000
Sell the patent	£150,000

In this case the company would choose to manufacture and sell the product.

Question 2

A decision tree is a useful way to lay out the decision-making problem in a visual way – see the figure below.

Decision tree of HR information system problem

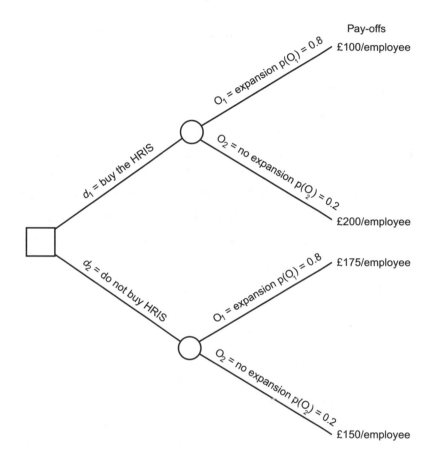

From the decision tree, the expected monetary values of the two alternative decisions can be calculated.

The expected monetary value for the 'buy' decision

$$= (0.8 \times 100) + (0.2 \times 200) = £120$$

The expected monetary value for the 'not to buy' decision

$$= (0.8 \times 175) + (0.2 \times 150) = £170$$

As these are costs, the lowest EMV would selected, leading to the decision to buy the HR information system.

References

ACKOFF, R. L. (1967) Management misinformation systems. *Management Science.* Vol. 14 No. 4, December.

ALAVI, M. (1997) *KPMG Peat Marwick U.S.: One Giant Brain*, Harvard Business School, Case 9-39-08, Boston, Mass.: Harvard Business School Press.

ALAVI, M. and LEIDNER, D. (2001) Knowledge management and knowledge management systems: conceptual foundations and research issues. *MIS Quarterly.* Vol. 25, No.1.

ANDERSON, D. R., SWEENEY, D. J. and WILLIAMS, D. A. (2001) *Statistics for business and economics.* 8th ed. St Paul/Minnesota: South Western College Publishing.

BEAZLEY, H., BOENISCH, J. and HARDEN, D. (2002) *Continuity management.* New York: Wiley.

BEE, F. and BEE, R. (2003) *Learning needs analysis and evaluation.* 2nd ed. London: CIPD.

BEE, R and BEE F (1990) *Mangement information systems and statistics.* London: CIPD

BEE, R. and BEE, F. (1997) *Project management: the people challenge.* London: CIPD.

BISSON. S. (2004) Quick recovery. *Guardian* 21 October.

BOCIJ, P., CHAFFEY, D., GREASLEY, A. and HICKIE, S. (2003) *Business information systems.* 2nd ed. Harlow: Pearson Education.

CARRINGTON, L. (2002) Oiling the wheels. *People Management.* 27 June, pp31–34.

CHECKLAND, P. B. (1981) *Systems thinking, systems practice.* Chichester: Wiley.

CHECKLAND, P. and HOLWELL, S. (1998) *Information, systems and information systems: making sense of the field.* Chichester: Wiley.

CHECKLAND, P. and SCHOLES, J. (1999) *Soft systems methodology in action.* Chichester: Wiley.

CHARTERED INSTITUTE OF PERSONNEL AND DEVELOPMENT (CIPD) (2003) *People and technology.* London: CIPD.

CHARTERED INSTITUTE OF PERSONNEL AND DEVELOPMENT (CIPD) (2004) *Recruitment, retention and turnover 2004.* London: CIPD.

DRUCKER, P. F. (1993) *Post-capitalist society.* New York: HarperCollins.

DRUCKER, P. F. (1999) *Management challenges of the 21st century.* New York: HarperCollins.

DYER, J. H. and OUCHI, W. G. (2002) Japanese-style partnerships. In J. HENRY and D. MAYLE (eds), *Managing innovation and change.* London: Sage.

EDWARDS, C., WARD, J. and BYTHEWAY, A. (1995) *The essence of information systems.* Prentice-Hall.

EVANS, P. and WURSTER, T. S. (2000) *Blown to bits: how the new economics of information transforms strategy,* Boston, Mass.: Harvard Business School Press.

FINNERAN, T. (2004) A component-based knowledge management system. *Data Administration Newsletter*, available online at: www.TDAN.com [USA, Robert S. Seiner] (accessed 30 May 2005).

FUTURE FOUNDATION (2004) *The digital divide in 2025*. London: Future Foundation.

HALL, S. (2004) CSA chief goes amid computer chaos. *Guardian*. 18 November.

HANDY, C. (1989) *The age of unreason.* London: Business Books.

HARRY, M. (1997) *Information systems in business.* 2nd ed. London: Pitman.

HIGGS, D. (2003) *Independent review of non-executive directors.* London: Department of Trade and Industry (DTI). Also available online at: http://www.dti.gov.uk/cld/non_exec_review/ (accessed 19 May 2005).

INCOME DATA SERVICES (IDS) (2002) *Human resource management systems.* IDS Studies. London: IDS.

JOHNSON, G. and SCHOLES, K. (2002) *Explaining corporate strategy.* 6th ed. Harlow: Pearson Education.

KETTLEY, P. and REILLY, P. (2003) *eHR: an introduction.* Report 398. Brighton: Institute for Employment Studies.

LAUDON, K. C. and LAUDON, J. P. (2003) *Essentials of management information systems.* 5th ed. USA: Pearson Education.

LEWIS, K.. and LYTTON, S. (2002) The way forward: partnership sourcing. In J. HENRY and D. MAYLE (eds), *Managing innovation and change.* London: Sage.

LUCEY, T. (1997) *Management information systems.* 8th ed. London: Letts Educational.

MALHOLTRA, Y. (2004) Why knowledge management systems fail? In M. E. D. KOENIG and T. K. SRIKANTAIAH (eds), *Knowledge management lessons learned: what works and what doesn't.* USA: Information Today.

MANAGER. (2004) Skills shortage behind project failures. *Manager.* January/February, p7.

MARCHAND, D. A., KETTINGER, W. and ROLLINS, J. D. (2000) Information orientation: people, technology and bottom line. *Sloan Management Review.* Summer.

NONAKA, I. and TAKEUCHI, H. (2001) Organisational knowledge creation. In J. HENRY (ed.), *Creative management.* London: Sage.

POLICE STANDARDS UNIT (2004) *Police Performance Monitoring 2003/2004.* London: Home Office.

PORTER, M. E. (2004) *Competitive strategy: techniques for analyzing industries and competitors.* Rev. ed. New York: Free Press.

ROTHWELL, R,. 2002 Towards the fifth-generation innovation process. In J. HENRY and D. MAYLE (eds), *Managing innovation and change.* London: Sage.

SCHULTHEIS, R. A. and SUMNER, M. (1998) *Management information systems: the manager's view.* 4th ed. USA: Irwin/McGraw-Hill.

SKAPINKER, M. (2003) *Change agenda: knowledge management.* London: CIPD.

SLOMAN, M. (2001) *The e-learning revolution.* London: CIPD.

References

STONICH, P. J. (1985) *Implementing strategy.* HarperBusiness.

STUART, L. (2004) Work this way. *Guardian.* 25 September.

WARD, J. (1995) *Principles of information systems management.* London: Routledge.

WARD, J. and PEPPARD, J. (2002) *Strategic planning for information systems.* 3rd ed. Chichester: Wiley.

WEAVER, P. L., LAMBROU, N. and WALKLEY, M. (2004) *Practical business systems development using SSADM Version 4: a complete tutorial guide.* London: FT Prentice Hall.

www.socitm.gov.uk (accessed 6 June 2005).

USEFUL WEBSITES

www.gov.uk

www.informationcommissioner.gov.uk.

www.softwaresource.co.uk

www.statistics.gov.uk

Index

A

alternative hypothesis 180
arrays 125–6
artificial intelligence 103
average (mean) 145–9

B

bankers automated clearing systems (BACS)
    108
bar diagram (chart) 131–3
    stacked bar diagram 132–3
    using Excel™ 243–4
bottom up forecasting 206
business continuity plans 76

C

central limit theorem 174
centred moving averages 214–5
chi-squared
    distribution 186,188
    goodness of fit tests 186–9
    independence tests 189–91
closed-loop systems 43–4, 46
cluster sampling 170
coefficient of determination 198–200
    using Excel™ 248–9
competitive advantage 13, 94, 104, 109
    differentiation 13
    focus 14
    knowledge management 94
    overall cost leadership 13
complexity 25, 29–30
computer-aided design (CAD) 113
computer-aided manufacture (CAM) 113
computer-aided software (CASE) 113
computer-based training (CBT) 113
computer-integrated manufacturing (CIM) 113
computer numerical control (CNC) 113
Computer Misuse Act 1990 (CMA) 78
confidence limits (or interval) 173–8
    of a sample mean 176
    of a sample proportion 178
    using Excel™ 246–7

consumers' price index (CPI) 225
contingency table 190
continuous probability distribution 162–5
continuous random variable 162
control systems 42–7
    elements 42
    human aspects 46–7
convenience sampling 171
correlation 193, 199–201
    coefficient 199–200
    using Excel™ 248–9
critical path
    definition 70
    analysis (CPA) 38–9
cumulative frequency distribution 128–9
curvilinear relationship 201
cyclical element (of a time series) 208

D

database 12, 50–5
database management system (DBMS) 13, 51
database structures 51–5
    hierarchical 53–4
    network 53
    object-oriented database (OODB) 53, 55
    relational 53, 81
data collection and storage 48–50
data flow diagram (DFD) 64, 66
Data Protection Act 1998 (DPA) 50, 77
    principles 77
    Employment Practices Data Protection
        Code 77
data security 73–9
    protection 74–5
    recovery 76
    UK law 77–8
data sources
    external 48, 229–32
    internal 48, 229–32
    primary 229
    secondary 229–32
deciles 151
decision analysis 234

decision-making
  and information systems 15–18, 46
  disorder in 17
  hard systems methodology 24, 27–9
  limited rationality 17
  logical incrementalism 17
  rational 17, 18
  soft systems methodology 24–9
decision support systems (DSSs) 113–14
decision theory 234–40
  certainty 16
  definition 234
  risk 16, 114, 239–40
  uncertainty 16–18
  utilty 239–40
decision tree 237–9
dedicated system 12
Delphi approach 205
dependent variable 193, 202
descriptive statistics 123
deseasonalising 214–6
desk top publishing (DTP) 113
diagrammatic methods 131–44
  using Excel™ 243–5
disaster recovery plan 75–6
double-loop feedback 43
Dow Jones Industrial Average Index 229
drilling down 81, 114, 116

E
econometric models 38
e-business 106–10
e-commerce 106–8
  business-to-business (B2B) 107
  business-to-consumer (B2C) 106
  consumer-to-consumer (C2C) 107
e-government 111–13
e-HR 110–11
e-learning 111
e-mail 105–6
e-mentoring 111
e-recruitment 110
electronic data interchange (EDI) 108
electronic funds transfer at point of sale
  (EFTPOS) 108
emergent decisions 17
emergent properties 22–3
Employment Practices Data Protection Code
  77
encryption 75

entity 65
entity life history 67
entropy 23
errors
  sampling 178
  Type 1 182
  Type 2 182
estimates 168
event 158–9
  definition 158
  probability 158–9
Excel™ (uses) 241–52
  correlation 248–9
  diagrammatic methods 243–5
  forecasting 250–2
  frequency distributions 242–3
  numerical methods 245–6
  regression analysis 248–9
  sampling 246–7
exception report 9
executive information system (EIS) 114
expected monetary value (EMV) 236–7
Expenditure and Food Survey 223, 230
expert system 102–3, 114, 120
exponential smoothing 209
exponential relationship 201

F
feedback 42–5
  negative 44
  positive 44
feedback loops 43–4
  actuator 43, 45
  comparator 43
  double-loop feedback 43
  higher-order feedback 43
  sensor 43
  single-loop feedback 43
feedforward loops 44–5
financial models 37–8
finite population adjustment 179
fire walls 75
focus groups 171
forecasting 204–18
  bottom up approach 206
  causal approach 205
  Delphi approach 205
  mean squared error 210–11
  pluralistic approach 206
  qualitative methods 205–6

quantitative methods 205
smoothing methods 209–11
time series approach 205, 206–17
top down approach 206
using Excel™ 250–2
Freedom of Information Act (2000) 77–8
frequency distribution 126–9
cumulative 128–9
relative 127–9
using Excel™ 242–3
frequency polygon 138–9
FT30 Index 229
FTSE All-Share Index 229
FTSE 100/250/350 Index 228–9
FTSE Small Cap Index 229

G
goodness of fit tests 186–9
government statistical publications 230–1
graphs 140–1

H
hackers 74
hard systems methodology 24, 27–9
higher-order feedback 43
histogram 136–8
using Excel™ 242–3
holism of systems 22–3
human resource information systems (HRIS) 80–93
core features 81–2
future 20
learning and development modules 90–2
other modules 92–3
recruitment modules 90
human resource (HR) planning 93
hypotheses 180–1
alternative, definition of 180
null, definition of 180
hypothesis testing 180–92

I
iconic models 37
independence tests (chi-squared tests) 189–91
independent variable 193, 201–2
index numbers 219–22
Information Commissioner 77
information culture 12–13

information independence 12
information management 3–19
information strategy 31–2
information systems (IS) strategy 31–2
ICT strategy 31–2
information systems
concepts 20–30
content 5
environmental disturbances 42–4, 47
for planning 31–41
for review and control 42–7
impact of organisational factors 10–12
information system design, development and maintenance 56–70
basic project model 57
evaluation 63
project initiation 57–8
requirements analysis 58–60, 64–7
Structured Systems Analysis and Design Methodology (SSADM) 63–4
system design 60
system build 60
system implementation and handover 62
system integration and testing 61
system review, amendment and maintenance 62–3
user acceptance testing 61
intelligent transport solution (ITS) 118
Internet 104–13
Interquartile range 152
intranet 82, 91, 99, 100–1
irregular element (of a time series) 207, 216

K
knowledge
creation/acquisition 97–8
conversion 98
definitions 95–7
explicit 96–8
operational 96
tacit 96–8
knowledge asset management 101
knowledge centres 100–1
knowledge communities 99–100
knowledge continuity management 101–2
knowledge management
definition 96–7
framework 97

process 98–9
knowledge management systems 94–103
    infrastructure for 98–99
    model 95

L
least squares method 195
linear regression 194–9
line of best fit 195
logical data modelling (LDM) 65–6
lower quartile 151

M
managing information
    condensation 6, 48
    filtration 6, 48
    presentation 5–7
    timeliness 8
management information reports
    exception 9
    request 9–10
    routine 8
    special 10
maximax/minimin criteria 235–6
maximin/minimax criteria 235
mean 145–9
    of a population 149
    of a random variable 160
    of a sample 149
    using Excel™ 245–6
mean squared error (MSE) 210–11
    using Excel™ 250–2
measures of dispersion 151–5
measures of location 145–51
median 149–51
    using Excel™ 245–6
mode 151
    using Excel™ 245–6
models
    econometric 38
    financial 37
    iconic 37
    symbolic 37
Monte Carlo method 39
Monthly Digest of Statistics 230
moving average forecast 209–11
    using Excel™ 250–2
multi-media training (MMT) 113
multinomial population 186
multiple regression 193, 201–2

N
navigators 108
neural networks 120
normal distribution 164–5
    features 164
    standard 165
null hypothesis 180
numerical methods 145–85
    using Excel™ 245–6

O
object oriented database (OODB) structures
    53, 55
ogive 139–40
one-tailed test 184
open-loop systems 43–44, 45, 46
operational planning 32–5
organisation culture 11
organisational structure 11, 14, 119

P
partnership sourcing 109–10
pay-off tables 234–6
    maximax/minimin criteria 235–6
    maximin/minimax criteria 235
percentiles 151
PERT (Project Evaluation Review Technique)
    38–9
personal digital assistant (PDA)/(XDA)
    116–17
pictograms 133–5
pie chart 113–14
    using Excel™ 243–4
planning
    information for 36–7
    levels 32
    problems 32–3
pluralistic approach to forecasting 206
point estimates 171–2
population, definition of 149
prediction error 194
probability
    classical method 158
    of an event 158–9
    relative frequency method 158
    rules of 157
    subjective method 158
probability density function 162
probability distributions 159–65
    continuous 162–5

discrete 159–62
procedure narrative 64–5
process analysis techniques 64
producers' price index 228
project model 57–63

Q

qualitative methods of forecasting 205–6
 bottom up approach 206
 Delphi approach 205
 top down approach 206
quantitative methods of forecasting
 causal approach 205,
 time series 205, 206–17
quartiles (upper and lower) 151
quota sampling 170

R

radio frequency identification (RFID) 50
random number table 169
random variable
 definition 159
 continuous 159
 discrete 159
 mean 160
 standard deviation 161
 variance 160–1
range 152
 using Excel™ 245–6
regression analysis 193–8
 dopondcnt variable 193, 202
 independent variable 193, 201–2
 linear 194–9
 multiple 193, 201–2
 using Excel™ 248–9
relative frequency distribution 127–9
request reports 9–10
requirements analysis (see also SSADM) 57,
 58–60, 64–7
Retail Price Index (RPI) 222–5
 table 224
 use of 225–8
rich picture 26–8
risk and utility 239–40
robotics 118
root definition 27
routine reports 8

S

sample, definition of 149

sample size calculation 178–9
sampling
 distributions 173–7
 frame 167
 methods of 168–71
scatter diagram 140–1, 194–5, 200
 using Excel™ 248–9
search engine 105
seasonal element (of a time series) 208
secondary data 229–32
sensitivity analysis 40
simple linear regression 194–9
simple random sampling 168–70, 178
simulation 114
single-loop feedback 43
skewed 149
smoothing methods 209–11
 moving average 209–11
 exponential 209
snowball sampling 171
soft systems methodology (SSM) 24–9
 seven stages 25–7
 rich picture 26–8
 root definition 27
 Weltanschauungen (world-views) 27
special reports 10
SPSS™ 241
SSADM™ (structured systems analysis and
 design methodology) 63–4, 67, 70
stacked bar diagram (chart) 132–3
 uslng Excel ™ 243–5
standard deviation 152–5
 of a population 154
 of a random variable 161
 of a sample 154
 using Excel™ 245–6
standard normal distribution 165
statistical inference 160, 167, 180
statistical process control 184
stock market indices 228–9
storage devices 48–50
strategic planning 32–5
stratified random sampling 170
structured query language (SQL) 51
symbolic models 37
system design 56–69
system implementation and handover 62
system integration and testing 61
system test plan 60, 61
systematic sampling 170

systems
  boundaries 21
  definition 20
  emergent properties 22–3
  entropy 23
  environment 21
  hard and soft properties 23–4
  holism 22
  open and closed 22
systems approach 20
  complexity 25, 29–30
  definition of 20–1
  hard systems methodology 24
  key features 21
  soft systems methodology (SSM) 24–9

T
tabulations 125–30
tactical planning 32–5
time series structure 206–9
  cyclical element 208
  irregular element 209
  seasonal element 208
  trend element 207–8
top down forecasting 206

tree diagram 157, 237–9
trend element (of a time series) 207–8
trend projections 211–14
two-tailed test 182
type 1 and 2 errors 182

U
uniform distribution 162–3
upper control limit (UCL) 184
upper quartile 151
user-acceptance testing 60–1
utility 239

V
variance 152–5
  of a population 154
  of a random variable 160–1
  of a sample 154
  using Excel™ 245–6
virtual reality 117–18
viruses 74–5
voice over internet protocol (VoIP) 117

W
world wide web (WWW) 105

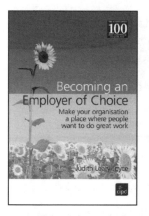

Also from CIPD Publishing . . .

Personal Effectiveness

Diana Winstanley

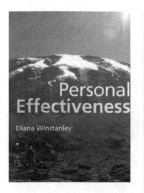

Written by a leading author in this field, this new text on Personal Effectiveness is designed to give students a basic understanding of study skills and management skills, and to give context to other studies.

Suitable for use on a range of undergraduate and postgraduate modules, including those relating to self development, personal skills, learning and development, management skills, study skills and coaching modules, and as part of general business or HR degrees, this text seeks to be both comprehensive and accessible through the use of learning aids.

Each chapter includes:
- learning objectives and a synopsis of content;
- vignette examples to illustrate key points;
- exercises with feedback;
- a self-check exercise and synopsis at the end of the chapter; and
- references and further sources of information.

Order your copy now online at www.cipd.co.uk/bookstore or call us on 0870 800 3366

Diana Winstanley has over 15 years experience of training staff, students and managers in personal effectiveness, as well as in human resource management, and is already a well respected author of a number of books and articles. She has also led, designed and supported a number of PhD and postgraduate programmes in transferable skills and personal effectiveness, and is currently Professor of Management and Director of Postgraduate Programmes at Kingston Business School. Previously she has been Senior Lecturer in Management and Personal Development, Deputy Director of the full-time MBA programme and Senior Tutor at Tanaka Business School, Imperial College London. She also has professional qualifications as a humanistic counsellor.

| Published 2005 | 1 84398 002 9 | Paperback | 256 pages |

The Chartered Institute of Personnel and Development is the leading publisher of books and reports for personnel and training professionals, students and all those concerned with the effective management and development of people at work.

Also from CIPD Publishing . . .

Developing and Applying Study Skills:

Writing assignments, dissertations and management reports

Donald Currie

Having trouble writing your assignment?

Do you want to improve your study skills and write successful reports?

Help is at hand with this latest title from CIPD Publishing. A practical guide to help you prepare, write and complete assignments, dissertations and management reports. This text looks at the skills required to produce successful documents, how to gain these skills and how and when to use them.

Taking a straight forward, hands-on approach, you can use this book as an ongoing tool to aid you in your studies. It offers guidance on getting the best from lectures, tutorials, seminars, structured learning sessions and group work.

Included throughout the book are exercises, case studies and self-test questions that can help you increase your experience of tackling organisation-based problems, addressing issues, increasing your academic understanding and monitoring your progress.

Order your copy now online at www.cipd.co.uk/bookstore or call us on 0870 800 3366

Donald Currie worked as a personnel officer for more than 15 years before joining the Southampton Institute as a Lecturer in personnel management. In 1990 he was appointed Fellow In Human Resource Management and for more than 10 years led the CIPD Professional Education Scheme. Donald continues to work as a consulatnt to the Southampton Business School, and has been running the CIPD CPP course since 1995.

Published 2005   1 84398 064 9   Paperback   240 pages

The Chartered Institute of Personnel and Development is the leading publisher of books and reports for personnel and training professionals, students, and for all those concerned with the effective management and development of people at work.

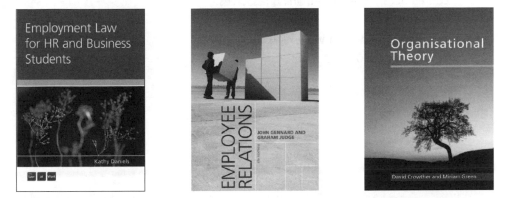

Membership has its rewards

Join us online today as an Affiliate member and get immediate access to our member services. As a member you'll also be entitled to special discounts on our range of courses, conferences, books and training resources.

To find out more, visit www.cipd.co.uk/affiliate or call us on 020 8612 6208.